中华人民共和国
民法典

汉英双语版

Civil Code
of
the People's Republic of China

Chinese-English Edition

全国人大常委会法制工作委员会·审定
English text finalized by the Legislative Affairs Commission of the Standing Committee of the National People's Congress of the People's Republic of China

法律出版社
LAW PRESS · CHINA
北京

图书在版编目(CIP)数据

中华人民共和国民法典：汉英双语版／全国人大常委会法制工作委员会审定. -- 北京：法律出版社，2021（2025.5 重印）

ISBN 978-7-5197-5633-8

Ⅰ. ①中… Ⅱ. ①全… Ⅲ. ①民法–法典–中国–汉、英 Ⅳ. ①D923

中国版本图书馆 CIP 数据核字（2021）第 093063 号

中华人民共和国民法典：汉英双语版
ZHONGHUA RENMIN GONGHEGUO MINFADIAN: HANYING SHUANGYU BAN

全国人大常委会法制工作委员会 审定

策划编辑 朱 峰
责任编辑 韩泓宇
装帧设计 鲁 娟

出版发行 法律出版社
编辑统筹 辞书·融出版编辑部 法律翻译与出版研究中心
责任校对 马秋婧
责任印制 吕亚莉
经　　销 新华书店

开本 710 毫米×1000 毫米 1/16
印张 30.25 **字数** 415 千
版本 2021 年 6 月第 1 版
印次 2025 年 5 月第 4 次印刷
印刷 天津嘉恒印务有限公司

地址：北京市丰台区莲花池西里 7 号（100073）
网址：www.lawpress.com.cn
投稿邮箱：info@lawpress.com.cn
举报盗版邮箱：jbwq@lawpress.com.cn

销售电话：010-83938349
客服电话：010-83938350
咨询电话：010-63939796

书号：ISBN 978-7-5197-5633-8 **定价**：158.00 元

凡购买本社图书，如有印装错误，我社负责退换。电话：010-83938349

Preface

Civil Code of the People's Republic of China is a milestone legislation as it is the first law promulgated with the name of Code since the establishment of the People's Republic of China, and it is an important achievement of developing the socialist rule of law with Chinese characteristics for a new era. By improving the law-based governance, it will help create an enabling environment for business and further unleash China's economic potential. In particular, with the highlight of a people-centered philosophy, the Code will play a pivotal role in protecting people's rights and interests, developing China's human rights cause as well as modernizing the country's governance capacity.

Letting the rest of the world know better about the *Civil Code* is a significant way to facilitate the communication of China's legal system with foreign countries and regions. Thus, the Standing Committee of the National People's Congress and its Legislative Affairs Commission (LAC) attach great importance to the translation of the Code to make it reach the rest of the world.

Acknowledgments. In the translation process, we were confronted with many challenges due to the difference of the two languages and some concepts that only exist in China's legal system. It is difficult, therefore, to complete the translation within a limited time period. It would be impossible to find a way out without the efforts by the Expert Team for the Translation of the Civil Code under LAC, including Gao Lingyun, Chen Weizuo, Jiang Junlu, Tong Xiaohua, Li Mingqian, Ma Jing, Zhang Falian, Xia Jihong, Da Ji, Mao Yu and Chengzhou

Ludan. We are grateful for their contributions in the translation, especially for their efforts in offering constructive suggestions on legal terms and making the translation more idiomatic. We also wish to express our sincere thanks to all the persons and organizations that contributed to the publication of this book.

In spite of the great care taken by the translators and editors to produce an accurate translation, shortcomings and oversights are hardly avoidable, and criticism from readers will be appreciated.

Special Notes to Readers. This translation is for reference only. In case of discrepancy between the English translation and the original Chinese text, the Chinese edition of the Code shall prevail. Besides, to make the text concise, we decided to use the third-person singular male pronouns to include the corresponding female and neuter pronouns except where the context clearly requires otherwise.

Legislative Affairs Commission of
the Standing Committee of
the National People's Congress
March 2021

序　言

《中华人民共和国民法典》(以下简称《民法典》)是中华人民共和国成立以来第一部以"法典"命名的法律,是新时代中国特色社会主义法治建设的重大成果,具有里程碑意义。《民法典》在中国特色社会主义法律体系中具有重要地位,是一部固根本、稳预期、利长远的基础性法律。《民法典》的颁布与实施对全面推进依法治国、加快建设社会主义法治国家,对发展社会主义市场经济、巩固社会主义基本经济制度具有重大意义;在坚持以人民为中心的发展思想、依法维护人民权益、推动我国人权事业发展以及推进国家治理体系和治理能力现代化方面发挥举足轻重的作用。

做好《民法典》的海外宣传介绍工作,是推进我国法律制度对外宣传和交流、讲好中国立法故事的一项重要举措。更好地将《民法典》介绍给世界,是增进中国同世界上其他国家和地区法律体系间交流的重要方式。因此,全国人大常委会及其法制工作委员会领导高度重视《民法典》的翻译和对外宣介工作。

致谢:由于汉英两种语言存在差异,中国法律体系中存在特有的法律概念,我们在翻译《民法典》时面临诸多挑战,在有限的时间内完成《民法典》的翻译工作是一项艰巨的任务。全国人大常委会法制工作委员会成立了《民法典》英文翻译工作组,成员包括高凌云、陈卫佐、姜俊禄、童孝华、李明倩、马静、张法连、夏继红、达吉、毛雨和程周鲁丹。在各位工作组成员的努力下,《民法典》的翻译工作才得以圆满完成。我们感谢各位工作组成员在《民法典》翻译过程中所作的贡献,特别是他们为《民法典》中法律术语的翻译提供了很多建设性建议,使《民法典》译文更加地道。我们也要向出版本书的出版社和编辑表示衷心的感谢。

尽管本书的译者和编辑尽其所能，审慎翻译，但错误和疏漏在所难免，敬请广大读者批评指正。

读者须知：本译文仅供参考。当《民法典》英文译文与中文原文表述不一致时，以《民法典》中文版为准。此外，除非上下文另有要求，译文中第三人称单数代词均使用“他”，代指“她”和“它”，以使译文简明扼要。

全国人民代表大会常务委员会

法制工作委员会

2021 年 3 月

TABLE OF CONTENTS

Book Two Real Rights

Book Three　Contracts

目　录

第二编　物　　权

第三编　合　　同

第四编　人　格　权

第五编　婚姻家庭

第六编　继　　承

第七编　侵权责任

CIVIL CODE
OF
THE PEOPLE'S REPUBLIC OF CHINA

NOTES

1. This translation is for reference only. In case of discrepancy between the English translation and the original Chinese text, the Chinese text shall prevail.

2. In this translation, third-person singular male pronouns should be construed to include the corresponding female and neuter pronouns except where the context clearly requires otherwise.

Order of the President of the People's Republic of China

No. 45

Civil Code of the People's Republic of China, adopted at the Third Session of the Thirteenth National People's Congress of the People's Republic of China on May 28, 2020, is hereby promulgated and shall go into effect as of January 1, 2021.

XI Jinping

President of the People's Republic of China

May 28, 2020

CIVIL CODE
OF
THE PEOPLE'S REPUBLIC OF CHINA

(Adopted at the Third Session of the Thirteenth National People's Congress on May 28, 2020)

Contents

Book One General Part

Chapter I General Provisions

Article 1 This Code is formulated in accordance with the Constitution of the People's Republic of China for the purposes of protecting the lawful rights and interests of the persons of the civil law, regulating civil-law relations, maintaining social and economic order, meeting the needs for developing socialism with Chinese characteristics, and carrying forward the core socialist values.

Article 2 The civil law regulates personal and proprietary relationships among the persons of the civil law, namely, natural persons, legal persons, and unincorporated organizations that are equal in status.

Article 3 The personal rights, proprietary rights, and other lawful rights and interests of the persons of the civil law are protected by law and free from infringement by any organization or individual.

Article 4 All persons of the civil law are equal in legal status when conducting civil activities.

Article 5 When conducting a civil activity, a person of the civil law shall, in compliance with the principle of voluntariness, create, alter, or terminate a civil juristic relationship according to his own will.

Article 6 When conducting a civil activity, a person of the civil law shall, in compliance with the principle of fairness, reasonably establish the rights and obligations of each party.

Article 7 When conducting a civil activity, a person of the civil law shall, in compliance with the principle of good faith, uphold honesty and honor commitments.

Article 8 When conducting a civil activity, no person of the civil law may violate the law, or offend public order or good morals.

Article 9 When conducting a civil activity, a person of the civil law shall act in a manner that facilitates conservation of resources and protection of the ecological environment.

Article 10 Civil disputes shall be resolved in accordance with law. Where the law does not specify, custom may be applied, provided that public order and good morals may not be offended.

Article 11 Where there are other laws providing special provisions regulating civil-law relations, such provisions shall be followed.

Article 12 The laws of the People's Republic of China shall apply to the civil activities taking place within the territory of the People's Republic of China, except as otherwise provided by law.

Chapter II Natural Persons

Section 1 Capacity for Enjoying Civil-law Rights and Capacity for Performing Civil Juristic Acts

Article 13 A natural person shall, from the time of birth until the time of death, have the capacity for enjoying civil-law rights, and may enjoy civil-law rights and assume civil-law duties in accordance with law.

Article 14 All natural persons are equal in their capacity for enjoying civil-law rights.

Article 15 The time of birth and time of death of a natural person are determined by the time recorded on his birth or death certificate as applied, or, if there is no birth or death certificate, by the time recorded in the natural person's household registration or other valid identity certificate. If there is sufficient evidence overturning the time recorded in the aforementioned documents, the time that is established by such evidence shall prevail.

Article 16 A fetus is deemed as having the capacity for enjoying civil-law rights in estate succession, acceptance of gift, and other situations where protection of a fetus' interests is involved. Provided, however, that a stillborn fetus does not have such capacity *ab initio*.

Article 17 A natural person aged eighteen or above is an adult. A natural person under the age of eighteen is a minor.

Article 18 An adult has full capacity for performing civil juristic acts and may independently perform civil juristic acts.

A minor aged sixteen or above whose main source of support is the income from his own labor is deemed as a person with full capacity for performing civil juristic acts.

Article 19 A minor aged eight or above has limited capacity for performing civil juristic acts and may perform a civil juristic act through or upon consent or ratification of his legal representative, except that such a minor may independently perform a civil juristic act that is purely beneficial to him or that is appropriate to his age and intelligence.

Article 20 A minor under the age of eight has no capacity for performing civil juristic acts, and may perform a civil juristic act only through his legal representative.

Article 21 An adult unable to comprehend his own conduct has no capacity for performing civil juristic acts, and may perform a civil juristic act only through his legal representative.

The preceding paragraph is applicable to a minor aged eight or above who is unable to comprehend his own conduct.

Article 22 An adult unable to fully comprehend his own conduct has limited capacity for performing civil juristic acts and may perform a civil juristic act through or upon consent or ratification of his legal representative, except that such an adult may independently perform a civil juristic act that is purely beneficial to him or that is appropriate to his intelligence and mental status.

Article 23 The guardian of a person who has no or limited capacity for performing civil juristic acts is the legal representative of the person.

Article 24 Where an adult is unable to comprehend or fully comprehend his conduct, any interested person of such an adult or a relevant organization may request the people's court to declare that the said adult be identified as a person with no or limited capacity for performing civil juristic acts.

Where a person has been identified by the people's court as a person with no or limited capacity for performing civil juristic acts, the people's court may, upon request of the person, an interested person thereof, or a relevant organization, and based on the recovery of his intelligence and mental health, declare that the said person becomes a person with limited or full capacity for performing civil juristic acts.

A relevant organization referred to in this Article includes a residents' committee, a villagers' committee, a school, a medical institution, the women's federation, the disabled person's federation, a legally established organization for senior people, the civil affairs department, and the like.

Article 25 The domicile of a natural person is the residence recorded in his household registration or other valid identification registration system; if a natural person's habitual residence is different from his domicile, the habitual residence is deemed as his domicile.

Section 2 Guardianship

Article 26 Parents have the duty to raise, educate, and protect their minor children.

Adult children have the duty to support, assist, and protect their parents.

Article 27 The parents of a minor are his guardians.

Where the parents of a minor are deceased or incompetent to be his guardians, the following persons, if competent, shall act as his guardians in the following order:

(1) his paternal grandparents and maternal grandparents;

(2) his elder brothers and elder sisters; or

(3) any other individual or organization that is willing to act as his guardian, provided that consent must be obtained from the residents' committee, the villagers' committee, or the civil affairs department in the place where the minor's domicile is located.

Article 28 For an adult who has no or limited capacity for performing civil juristic acts, the following persons, if competent, shall act as his guardians in the following order:

(1) his spouse;

(2) his parents and his children;

(3) any other close relatives of his; or

(4) any other individual or organization that is willing to act as his guardian, provided that consent must be obtained from the residents' committee, the villagers' committee, or the civil affairs department in the place where the adult's domicile is located.

Article 29 A parent who is the guardian of his child may, in his will, designate a succeeding guardian for his child.

Article 30 A guardian may be determined through agreement among the persons who are legally qualified to be guardians. The true will of the ward shall be respected in determining the guardian through agreement.

Article 31 Where a dispute arises over the determination of a guardian, the guardian shall be appointed by the residents' committee, the villagers' committee, or the civil affairs department in the place where the ward's domicile is located, and a party not satisfied with such an appointment may request the people's court to appoint a guardian; the relevant parties may also directly request the people's court to make such an appointment.

When appointing a guardian, the residents' committee, the villagers' committee, the civil affairs department, or the people's court shall respect the true will of the ward and appoint a guardian in the best interest of the ward from among the legally qualified persons.

Where the personal, proprietary, and other lawful rights and interests of a ward are not under any protection before a guardian is appointed in accordance with the first paragraph of this Article, the residents' committee, the villagers' committee, a relevant organization designated by law, or the civil affairs department in the place where the ward's domicile is located shall act as a temporary guardian.

Once appointed, a guardian may not be replaced without authorization; where a guardian has been replaced without authorization, the responsibility of the originally appointed guardian is not discharged.

Article 32 Where there is no person legally qualified to be a guardian, the civil affairs department shall act as the guardian, and the residents' committee or villagers' committee in the place where the ward's domicile is located may also act as the guardian if they are competent in performing the duties of guardian.

Article 33 An adult with full capacity for performing civil juristic acts may, in anticipation of incapacity in the future, consult his close relatives, or other individuals or organizations willing to be his guardian, and appoint in writing a guardian for himself, who shall perform the duties of guardian when the adult loses all or part of his capacity for performing civil juristic acts.

Article 34 The duties of a guardian are to represent the ward to perform civil juristic acts and to protect the personal, proprietary, and other lawful rights and interests of the ward.

A guardian's rights arising from performance of his duties as required by law are protected by law.

A guardian who fails to perform his duties or infringes upon the lawful rights or interests of the ward shall bear legal liability.

Where a guardian is temporarily unable to perform his duties owing to an emergency such as an unexpected incident, thus leaving the ward in an unattended situation, the residents' committee, the villagers' committee, or the civil affairs department in the place where the ward's domicile is located shall make arrangement as a temporary measure to provide necessary life care for the ward.

Article 35 A guardian shall perform his duties in the best interest of the ward. A guardian may not dispose of the ward's property unless it is for protecting the interests of the ward.

When performing his duties and making decisions relating to a minor's interests, a guardian of a minor shall respect the true will of the minor based on the latter's age and intelligence.

When performing his duties, a guardian of an adult shall respect the true will of the adult to the greatest extent possible, and ensure and aid the ward in performing civil juristic acts appropriate to his intelligence and mental status. The guardian may not interfere with the matters that the ward is capable of independently managing.

Article 36 Where a guardian has performed any of the following acts, the people's court shall, upon request of a relevant individual or organization, disqualify the guardian, adopt necessary temporary measures, and appoint a new guardian in the best interest of the ward in accordance with law:

(1) engaging in any act which severely harms the physical or mental health

of the ward;

(2) being indolent in performing the duties of guardian, or being unable to perform such duties but refusing to delegate all or part of the duties to others, thus placing the ward in a desperate situation; or

(3) engaging in any other act which severely infringes upon the lawful rights and interests of the ward.

The relevant individual and organization referred to in this Article include any other person legally qualified to be a guardian, the residents' committee, the villagers' committee, a school, a medical institution, the women's federation, the disabled persons' federation, a child protection organization, a legally established organization for senior people, the civil affairs department, and the like.

Where the aforementioned individual and organization other than the civil affairs department, as stated in the preceding paragraph, fail to request the people's court to disqualify the guardian in a timely manner, the civil affairs department shall initiate such a request to the people's court.

Article 37 A parent, child, or spouse legally obligated to pay for his ward's support shall continue to perform such obligations after being disqualified as a guardian by the people's court.

Article 38 Where a ward's parent or child, who has been disqualified as a guardian by the people's court for reasons other than having committed an intentional crime against the ward, and who has truly repented and mended his ways, applies to the people's court for reinstatement, the people's court may, upon considering the actual situation and upon the satisfaction of the prerequisite that the true will of the ward is respected, reinstate the guardian, and the guardianship between the ward and the guardian appointed by the people's court after the disqualification of the original guardian shall thus be terminated simultaneously.

Article 39 A guardianship is terminated under any of the following circumstances:

(1) the ward has obtained or regained full capacity for performing civil juristic acts;

(2) the guardian has become incompetent to be a guardian;

(3) the ward or the guardian deceases; or

(4) any other circumstance in which the people's court determines to terminate the guardianship.

Where a ward is still in need of a guardian after the termination of the guardianship, a new guardian shall be appointed in accordance with law.

Section 3 Declaration of a Missing Person and Declaration of Death

Article 40 If a natural person's whereabouts have been unknown for two years, an interested person may request the people's court to declare the natural person as a missing person.

Article 41 The period of time during which a natural person's whereabouts is unknown shall be counted from the date when the natural person has not been heard of ever since. If a person is missing during wartime, the time of his whereabouts becoming unknown shall be counted from the date the war ends or from the date as determined by the relevant authority.

Article 42 A missing person's property shall be placed in the custody of his spouse, adult children, parents, or any other person willing to take such custody.

Where a dispute arises over the custody of a missing person's property, or the persons provided in the preceding paragraph are unavailable or incompetent for such a purpose, the property shall be placed in the custody of a person appointed by the people's court.

Article 43 A custodian shall properly manage the missing person's property and safeguard his proprietary interests.

The taxes, debts, and other due payment obligations owed by a missing person, if any, shall be paid by the custodian out of the missing person's property.

A custodian who, intentionally or due to gross negligence, causes damage to the property of the missing person shall be liable for compensation.

Article 44 Where a custodian fails to perform his duties of custodian, infringes upon the proprietary rights or interests of the missing person, or if the custodian becomes incompetent to be a custodian, an interested person of the missing person may request the people's court to replace the custodian.

A custodian may, with just cause, request the people's court to appoint a new custodian to replace himself.

Where the people's court appoints a new custodian, the new custodian is entitled to request the former custodian to deliver the relevant property and a property management report in a timely manner.

Article 45 Where a missing person reappears, the people's court shall, upon request of the said person or an interested person thereof, revoke the declaration of his being missing.

A missing person who reappears is entitled to request the custodian to deliver the relevant property and a property management report in a timely manner.

Article 46 An interested person may request the people's court to make a declaration of the death of a natural person under either of the following circumstances:

(1) the natural person's whereabouts have been unknown for four years; or

(2) the natural person's whereabouts have been unknown for two years as a result of an accident.

The two-year requirement for a natural person to be declared dead does not apply where the person's whereabouts have been unknown as a result of an accident and if a relevant authority certifies that it is impossible for the said natural person to survive.

Article 47 Where an interested person requests the people's court to declare the death of a natural person, while another interested person requests to declare the person being missing, the people's court shall declare that the person is dead if the conditions for declaration of death as provided in this Code are satisfied.

Article 48 For a person declared dead, the date when the people's court makes a judgment declaring his death is deemed as the date of his death; for a person declared dead because his whereabouts is unknown as a result of an accident, the date of the occurrence of the accident is deemed as the date of his death.

Article 49 The declaration of the death of a natural person who is still alive does not affect the effects of the civil juristic acts performed by the person during the period the death declaration is effective.

Article 50 Where a person declared dead reappears, the people's court shall, upon request of the person or an interested person thereof, revoke the declaration of his death.

Article 51 The marital relationship with a person declared dead ceases to exist from the date the declaration of his death is made. Where the declaration of death is revoked, the aforementioned marital relationship shall be automatically resumed from the date the declaration of death is revoked, unless the spouse has married to someone else or states in writing to the marriage registration authority the unwillingness to resume the marriage.

Article 52 Where a child of a person declared dead has been legally adopted by others during the period when the declaration of death is effective, the person declared dead may not, after the declaration of his death is revoked, claim that the adoption is invalid on the ground that his child is adopted without his consent.

Article 53 Where a declaration of the death of a person is revoked, the person is entitled to request those who have obtained his property under Book Six of this Code to return the property, or make appropriate compensation if the property cannot be returned.

Where an interested person conceals the true information and causes a natural person to be declared dead so as to obtain the latter's property, the interested person shall, in addition to returning the wrongfully obtained property, make compensation for any loss thus caused.

Section 4 Individual-run Industrial and Commercial Households and Rural-land Contractual Management Households

Article 54 A natural person who operates an industrial or commercial business may register it, in accordance with law, as an individual-run industrial and commercial household. An industrial and commercial household may have a trade name.

Article 55 Members of a rural economic collective who, in accordance with law, have been granted an original contract to operate a lot of rural land and engage in the operation of the land on a household basis form a rural-land contractual management household.

Article 56 The debts of an individual-run industrial and commercial household shall be paid from the assets of the individual who operates the business in his own name or from the individual's family assets if the business is operated in the name of the household, or, if it is impossible to determine whether the business is operated in the name of the individual or in the name of the individual's household, from the individual's family assets.

The debts of a rural-land contractual management household shall be paid from the assets of the household that is engaged in the operation on the contracted rural land, or from the portion of the assets of the family members who actually engage in such operation.

Chapter Ⅲ Legal Persons

Section 1 General Rules

Article 57 A legal person is an organization that has the capacity for enjoying civil-law rights and the capacity for performing civil juristic acts, and that independently enjoys civil-law rights and assumes civil-law obligations in accordance with law.

Article 58 A legal person shall be established in accordance with law.

A legal person shall have its own name, governance structure, domicile, and assets or funds. The specific conditions and procedures for the establishment of a legal person shall be in accordance with laws and administrative regulations.

Where there are laws or administrative regulations providing that the establishment of a legal person shall be subject to approval of a relevant authority, such provisions shall be followed.

Article 59 A legal person's capacity for enjoying civil-law rights and capacity for performing civil juristic acts are acquired when the legal person is established, and cease when the legal person is terminated.

Article 60 A legal person independently assumes civil liability to the extent of all of its assets.

Article 61 The person with the responsibility of representing a legal person in conducting civil activities in accordance with law or the legal person's articles of association is the legal representative of the legal person.

The legal consequences of the civil activities conducted by the legal representative in the legal person's name shall be assumed by the legal person.

Any restrictions on the legal representative's power to represent the legal person which is stipulated in the articles of association or imposed by the governing body of the legal person may not be asserted against a *bona fide* counterparty.

Article 62 Where a legal representative of a legal person causes damage to others while performing his responsibilities, the civil liability thus incurred shall be assumed by the legal person.

After assuming the aforementioned civil liability, the legal person has the right to indemnification, in accordance with law or its articles of association, against its legal representative who is at fault.

Article 63 The domicile of a legal person is the place where its principal administrative office is located. Where a legal person is required by law to be registered, the place of its principal administrative office shall be registered as its domicile.

Article 64 Where, during the term of existence of a legal person, there is any change in a matter that has been recorded upon its registration, the legal person shall apply to the registration authority for modification of the registration in accordance with law.

Article 65 The actual situation of a legal person, which is inconsistent with what is recorded upon registration, may not be asserted against a *bona fide* counterparty.

Article 66 The registration authority shall, in accordance with law, post in a timely manner a public notice of the information recorded by a legal person upon registration.

Article 67 In case of a merger between or among legal persons, the rights and obligations of such legal persons shall be enjoyed and assumed by the surviving legal person.

In case of a division of a legal person, the rights and obligations of the legal person shall be enjoyed and assumed jointly and severally by the legal persons established after division, unless otherwise agreed by its creditors and debtors.

Article 68 If any of the following causes exists, a legal person is terminated after it has completed liquidation and de-registration in accordance with law:

(1) the legal person is dissolved;

(2) the legal person is declared bankrupt; or

(3) there exists any other cause as provided by law.

Where there are laws or administrative regulations providing that the termination of a legal person shall be subject to approval of the relevant authority, such provisions shall be followed.

Article 69 A legal person is dissolved under any of the following circumstances:

(1) the term stipulated in its articles of association expires, or there exists any other cause for dissolution as is stipulated in the articles of association;

(2) the governing body of the legal person makes a resolution to dissolve the legal person;

(3) the legal person has to be dissolved because of a merger or division;

(4) the legal person's business license or registration certificate is legally revoked, or the legal person has received an order of closure or been dissolved; or

(5) there exists any other circumstance as provided by law.

Article 70 Where a legal person is dissolved for reasons other than a merger or division, a liquidation committee shall be formed in a timely manner by the persons with the duty of liquidation to liquidate the legal person.

Unless otherwise provided by laws or administrative regulations, members of the legal person's executive or decision-making body, such as the directors or councilors, are the persons with the duty to liquidate the legal person.

The persons with the duty to liquidate the legal person who fail to perform their duties in time and thus cause damage to others shall bear civil liability; the competent authority or an interested person may request the people's court to appoint the relevant persons to form a liquidation committee to liquidate the legal person.

Article 71 The procedure for liquidating a legal person and the authorities of a liquidation committee shall be in compliance with the provisions of relevant laws; in the absence of such a provision, the relevant rules provided in corporate laws shall be applied *mutatis mutandis*.

Article 72 During the period of liquidation, a legal person continues to exist but may not engage in any activity unrelated to the liquidation.

Unless otherwise provided by law, upon completion of the liquidation, any residual assets of a liquidated legal person shall be distributed in accordance with its articles of association or the resolution made by its governing body.

A legal person is terminated after liquidation and de-registration is completed; a legal person that is not required by law to be registered is terminated upon completion of the liquidation.

Article 73 A legal person declared bankrupt is terminated upon completion of the bankruptcy liquidation and de-registration in accordance with law.

Article 74 A legal person may establish branches in accordance with law. Where there are laws or administrative regulations providing that such a branch shall be registered, such provisions shall be followed.

A branch of a legal person engages in civil activities in its own name and the civil liability thus incurred shall be assumed by the legal person; alternatively, the civil liability may also be paid first from the assets managed by the branch, and any deficiency shall be paid by the legal person.

Article 75 The legal consequences of the civil activities conducted by an incorporator for the purpose of establishing a legal person shall be assumed by the legal person; or, in the event that no legal person is successfully established, by the incorporator, or the incorporators jointly and severally if there are two or more of them.

Where an incorporator engages in civil activities in his own name for the purpose of establishing a legal person and thus incurs civil liability, a third person creditor may elect to request either the legal person or the incorporator to bear the liability.

Section 2 For-profit Legal Persons

Article 76 A for-profit legal person is a legal person established for the purpose of making profits and distributing the profits among its shareholders and other capital contributors.

For-profit legal persons include limited liability companies, joint stock companies limited by shares, and other enterprises that have the legal person status.

Article 77 A for-profit legal person is established upon registration in accordance with law.

Article 78 The registration authority shall issue a business license to a legally established for-profit legal person. The date of issuance of the business license is the date of establishment of the for-profit legal person.

Article 79 To establish a for-profit legal person, there shall be articles of association formulated in accordance with law.

Article 80 A for-profit legal person shall establish a governing body.

The governing body has the authority to revise the articles of association of the legal person, elect or replace members of the executive or supervisory body, and perform other responsibilities stipulated in the articles of association.

Article 81 A for-profit legal person shall establish an executive body.

The executive body has the authority to convene meetings of the governing body, decide on business and investment plans, establish internal management structure, and perform other responsibilities stipulated in the articles of association of the legal person.

Where the executive body of a legal person is the board of directors or the executive director, the legal representative shall be the chairman of the board of directors, the executive director, or the manager, as is stipulated in the articles of association. Where there is no board of directors or executive director established, the person with the principal responsibilities as stipulated in the articles of association shall be the executive body and the legal representative of the legal person.

Article 82 Where a for-profit legal person establishes a supervisory body such as a board of supervisors or a supervisor, the supervisory body has, in accordance with law, the authority to inspect the financial matters of the legal person, supervise the performance of duty by the members of the executive body and the senior management officers of the legal person, and perform other responsibilities stipulated in the articles of association.

Article 83 A capital contributor of a for-profit legal person may not abuse his rights as such to harm the interests of the legal person or any other capital contributor. A capital contributor abusing such rights and causing harm to the legal person or any other capital contributor shall bear civil liability in accordance with law.

A capital contributor of a for-profit legal person may not abuse the legal person's independent status and his own limited liability status to harm the interests of the legal person's creditors. A capital contributor abusing the legal person's independent status or its own limited liability status to evade repayment of debts and thus severely harming the interests of the legal person's creditors shall be jointly and severally liable for the legal person's obligations.

Article 84 The controlling capital contributors, actual controllers, directors, supervisors, and senior management officers of a for-profit legal person may not harm the legal person's interests by taking advantage of any affiliated relations, and shall compensate for any loss thus caused to the legal person.

Article 85 A capital contributor of a for-profit legal person may request the people's court to revoke a resolution which is made at a meeting of the governing body or executive body of the legal person if the procedure for convening the meeting or the voting method thereof is in violation of the laws, administrative regulations, or the legal person's articles of association, or, if the content of the resolution violates the articles of association. Provided, however, that any civil juristic relationship already formed between the legal person and a *bona fide* counterparty based on such a resolution may not be affected.

Article 86 A for-profit legal person shall, when engaging in operational activities, observe commercial ethics, maintain the security of transactions, subject itself to the supervision of the government and the public, and assume social responsibilities.

Section 3 Non-profit Legal Persons

Article 87 A non-profit legal person is a legal person established for public welfare or other non-profit purposes which may not distribute any profit to its capital contributors, incorporators, or members.

Non-profit legal persons include public institutions, social organizations, foundations, social service institutions, and the like.

Article 88 A public institution established for the purpose of providing public services to meet the needs for economic and social development attains the status of a public-institution legal person if it satisfies the requirements for being a legal person and is legally registered as such; where the law does not require such a public institution to be registered, it attains the status of a public-institution legal person from the date of its establishment.

Article 89 Where a public-institution legal person establishes a council, the council is its decision-making body unless otherwise provided by law. The legal representative of a public-institution legal person is elected in accordance with the provisions of laws, administrative regulations, or the legal person's articles of association.

Article 90 A social organization established upon the common will of its members for a non-profit purpose, such as public welfare or the common interest of all members, attains the status of a social-organization legal person if it satisfies the requirements for being a legal person and is legally registered as such. Where the law does not require such a social organization to be registered, it attains the status of a social-organization legal person from the date of its establishment.

Article 91 To establish a social-organization legal person, there shall be articles of association formulated in accordance with law.

A social-organization legal person shall establish a governing body such as a members' assembly or a meeting of the members' representatives.

A social-organization legal person shall establish an executive body such as a council. The chairman of the council, the president, or an individual with similar responsibilities shall, in accordance with the articles of association, act as the legal representative of the legal person.

Article 92 A foundation, social service institution, or any other institution established with donated property for the purpose of public welfare attains the status of a donation-funded legal person if it meets the requirements for being a legal person and is legally registered as such.

A site legally established to hold religious activities may be registered as a legal person and attains the status of a donation-funded legal person if it meets the requirements for being a legal person. Where there are laws or administrative regulations providing for the religious sites, such provisions shall be followed.

Article 93 To establish a donation-funded legal person, there shall be articles of association formulated in accordance with law.

A donation-funded legal person shall establish a decision-making body such as a council or any other form of democratic management body, and an executive body. The chairman of the council or an individual with similar responsibilities shall, in accordance with the articles of association, act as the legal representative of the legal person.

A donation-funded legal person shall establish a supervisory body such as a board of supervisors.

Article 94 A donor has the right to inquire into and provide comments and suggestions on the expenditure and management of the property he has donated to a donation-funded legal person, and the donation-funded legal person shall respond honestly and in a timely manner.

Where a decision is made by the decision-making body, executive body, or the legal representative of a donation-funded legal person, if the decision-making procedure is in violation of the laws, administrative regulations, or the legal person's articles of association, or, if the content of the decision violates the articles of association, a donor or any other interested person, or the competent authority may request the people's court to revoke the decision. Provided, however, that any civil juristic relationship already formed between the donation-funded legal person and a *bona fide* counterparty based on such a decision may not be affected.

Article 95 Upon termination, a non-profit legal person established for the purpose of public welfare may not distribute the residual assets among its capital contributors, incorporators, or members. The residual assets shall continue to be used for the purpose of public welfare, as is stipulated in the articles of association or the resolution made by the governing body; where it is not possible to dispose of such residual assets in accordance with the articles of association or the resolution made by the governing body, the competent authority shall take the charge transferring the assets to another legal person with the same or similar purposes and then make a public notice.

Section 4 Special Legal Persons

Article 96 For the purposes of this Section, State-organ legal persons, rural economic collective legal persons, urban and rural cooperative economic organization legal persons, and primary-level self-governing organization legal persons are special types of legal persons.

Article 97 A State organ with independent budgets or a legally chartered institution assuming administrative functions is qualified as a State-organ legal person from the date of its establishment and may engage in civil activities that are necessary for the performance of its responsibilities.

Article 98 A State-organ legal person is terminated when the State organ is closed, and its civil-law rights and obligations are enjoyed and assumed by the succeeding State-organ legal person; in the absence of a succeeding State organ, the said rights and obligations shall be enjoyed and assumed by the State-organ legal person that has made the decision to close it.

Article 99 A rural economic collective attains the status of a legal person in accordance with law.

Where there are laws or administrative regulations providing for rural economic collectives, such provisions shall be followed.

Article 100 An urban or rural economic cooperative attains the status of a legal person in accordance with law.

Where there are laws or administrative regulations providing for urban and rural economic cooperatives, such provisions shall be followed.

Article 101 An urban residents' committee or a villagers' committee, as a primary-level self-governing organization, attains the status of a legal person, and may engage in civil activities necessary for the performance of their responsibilities.

Where there is no village economic collective established, the villagers' committee may, in accordance with law, perform the responsibilities of a village economic collective.

Chapter Ⅳ Unincorporated Organizations

Article 102 An unincorporated organization is an organization which does not have the legal person status but may engage in civil activities in its own name in accordance with law.

Unincorporated organizations include sole proprietorships, partnerships, professional service institutions that do not have the legal person status, and the like.

Article 103 Unincorporated organizations shall be registered in accordance with law.

Where laws or administrative regulations provide that establishment of an unincorporated organization shall be subject to approval by the relevant authority, such provisions shall be followed.

Article 104 Where an unincorporated organization becomes insolvent, its capital contributors or founders shall assume unlimited liability for the debts of the organization, unless otherwise provided by law.

Article 105 An unincorporated organization may designate one or more members to represent the organization to engage in civil activities.

Article 106 An unincorporated organization shall be dissolved under any of the following circumstances:

(1) the term stipulated in its articles of association expires or any other cause for dissolution as is stipulated in the articles of association occurs;

(2) its capital contributors or founders decide to dissolve it; or

(3) dissolution is required under any other circumstance as provided by law.

Article 107 Upon dissolution, an unincorporated organization shall be liquidated in accordance with law.

Article 108 In addition to the provisions in this Chapter, the provisions in Section 1 of Chapter Ⅲ of this Book shall be applied to unincorporated organizations *mutatis mutandis*.

Chapter V Civil-law Rights

Article 109 The personal liberty and dignity of a natural person is protected by law.

Article 110 A natural person enjoys the right to life, the right to corporeal integrity, the right to health, the right to name, the right to likeness, the right to reputation, the right to honor, the right to privacy, and the right to freedom of marriage.

A legal person or an unincorporated organization enjoys the right to entity name, the right to reputation, and the right to honor.

Article 111 A natural person's personal information is protected by law. Any organization or individual that needs to access other's personal information may only do so in accordance with law and guarantee the safety of such information, and may not illegally collect, use, process, or transmit other's personal information, or illegally trade, provide, or publicize such information.

Article 112 The personal rights of a natural person arising from a marital or familial relationship are protected by law.

Article 113 The proprietary rights of the persons of the civil law are equally protected by law.

Article 114 Persons of the civil law enjoy real rights in accordance with law.

Real rights are the rights to directly and exclusively control a specific thing by the right holder in accordance with law, which consist of the ownership, right to usufruct, and security interests in the property.

Article 115 Property consists of immovable and movable property. Where the law provides that a right shall be treated as property over which a real right lies, such provisions shall be followed.

Article 116 The categories and contents of the real rights are provided by law.

Article 117 Where, for the purpose of public interests, immovable or movable property is expropriated or requisitioned according to the scope of authority and the procedure provided by law, fair and reasonable compensation shall be paid.

Article 118 Persons of the civil law have rights *in personam* in accordance with law.

A right *in personam* is the right of an obligee to request a specific obligor to do or not to do a certain act, as arising from a contract, a tortious act, a *negotiorum gestio*, or unjust enrichment, or otherwise arising by operation of law.

Article 119 A contract formed in accordance with law is legally binding on the parties to the contract.

Article 120 Where a person's civil-law rights and interests are infringed upon due to a tortious act, the person is entitled to request the tortfeasor to bear tort liability.

Article 121 A person who, without a statutory or contractual obligation, engages in management activities to prevent another person from suffering loss of interests, is entitled to request the said other person who receives benefit therefrom to reimburse the necessary expenses thus incurred.

Article 122 Where a person obtains unjust interests at the expense of another person's loss without a legal cause, the person thus harmed is entitled to request the enriched person to make restitution.

Article 123 A person of the civil law enjoys intellectual property rights in accordance with law.

Intellectual property rights are the exclusive rights enjoyed by the right holders in accordance with law over the following subject matters:

(1) works;

(2) inventions, new utility models, or appearance designs;

(3) trademarks;

(4) geographical indications;

(5) trade secrets;

(6) layout designs of integrated circuits;

(7) new plant varieties; and

(8) the other subject matters as provided by law.

Article 124 A natural person has the right to succession in accordance with law.

Private property lawfully owned by a natural person may be transferred through inheritance in accordance with law.

Article 125 The persons of the civil law enjoy shareholder rights and other investor rights in accordance with law.

Article 126 The persons of the civil law enjoy other civil-law rights and interests as provided by law.

Article 127 Where there are laws particularly providing for the protection of data and online virtual assets, such provisions shall be followed.

Article 128 Where there are laws particularly providing for the protection of the civil-law rights of the minors, the elderly, the disabled, women, or the consumers, such provisions shall be followed.

Article 129 Civil-law rights may be acquired through the performance of a civil juristic act, the occurrence of an act *de facto*, the occurrence of an event as provided by law, or by other means provided by law.

Article 130 The persons of the civil law enjoy their civil-law rights according to their own will and in accordance with law free from any interference.

Article 131 While exercising civil-law rights, the persons of the civil law shall perform their obligations which are provided by law and agreed with the other parties.

Article 132 No person of the civil law shall abuse his civil-law rights and harm the interests of the State, the public interests, or the lawful rights and interests of others.

Chapter Ⅵ Civil Juristic Acts

Section 1 General Rules

Article 133 A civil juristic act is an act through which a person of the civil law, by expression of intent, creates, alters, or terminates a civil juristic relationship.

Article 134 A civil juristic act may be accomplished through a consensus of expression of intent of two or more parties, or through one party's unilateral expression of intent.

Where a legal person or an unincorporated organization makes a resolution in accordance with the procedure and voting method provided by law or stipulated in its articles of association, such a resolution is accomplished as a civil juristic act.

Article 135 A civil juristic act may be done in writing, orally, or in any other form; where a specific form is required by laws or administrative regulations, or agreed by the parties, it shall be done in such a form.

Article 136 Unless otherwise provided by law or agreed by the parties, a civil juristic act takes effect at the time it is accomplished.

A person that performs a civil juristic act may not change or revoke the act without authorization, unless doing so is in compliance with law or as consented to by the other party.

Section 2 Expression of Intent

Article 137 An expression of intent made through real-time communication becomes effective from the time the person to whom the intent is expressed is aware of its content.

An expression of intent made in a form other than real-time communication becomes effective from the time it reaches the person to whom the intent is expressed. Where such an expression of intent is made through an electronic data message and the person to whom the intent is expressed has designated a specific data-receiving system, it becomes effective from the time such a data message enters that system; where no data-receiving system is specifically designated, it becomes effective from the time the person to whom the intent is expressed knows or should have known that the data message has entered the system. Where the parties have agreed otherwise on the effective time of the expression of intent made in the form of an electronic data message, such an agreement shall prevail.

Article 138 Where an expression of intent is not made to any specific person, it becomes effective when the expression is completed, unless otherwise provided by law.

Article 139 An expression of intent made through public notice becomes effective upon the time the public notice is posted.

Article 140 A person performing a civil juristic act may make an expression of intent either expressly or implicitly.

Silence is deemed as an expression of intent only when it is so provided by law, agreed by the parties, or accords with the course of dealing between the parties.

Article 141 A person performing a civil juristic act may withdraw an expression of intent. The notice of withdrawal of the expression of intent shall reach the counterparty prior to or at the same time with the counterparty's receipt of the expression of intent.

Article 142 Where an expression of intent is made to a specific person, the meaning of the expression shall be interpreted according to the words and sentences used, with reference to the relevant terms, the nature and purpose of the civil juristic act, the custom, and the principle of good faith.

Where an expression of intent is not made to any specific person, the true intent of the person performing a civil juristic act may not be interpreted solely on the words and sentences used, but along with the relevant terms, the nature and purpose of the civil juristic act, custom, and the principle of good faith.

Section 3 Effect of a Civil Juristic Act

Article 143 A civil juristic act is valid if the following conditions are satisfied:

(1) the person performing the act has the required capacity for performing civil juristic acts;

(2) the intent expressed by the person is true; and

(3) the act does not violate any mandatory provisions of laws or administrative regulations, nor offend public order or good morals.

Article 144 A civil juristic act performed by a person who has no capacity for performing civil juristic acts is void.

Article 145 A civil juristic act, performed by a person with limited capacity for performing civil juristic acts, which is purely beneficial to the person or is appropriate to the age, intelligence, or mental status of the person is valid; any other civil juristic act performed by such a person is valid if a consent or ratification is obtained from his legal representative.

A third person involved in the act performed by a person with limited capacity for performing civil juristic acts may request the legal representative of the latter to ratify the act within 30 days from receipt of the notification. Inaction of the legal representative is deemed as refusal of ratification. Before such an act is ratified, a *bona fide* third person is entitled to revoke the act. The revocation shall be made by notice.

Article 146 A civil juristic act performed by a person and another person based on a false expression of intent is void.

Where an expression of intent deliberately conceals a civil juristic act, the validity of the concealed act shall be determined in accordance with the relevant laws.

Article 147 Where a civil juristic act is performed based on serious misunderstanding, the person who performs the act has the right to request the people's court or an arbitration institution to revoke the act.

Article 148 Where a party by fraudulent means induces the other party to perform a civil juristic act against the latter's true intention, the defrauded party has the right to request the people's court or an arbitration institution to revoke the act.

Article 149 Where a party knows or should have known that a civil juristic act performed by the other party is based on a third person's fraudulent act and is against the other party's true intention, the defrauded party has the right to request the people's court or an arbitration institution to revoke the civil juristic act.

Article 150 Where a party performs a civil juristic act against its true intention owing to duress of the other party or a third person, the coerced party has the right to request the people's court or an arbitration institution to revoke the civil juristic act.

Article 151 In situations such as where one party takes advantage of the other party that is in a desperate situation or lacks the ability of making judgment, and as a result the civil juristic act thus performed is obviously unfair, the damaged party is entitled to request the people's court or an arbitration institution to revoke the act.

Article 152 A party's right to revoke a civil juristic act is extinguished under any of the following circumstances:

(1) the party has failed to exercise the right to revocation within one year from the date when it knows or should have known of the cause for revocation, or within 90 days from the date when the party who has performed the act with serious misunderstanding knows or should have known of the cause for revocation;

(2) the party acting under duress has failed to exercise the right to revocation within one year from the date when the duress ceases; or

(3) the party who becomes aware of the cause for revocation waives the right to revocation expressly or through its own conduct.

The right to revocation is extinguished if the party fails to exercise it within five years from the date when the civil juristic act has been performed.

Article 153 A civil juristic act in violation of the mandatory provisions of laws or administrative regulations is void, unless such mandatory provisions do not lead to invalidity of such a civil juristic act.

A civil juristic act that offends the public order and good morals is void.

Article 154 A civil juristic act is void if it is conducted through malicious collusion between the actor and a counterparty and thus harms the lawful rights and interests of another person.

Article 155 A void or revoked civil juristic act does not have any legal force *ab initio*.

Article 156 If invalidation of a part of a civil juristic act does not affect the validity of the other part, the other part of the act remains valid.

Article 157 Where a civil juristic act is void, revoked, or is determined to have no legal effect, the property thus obtained by a person as a result of the act shall be returned, or compensation be made based on the appraised value of the property if it is impossible or meaningless to return the property. Unless otherwise provided by law, the loss thus incurred upon the other party shall be compensated by the party at fault, or, if both parties are at fault, by the parties proportionally.

Section 4 A Civil Juristic Act Subject to a Condition or a Term

Article 158 A condition may be attached to a civil juristic act unless the nature of the act denies such an attachment. A civil juristic act subject to a condition precedent becomes effective when the condition is fulfilled. A civil juristic act subject to a condition subsequent becomes invalid when the condition is fulfilled.

Article 159 Where a condition is attached to a civil juristic act, if a party, for the sake of its own interests, improperly obstructs the fulfillment of the condition, the condition is deemed as having been fulfilled; if a party improperly facilitates the fulfillment of the condition, the condition is deemed as not having been fulfilled.

Article 160 A term may be attached to a civil juristic act, unless the nature of such act denies such an attachment. A civil juristic act subject to a term of effectiveness becomes effective when the term begins. A civil juristic act subject to a term of termination becomes ineffective upon expiration of the term.

Chapter Ⅶ Agency

Section 1 General Rules

Article 161 A person of the civil law may perform a civil juristic act through his agent.

A civil juristic act may not be performed through an agent if the act must be performed by the principal himself in accordance with law, as agreed by the parties, or based on the nature of the act.

Article 162 A civil juristic act performed by an agent in the principal's name within the scope of authority is binding on the principal.

Article 163 Agency consists of agency by agreement and agency by operation of law.

An agent under agreement shall act in accordance with the principal's authorization. An agent by operation of law shall act in accordance with law.

Article 164 An agent who fails to perform or fully perform his duty and thus causes harm to the principal shall bear civil liability.

Where an agent maliciously colludes with a third person, thus harming the lawful rights and interests of the principal, the agent and the third person shall bear joint and several liability.

Section 2 Agency by Agreement

Article 165 In an agency by agreement, if authority is conferred in writing, it shall clearly state in the letter of authorization the name of the agent, the authorized matters, as well as the scope and duration of the authority, and it shall be signed or sealed by the principal.

Article 166 Where two or more agents are authorized to deal with the same matter for the principal, the agents shall jointly exercise the authority unless otherwise agreed by the parties.

Article 167 Where an agent knows or should have known that handling the authorized matter is in violation of law but still acts as authorized, or, if a principal knows or should have known that an act of the agent is in violation of law but raises no objection, the principal and the agent shall bear joint and several liability.

Article 168 An agent may not, in the principal's name, perform a civil juristic act with himself, unless it is consented to or ratified by the principal.

An agent who has been designated by two or more principals may not in the name of one principal perform a civil juristic act with another principal whom he concurrently represents, unless it is consented to or ratified by both principals.

Article 169 Where an agent needs to re-delegate his authority to a third person, he shall obtain consent or ratification from the principal.

If the re-delegation of authority to a third person is consented to or ratified by the principal, the principal may directly instruct the third person to do the authorized task, and the agent shall be liable only for the selection of such a third person and the instructions given to the third person by the agent himself.

If re-delegation of authority to a third person is not consented to or ratified by the principal, the agent shall be liable for the acts performed by the third person, unless the agent re-delegates his authority to a third person in an emergency situation in order to protect the interests of the principal.

Article 170 A civil juristic act performed by a person for fulfilling his responsibilities assigned by a legal person or an unincorporated organization, within the scope of authority and in the name of the legal person or the unincorporated organization, is binding on the legal person or unincorporated organization.

Restrictions imposed by a legal person or an unincorporated organization on the scope of authority of a person who performs the responsibilities assigned by the legal person or unincorporated organization are not effective against a *bona fide* counterparty.

Article 171 An act performed by a person without authority, beyond the authority, or after the authority is terminated is not effective against the principal who has not ratified it.

A counterparty may urge the principal to ratify such an act within 30 days after receipt of the notification. Inaction of the principal is deemed as a refusal of ratification. Before such an act is ratified, a *bona fide* counterparty has the right to revoke the act. The revocation shall be made by notice.

Where the aforementioned act is not ratified, a *bona fide* counterparty has the right to request the person who has performed the act to fulfill the obligations or compensate for the loss thus incurred. Provided, however, that the amount of compensation may not exceed the amount of benefit the counterparty would have received had the principal ratified the act.

Where a counterparty knows or should have known that the person performing the act has no authority, the counterparty and the said person shall bear the liability in proportion to their fault.

Article 172 An act performed by a person without authority, beyond the authority, or after the authority is terminated is effective if the counterparty has reasons to believe that the said person has authority.

Section 3 Termination of Agency

Article 173 An agency by agreement is terminated under any of the following circumstances:

(1) the term of agency expires or the authorized tasks have been completed;

(2) the principal revokes the agency or the agent resigns;

(3) the agent loses his capacity for performing civil juristic acts;

(4) the agent or the principal deceases; or

(5) the legal person or unincorporated organization who is the agent or the principal is terminated.

Article 174 An act performed by an agent under agreement after the principal deceases remains valid under any of the following circumstances:

(1) the agent does not know or should not have known of the death of the principal;

(2) the act is ratified by the heirs of the principal;

(3) it is clearly stated in the letter of authorization that the agency is terminated only upon completion of the authorized tasks; or

(4) the agent has started the act before the principal deceases and continues to act in the interests of the heirs of the principal.

The preceding paragraph shall be applied *mutatis mutandis* where the principal who is a legal person or an unincorporated organization is terminated.

Article 175 An agency by operation of law is terminated under any of the following circumstances:

(1) the principal obtains or regains full capacity for performing civil juristic acts;

(2) the agent loses the capacity for performing civil juristic acts;

(3) the agent or the principal deceases; or

(4) there exists any other circumstance as provided by law.

Chapter Ⅷ Civil Liability

Article 176 A person of the civil law shall perform civil-law obligations and bear civil liability in accordance with law or the agreement of the parties.

Article 177 Where two or more persons assume shared liability in accordance with law, each person shall bear the liability in proportion to their respective share of fault if such share can be determined, or in equal share if such share cannot be determined.

Article 178 Where two or more persons assume joint and several liability in accordance with law, the right holder has the right to request some or all of them to bear the liability.

The persons subjected to joint and several liability shall each bear the liability in proportion to their respective share of fault, or in equal share if such share cannot be determined. A person who has assumed the liability more than his share of fault has the right to contribution against the other person(s) subjected to the joint and several liability.

Joint and several liability shall be either provided by law or agreed upon by the parties.

Article 179 The main forms of civil liability include:

(1) cessation of the infringement;

(2) removal of the nuisance;

(3) elimination of the danger;

(4) restitution;

(5) restoration;

(6) repair, redoing, or replacement;

(7) continuance of performance;

(8) compensation for losses;

(9) payment of liquidated damages;

(10) elimination of adverse effects and rehabilitation of reputation; and

(11) extension of apologies.

Where punitive damages are available as provided by law, such provisions shall be followed.

The forms of civil liability provided in this Article may be applied separately or concurrently.

Article 180 A person who is unable to perform his civil-law obligations due to *force majeure* bears no civil liability, unless otherwise provided by law.

"*Force majeure*" means objective conditions which are unforeseeable, unavoidable, and insurmountable.

Article 181 A person who causes harm to the tortfeasor out of a justifiable defense bears no civil liability.

A person who, when acting out of justifiable defense, exceeds the necessary limit and thus causes undue harm to the tortfeasor shall bear appropriate civil liability.

Article 182 Where a person when seeking to avoid a peril in response to an emergency causes harm to others, the person who creates the peril shall bear civil liability.

Where the peril is caused by natural forces, the person who causes harm to others when seeking to avoid the peril bears no civil liability, but may make appropriate compensation.

Where the measures adopted by a person seeking to avoid a peril in response to an emergency are improper or exceed the necessary limit and thus cause undue harm to others, the person shall bear appropriate civil liability.

Article 183 Where a party is injured for protecting the civil-law rights and interests of another person, the tortfeasor shall bear civil liability, and the beneficiary may make appropriate compensation to the injured person. In the absence of a tortfeasor, or if the tortfeasor flees or is incapable of assuming civil liability, upon request of the injured person, the beneficiary shall make appropriate compensation.

Article 184 A person who voluntarily engages in rescuing another person in an emergency situation and thus causes harm to the latter person bears no civil liability.

Article 185 A person who infringes upon the name, likeness, reputation, or honor of a hero or a martyr and thus harms the social public interests shall bear civil liability.

Article 186 Where a party's breach of contract causes harm to the other party's personal or proprietary rights and interests, the latter party may elect to request the former to bear liability either for breach of contract or for commission of tort.

Article 187 Where a person of the civil law has to concurrently bear civil, administrative, and criminal liabilities as a result of the same act performed by him, the assumption of administrative or criminal liabilities by the person may not affect the civil liability he should bear. If the assets of the person are insufficient to pay for all the liabilities, the civil liability shall be paid first.

Chapter IX Limitation of Action

Article 188 The limitation period for a person to request the people's court to protect his civil-law rights is three years, unless otherwise provided by law.

Unless otherwise provided by law, the limitation period begins from the date when the right holder knows or should have known that his right has been harmed and that who is the obligor. However, no protection to a right is to be granted by the people's court if 20 years have lapsed since the date when the injury occurs, except that the people's court may, upon request of the right holder, extend the limitation period under special circumstances.

Article 189 Where the parties agree on payment of a debt by installment, the limitation period begins from the date when the last installment is due.

Article 190 The limitation period for a person with no or limited capacity for performing civil juristic acts to bring a claim against his legal representative begins from the date when the agency by operation of law is terminated.

Article 191 The limitation period for a minor to bring a sexual molestation claim against the offender begins from the date when the minor reaches the age of eighteen.

Article 192 Expiration of the limitation period may be used by an obligor as a defense against a claim of non-performance.

An obligor who agrees to perform a prior obligation after the limitation period expires may not later on use the expiration of the limitation period as a defense, and an obligor who has voluntarily performed such a prior obligation may not later on demand for restitution.

Article 193 The people's court may not apply the provisions on limitation periods on its own initiative.

Article 194 The limitation period is suspended if, within the last six months of the limitation period, a right holder is unable to exercise the right to claim owing to the existence of one of the following obstacles:

(1) where there is *force majeure*;

(2) where the right holder with no or limited capacity for performing civil juristic acts has no legal representative, or his legal representative deceases or loses the capacity for performing civil juristic acts or the right to representation;

(3) where no heir or administrator of an estate has been determined after the opening of succession;

(4) where the right holder is controlled by the obligor or another person; or

(5) where there are other obstacles that cause the right holder unable to exercise the right to claim.

The limitation period shall expire six months after the date when the cause for suspension is removed.

Article 195 A limitation period is interrupted under any of the following circumstances, and the limitation period shall run anew from the time of interruption or the time when the relevant proceeding is completed:

(1) the right holder requests the obligor to perform the obligation;

(2) the obligor agrees to perform the obligation;

(3) the right holder initiates a lawsuit or arbitration proceeding against the obligor; or

(4) there exists any other circumstance that has the same effect as initiating a lawsuit or arbitration proceeding by the right holder.

Article 196 The limitation period does not apply to the following rights to claim:

(1) a claim for cessation of the infringement, removal of the nuisance, or elimination of the danger;

(2) a claim for return of property of a person who has a real right in immovable or registered movable property;

(3) a claim for payment of child support or support for other family members; or

(4) any other claim to which the limitation period is not applicable in accordance with law.

Article 197 The time period, counting methods, and the grounds for suspension and interruption of the limitation period are provided by law, and any arrangement otherwise agreed by the parties is void.

An anticipatory waiver of one's interests in the limitation period made by the parties is void.

Article 198 Any provisions of law regulating the limitation period for arbitration shall be followed; in the absence of such provisions, the provisions on limitation period for litigation provided herein shall be applied *mutatis mutandis*.

Article 199 The time period within which a right holder may exercise certain rights, such as the right to revocation and the right to rescission, which are provided by law or agreed by the parties shall begin, unless otherwise provided by law, from the date when the right holder knows or should have known that he has such a right, and the provisions on the suspension, interruption, or extension of the limitation period are not be applicable. Upon expiration of the time period, the right to revocation, the right to rescission, and the like rights are extinguished.

Chapter X Counting of Periods of Time

Article 200 Time periods referred to in the civil law are counted by year, month, day, and hour according to the Gregorian calendar.

Article 201 Where a time period is counted by year, month, and day, the day on which the time period begins is not counted in and the period runs from the following day.

Where a time period is counted by hour, the period begins to run from the hour as provided by law or agreed by the parties.

Article 202 Where a time period is counted by year and month, the corresponding date of the due month is the last day of the time period; in the absence of such a corresponding date, the last day of that month is the last day of the time period.

Article 203 Where the last day of a time period falls on a legal holiday, the day after the holiday is deemed as the last day of the period.

The last day shall end at 24 : 00; where a business hour is applied, the last day shall end at the time the business is closed.

Article 204 The counting of a time period shall be governed by the provisions of this Code, unless otherwise provided by law or agreed by the parties.

Book Two Real Rights

Part One General Provisions

Chapter I General Rules

Article 205 This Book regulates the civil-law relations arising from the attribution and utilization of things.

Article 206 The State upholds and improves the fundamental socialist economic systems, such as the ownership system under which diverse forms of ownership co-develop with public ownership as the mainstay, the distribution system under which multiple forms of distribution co-exist with distribution according to work as the mainstay, as well as the system of socialist market economy.

The State consolidates and develops the public sector of the economy, and encourages, supports, and guides the development of the non-public sector of the economy.

The State implements a socialist market economy and protects the equal legal status and development rights of all market participants.

Article 207 The real rights of the State, collectives, private individuals, and the other right holders are equally protected by law and free from infringement by any organization or individual.

Article 208 The creation, alteration, transfer, or extinguishment of the real rights in immovable property shall be registered in accordance with law. The creation and transfer of real rights in movable property shall be subject to the delivery of the movable property in accordance with law.

Chapter Ⅱ Creation, Alteration, Transfer, and Extinguishment of Real Rights

Section 1 Registration of Immovable Property

Article 209 The creation, alteration, transfer, or extinguishment of a real right in immovable property shall become effective upon registration in accordance with law, and does not take effect without registration, unless otherwise provided by law.

Ownership registration is not required for natural resources that are provided by law to be owned by the State.

Article 210 The registration of immovable property shall be handled by the registration authority at the place where the immovable property is located.

The State implements a unified registration system with respect to immovable property. The scope, authorities, and measures for the unified registration shall be specified by laws and administrative regulations.

Article 211 When applying for registration of immoveable property, an applicant shall, in light of the different items to be registered, provide necessary materials such as the proof of real rights, metes and bounds, and the area of the immovable property.

Article 212 The registration authority shall perform the following responsibilities:

(1) to examine the proof of real rights and other necessary materials provided by the applicant;

(2) to inquire of the applicant regarding the relevant items for registration;

(3) to register the relevant items truthfully and in a timely manner; and

(4) to perform other responsibilities as provided by laws and administrative regulations.

Where further proof is required for the relevant information of the immovable property to be registered, the registration authority may require the applicant to provide supplementary materials, and may conduct onsite inspection where necessary.

Article 213 A registration authority may not engage in the following acts:

(1) to require an appraisal of the immovable property;

(2) to carry out repeated registration in the name of annual inspection, and the like; or

(3) to engage in other acts that exceed the scope of its responsibilities for registration.

Article 214 The creation, alteration, transfer, or extinguishment of a real right of the immovable property that is required by law to be registered becomes effective at the time when it is recorded in the register of immovable property.

Article 215 A contract concluded by the parties on the creation, alteration, transfer, or extinguishment of a real right becomes effective upon its formation, unless it is otherwise provided by law or agreed upon by the parties, and the validity of the contract is not affected by the fact that the real right registration is not completed.

Article 216 The register of immovable property is the basis for determining the attribution and contents of the real rights in immovable property.

The register of immovable property shall be kept by the registration authority.

Article 217 The real right certificate for immovable property is a proof of a right holder's entitlement to the real right in the immovable property. The items recorded in the real right certificate for immovable property shall be consistent with what are recorded in the register of immovable property; in case of inconsistency between the two, what is recorded in the register of immovable property shall prevail, unless there is evidence establishing a clear error in the register of immovable property.

Article 218 A right holder or an interested person may apply for retrieving and making copies of the information of the registered immovable property, and the registration authority shall provide the information.

Article 219 An interested person may not disclose or illegally use the registered information of a right holder's immovable property.

Article 220 A right holder or an interested person may apply for rectification of the registration if he believes that an item is incorrectly recorded in the register of immovable property. Where the right holder as recorded in the register of immovable property agrees in writing to make rectification, or where there is evidence establishing a clear error in the register, the registration authority shall rectify it.

Where the right holder as recorded in the register of immovable property does not agree to make rectification, an interested person may apply for registration of a demurrer. Where the registration authority registers the demurrer but the applicant fails to file a lawsuit within 15 days from the date of such a registration, the registration of demurrer becomes ineffective. Where a demurrer is improperly registered and damage is thus caused to the right holder, the right holder may request the applicant to pay damages.

Article 221 Where the parties enter into an agreement for the sale of a house or on any other real right in immovable property, they may apply for registration of a priority notice to a registration authority in accordance with the agreement so as to ensure the realization of the real right in the future. Where, after the priority notice is registered, the immovable property is disposed of without the consent of the right holder as registered in the priority notice, the disposition is not effective in terms of the real right.

Where, after the priority notice is registered, no application for registration of the real right of immovable property has been made within 90 days from the date on which the creditor's claim extinguishes or the immovable property is eligible for registration, the registration of the priority notice becomes ineffective.

Article 222 A party who provides false materials upon application for registration and thus causes damage to another person shall be liable for compensation.

Where damage is caused to another person due to an error upon registration, the registration authority shall be liable for compensation. After having made such compensation, the registration authority has the right to indemnification against the person who has made the error.

Article 223 The fee for the registration of immovable property shall be collected on a piece-by-piece basis and may not be collected in proportion to the area, size, or purchase price of the immovable property.

Section 2 Delivery of Movable Property

Article 224 The creation or transfer of a real right in movable property shall take effect upon delivery, unless otherwise provided by law.

Article 225 The creation, alteration, transfer, or extinguishment of the real rights in vessels, aircrafts, motor vehicles, and the like, that have not been registered, is not effective against a *bona fide* third person.

Article 226 Where a right holder is already in possession of a movable property before a real right in the movable property is created or transferred, the real right in the movable property becomes effective at the time when the civil juristic act is effected.

Article 227 Where a third person is in possession of a movable property before a real right in the movable property is created or transferred, the person obligated to deliver the movable property may transfer his right to restitution against the third person as substitute for delivery.

Article 228 Where, upon transfer of a real right in movable property, the parties agree that the transferor continues to be in possession of the movable property, the real right in the movable property becomes effective at the time when such an agreement enters into effect.

Section 3 Other Rules

Article 229 Where a real right is created, altered, transferred, or extinguished as a result of a legal document issued by the people's court or an arbitration institution, or based on an expropriation decision made by the people's government, the creation, alteration, transfer, or extinguishment of the real right becomes effective at the time when the legal document or expropriation decision enters into effect.

Article 230 Where a real right is acquired through succession, the real right as inherited becomes effective at the time when the succession opens.

Article 231 Where a real right is created or extinguished as a result of a *de facto* act such as lawful construction or demolition of a house, the creation or extinguishment of the real right becomes effective when the *de facto* act is accomplished.

Article 232 Where disposition of a real right in immovable property as provided in this Section is required by law to be registered, the disposition of the real right, if not so registered, is not effective.

Chapter Ⅲ Protection of Real Rights

Article 233 Where a real right is infringed upon, the right holder may have the problem solved by means of settlement, mediation, arbitration, litigation, and the like.

Article 234 Where a dispute arises over the attribution or contents of a real right, an interested person may request for confirmation of the right.

Article 235 Where immovable or movable property is possessed by a person not entitled to do so, the right holder may request for restitution.

Article 236 Where there is a nuisance or a potential nuisance against a real right, the right holder may request for removal of the nuisance or elimination of the danger.

Article 237 Where immovable or movable property is destructed or damaged, the right holder may request for repair, redoing, replacement, or restoration to the original condition in accordance with law.

Article 238 Where a real right is infringed upon and damage is thus caused, the right holder may, in accordance with law, request the infringing person to pay damages or bear other civil liabilities.

Article 239 The forms of real right protection provided in this Chapter may be applied either separately or concurrently according to the circumstances of the infringement of a right.

Part Two Ownership

Chapter IV General Rules

Article 240 An owner is entitled to possess, use, benefit from, and dispose of his own immovable or movable property in accordance with law.

Article 241 An owner of immovable or movable property is entitled to create a right to usufruct and a security interest on his own immovable or movable property. A usufructuary or security interest holder, when exercising his rights, may not harm the rights and interests of the owner.

Article 242 Where immovable or movable property is provided by law to be exclusively owned by the State, no organization or individual may acquire ownership of it.

Article 243 For the need of the public interest, the collectively-owned land and the houses and other immovable property of an organization or individual may be expropriated within the scope of authority and pursuant to the procedures provided by law.

In the case of expropriation of collectively-owned land, land compensation fees, resettlement subsidies, and compensation fees for rural villagers' dwellings and other ground attachments as well as young crops shall be paid in full in a timely manner in accordance with law, and social security premiums of the farmers whose land has been expropriated shall be arranged, their lives secured, and their lawful rights and interests safeguarded.

In the case of expropriation of houses or other immovable property of organizations or individuals, compensation for the expropriation shall be made in accordance with law in order to safeguard the lawful rights and interests of the person whose immovable property has been expropriated. In the case of expropriation of individuals' dwelling houses, the housing conditions of such individuals shall also be guaranteed.

No organization or individual may embezzle, misappropriate, secretly distribute, intercept, default on the payment of the expropriation compensation fees, or the like.

Article 244 The State provides special protection to cultivated land, strictly restricts the conversion of agricultural land into land used for construction purposes, and controls the overall volume of the land used for construction purposes. Collectively-owned land may not be expropriated exceeding the scope of authority or in violation of the procedures provided by law.

Article 245 The immovable or movable property of an organization or individual may, in response to an emergency such as providing disaster relief and preventing and controlling pandemics, be requisitioned within the scope of authority and pursuant to the procedures provided by law. The requisitioned immovable or movable property shall be returned to the aforementioned organization or individual after use. Where the immovable or movable property of an organization or individual is requisitioned, or where it is destructed, damaged, or lost after being requisitioned, compensation shall be made.

Chapter V State Ownership, Collective Ownership, and Private Ownership

Article 246 Where a property is provided by law to be owned by the State, the property belongs to the State, namely, to the whole people.

The ownership rights over the State-owned property shall be exercised by the State Council on behalf of the State, unless otherwise provided by law.

Article 247 Mineral deposits, waters, and sea areas are owned by the State.

Article 248 Uninhabited islands are owned by the State, and the State Council exercises the ownership rights over the uninhabited islands on behalf of the State.

Article 249 Urban land is owned by the State. Land in rural and urban suburbs that is provided by law to be owned by the State is owned by the State.

Article 250 Natural resources, such as forests, mountain ridges, grass-lands, unreclaimed land, and mudflats, other than those provided by law to be collectively-owned, are owned by the State.

Article 251 The wild animal and plant resources that are provided by law to be owned by the State are owned by the State.

Article 252 Radio-frequency spectrum resources are owned by the State.

Article 253 The cultural relics that are provided by law to be owned by the State are owned by the State.

Article 254 The assets for national defense are owned by the State.

Infrastructures such as railways, roads, electric power facilities, telecommunication facilities, as well as oil and gas pipelines that are provided by law to be owned by the State are owned by the State.

Article 255 A State organ has the right to possess and use the immovable and movable property directly under its control and to dispose of such property in accordance with law and the relevant regulations made by the State Council.

Article 256 A public institution established by the State has the right to possess and use the immovable and movable property directly under its control, and to benefit from and dispose of such property in accordance with law and the relevant regulations made by the State Council.

Article 257 With respect to enterprises invested by the State, the State Council and the local people's governments shall, on behalf of the State, perform the investor's duties and enjoy the investor's rights and interests respectively in accordance with laws and administrative regulations.

Article 258 The State-owned property is protected by law, and no organization or individual may misappropriate, loot, secretly distribute, intercept, or destroy such property.

Article 259 Institutions and their staff with the duties of administration and supervision over the State-owned property shall strengthen the administration and supervision of the State-owned property in accordance with law, strive to preserve and increase the value of such property and prevent any loss thereof; they shall assume legal liabilities in accordance with law if losses are caused to the State-owned property as a result of their abuse of powers or dereliction of duties.

A person, who causes losses to the State-owned property by transferring it at low prices, secretly distributing it in conspiracy with other persons, creating a security interest on it without authorization, or by other means in the course of enterprise restructuring, merger or division, affiliated transactions, and the like, in violation of the provisions on the administration of the State-owned property, shall bear legal liability in accordance with law.

Article 260 The collectively-owned immovable and movable property include:

(1) the land, forests, mountain ridges, grasslands, unreclaimed land, and mudflats that are provided by law to be owned by collectives;

(2) the buildings, production facilities, and farmland water conservancy facilities that are owned by collectives;

(3) the educational, scientific, cultural, public health, sports, and other facilities that are owned by collectives; and

(4) any other immovable and movable property that are owned by collectives.

Article 261 The immovable and movable property of a farmer collective are collectively owned by the members of this collective.

The following matters shall be decided by the collective's members in accordance with statutory procedures:

(1) land contracting schemes, and the contracting of land to any organization or individual outside this collective;

(2) adjustment to the contracted land among the persons who have the right to contractual management of land;

(3) methods for the use and distribution of funds such as land compensation fees;

(4) matters such as changes in the ownership of enterprises invested by the collective; and

(5) other matters as provided by law.

Article 262 With respect to the collectively-owned land, forests, mountain ridges, grasslands, unreclaimed land, mudflats, and the like, the ownership thereof shall be exercised in accordance with the following provisions:

(1) where they are owned by the farmer collective of a village, the ownership shall be exercised collectively by the collective economic organization of the village or the villagers' committee on behalf of the collective in accordance with law;

(2) where they are owned by two or more farmer collectives within a village, the ownership shall be exercised by the respective collective economic organizations or the villagers' groups on behalf of the collectives in accordance with law; and

(3) where they are owned collectively by the farmer collective of a rural-town, the ownership shall be exercised by the economic organizations of the town on behalf of the collective.

Article 263 With respect to the immovable and movable property owned by an urban-town collective, the collective is entitled to possess, use, benefit from, and dispose of such property in accordance with laws and administrative regulations.

Article 264 Rural collective economic organizations, villagers' committees, and villagers' groups shall make the situation of the collectively-owned property known to the members of this collective in accordance with laws, administrative regulations, and their articles of association, as well as the local covenants. Members of the collective have the right to retrieve and make copies of the relevant materials.

Article 265 The property owned by a collective is protected by law, and no organization or individual may misappropriate, loot, secretly distribute, or destruct such property.

Where a decision made by a rural collective economic organization, a villagers' committee, or the person in charge thereof infringes upon the lawful rights and interests of a member of the collective, the infringed member may request the people's court to revoke the decision.

Article 266 A private individual has the right to own his lawful income, houses, articles for daily use, production tools, raw materials, as well as other immovable and movable property.

Article 267 The property lawfully owned by a private individual is protected by law, and no organization or individual may misappropriate, loot, or destruct such property.

Article 268 The State, collectives, and private individuals may establish companies with limited liabilities, joint stock companies limited by shares, or other enterprises through making capital contributions in accordance with law. Where the immovable or movable property of the State, collectives, and private individuals are invested in an enterprise, the investors are, in accordance with their agreement or in proportion to their investment, entitled to receive returns on the assets, make major decisions, and select business managers, and obligated to perform their duties.

Article 269 A for-profit legal person has the right to possess, use, benefit from, and dispose of its immovable and movable property in accordance with laws, administrative regulations, and its articles of association.

The provisions of the relevant laws, administrative regulations, and articles of association shall apply to the rights of a legal person other than a for-profit legal person with respect to its immovable and movable property.

Article 270 The immovable and movable property that is lawfully owned by a social-organization legal person or a donation-funded legal person is protected by law.

Chapter Ⅵ Ownership of a Building's Units

Article 271 A unit owner has the ownership over an exclusive unit of a building, such as a dwelling space or a space used for operating businesses, and has the right to co-own and jointly manage the common space other than the exclusive units.

Article 272 A unit owner has the right to possess, use, benefit from, and dispose of his exclusive unit of a building. The unit owner may not, when exercising his rights, endanger the safety of the building or impair the lawful rights and interests of other unit owners.

Article 273 A unit owner has rights and assumes duties with respect to the common space other than the exclusive units of the building, and may not refuse to perform such duties on the ground that he has waived such rights.

Where a unit owner transfers a dwelling space or a space used for business operations owned by him in a building, his rights to co-own and jointly manage the common space therein shall be transferred concomitantly.

Article 274 Roads within the construction zone are co-owned by all unit owners, except for those that are part of the urban public roads. Green spaces within the construction zone are co-owned by all unit owners, except for those that are part of the urban public green spaces and those expressly indicated to be owned by private individuals. Other public places, public facilities, and spaces used for property management service within the construction zone are co-owned by all unit owners.

Article 275 The ownership of the parking spaces and garages planned for parking vehicles within the construction zone shall be agreed upon by the parties by way of selling, giving away as gifts, leasing, and the like.

The parking spaces for parking vehicles that occupy the roads or other spaces co-owned by all unit owners are co-owned by all unit owners.

Article 276 The parking spaces and garages planned for parking vehicles within the construction zone shall first meet the needs of the unit owners.

Article 277 The unit owners may establish the owners' assembly and elect the members of the owners' committee. The specific conditions of and procedures for the establishment of the owners' assembly and the owners' committee shall be in accordance with laws and regulations.

The relevant department of the local people's government and the residents' committee shall provide guidance to and assistance in the establishment of the owners' assembly and the election of the members of the owners' committee.

Article 278 The following matters shall be jointly decided by the unit owners:

(1) to formulate and amend the procedural rules of the owners' assembly;

(2) to formulate and amend the covenants on management;

(3) to elect or replace members of the owners' committee;

(4) to employ and remove the property management service enterprise or other managers;

(5) to use maintenance funds for buildings and auxiliary facilities thereof;

(6) to raise maintenance funds for buildings and auxiliary facilities thereof;

(7) to renovate and reconstruct buildings and auxiliary facilities thereof;

(8) to change the intended use of the co-owned space or making use of the co-owned space to engage in business activities; and

(9) to handle other major matters relating to co-ownership and the right to joint management.

The quorum for matters subject to the unit owners' joint decision shall be two thirds or more of the exclusive units both by area and by number of unit owners. Decisions of matters provided in Subparagraphs (6) through (8) shall be subject to the consent of the unit owners representing three quarters or more of the participating exclusive units both by area and by number of unit owners. Decisions of other matters provided in the preceding paragraph shall be subject to the consent of the unit owners representing more than half of the participating exclusive units both by area and by number of unit owners.

Article 279 No unit owner may turn a dwelling space into a space used for operating businesses in violation of laws, regulations, or the covenants on management. A unit owner who intends to turn a dwelling space into a space used for operating businesses shall, in addition to abiding by laws, regulations, and the covenants on management, obtain unanimous consent from all interested unit owners.

Article 280 Decisions of the owners' assembly or the owners' committee are legally binding on unit owners.

Where a decision made by the owners' assembly or the owners' committee infringes upon the lawful rights and interests of a unit owner, the infringed owner may request the people's court to revoke it.

Article 281 The maintenance funds for buildings and their auxiliary facilities are co-owned by the unit owners. The funds may, upon joint decision of the unit owners, be used for the maintenance, renewal, and renovation of the co-owned spaces, such as elevators, roofs, exterior walls, and barrier-free facilities. Information on raising and using the maintenance funds for buildings and their auxiliary facilities shall be publicized on a regular basis.

Where a building and its auxiliary facilities need to be maintained in an emergency situation, the owners' assembly or the owners' committee may, in accordance with law, apply for the use of the maintenance funds for the building and its auxiliary facilities.

Article 282 The income generated from the space co-owned by the unit owners that is received by the developer, the property management service enterprise, or other managers is co-owned by all unit owners after reasonable costs are deducted.

Article 283 Where there is an agreement on matters such as allocation of expenses on and distribution of income gained from a building and its auxiliary facilities, such matters shall be determined in accordance with the agreement; where there is no agreement or the relevant agreement is unclear, such matters shall be determined in proportion to the area of each unit owner's exclusive unit to the total area.

Article 284 The unit owners may either manage the buildings and the auxiliary facilities on their own, or entrust a property management service enterprise or another manager for such a purpose.

The unit owners have the right to replace, in accordance with law, the property management service enterprise or the other managers employed by the developer.

Article 285 The property management service enterprise or otherwise a manager shall, as entrusted by the unit owners, manage the buildings and their auxiliary facilities within the construction zone in accordance with the provisions of Book Three of this Code relating to contracts for property management service, subject itself to the supervision of the unit owners, and respond to the unit owners' inquiries about property management services in a timely manner.

The property management service enterprise or other managers shall carry out emergency measures and other management measures implemented by the government in accordance with law and actively cooperate in the performance of the relevant work.

Article 286 The unit owners shall abide by laws, regulations, and the covenants on management, and their relevant acts shall meet the requirements of conserving resources and protecting the ecological environment. With respect to the emergency measures and other management measures implemented by the government in accordance with law that are carried out by the property management service enterprise or other managers, the unit owners shall, in accordance with law, be cooperative.

With respect to an act impairing the lawful rights and interests of others, such as arbitrarily discarding garbage, discharging pollutants or noises, feeding and keeping animals in violation of the regulations, constructing structures against rules and regulations, encroaching on passages, and refusing to pay property management fees, the owners' assembly or the owners' committee has the right to request the actor to discontinue such infringements, remove the nuisance, eliminate the danger, restore to the original condition, and compensate for the losses thus caused.

Where a unit owner or an actor refuses to perform the relevant duties, the party concerned may make a report to, or lodge a complaint with the competent administrative department, which shall handle the case in accordance with law.

Article 287 A unit owner has the right to request the developer, the property management service enterprise or other managers, and other unit owners to bear civil liability for any act done by them that infringes upon his lawful rights and interests.

Chapter Ⅶ Adjacent Relationships

Article 288 The persons entitled to adjacent rights in immovable property shall properly deal with adjacent relationships in accordance with the principles of facilitation to production, convenience for daily lives, solidarity and mutual assistance, and fairness and reasonableness.

Article 289 Where there are laws and regulations providing for adjacent relationships, those provisions shall be applied. Where there are no such provisions, local customs may be followed.

Article 290 A person entitled to the real rights in immovable property shall provide a person entitled to an adjacent right in the immovable property the necessary convenience for the use of water or drainage.

The right to utilization of natural flowing water shall be reasonably allocated among the persons entitled to the adjacent rights in the immovable property. When discharging the water, the direction of the natural water flow shall be respected.

Article 291 A person entitled to the real rights in immovable property shall provide necessary convenience for the persons entitled to an adjacent right who have to utilize his land for passage, and the like.

Article 292 Where a person entitled to the real rights in immovable property has to utilize the adjacent land or building for constructing or maintaining a building, or for laying electrical wires, cables, or the pipelines for water, heating, gas, or the like, the person entitled to the real rights in the adjacent land or building shall provide necessary convenience.

Article 293 The construction of a building may not violate the relevant construction standards of the State or obstruct the ventilation, lighting, or sunlight of the adjacent buildings.

Article 294 A person entitled to the real rights in immovable property may not, in violation of the regulations of the State, discard solid wastes or emit harmful substances such as atmospheric pollutants, water pollutants, soil pollutants, noises, light radiation, or electromagnetic radiation.

Article 295 A person entitled to the real rights in immovable property may not endanger the safety of the adjacent immovable property when excavating land, constructing buildings, laying pipelines, installing facilities, or the like.

Article 296 A person entitled to the real rights in immovable property who utilizes the adjacent immovable property for the purpose of using water, drainage, passage, laying pipelines, or the like, shall spare no effort to avoid causing damage to the person entitled to the real rights in the adjacent immovable property.

Chapter Ⅷ Co-ownership

Article 297 Immovable or movable property may be co-owned by two or more organizations or individuals. Co-ownership consists of co-ownership by shares and joint co-ownership.

Article 298 Co-owners by shares have the ownership of the co-owned immovable or movable property according to their shares.

Article 299 Joint co-owners jointly have the ownership of the co-owned immovable or movable property.

Article 300 The co-owners shall manage the co-owned immovable or movable property in accordance with their agreement. Where there is no agreement or the relevant agreement is unclear, each co-owner is entitled and obligated to manage it.

Article 301 Unless otherwise agreed by the co-owners, any disposition of the co-owned immovable or movable property, or any major repair or change of the nature or intended use of the co-owned immovable or movable property shall be subject to the consent of the co-owners by shares whose shares account for two thirds or more of the total shares, or to the consent of all joint co-owners.

Article 302 The management expenses of and other burdens on a thing co-owned by the co-owners shall be borne according to the agreement among the co-owners where there is such an agreement; where there is no agreement or the relevant agreement is unclear, these expenses shall be borne by the co-owners by shares proportionally, and by the joint co-owners jointly.

Article 303 Where the co-owners have agreed not to partition the co-owned immovable or movable property in order to maintain the co-ownership, the agreement shall be followed, except that a co-owner may request partition if there is a compelling reason for partition. Where there is no agreement or the relevant agreement is unclear, a co-owner by shares may request partition at any time, whereas a joint co-owner may request partition in case the basis for the joint ownership ceases to exist or there is a compelling reason for partition. Compensation shall be made if partition causes damage to the other co-owners.

Article 304 The co-owners may determine through negotiation the way of partition of the co-owned thing. Where they fail to reach an agreement, and where the co-owned immovable or movable property is divisible and its value is not diminished upon division, partition in kind shall be effected; where it is difficult to divide the co-owned thing or where its value would be impaired upon division, partition shall be carried out through dividing the proceeds based on appraisal or obtained from auction or a sale of it.

Where the immovable or movable property acquired by a co-owner by means of partition is defective, the other co-owners shall share the losses.

Article 305 A co-owner by shares may transfer the portion of shares he owned in the co-owned immovable or movable property. The other co-owners have the right of pre-emption to buy the shares under equivalent conditions.

Article 306 Where a co-owner by shares transfers the portion of shares he owned in the co-owned immovable or movable property, he shall notify the other co-owners of the conditions of transfer in a timely manner. The other co-owners shall exercise their right of pre-emption within a reasonable period of time.

Where two or more co-owners assert their rights of pre-emption, they shall determine through negotiation the proportion of shares each may purchase; where no agreement is reached, they shall exercise their right of pre-emption in proportion to the shares they each own at the time of transfer.

Article 307 In terms of external relations, the co-owners are jointly and severally entitled to claims and are jointly and severally obligated to perform obligations arising from the co-owned immovable or movable property, unless it is otherwise provided by law or where the third person is aware that the co-owners are not in a relationship of joint and several claims and obligations. In terms of internal relations, unless otherwise agreed by the co-owners, the co-owners by shares are entitled to claims and obligated to perform obligations in proportion to the shares they each own, and the joint co-owners are jointly entitled to claims and obligated to perform obligations. A co-owner by shares who has performed the obligation in excess of his shares has the right to contribution against the other co-owners.

Article 308 Where there is no agreement among the co-owners or the relevant agreement is unclear as to whether the co-owned immovable or movable property is under co-ownership by shares or under joint co-ownership, the immovable or movable property shall be deemed to be under co-ownership by shares, unless the co-owners are in a relationship such as a familial relationship or the like.

Article 309 The share of a co-owner by shares in the immovable or movable property shall be determined according to his capital contribution where there is no agreement or the relevant agreement is unclear. Where it is impossible to determine the amount of capital contribution, each co-owner by shares shall be entitled to an equal share.

Article 310 The relevant provisions of this Chapter shall be applied *mutatis mutandis* to the situation where two or more organizations or individuals are jointly entitled to a right to usufruct or a security interest.

Chapter IX Special Provisions on the Acquisition of Ownership

Article 311 Where a person with no right to dispose of immovable or movable property transfers it to another person, the owner has the right to recover it; unless otherwise provided by law, the transferee acquires the ownership of the immovable or movable property under the following circumstances:

(1) the transferee is in good faith at the time when the immovable or movable property is transferred to him;

(2) the transfer is made at a reasonable price; and

(3) the transferred immovable or movable property has been registered as required by law, or has been delivered to the transferee where registration is not required.

Where a transferee acquires the ownership of the immovable or movable property in accordance with the provisions of the preceding paragraph, the original owner has the right to claim damages against the person who disposes of the property without a right.

Where a party acquires, in good faith, a real right other than ownership, the provisions of the preceding two paragraphs shall be applied *mutatis mutandis*.

Article 312 An owner or any other right holder has the right to recover a lost thing. Where the lost thing is possessed by another person by way of transfer, the right holder has the right to claim damages against the person who disposes of the thing without the right to disposition, or to request the transferee to return the original thing within two years from the date on which the right holder knows or should have known of the transferee; provided, however, that where the transferee has acquired the lost thing at auction or from a qualified business operator, the right holder shall, at the time of requesting the return of the original thing, reimburse the expenses that have been paid by the transferee. The right holder has, after having reimbursed the expenses paid by the transferee, the right to indemnification against the person who disposes of the thing without the right to disposition.

Article 313 After a *bona fide* transferee acquires the movable property, the original rights in the movable property are extinguished, unless the *bona fide* transferee knows or should have known of such rights at the time of the transfer.

Article 314 Where a lost thing is found, it shall be returned to its right holder. The finder shall, in a timely manner, notify its right holder or hand it over to the relevant departments such as the department for public security.

Article 315 Where the relevant department receives a lost thing and knows who is its right holder, the department shall, in a timely manner, notify him to collect the lost thing; where the department does not know who is the right holder, it shall issue a lost-and-found notice in a timely manner.

Article 316 A finder shall well keep a lost thing before it is delivered to the relevant department, and the relevant department shall well keep it before it is collected. A person who, intentionally or by gross negligence, causes the lost thing under his custody destructed, damaged, or lost shall bear civil liability.

Article 317 The right holder of a lost thing shall, at the time of collecting it, pay to the finder or the relevant department the necessary expenses, such as the expense for safekeeping the lost thing.

Where a right holder has offered a reward for finding the lost thing, he shall, at the time of collecting the lost thing, perform his obligations as promised.

Where a finder misappropriates the lost thing, he is neither entitled to request reimbursement of expenses such as the expense for safekeeping the lost thing, nor entitled to request the right holder to perform the obligations as promised.

Article 318 Where a lost thing has not been claimed by anybody within one year from the date the lost-and-found notice is publicized, the lost thing is to be escheated to the State.

Article 319 Where a drifting thing is found or a thing buried underground or hidden is discovered, the provisions relating to the finding of lost things shall be applied *mutatis mutandis*, unless otherwise provided by law.

Article 320 Where a principal thing is transferred, the accessary thereof shall be transferred concomitantly, unless otherwise agreed by the parties.

Article 321 Unless otherwise agreed by the parties, the natural fruits of a thing shall be acquired by the owner of the thing, or by a usufructuary if there are both an owner and a usufructuary of the thing.

The civil fruits of a thing shall be acquired as agreed by the parties if there is such an agreement, or, where there is no agreement or the relevant agreement is unclear, in accordance with the course of dealing.

Article 322 A thing, that is created as a result of processing, or combining or mixing with another thing or things, shall be owned as agreed if there is such an agreement, or in accordance with law if there is no agreement or the relevant agreement is unclear, or, in the absence of any provisions in law, be determined in compliance with the principles of making full use of the thing and protecting the party without fault. Where damage is caused to another party owing to one party's fault or owing to the determination of the attribution of the thing, indemnity or compensation shall be paid.

Part Three Rights to Usufruct

Chapter X General Rules

Article 323 A usufructuary has the right to possess, use, and benefit from the immovable or movable property owned by another person in accordance with law.

Article 324 Organizations and individuals may, in accordance with law, possess, use, and benefit from the natural resources owned by the State, the State-owned natural resources that are used by collectives, and the natural resources that are owned by collectives as provided by law.

Article 325 The State implements a system of compensation for the use of natural resources, unless otherwise provided by law.

Article 326 A usufructuary shall, when exercising his right, abide by the provisions of laws on the protection, rational exploitation, and utilization of resources and the protection of the ecological environment. The owner may not interfere with the exercise of such rights by the usufructuary.

Article 327 Where a right to usufruct is extinguished or adversely affected due to expropriation or requisition of the immovable or movable property, the usufructuary has the right to compensation according to the provisions of Articles 243 and 245 of this Code.

Article 328 The right to use the sea areas that is acquired in accordance with law is protected by law.

Article 329 The right to explore and mine minerals, to draw water, and to use waters and mudflats to engage in aquaculture or fishing that are acquired in accordance with law is protected by law.

Chapter XI Rights to Contractual Management of Land

Article 330 Rural collective economic organizations shall adopt a two-tier management system, with household contractual management as the basis and integrated with the collective management.

A system of contractual management of land is adopted in accordance with law for cultivated land, forestland, grassland, and other land used for agricultural purposes which are owned by farmers collectively, or owned by the State and used by farmers collectively.

Article 331 A person who has the right to contractual management of land is, in accordance with law, entitled to possess, use, and benefit from the cultivated land, forestland, and grassland contracted and managed by him, and to engage in agricultural production such as crop cultivation, forestry, and animal husbandry.

Article 332 The term of a contract for cultivated land is 30 years. The term of a contract for grassland ranges from 30 to 50 years. The term of a contract for forestland ranges from 30 to 70 years.

Upon expiration of the term of contract as provided in the preceding paragraph, the person with the right to contractual management of land is entitled to renew the contract in accordance with the provisions of laws on rural land contracting.

Article 333 A right to contractual management of land is created at the time when the contract on the right to contractual management of land enters into effect.

The registration authority shall issue a certificate, such as a certificate of the right to contractual management of land, a certificate of the right to forestry, and the like, to the person entitled to the respective right to contractual management of land, and establish a register for this purpose to record and confirm such rights.

Article 334 The persons with the rights to contractual management of land are entitled to exchange or transfer such rights in accordance with law. The contracted land may not be used for non-agricultural construction purposes without being approved in accordance with law.

Article 335 Where the rights to contractual management of land are exchanged or transferred, the parties may apply to the registration authority for registration; without registration, such exchange or transfer may not be asserted against a *bona fide* third person.

Article 336 Within the term of contract, the party offering the contract may not adjust the contracted land.

Under special circumstances such as severe deterioration on the contracted land caused by natural disasters, appropriate adjustments shall be made in accordance with the provisions of laws on rural land contracting where necessary.

Article 337 Within the term of contract, the party offering the contract may not take back the contracted land unless otherwise provided by law.

Article 338 Where the contracted land is expropriated, the affected person with the right to contractual management of land is entitled to the corresponding compensation according to the provisions of Article 243 of this Code.

Article 339 A person with the right to contractual management of land may decide on his own to transfer the right to management of land to others by leasing, contributing it as shares, or other means in accordance with law.

Article 340 Within the time limit as agreed in the contract, the person with the right to management of land is entitled to possess the rural land, to carry out agricultural production and operation on his own, and to benefit therefrom.

Article 341 The right to management of land which is transferred for a term of five years or longer is created when the contract for the transfer enters into force. The parties may apply to the registration authority for registration of the right to management of land; without registration, such a right may not be asserted against a *bona fide* third person.

Article 342 Where rural land is contracted by means including bidding, auction, or open negotiation, for which a title certificate is obtained through registration in accordance with law, the right to manage such land may, in accordance with law, be transferred by means of leasing, contributing it as shares, mortgaging, or by other means.

Article 343 Where contractual management is adopted for the State-owned land that is used for agricultural purposes, the relevant provisions of this Book shall be applied *mutatis mutandis*.

Chapter XII Rights to Use Land for Construction Purposes

Article 344 With respect to the State-owned land zoned for construction purposes, a person with the right to use a lot of such land is entitled to possess, use, and benefit from the lot, and to use it to construct buildings, structures, and auxiliary facilities.

Article 345 The right to use a lot of land for construction purposes may be created separately on the surface of, above, or below the lot of land.

Article 346 The right to use a lot of land for construction purposes shall be created in conformity with the requirements for conservation of resources and protection of the ecological environment, and in compliance with the provisions of laws and administrative regulations on the planned use of the lot, and may not impair the rights to usufruct already created thereon.

Article 347 The right to use a lot of land for construction purposes may be created by way of transfer or gratuitous grant.

The bidding, auction, or other means of public bidding shall be adopted in transferring a lot of land used for business purposes, such as for industrial, commercial, tourism, recreational, and commercial residential purposes, or where there are two or more intended users competing for the right to use the same lot of land.

The creation of a right to use a lot of land for construction purposes by way of gratuitous grant is strictly restricted.

Article 348 Where a right to use a lot of land for construction purposes is created through bidding, auction, agreement, or other means of transfer, the parties shall enter into a contract in writing for the transfer of the right to use the lot of land for construction purposes.

A contract for the transfer of the right to use a lot of land for construction purposes generally contains the following clauses:

(1) the name and address of each party;

(2) the metes and bounds and area of the lot of land;

(3) the space occupied by the buildings, structures, and the auxiliary facilities thereof;

(4) the planned use and zoning conditions of the lot;

(5) the term of the right to use the lot of land for construction purposes;

(6) the transfer fee and other fees, and the mode of payment thereof; and

(7) the means of dispute resolution.

Article 349 To create a right to use a lot of land for construction purposes, application shall be filed with the registration authority for the registration of the right. The right to use a lot of land for construction purposes is created upon registration. The registration authority shall issue a title certificate to the person entitled to the right.

Article 350 A person who has the right to use a lot of land for construction purposes shall make reasonable use of the lot and may not change its planned use. Where it is necessary to change the planned use of the lot, approval shall be obtained from the competent administrative department in accordance with law.

Article 351 A person who has the right to use a lot of land for construction purposes shall pay the transfer fee and other fees in accordance with law and the contract.

Article 352 The ownership of buildings, structures, and auxiliary facilities thereof constructed by a person with the right to use the lot of land for construction purposes belongs to the person, unless it is proved by evidence to the contrary.

Article 353 Unless otherwise provided by law, the persons with a right to use a lot of land for construction purposes are entitled to transfer, exchange, offer as capital contribution, give away as a gift, or mortgage their rights.

Article 354 Where a right to use a lot of land for construction purposes is transferred, exchanged, offered as capital contribution, given away as a gift, or mortgaged, the parties shall enter into a contract thereon in writing. The term of the use shall be agreed upon by the parties, provided that it may not exceed the remaining term of the right to use the lot of land for construction purposes.

Article 355 Where a right to use a lot of land for construction purposes is transferred, exchanged, offered as capital contribution, or given away as a gift, an application for registration of the change shall be filed with the registration authority.

Article 356 Where a right to use a lot of land for construction purposes is transferred, exchanged, offered as capital contribution, or given away as a gift, the buildings, structures, and auxiliary facilities thereof attached to the land shall be disposed of concomitantly.

Article 357 Where a building or structure, and auxiliary facilities thereof are transferred, exchanged, offered as capital contribution, or given away as a gift, the right to use the lot of land for construction purposes in the lot of land occupied by the building, structure, and auxiliary facilities thereof shall be disposed of concomitantly.

Article 358 Where a right to use a lot of land for construction purposes needs to be taken back prior to expiration of its term for public interest purposes, compensation shall be paid for the houses and other immovable property on the land according to the provisions of Article 243 of this Code, and the portion of the unused transfer fee shall be refunded.

Article 359 The right to use a lot of land for construction of residential buildings is automatically renewed upon expiration of the term. The payment, reduction, or exemption of the renewal fees shall be dealt with in accordance with the provisions of laws and administrative regulations.

The renewal of the right to use a lot of land for construction of buildings other than residences, upon expiration of the term, shall be dealt with in accordance with the provisions of the laws. The ownership of the buildings and other immovable property on such lot of land shall be determined in accordance with the agreement, or, where there is no agreement or the relevant agreement is unclear, in accordance with the provisions of laws and administrative regulations.

Article 360 Where a right to use a lot of land for construction purposes is extinguished, the transferor of the right shall deregister the right in a timely manner. The registration authority shall withdraw the title certificate thereof.

Article 361 The using of a lot of collectively-owned land for construction purposes shall be dealt with in accordance with the provisions of the laws on land administration.

Chapter XIII Rights to Use House Sites

Article 362 A person who has the right to use a house site is entitled to possess and use the lot of land owned by the collective, and to utilize such lot of land to build a dwelling and auxiliary facilities in accordance with law.

Article 363 The acquisition, exercise, and transfer of the right to use a house site are governed by the laws on land administration and the relevant regulations of the State.

Article 364 Where a house site is destroyed due to a natural disaster or for other reasons, the right to use the house site is extinguished. A new house site shall be allocated in accordance with law to the villagers who have lost their house site.

Article 365 Where a registered right to use a house site is transferred or extinguished, registration of the change or deregistration of the right shall be made in a timely manner.

Chapter XIV Rights of Habitation

Article 366 A person with a right of habitation is entitled to the right to usufruct of possessing and using another person's dwelling as agreed in the contract, so as to meet his needs of habitation.

Article 367 To create a right of habitation, the parties shall enter into a contract on such a right in writing.

A contract on a right of habitation generally contains the following clauses:

(1) the name and address of each party;

(2) the location of the dwelling;

(3) the conditions and requirements for the habitation;

(4) the duration of the right of habitation; and

(5) the means of dispute resolution.

Article 368 A right of habitation shall be created free of charge, unless otherwise agreed by the parties. To create a right of habitation, an application for the registration of the right shall be filed with the registration authority. The right of habitation is created upon registration.

Article 369 A right of habitation may not be transferred or inherited. The dwelling in which a right of habitation is created may not be let on lease, unless otherwise agreed by the parties.

Article 370 A right of habitation is extinguished if the term of the right expires, or if the person entitled to the right deceases. Where a right of habitation is extinguished, deregistration of the right shall be made in a timely manner.

Article 371 Where a right of habitation is created by will, the relevant provisions of this Chapter shall be applied *mutatis mutandis*.

Chapter XV Easements

Article 372 A person who has a right to easement is entitled to utilize the immovable property of another person as agreed in a contract so as to enhance the efficiency of his own immovable property.

The immovable property of another person referred to in the preceding paragraph is the servient land, and the immovable property of the person entitled to the easement is the dominant land.

Article 373 To create an easement, the parties shall enter into an easement contract in writing.

An easement contract generally contains the following clauses:

(1) the name and address of each party;

(2) the location of the servient land and the dominant land;

(3) the purposes and methods of utilizing the servient land;

(4) the duration of the easement;

(5) the fees and the mode of payment; and

(6) the means of dispute resolution.

Article 374 An easement is created at the time the easement contract enters into effect. Where the parties request for registration, applications may be filed with the registration authority for the registration of the easement; without registration, such an easement may not be asserted against a *bona fide* third person.

Article 375 A right holder of the immovable property served as the servient land shall allow the person entitled to an easement to utilize the immovable property as agreed in the contract and may not interfere with the exercise of the right to easement by such person.

Article 376 A person entitled to an easement shall utilize the servient land in accordance with the purposes and methods of utilization as agreed in the contract, and minimize restrictions on the real rights of the right holder in the servient land.

Article 377 The term of an easement shall be agreed upon by the parties, provided that it may not exceed the remaining term of the right to usufruct, such as the right to contractual management of land or the right to use a lot of land for construction purposes.

Article 378 Where an owner of a lot of land is entitled to or is encumbered with an easement, when a right to usufruct, such as a right to contractual management of land or a right to use a house site is created on the lot of land, the usufructuary shall continue to be entitled to or be encumbered with the easement thereon that has already been created.

Article 379 Where a right to usufruct, such as a right to contractual management of land, a right to use a lot of land for construction purposes, and a right to use a house site, has already been created on a lot of land, the owner of the lot of land may not create an easement on the lot without the consent of the usufructuary.

Article 380 An easement may not be transferred separately. Where a right to contractual management of land, a right to use a lot of land for construction purposes, and the like rights are transferred, the easement shall be transferred concomitantly, unless otherwise agreed in the contract.

Article 381 An easement may not be mortgaged separately. Where a right to contractual management of land, a right to use a lot of land for construction purposes, and the like rights are mortgaged, the easement shall be transferred concomitantly upon enforcement of the mortgage.

Article 382 Where a right to easement is involved when the dominant land and a right to contractual management of land, a right to use a lot of land for construction purposes, and the like rights thereon are partially transferred, the transferee is simultaneously entitled to the easement.

Article 383 Where a right to easement is involved when the servient land and a right to contractual management of land, a right to use a lot of land for construction purposes, and the like rights thereon are partially transferred, the easement is legally binding on the transferee.

Article 384 Where a person entitled to an easement is under either of the following circumstances, the person who has the right in the servient land is entitled to rescind the easement contract to extinguish the easement:

(1) abusing the right to easement in violation of the provisions of laws or the contract; or

(2) in case of paid use of the servient land, failing to pay the relevant fees despite of receipt of two warning notices within a reasonable period of time after the payment is due according to the agreement.

Article 385 Where a registered easement is altered, transferred, or extinguished, the registration of the change or deregistration shall be made in a timely manner.

Part Four Security Interests

Chapter XVI General Rules

Article 386 Where a debtor fails to perform his obligation due, or any event upon the occurrence of which a security interest is to be enforced as agreed upon by the parties occurs, the person entitled to the security interest has priority to be paid from the collateral in accordance with law, unless otherwise provided by law.

Article 387 Where a creditor needs to secure his claims in a civil activity such as lending, buying and selling, and the like, he may create a security interest in accordance with the provisions of this Code and other laws.

Where a third person provides security to the creditor for the debtor, the debtor may be requested to provide a counter-security. Counter-securities shall be governed by the provisions of this Code and other laws.

Article 388 To create a security interest, a security contract shall be entered into in accordance with the provisions of this Code and other laws. Security contracts include mortgage contracts, pledge contracts, and other contracts with a function of security. A security contract is a contract secondary to the principal contract under which the principal claims and obligations arise. Where the principal contract is void, the security contract is also void, unless otherwise provided by law.

Where a security contract is determined to be void, if the debtor, the security provider, and the creditor are at fault, they shall each bear civil liability in proportion to their fault.

Article 389 Unless otherwise agreed by the parties, the scope covered by a security interest includes the principal claim and its interests based on the principal contract, liquidated damages, compensatory damages, and the expenses arising from safekeeping the collateral and enforcing the security interests.

Article 390 Where a collateral is destructed, damaged, or lost, or is expropriated during the secured period, the person entitled to a security interest has priority to be paid from the insurance payment, compensation, or indemnity received on the collateral. Where the collateral is destructed, damaged, or lost, or is expropriated prior to the due date of performance of the secured claim, the insurance payment, compensation, or indemnity may also be placed in escrow.

Article 391 Where a third person provides security and the creditor allows the debtor to transfer all or part of the secured obligations without the third person's written consent, the security provider is no longer liable for securing the part of the obligations so transferred.

Article 392 Where a claim is secured by both a collateral and a surety, and the debtor fails to perform his obligation due or any event upon which a security interest is to be enforced as agreed upon by the parties occurs, the creditor shall enforce the claim in accordance with the agreement. Where there is no agreement or the relevant agreement is unclear, if the collateral is provided by the debtor, the creditor shall first enforce the claim against the collateral, and if the collateral is provided by a third person, the creditor may elect to enforce the claim against the collateral or request the surety to assume liability. After the third person who provides security has assumed such liability, he has the right to indemnification against the debtor.

Article 393 A security interest is extinguished under any of the following circumstances:

(1) the claim under the principal contract is extinguished;

(2) the security interest is enforced;

(3) the creditor waives his security interest; or

(4) there exists any other circumstance in which the security interest is extinguished as provided by law.

Chapter XVII Mortgage

Section 1 General Mortgage

Article 394 Where a debtor or a third person, in order to secure the performance of an obligation, mortgages his property to the creditor without relinquishing the possession of the property, the creditor has priority to be paid from the collateral if the debtor fails to perform his obligation due or an event upon the occurrence of which the security interest in the collateral is to be enforced as agreed by the parties occurs.

The debtor or the third person as specified in the preceding paragraph is the mortgagor, the creditor is the mortgagee, and the collateral mortgaged to secure the claim is the mortgaged property.

Article 395 The following property, which the debtor or a third person is entitled to dispose of, may be mortgaged:

(1) buildings and other things attached to the land;

(2) the right to use a lot of land for construction purposes;

(3) the right to use the sea areas;

(4) production equipment, raw materials, work in process, and finished products;

(5) buildings, vessels, and aircrafts under construction;

(6) vehicles for transport; and

(7) any other property not prohibited by laws or administrative regulations from being mortgaged.

A mortgagor may mortgage the property listed in the preceding paragraph concurrently.

Article 396 An enterprise, an individual-run industrial and commercial household, or an agricultural production operator may mortgage their production equipment, raw materials, work in process, or finished products that they currently own or thereafter acquired, and if the debtor fails to perform his obligation due or any event upon the occurrence of which the security interest in the mortgaged property is to be enforced as agreed by the parties occurs, the creditor has priority to be paid from the movable property determined at the time when the mortgaged property is ascertained.

Article 397 Where a building is mortgaged, the right to use the lot of land for construction purposes in the area occupied by the building shall be mortgaged concomitantly. Where a right to use a lot of land for construction purposes is mortgaged, any building on the lot of land shall be mortgaged concomitantly.

Where a mortgagor fails to concomitantly mortgage the property as provided in the preceding paragraph, the unmortgaged property in question shall be deemed to be concomitantly mortgaged.

Article 398 A right to use a lot of land for construction purposes of a township or village enterprise may not be mortgaged separately. Where the factory premises or any other buildings of a township or village enterprise are mortgaged, the right to use the lot of land for construction purposes in the area occupied by the buildings shall be concomitantly mortgaged.

Article 399 The following property may not be mortgaged:

(1) land ownership;

(2) the right to use the land owned by a collective, such as house sites, land and hills retained for household use, unless it may be mortgaged as provided by law;

(3) educational facilities, medical and health facilities, and other public welfare facilities of non-profit legal persons established for public welfare purposes, such as schools, kindergartens, and medical institutions;

(4) property of which the ownership or right to the use is unclear or disputed;

(5) property that has been sealed up, detained, or placed under custody in accordance with law; and

(6) any other property that may not be mortgaged as provided by laws or administrative regulations.

Article 400 To create a mortgage, the parties shall enter into a mortgage contract in writing.

A mortgage contract generally contains the following clauses:

(1) the type and amount of the secured claim;

(2) the term during which the debtor shall perform obligations;

(3) such particulars as the name and quantity of the mortgaged property; and

(4) the scope of the security interest covered.

Article 401 Where, prior to the due date of performance of an obligation, the mortgagee reaches an agreement with the mortgagor under which the mortgaged property belongs to the creditor in the event that the debtor fails to perform the obligation due, the mortgagee, regardless, may only have priority to be paid from the mortgaged property in accordance with law.

Article 402 To create a mortgage on the property as specified in Subparagraphs (1) through (3) of the first paragraph of Article 395, or on the building under construction as specified in Subparagraph (5) of the first paragraph of Article 395 of this Code, registration shall be made for the mortgage. The mortgage shall be created upon registration.

Article 403 A mortgage on movable property shall be created at the time when the mortgage contract enters into effect; without registration, such a mortgage may not be asserted against a *bona fide* third person.

Article 404 A mortgage on movable property may not be asserted against a buyer who has paid a reasonable purchase price and acquired the mortgaged property in the ordinary course of business.

Article 405 Where mortgaged property has been let to and possessed by another person prior to creation of the mortgage, the lease relationship is not affected by the mortgage.

Article 406 A mortgagor may transfer the mortgaged property to another person during the term of the mortgage unless otherwise agreed by the parties. The transfer of the mortgaged property does not affect the mortgage.

A mortgagor who transfers the mortgaged property to another person shall notify the mortgagee in a timely manner. The mortgagee may request the mortgagor to apply the proceeds of the transfer to pay off the obligation before it is due, or place such proceeds in escrow where he may establish that the transfer of the mortgaged property may impair his right to the mortgage. The portion of the proceeds obtained from the transfer in excess of the amount of the obligation owed shall belong to the mortgagor, whereas any deficiency balance shall be paid by the debtor.

Article 407 A mortgage may not be transferred separately from the underlying claim or be used as security for another claim. Where a claim is transferred, the mortgage securing the claim shall be transferred concomitantly with it, unless otherwise provided by law or agreed by the parties.

Article 408 Where an act of a mortgagor suffices to reduce the value of the mortgaged property, the mortgagee is entitled to request the mortgagor to refrain from performing such an act. Where the value of the mortgaged property is reduced, the mortgagee is entitled to request the mortgagor to restore its value or provide additional security to the extent of the reduced value. Where the mortgagor neither restores the original value of the mortgaged property, nor provides additional security, the mortgagee is entitled to request the debtor to pay off the debt before it is due.

Article 409 A mortgagee may waive his right to the mortgage, or waive his priority order in the line of the mortgagees. A mortgagee and the mortgagor may reach an agreement to change such things as the mortgagee's priority order in the line of the mortgagees and the amount of the secured claim, provided that any change to the mortgage may not adversely affect the other mortgagees without their written consent.

Where a debtor creates a mortgage on his own property, and the mortgagee waives his right to the mortgage and his priority order in the line of the mortgagees, or changes the mortgage, the other security providers shall be exempted from the security liability to the extent of the rights and interests of the mortgagee that are forfeited owing to the waiver of his priority to be paid from the mortgaged property, unless the other security providers are committed to still provide security.

Article 410 Where a debtor fails to perform his obligation due or an event upon the occurrence of which a mortgage is to be enforced as agreed upon by the parties occurs, the mortgagee may, upon agreement with the mortgagor, have the priority right to appraise and accept the mortgaged property, or apply the proceeds obtained from auction or sale of the mortgaged property to satisfy his claim against the mortgagor. Where the agreement is detrimental to the interests of other creditors, the other creditors may request the people's court to rescind the agreement.

Where a mortgagee and a mortgagor fail to reach an agreement on the methods of enforcing the mortgage, the mortgagee may request the people's court to have the mortgaged property sold at auction or in a sale.

The appraisal or sale of the mortgaged property shall be based on the market price.

Article 411 Where a mortgage is created in accordance with the provisions of Article 396 of this Code, the mortgaged property shall be ascertained at the time when one of the following circumstances occurs:

(1) the claim is not satisfied upon expiration of the period of performance of the obligation;

(2) the mortgagor is declared bankrupt or dissolved;

(3) an event upon the occurrence of which the mortgage is to be enforced as agreed upon by the parties occurs; or

(4) there exists any other circumstance that seriously affects the enforcement of the claim.

Article 412 Where a debtor fails to perform his obligation due or an event upon the occurrence of which a mortgage is to be enforced as agreed upon by the parties occurs, resulting in the seizure of the mortgaged property by the people's court in accordance with law, the mortgagee is entitled to collect the natural fruits or civil fruits accrued from the mortgaged property as of the date of the seizure, unless the mortgagee fails to notify the person who is obligated to pay off the civil fruits.

The fruits and proceeds as specified in the preceding paragraph shall first be applied to offset the expenses of collecting them.

Article 413 Where the appraised value of mortgaged property or the proceeds obtained from auction or sale of it is in excess of the amount of the obligation owed, any excess shall belong to the mortgagor, whereas any deficiency balance shall be paid by the debtor.

Article 414 Where a property is mortgaged to two or more creditors, the proceeds obtained from auction or sale of the mortgaged property shall be applied to repay the debts in accordance with the following provisions:

(1) where the mortgages have all been registered, the priority order of payment is based on the priority in time of registration;

(2) a registered mortgage has priority over an unregistered mortgage to be paid; and

(3) where none of the mortgages are registered, payment shall be made on a *pro rata* basis against the claims.

The preceding paragraph shall be applied *mutatis mutandis* with regard to the priority order of payment for other security interests that are registrable.

Article 415 Where both a mortgage and a pledge are created on the same property, the priority order of repayment with the proceeds obtained from auction or sale of the property shall be based on the priority in time of registration and delivery of the property.

Article 416 Where a principal claim secured by a mortgage on movable property is the purchase price of the mortgaged property, and registration for the mortgage is made within 10 days after delivery of the property, the mortgagee has the priority to be paid over the other persons, other than a lienholder, who have security interests thereon in relation to the purchaser of the mortgaged property.

Article 417 Where a right to use a lot of land for construction purposes is mortgaged, any newly added buildings on the lot of land are not part of the mortgaged property. Upon enforcement of the mortgage on the right to use the lot of land for construction purposes, the newly added buildings on such land shall be disposed of concomitantly with the right to use such land for construction purposes. Provided, however, that the mortgagee has no priority to be paid from the proceeds obtained from disposition of the newly added buildings.

Article 418 Where a right to use a lot of land owned by a collective is mortgaged in accordance with law, the nature of the ownership and the purpose of use of the land may not be altered without going through statutory procedures after the mortgage is enforced.

Article 419 A mortgagee shall exercise his right to mortgage within the limitation period for claiming against the principal obligation; otherwise no protection may be provided by the people's court.

Section 2 Maximum Mortgage for Floating Claims

Article 420 Where a debtor or a third person provides a collateral for future claims that will arise consecutively within a certain period of time to secure performance of the obligations, if the debtor fails to perform an obligation due or an event upon the occurrence of which such a mortgage is to be enforced as agreed upon by the parties occurs, the mortgagee has the priority to be paid from the mortgaged property up to the maximum amount of his claims.

A claim that exists prior to the creation of the maximum mortgage for floating claims may, upon consent of the parties, be included in the claims secured by such a mortgage.

Article 421 Before the claims secured by the maximum mortgage for floating claims are ascertained, where part of the claims are transferred, the mortgage may not be transferred unless otherwise agreed by the parties.

Article 422 Before the claims secured by a maximum mortgage for floating claims are ascertained, the mortgagee and the mortgagor may change by agreement the period of time for the ascertainment of the claims, the scope of the claims, and the maximum amount of the claims, provided that such changes may not adversely affect other mortgagees.

Article 423 The claims of the mortgagee are ascertained under any of the following circumstances:

(1) where the agreed period of time for the claims to be ascertained expires;

(2) where there is no agreement on the period of time for the claims to be ascertained or the relevant agreement is unclear, and the mortgagee or the mortgagor requests for ascertainment of the claims after the lapse of two years from the date of the creation of the mortgage;

(3) where it is impossible for a new claim to arise;

(4) where the mortgagee knows or should have known that the mortgaged property has been sealed up or detained;

(5) where the debtor or the mortgagor is declared bankrupt or dissolved; or

(6) there exists any other circumstance under which the claims are to be ascertained as provided by law.

Article 424 In addition to the provisions of this Section, the relevant provisions of Section 1 of this Chapter shall be applied to the maximum mortgage for floating claims.

Chapter XVIII Pledge

Section 1 Pledge in Movable Property

Article 425 Where a debtor or a third person pledges his movable property to the creditor for possession in order to secure the performance of an obligation, if the debtor fails to perform the obligation due or an event upon the occurrence of which the pledge is to be enforced as agreed upon by the parties occurs, the creditor has priority to be paid from the movable property.

The debtor or third person as specified in the preceding paragraph is the pledgor, the creditor is the pledgee, and the movable property delivered is the pledged property.

Article 426 Movable property may not be pledged where its transfer is prohibited by laws or administrative regulations.

Article 427 To create a pledge, the parties shall enter into a pledge contract in writing.

A pledge contract generally contains the following clauses:

(1) the type and amount of the secured claim;

(2) the term for the debtor to perform the obligation;

(3) such particulars as the name and quantity of the pledged property;

(4) the scope of the security covered; and

(5) the time for and the mode of the delivery of the pledged property.

Article 428 Where, prior to the due date of performance of an obligation, the pledgee reaches an agreement with the pledgor under which the pledged property belongs to the creditor in the event that the debtor fails to perform the obligation due, the pledgee, regardless, may only have priority to be paid from the pledged property in accordance with law.

Article 429 A pledge is created upon delivery of the pledged property by the pledgor.

Article 430 A pledgee has the right to collect the fruits and proceeds accrued from the pledged property unless otherwise agreed in the contract.

The fruits and proceeds as specified in the preceding paragraph shall first be applied to offset the expenses of collection of them.

Article 431 A pledgee who, during the effective period of the pledge, uses or disposes of the pledged property without the consent of the pledgor and thus causes damage to the latter shall be liable for compensation.

Article 432 A pledgee is obligated to well keep the pledged property, and shall be liable for compensation where the pledged property is destructed, damaged, or lost due to his improper custody.

Where a pledgee's act is likely to cause the pledged property to be destructed, damaged, or lost, the pledgor may request the pledgee to place the pledged property in escrow, or request the pledgee to allow him to discharge the obligation before it is due and return the pledged property.

Article 433 Where, due to a cause the pledgee is not responsible for, the pledged property is likely to be damaged or significantly diminished in value which suffices to jeopardize the pledgee's rights, the pledgee has the right to request the pledgor to provide additional security; where the pledgor fails to do so, the pledgee may have the pledged property sold at auction or in a sale and may, by agreement with the pledgor, apply the proceeds obtained from the auction or sale to discharge the obligation before it is due or place such proceeds in escrow.

Article 434 A pledgee shall be liable for compensation where he, during the effective period of the pledge, repledges the pledged property without the consent of the pledgor to a third person and thus causes destruction, damage, or loss to the pledged property.

Article 435 A pledgee may waive his right to the pledge. Where a debtor creates a pledge on his own property and the pledgee waives his right to the pledge, the other security providers shall be exempted from the security liability to the extent of the rights and interests of the pledgee that are forfeited owing to the waiver of his priority to be paid from the collateral, unless the other security providers are committed to still provide security.

Article 436 A pledgee shall return the pledged property after the debtor has performed his obligation or the pledgor has paid the secured claim before it is due.

Where a debtor fails to perform an obligation due or an event upon the occurrence of which a pledge is to be enforced as agreed upon by the parties occurs, the pledgee may, by agreement with the pledgor, appraise and accept the pledged property as satisfaction of his claim, or have priority to be paid from the proceeds obtained from auction or sale of the pledged property.

The appraisal or sale of the pledged property shall be based on the market price.

Article 437 A pledgor may request the pledgee to timely enforce the pledge after expiration of the period of performance of the obligation; where the pledgee fails to do so, the pledgor may request the people's court to have the pledged property sold at auction or in a sale.

Where a pledgor requests the pledgee to timely enforce the pledge and damage is caused to the pledgor owing to the pledgee's indolence in doing so, the pledgee shall be liable for compensation.

Article 438 After a pledged property is appraised, or is sold at auction or in a sale, where the value of the pledged property as appraised or the proceeds obtained from auction or sale is in excess of the amount of the obligation owed, any excess shall belong to the pledgor, whereas any deficiency balance shall be paid by the debtor.

Article 439 A pledgor and a pledgee may create a maximum pledge for floating claims upon agreement.

In addition to the relevant provisions of this Section, the relevant provisions of Section 2 of Chapter XVII of this Book shall be applied *mutatis mutandis* to the maximum pledge for floating claims.

Section 2 Pledge on a Right

Article 440 The following rights, which a debtor or a third person is entitled to dispose of, may be pledged:

(1) bills of exchange, promissory notes, and checks;

(2) bonds and certificates of deposits;

(3) warehouse receipts and bills of lading;

(4) transferable fund shares and equity;

(5) transferable proprietary rights consisted in intellectual property such as the right to the exclusive use of registered trademarks, patent rights, and copyrights;

(6) existing and after-acquired accounts receivable; and

(7) any other proprietary right that may be pledged in accordance with the provisions of laws and administrative regulations.

Article 441 Unless otherwise provided by law, a pledge on a bill of exchange, promissory note, check, bond, certificate of deposits, warehouse receipt, or bill of lading is created at the time when the certificate of such a right is delivered to the pledgee, or, in the absence of such a certificate, at the time when the pledge is registered.

Article 442 Where the maturity date for the payment or the delivery of goods against a pledged bill of exchange, promissory note, check, bond, certificate of deposit, warehouse receipt, or bill of lading precedes the due date of the principal claim, the pledgee may cash the certificate or take delivery of the goods, and, upon agreement with the pledgor, apply the purchase price or the goods accepted to discharge the obligation before it is due or place it in escrow.

Article 443 A pledge on fund shares or equity is created upon registration of the pledge.

The fund shares or equity, after being pledged, may not be transferred unless otherwise agreed by the pledgor and the pledgee through consultation. The proceeds obtained by the pledgor from the transfer of the pledged fund shares or equity shall be applied to pay to the pledgee to discharge the obligation before it is due or be placed in escrow.

Article 444 A pledge on a proprietary right in intellectual property, such as the right to the exclusive use of a registered trademark, a patent right, or copyright, is created upon registration.

A proprietary right in intellectual property, after being pledged, may not be transferred or licensed by the pledgor to another person, unless otherwise agreed by the pledgor and the pledgee through consultation. The proceeds obtained by the pledgor from the transfer or licensing of the proprietary right in the pledged intellectual property shall be applied to pay to the pledgee to discharge the obligation before it is due or be placed in escrow.

Article 445 A pledge on an account receivable is created upon registration.

An account receivable, after being pledged, may not be transferred unless otherwise agreed by the pledgor and the pledgee through consultation. The proceeds obtained by the pledgor from the transfer of the account receivable shall be applied to pay to the pledgee to discharge the obligation before it is due or be placed in escrow.

Article 446 In addition to the provisions of this Section, the relevant provisions of Section 1 of this Chapter shall be applied to the pledge on rights.

Chapter XIX Lien

Article 447 Where a debtor fails to perform his obligation due, the creditor may retain the debtor's movable property which is already in the lawful possession of the creditor and has priority to be paid from such movable property.

The creditor as specified in the preceding paragraph is the lienholder, the movable property in his possession for this purpose is the property under lien.

Article 448 The movable property retained under a lien by the creditor shall be in the same legal relationship as the underlying claim, unless the lienholder and the debtor are both enterprises.

Article 449 Movable property that may not be retained under a lien as provided by law or agreed by the parties may not be so retained.

Article 450 Where the property retained under a lien is a divisible thing, the value of the retained property shall be equivalent to the amount of the obligation.

Article 451 A lienholder is obligated to well keep the retained property and shall be liable for compensation where the retained property is destructed, damaged, or lost due to improper custody.

Article 452 A lienholder has the right to collect the fruits and proceeds accrued from the property retained under a lien.

The fruits and proceeds as specified in the preceding paragraph shall first be applied to offset the expenses for collection of them.

Article 453 A lienholder and the debtor shall reach an agreement on the period of performance of the obligation after the property is retained under the lien; where there is no agreement or the relevant agreement is unclear, the lienholder shall give the debtor a period of 60 or more days as the term of performance, unless the retained movable property is fresh, living, or perishable so that it is hard to keep it for long. Where a debtor defaults upon expiration of the term of performance, the lienholder may, upon agreement with the debtor, appraise the retained property, or be paid with priority from the proceeds obtained from auction or sale of the retained property.

The appraisal or sale of the retained property shall be based on the market price.

Article 454 A debtor may request the lienholder to enforce the lien after expiration of the period of performance of the obligation; where the lienholder fails to do so, the debtor may request the people's court to have the retained property sold at auction or in a sale.

Article 455 After the property retained under a lien is appraised and accepted by the lienholder as full or partial satisfaction of his claim, or is sold at auction or in a sale, where the value of the retained property or the proceeds obtained from auction or sale of the retained property is in excess of the amount of the obligation owed, any excess shall belong to the debtor, whereas any deficiency balance shall be paid by the debtor.

Article 456 Where a lien is created on movable property on which a mortgage or pledge has already been created, the lienholder has priority to be paid.

Article 457 A lien is extinguished where the lienholder loses possession of the retained property or accepts another form of security provided by the debtor.

Part Five Possession

Chapter XX Possession

Article 458 In the case of possession of immovable or movable property based on a contractual relationship, matters such as the use of the immovable or movable property, the benefits therefrom, and the default liability shall be subject to the agreement in the contract; where there is no agreement thereon in the contract or the relevant agreement is unclear, the relevant provisions of laws shall be followed.

Article 459 Where damage is caused to immovable or movable property by its possessor as a result of use of the property, a *mala fide* possessor shall be liable for compensation.

Article 460 Where immovable or movable property is in the possession of another person, a person holding a right in the property may request the possessor to return the original property and its fruits and proceeds, provided that the necessary expenses incurred by a *bona fide* possessor for the maintenance of the immovable or movable property shall be paid.

Article 461 Where immovable or movable property in another person's possession is destructed, damaged, or lost, and a person holding a right in the property requests for compensation, the possessor shall return to the right holder the amount of insurance payment, compensation or indemnity he has received for the property destructed, damaged, or lost; where the right holder has not been fully compensated, a possessor *mala fide* shall also compensate for the loss.

Article 462 Where immovable or movable property is trespassed or converted, its possessor is entitled to request restitution. Where there is a nuisance against the possession, the possessor has the right to request the removal of the nuisance or the elimination of the danger. Where damage is caused as a result of the trespass, conversion, or nuisance, the possessor has the right to request compensatory damages in accordance with law.

The possessor's right to request for restitution is extinguished if such a right has not been exercised within one year from the date the trespass or conversion occurs.

Book Three Contracts

Part One General Provisions

Chapter Ⅰ General Rules

Article 463 This Book regulates the civil-law relations arising from contracts.

Article 464 A contract is an agreement on the establishment, modification, or termination of a civil juristic relationship between persons of the civil law.

An agreement on establishing a marriage, adoption, guardianship, or the like personal relationships shall be governed by the provisions of laws providing for such personal relationships; in the absence of such provisions, the provisions of this Book may be applied *mutatis mutandis* according to the nature of such an agreement.

Article 465 A contract formed in accordance with law is protected by law.

A contract formed in accordance with law is legally binding only on the parties to the contract, unless otherwise provided by law.

Article 466 Where the parties have a dispute on the understanding of a contract clause, the meaning of the disputed clause shall be determined according to the provision in the first paragraph of Article 142 of this Code.

Where a contract is made in two or more languages which are agreed to be equally authentic, the words and sentences used in each text are presumed to have the same meaning. Where the words and sentences used in each text are inconsistent, interpretation shall be made in accordance with the related clauses, the nature, and the purpose of the contract, and the principle of good faith, and the like.

Article 467 For a contract not explicitly provided in this Code or other laws, the General Provisions of this Book shall be applied, and the provisions provided in this Book and other laws on a contract which is most similar to the said contract may be applied *mutatis mutandis*.

The laws of the People's Republic of China shall apply to the contracts of Sino-foreign equity joint venture, contracts of Sino-foreign contractual joint venture, or contracts of Sino-foreign cooperation in the exploration and exploitation of natural resources, that are to be performed within the territory of the People's Republic of China.

Article 468 For a creditor-debtor relation not arising from a contract, the provisions of laws relating to such relations shall be applied; in the absence of such provisions, the relevant provisions of the General Provisions of this Book shall be applied, unless they are not applicable due to the nature of the creditor-debtor relation.

Chapter Ⅱ Conclusion of Contracts

Article 469 The parties may conclude a contract in writing, orally, or in other forms.

A writing refers to any form that renders the content contained therein capable of being represented in a tangible form, such as a written agreement, letter, telegram, telex, facsimile, or the like.

A data message in any form, such as electronic data interchange and e-mails, that renders the content contained therein capable of being represented in a tangible form and accessible for reference and use at any time is deemed as a writing.

Article 470 The content of a contract shall be agreed by the parties and generally includes the following clauses:

(1) name or entity name and domicile of each party;

(2) objects;

(3) quantity;

(4) quality;

(5) price or remuneration;

(6) period, place, and manner of performance;

(7) default liability; and

(8) the means of dispute resolution.

The parties may consult with the various types of model contracts when concluding a contract.

Article 471 The parties may conclude a contract by making an offer and acceptance or through other means.

Article 472 An offer is an expression of intent to conclude a contract with another person, and the expression of intent shall satisfy the following conditions:

(1) the content shall be specific and definite; and

(2) it is indicated therein that the offeror is to be bound by his expression of intent upon acceptance thereof by an offeree.

Article 473 An invitation to offer is a manifestation that a person expects another person to make an offer to him. Auction announcements, bidding announcements, stock prospectuses, bond prospectuses, fund prospectuses, commercial advertisements and promotions, mailed price catalogs, and the like, are invitations to offer.

A commercial advertisement and promotion constitute an offer if their content satisfies the conditions for an offer.

Article 474 The time when an offer becomes effective is governed by the provisions of Article 137 of this Code.

Article 475 An offer may be withdrawn. The withdrawal of an offer is governed by the provisions of Article 141 of this Code.

Article 476 An offer may be revoked, unless under either of the following circumstances:

(1) the offeror has explicitly indicated that the offer is irrevocable by specifying a time limit for acceptance or in any other manner; or

(2) the offeree has reasons to believe that the offer is irrevocable and has made reasonable preparations for performing the contract.

Article 477 Where an expression of intent to revoke an offer is made through real-time communication, the content of such expression of intent shall be known to the offeree before the offeree makes an acceptance; where an expression of intent to revoke an offer is not made through real-time communication, it shall reach the offeree before the offeree makes an acceptance.

Article 478 An offer becomes invalid under any of the following circumstances:

(1) the offer is rejected;

(2) the offer is revoked in accordance with law;

(3) the offeree makes no acceptance prior to expiration of the time limit for acceptance; or

(4) the offeree materially alters the content of the offer.

Article 479 An acceptance is an expression of intent of the offeree to accept an offer.

Article 480 An acceptance shall be made by means of notice, except that an acceptance may be made by performing an act according to the parties' course of dealing or as indicated in the offer.

Article 481 An acceptance shall reach the offeror within the time limit specified in the offer.

Where no time limit for acceptance is specified in the offer, an acceptance shall reach the offeror in accordance with the following provisions:

(1) where an offer is made through real-time communication, acceptance shall be made promptly; or

(2) where an offer is not made through real-time communication, the acceptance shall reach the offeror within a reasonable period of time.

Article 482 Where an offer is made through a letter or a telegram, the time limit for acceptance shall be counted from the date shown on the letter or the date the telegram is handed in for dispatch or, if no such a date is shown on the letter, from the mailing date shown by the postmark of the letter. Where an offer is made by means of instantaneous communications such as telephone calls, facsimiles, or e-mails, the time limit for acceptance shall be counted from the moment the offer reaches the offeree.

Article 483 A contract is formed at the time when an acceptance becomes effective, unless otherwise provided by law or agreed by the parties.

Article 484 Where an acceptance is made by means of notice, the time when an acceptance becomes effective is governed by the provisions of Article 137 of this Code.

Where notice is not required for making acceptance, an acceptance becomes effective when an act of acceptance is performed according to the parties' course of dealing or as indicated in the offer.

Article 485 An acceptance may be withdrawn. The withdrawal of an acceptance is governed by the provisions of Article 141 of this Code.

Article 486 Where an offeree makes an acceptance beyond the time limit for acceptance, or an acceptance is made within the time limit for acceptance but it cannot reach the offeror in time under normal circumstances, such an acceptance constitutes a new offer unless the offeror timely notifies the offeree that the acceptance is effective.

Article 487 Where an offeree makes an acceptance within the time limit for acceptance, if it would have reached the offeror in time under normal circumstances but reaches the offeror beyond the time limit for other reasons, the acceptance shall be effective unless the offeror timely notifies the offeree that the acceptance is not accepted as it exceeds the time limit for acceptance.

Article 488 The content of an acceptance shall be consistent with the content of the offer. Where an offeree proposes in the acceptance any material alteration to the content of the offer, it constitutes a new offer. An alteration concerning the object of the contract, the quantity, quality, price or remuneration, period of performance, place and manner of performance, default liability, the means of dispute resolution, or the like is a material alteration to the content of an offer.

Article 489 Where an acceptance makes a non-material alteration to the offer, the acceptance shall be effective and the content of the contract shall be as altered by the acceptance, unless the offeror objects in time, or the offer indicates that an acceptance may not make any alteration to the content of the offer.

Article 490 Where the parties conclude a contract in the form of a written agreement, the contract is formed at the time when the parties all sign, stamp, or put their fingerprints on the written agreement. Prior to signing, stamping, or putting their fingerprints thereon, where one of the parties has already performed the principal obligation and the other party has accepted the performance, the contract is formed at the time of such acceptance.

Where a contract is required to be concluded in writing in accordance with laws or administrative regulations or agreed by the parties and the parties fail to make the contract in writing, if one of the parties has already performed the principal obligation and the other party has accepted the performance, the contract is formed at the time the performance is accepted.

Article 491 Where the parties conclude a contract in the form of a letter, data message, or the like, and a confirmation letter is required to be signed, the contract is formed when the confirmation letter is signed.

Where the information about goods or services published by a party *via* information network, such as internet, satisfies the conditions for an offer, unless otherwise agreed by the parties, a contract is formed at the time when the other party selects such product or service and successfully submits the order.

Article 492 The place where an acceptance becomes effective is the place where the contract is formed.

Where a contract is concluded in the form of data message, unless otherwise agreed by the parties, the recipient's principal place of business is the place where the contract is formed; in the absence of a principal place of business, the recipient's domicile is the place where the contract is formed.

Article 493 Where the parties conclude a contract in the form of a written agreement, unless otherwise agreed by them, the place where the written agreement is finally signed, stamped, or fingerprinted is the place where the contract is formed.

Article 494 Where the State issues a State purchase order or a mandatory assignment in accordance with the needs such as emergency and disaster relief, pandemic prevention and control, or the like, the persons of the civil law concerned shall conclude a contract in accordance with the rights and obligations provided by the relevant laws and administrative regulations.

A party that has an obligation to make an offer in accordance with the provisions of laws and administrative regulations shall make a reasonable offer in a timely manner.

A party that has an obligation to make an acceptance in accordance with the provisions of laws and administrative regulations may not reject the reasonable request of the other party to conclude a contract.

Article 495 A letter of subscription, letter of order, letter of reservation, or the like, in which the parties agree to conclude a contract within a certain period of time in the future, constitutes a preliminary contract.

Where one of the parties fails to perform the obligation to conclude a contract agreed in the preliminary contract, the other party may request such party to bear the liability for breach of the preliminary contract.

Article 496 A standard clause refers to a clause formulated in advance by a party for repeated use which has not been negotiated with the other party when concluding the contract.

Upon concluding a contract, where a standard clause is used, the party providing the standard clause shall determine the parties' rights and obligations in compliance with the principle of fairness, and shall, in a reasonable manner, call the other party's attention to the clause concerning the other party's major interests and concerns, such as a clause that exempts or alleviates the liability of the party providing the standard clause, and give explanations of such clause upon request of the other party. Where the party providing the standard clause fails to perform the aforementioned obligation of calling attention or giving explanations, thus resulting in the other party's failure to pay attention to or understand the clause concerning its major interests and concerns, the other party may claim that such clause does not become part of the contract.

Article 497 A standard clause is void under any of the following circumstances:

(1) existence of a circumstance under which the clause is void as provided in Section 3 of Chapter Ⅵ of Book One and Article 506 of this Code;

(2) the party providing the standard clause unreasonably exempts or alleviates itself from liability, imposes heavier liability on the other party, or restricts the main rights of the other party; or

(3) the party providing the standard clause deprives the other party of its main rights.

Article 498 Where a dispute arises over the understanding of a standard clause, the clause shall be interpreted in accordance with its common understanding. Where there are two or more interpretations of a standard clause, the clause shall be interpreted against the party providing the standard clause. Where a standard clause is inconsistent with a non-standard clause, the non-standard clause shall prevail.

Article 499 Where a rewarder through making an announcement promises to pay a reward to anyone who has completed a particular act, the person who has completed the act may request the rewarder to pay the reward.

Article 500 During the course of concluding a contract, the party that falls under any of the following circumstances and causes losses to the other party shall bear the liability for compensation:

(1) under the guise of concluding a contract, engaging in consultation with malicious intention;

(2) intentionally concealing material facts or providing false information concerning the conclusion of the contract; or

(3) conducting any other act contrary to the principle of good faith.

Article 501 The parties may not disclose or improperly use the trade secrets or other confidential information that are obtained in the course of concluding a contract, regardless of whether the contract is ultimately formed or not. The party that discloses or improperly uses such trade secrets or information and thus causes losses to the other party shall bear the liability for compensation.

Chapter Ⅲ Effect of Contracts

Article 502 A contract formed in accordance with law becomes effective upon its formation, unless otherwise provided by law or agreed by the parties.

Where there are laws or administrative regulations providing that a contract shall be subject to approval or other procedures, such provisions shall be followed. Where failure to complete the approval or other procedures is to affect the effectiveness of the contract, the validity of the clauses concerning the performance of the obligation of filing for approval and the like procedures and the other relevant clauses in the contract are not affected. Where the party obligated to complete application for approval or other procedures fails to do so, the other party may request the said party to bear the liability for breach of such obligation.

Where there are laws or administrative regulations providing that modification, assignment, or rescission of a contract shall be subject to approval or other procedures, the provisions of the preceding paragraph shall be applied.

Article 503 Where a person without authority concludes a contract in the name of a principal, and if the principal has already started performing the contractual obligation or accepted the performance of the other party, the contract is deemed ratified.

Article 504 Where the legal representative of a legal person or the responsible person of an unincorporated organization concludes a contract *ultra vires*, such an act is effective and the contract is binding on the legal person or the unincorporated organization unless the other party knows or should have known that the legal representative or the responsible person acts *ultra vires*.

Article 505 Where the parties conclude a contract beyond their scope of business, the validity of the contract shall be determined according to the relevant provisions in Section 3 of Chapter Ⅵ of Book One of this Code and this Book, and the contract may not be determined as invalid solely on the ground that it is beyond their scope of business.

Article 506 An exculpatory clause in a contract exempting the following liabilities are void:

(1) the liability arising from physical injury inflicted on the other party; or

(2) the liability arising from losses caused to the other party's property due to an intentional act or by gross negligence.

Article 507 Where a contract does not take effect, or is void, revoked, or terminated, the validity of a clause in the contract concerning dispute resolution is not affected.

Article 508 The validity of a contract which is not covered by the provisions in this Book is governed by the relevant provisions in Chapter Ⅵ of Book One of this Code.

Chapter Ⅳ Performance of Contracts

Article 509 The parties shall fully perform their respective obligations as agreed in the contract.

The parties shall comply with the principle of good faith, and perform such obligations as sending notification, rendering assistance, and keeping confidentiality in accordance with the nature and purpose of the contract and the course of dealing.

The parties shall avoid wasting the resources, polluting the environment, or damaging the ecology in the course of performance of the contract.

Article 510 After a contract becomes effective, where the parties have not agreed on such contents as the quality, price or remuneration, or the place of performance, and the like, or the relevant agreement is unclear, the parties may make a supplementary agreement; where the parties fail to reach a supplementary agreement, such contents shall be determined according to the relevant clauses of the contract or the course of dealing.

Article 511 Where an agreement between the parties concerning the contents of their contract is unclear and such contents cannot be determined according to the provisions of the preceding Article, the following provisions shall be applied:

(1) where the quality requirements are not clearly stipulated, the contract shall be performed in accordance with a mandatory national standard, or a recommendatory national standard in the absence of a mandatory national standard, or the standard of the industry in the absence of a recommendatory national standard. In the absence of any national or industrial standard, the contract shall be performed in accordance with the general standard or a specific standard conforming to the purpose of the contract.

(2) where the price or remuneration is not clearly stipulated, the contract shall be performed in accordance with the market price in the place of performance at the time the contract is concluded. Where a government-set or government-guided price shall be applied as required by law, the contract shall be performed at such a price.

(3) where the place of performance is not clearly stipulated, the contract shall be performed at the place of the party receiving money where payment of money is involved, or, where real estate is to be delivered, at the place where the real estate is located. For other subject matters, the contract shall be performed at the place where the party performing the obligation is located.

(4) where the period of performance is not clearly stipulated, the debtor may perform the obligation at any time, and the creditor may request the debtor to perform at any time, provided that he shall give the debtor a period of time necessary for preparation;

(5) where the manner of performance is not clearly stipulated, the contract shall be performed in a manner conducive to realizing the purpose of the contract; and

(6) where the allocation of expenses for performance is not clearly stipulated, the expenses shall be borne by the party performing the obligation; where

the expenses for performance are increased due to the creditor's reason, the creditor shall bear the increased part of the expenses.

Article 512 Where the object of an electronic contract concluded through internet or other information network is the delivery of goods and the goods are to be delivered by express delivery services, the time of delivery is the time of acknowledging receipt of the goods by the recipient. Where the object of the said electronic contract is the provision of services, the time for provision of the service is the time stated in the automatically generated electronic certificate or physical certificate. Where there is no time stated in such a certificate or the time stated therein is inconsistent with the actual time for provision of the service, the actual time for provision of the service shall prevail.

Where the subject matter of the said electronic contract is delivered by online transmission, the time of delivery is the time when the subject matter of the contract enters the specific system designated by the other party and can be searched and identified.

Where the parties to the said electronic contract agree otherwise on the mode and time of delivery of goods or provision of services, such an agreement shall be complied with.

Article 513 Where a government-set or government-guided price is adopted in a contract, if the said price is adjusted within the delivery period agreed in the contract, the contract price shall be the price as adjusted at the time of delivery. Where an overdue delivery of the subject matter occurs, the contract price shall be the original price if the price rises at the time of delivery, or the price as adjusted if the price falls at the time of delivery. Where a delayed collection of the subject matter or an overdue payment occurs, the contract price shall be the price as adjusted if the price rises, or the original price if the price falls.

Article 514 Where an obligation is payment of money, unless otherwise provided by law or agreed by the parties, the creditor may request the debtor to perform the obligation by the lawful currency of the place of actual performance.

Article 515 Where a contract has multiple objects and the debtor is required to perform only one of them, the debtor has the right of choice to select the object to perform, unless otherwise provided by law or agreed by the parties, or otherwise determined by the course of dealing.

Where the party with the right of choice fails to make selection within the agreed period or upon expiration of the period of performance, and still fails to make selection within a reasonable period of time after being demanded, the right of choice shall be shifted to the other party.

Article 516 A party shall promptly notify the other party when exercising the right of choice, and the object of the contract to be performed shall be ascertained at the time when such notice reaches the other party. Once ascertained, the object may not be changed unless otherwise consented to by the other party.

Where one of the objects available for selection becomes impossible to perform, the party with the right of choice may not select such object to perform, unless the impossibility to perform is caused by the other party.

Article 517 Where there are two or more creditors, if the object is divisible and each creditor is entitled to the claim in proportion to his own share, then the claim is a claim by shares; where there are two or more debtors, if the object is divisible and each debtor assumes the obligation in proportion to his own share, then the obligation is an obligation by shares.

Where it is difficult to determine the share among the creditors with a claim by shares or the debtors with an obligation by shares, each is deemed to have or assume an equal share.

Article 518 Where there are two or more creditors, and any or all of the creditors may request the debtor to perform the obligation, their claim is a joint and several claim; where there are two or more debtors, and the creditor can request any or all of the debtors to perform the full obligation, the obligation is a joint and several obligation.

A joint and several claim or a joint and several obligation shall be provided by law or agreed by the parties.

Article 519 Where it is difficult to determine the share of obligation among the debtors subjected to joint and several liabilities, each debtor is deemed to owe an equal share.

A debtor subjected to joint and several liabilities who has assumed obligation in excess of his own share has the right to contribution against the other debtors subjected to joint and several liabilities to the extent of the share not performed by the other debtors, and accordingly shall be entitled to the rights of a creditor, provided that the other creditors' interests may not be harmed. The defenses of the other debtors subjected to joint and several liabilities against the creditor may be asserted against such a debtor.

Where a debtor subjected to joint and several liabilities against whom the right to contribution is claimed is unable to perform the share of obligation he is liable to bear, the other debtors subjected to joint and several liabilities shall be liable for the relevant part of the obligation on a *pro rata* basis.

Article 520 Where one of the debtors subjected to joint and several liabilities has performed his obligation, offset his obligation, or placed the subject matter of the obligation in escrow, the obligation of the other debtors owed to the creditor is extinguished to the corresponding extent, and such a debtor has the right to contribution against the other debtors in accordance with the provisions of the preceding Article.

Where the obligation of one of the debtors subjected to joint and several liabilities is exempted by the creditor, the obligation of the other debtors subjected to joint and several liabilities owed to the creditor is extinguished to the extent of the share of liability that such a debtor assumes.

Where the obligation of one of the debtors subjected to joint and several liabilities has merged with the claim of the creditor so that the obligation and the claim are held by the same person, after deducting such share of obligation, the creditor's claim against the other debtors subjected to joint and several liabilities continues to exist.

Where a creditor delays in accepting the performance of one of the debtors subjected to joint and several liabilities, such delay takes effect on the other debtors subject to joint and several liabilities.

Article 521 Where it is difficult to determine the share among the creditors with joint and several claims, each creditor is deemed to have an equal share of the claims.

A creditor who has accepted the performance of obligation shall reimburse the other creditors with joint and several claims with him on a *pro rata* basis.

The relevant provisions on joint and several obligations in this Chapter are applicable to a joint and several claim *mutatis mutandis*.

Article 522 Where the parties agree that the debtor shall perform the obligation to a third person, if the debtor fails to perform the obligation to the third person or the performance does not conform to the agreement, the debtor shall bear default liability to the creditor.

Where it is provided by law or agreed by the parties that a third person may directly request the debtor to perform the obligation to him, and the third person does not explicitly reject it within a reasonable period of time, if the debtor fails to perform the obligation to the third person or the performance does not conform to the agreement, the third person may request the debtor to bear default liability. The defenses that the debtor has against the creditor may be asserted against the third person.

Article 523 Where the parties agree that the obligation shall be performed by a third person to the creditor, if the third person fails to perform the obligation or the performance does not conform to the agreement, the debtor shall bear default liability to the creditor.

Article 524 Where a debtor fails to perform an obligation and a third person has a lawful interest in the performance of the obligation, the third person is entitled to perform it to the creditor on behalf of the debtor, unless the obligation may only be performed by the debtor based on the nature of the obligation, as agreed by the parties, or as provided by law.

After the creditor accepts the performance of such obligation by the third person, his claim against the debtor shall be assigned to the third person, unless otherwise agreed by the debtor and the third person.

Article 525 Where the parties mutually owe obligations to each other and the contract does not provide for a priority order of performance, the parties shall concurrently perform their obligations. Either party may reject the other party's request for performance before the other party performs. Either party may reject the other party's request for the corresponding performance if the other party's performance does not conform to the agreement.

Article 526 Where the parties mutually owe obligations to each other and the contract provides for a priority order of performance, if the party obligated to perform first fails to perform the obligation, the party obligated to perform later may reject the request for performance made by that party. Where the performance of the party obligated to perform first does not conform to the agreement, the party obligated to perform later may reject the request made by the former party for performance of the corresponding obligation.

Article 527 A party obligated to perform the obligation first may suspend the performance if there is clear evidence proving that the other party falls under any of the following circumstances:

(1) its operating conditions are seriously deteriorated;

(2) it transfers property or withdraws capital to evade debts;

(3) the good will of its business has been lost; or

(4) there exists any other circumstance under which it has lost or is losing its ability to perform the obligation.

A party that suspends the performance with no such clear evidence shall bear default liability.

Article 528 A party who suspends performance in accordance with the provisions of the preceding Article shall notify the other party in a timely manner. The performance shall be resumed if the other party provides an appropriate security. After a party suspends the performance, where the other party fails to restore its ability to perform the obligation and fails to provide an appropriate security within a reasonable period of time, the other party is deemed to indicate by act that it will not perform the principal obligation, and the party that suspends the performance may cancel the contract and may request the other party to bear default liability.

Article 529 Where a debtor's performance of an obligation has become difficult due to the fact that the creditor fails to notify the debtor that it has split into two or more entities, merges with another entity, or changed its domicile, the debtor may suspend performance or place the subject matter in escrow.

Article 530 A creditor may reject the debtor's early performance of the obligation, unless the early performance is not detrimental to the interests of the creditor.

Any additional expenses incurred to the creditor due to the debtor's early performance of the obligation shall be borne by the debtor.

Article 531 A creditor may reject the debtor's partial performance of the obligation, unless the partial performance is not detrimental to the interests of the creditor.

Any additional expenses incurred to the creditor due to the debtor's partial performance of the obligation shall be borne by the debtor.

Article 532 After a contract becomes effective, neither party may refuse to perform the contractual obligations on the ground that either party's name or entity name, legal representative, the responsible person, or the person handling the contract has been changed.

Article 533 After a contract is formed, where a fundamental condition upon which the contract is concluded is significantly changed which is unforeseeable by the parties upon conclusion of the contract and which is not one of the commercial risks, if continuing performance of the contract is obviously unfair to one of the parties, the party that is adversely affected may re-negotiate with the other party; where agreement cannot be reached within a reasonable period of time, the parties may request the people's court or an arbitration institution to rectify or rescind the contract.

The people's court or an arbitration institution shall, taking account of the actual circumstances of the case, rectify or rescind the contract in compliance with the principle of fairness.

Article 534 Where the parties take advantage of the contract to commit an act that endangers the State's interests or public interests, the market regulatory authority and other relevant administrative authorities shall be responsible for supervising and handling it in accordance with the provisions of laws and administrative regulations.

Chapter V Preservation of Contracts

Article 535 Where a debtor's right against a counterparty or an accessory right related thereto has not been claimed against the counterparty owing to the debtor's indolence, and the enforcement of the creditor's due claim is thus adversely affected, the creditor may request the people's court to allow him to exercise by subrogation the debtor's claim against the counterparty of the debtor in his own name, unless such claim belongs exclusively to the debtor himself.

The scope of the right of subrogation is limited to the creditor's due claim. The necessary expenses for the creditor to exercise the right of subrogation shall be borne by the debtor.

The counterparty's defenses against the debtor may be asserted against the creditor.

Article 536 Prior to the due date of the creditor's claim, where there exists a circumstance under which the limitation period for the debtor's principal claim against a counterparty or an accessory claim related thereto is to expire, or the debtor fails to timely declare his claim in a bankruptcy proceeding, and hence, the enforcement of the creditor's claim is adversely affected, the creditor may, by subrogation, request the counterparty of the debtor to perform its obligation to the debtor, declare the debtor's claim to the bankruptcy administrator, or take other necessary acts.

Article 537 Where the people's court determines that the right of subrogation has been established, the counterparty of the debtor shall perform the obligation to the creditor. After the performance is accepted by the creditor, the corresponding rights and obligations between the creditor and the debtor, and those between the debtor and the counterparty, are terminated. Where the debtor's claim or an accessory claim related thereto against the counterparty is subject to preservation or enforcement measures, or where the debtor becomes bankrupt, it shall be dealt with in accordance with the provisions of the relevant laws.

Article 538 Where a debtor gratuitously disposes of his proprietary rights and interests by waiving his claims, waiving the security for his claims, or transferring his property without consideration, and the like, or maliciously extends the period of performance of his due claim, and hence, the enforcement of the creditor's claim is adversely affected, the creditor may request the people's court to revoke the debtor's act.

Article 539 Where a debtor transfers his property at an obviously unreasonably low price, takes another's property at an obviously unreasonably high price, or provides security for another's obligation, and hence, the enforcement of the creditor's claim is adversely affected, the creditor may request the people's court to revoke the debtor's act if the counterparty of the debtor knows or should have known such circumstance.

Article 540 The scope of the right to revocation is limited to the extent of the creditor's claim. The expenses necessary for the creditor to exercise the right to revocation shall be borne by the debtor.

Article 541 The right to revocation shall be exercised within one year from the date on which the creditor knows or should have known the cause for the revocation. The right to revocation is extinguished where a creditor does not exercise such right within five years since the date on which the debtor conducts the relevant act.

Article 542 Where an act of the debtor adversely affecting the enforcement of the creditor's claim is revoked, such an act does not have legal effect *ab initio*.

Chapter Ⅵ Modification and Assignment of Contracts

Article 543 The parties may modify a contract upon agreement through consultation.

Article 544 Where an agreement between the parties to modify the content of a contract is unclear, it is presumed that the contract is not modified.

Article 545 A creditor may assign his claim in whole or in part to a third person, except that a claim may not be assigned where:

(1) it is not assignable by virtue of its nature;

(2) it is not assignable as agreed by the parties; or

(3) it is not assignable in accordance with law.

Where the parties agree that a non-pecuniary claim may not be assigned, such an agreement may not be asserted against a *bona fide* third person. Where the parties agree that a pecuniary claim may not be assigned, such an agreement may not be asserted against a third person.

Article 546 Where a creditor assigns his claim but fails to notify the debtor, the assignment is not effective against the debtor.

The notice of the assignment of a claim may not be revoked, unless consented to by the assignee.

Article 547 Where a creditor assigns his claim, the assignee acquires the accessory right related to the claim unless the accessory right belongs exclusively to the creditor.

Failure to register the assignment of the accessory right or failure to change the possession thereof does not affect the acquisition of the accessory right by the assignee.

Article 548 After a debtor receives a notice of assignment of a claim, the debtor's defenses against the assignor may be asserted against the assignee.

Article 549 A debtor may claim a set-off against the assignee under either of the following circumstances:

(1) when the debtor receives the notice of assignment of a claim, the debtor has a claim against the assignor which becomes due prior to or at the same time of the due date of the assigned claim; or

(2) the debtor's claim and the assigned claim are generated on the basis of the same contract.

Article 550 The expenses for performance increased due to the assignment of a claim shall be borne by the assignor.

Article 551 Where a debtor delegates his obligation in whole or in part to a third person, the consent of the creditor shall be obtained.

The debtor or the third person may demand the creditor to give his consent within a reasonable period of time. Where the creditor makes no indication, it shall be deemed as no consent given.

Article 552 Where a third person agrees with the debtor to join in the obligation and notifies the creditor thereof, or a third person indicates to the creditor his willingness to join in the obligation, if the creditor does not explicitly make a rejection within a reasonable period of time, the creditor may request the third person to assume the joint and several obligation with the debtor to the extent of the obligation the third person is willing to assume.

Article 553 Where a debtor delegates his obligation, the delegatee may assert a defense of the original debtor against the creditor; where the original debtor has a claim against the creditor, the delegatee may not claim a set-off against the creditor.

Article 554 Where a debtor delegates his obligation, the delegatee shall assume the accessory obligation related to the principal obligation, unless the accessory obligation belongs exclusively to the original debtor.

Article 555 A party may concomitantly assign his rights and delegate his obligations under a contract to a third person with the consent of the other party.

Article 556 Where the rights and obligations under a contract are assigned and delegated concomitantly, the provisions on assignment of claims and delegation of obligations shall be applied.

Chapter Ⅶ Termination of Rights and Obligations under a Contract

Article 557 A claim or obligation is terminated under any of the following circumstances:

(1) the obligation has been performed;

(2) the obligations are offset against each other;

(3) the debtor has placed the subject matter in escrow in accordance with law;

(4) the creditor has exempted the obligation;

(5) the claim and obligation are merged to be held by the same person; or

(6) there exists any other circumstance under which the claim or obligation is terminated as provided by law or agreed by the parties.

The relationship of rights and obligations under a contract is terminated upon rescission of the contract.

Article 558 After the parties' claims and obligations are terminated, the parties shall, in compliance with the principle of good faith and the like, perform such obligations as sending notification, rendering assistance, keeping confidentiality, and recycling the used articles according to the course of dealing.

Article 559 Upon termination of a claim and an obligation, a right accessory to the claim is extinguished concomitantly, unless otherwise provided by law or agreed by the parties.

Article 560 Where a debtor owes to a creditor multiple obligations of the same kind, and the debtor's payment is not sufficient to discharge all of the obligations, upon making performance, the debtor shall designate which obligation is to be discharged, unless otherwise agreed by the parties.

Where the debtor fails to make such a designation, the obligation that has become due shall be performed first. Where multiple obligations have become due, the obligation not secured or with the least security shall be performed first. Where none of the obligations are secured or the obligations are equally secured, the obligation with which the debtor assumes the heaviest burden shall be performed first. Where the burdens are the same, the obligations shall be performed in the priority order of their due dates. Where the due dates are the same, the obligations shall be performed on a *pro rata* basis.

Article 561 In addition to performing the principal obligation, a debtor shall pay to the creditor interests and other expenses related to the enforcement of the obligation. Where the payment is not sufficient to discharge all of the obligations, unless otherwise agreed by the parties, the debtor shall perform the obligations in accordance with the following order of priority:

(1) the relevant expenses incurred by the creditor for enforcing the claim;

(2) the interests; and

(3) the principal obligation.

Article 562 The parties may rescind the contract upon agreement through consultation.

The parties may agree on the causes for a party to rescind the contract. When a cause for rescission of contract arises, the party with the right to rescission may rescind the contract.

Article 563 The parties may rescind the contract under any of the following circumstances:

(1) the purpose of a contract cannot be achieved due to *force majeure*;

(2) prior to expiration of the period of performance, one of the parties explicitly expresses or indicates by act that it will not perform the principal obligation;

(3) one of the parties delays performance of the principal obligation and still fails to perform it within a reasonable period of time after being demanded;

(4) one of the parties delays performance of the obligation or has otherwise acted in breach of the contract, thus making it impossible to achieve the purpose of the contract; or

(5) there exists any other circumstance as provided by law.

For a contract under which the debtor is required to continuously perform an obligation for an indefinite period of time, the parties to the contract may rescind the contract at any time, provided that the other party shall be notified reasonably in advance.

Article 564 Where a time limit for exercising the right to rescind the contract is provided by law or agreed by the parties, if the party with the right to rescission has not exercised the right upon expiration of the period, such right is extinguished.

Where no time limit for exercising the right to rescind the contract is provided by law or agreed by the parties, such a right is extinguished if the party with the right to rescission has not exercised the right within one year after it knows or should have known the causes for rescission, or within a reasonable period of time after being demanded by the other party.

Article 565 Where one of the parties requests to rescind the contract in accordance with law, the other party shall be duly notified. The contract is rescinded at the time the notice reaches the other party, or, where the notice states that the contract is to be automatically rescinded if the debtor fails to perform his obligation within a specified period of time, the contract is rescinded when the debtor fails to perform the obligation upon expiration of the specified period of time. Where the other party has objections to the rescission of the contract, either party may request the people's court or an arbitration institution to determine the validity of the rescission.

Where one of the parties, without notifying the other party, requests the rescission of the contract by directly filing a lawsuit or applying for arbitration in accordance with law, and the people's court or arbitration institution confirms such request, the contract is rescinded when a duplicated copy of the complaint or the application letter for arbitration is served on the other party.

Article 566 After a contract is rescinded, where an obligation has not yet been performed, the performance shall cease; where an obligation has already been performed, the parties may, taking into account the performance status and the nature of the contract, request restoration to the original status or other remedial measures taken, and have the right to request for compensation for the losses.

Where a contract is rescinded due to a default, the party with the right to rescind the contract may request the breaching party to bear default liability, unless otherwise agreed by the parties.

After the principal contract is rescinded, a security provider shall still be obligated to secure the debtor's liability, unless otherwise agreed in the security contract.

Article 567 Termination of the relationship of rights and obligations under a contract does not affect the validity of the contract clauses regarding settlement and liquidation.

Article 568 Where the parties mutually owe obligations to each other, and the subject matters of the obligations are of the same kind and quality, any party may offset its obligation against the obligation of the other party that becomes due, unless the obligations cannot be offset by virtue of their nature, or in accordance with the agreements by the parties or the provisions of law.

A party who claims a set-off shall notify the other party. The notice becomes effective when it reaches the other party. No conditions or time limit may be attached to the set-off.

Article 569 Where the parties mutually owe obligations to each other and the subject matters of the obligations are not of the same kind or quality, the obligations may also be offset upon agreement by the parties through consultation.

Article 570 Where it is difficult to perform an obligation under any of the following circumstances, a debtor may place the subject matter in escrow:

(1) the creditor refuses to accept the performance without just cause;

(2) the creditor cannot be located;

(3) the creditor dies with his heirs or estate administrator not determined, or the creditor loses his capacity for performing civil juristic acts with no guardian determined; or

(4) there exists any other circumstance as provided by law.

Where the subject matter is not suitable for being placed in escrow or the expenses therefor are excessively high, the debtor may sell the subject matter through auction or sale and place the proceeds thus obtained in escrow in accordance with law.

Article 571 A subject matter or the proceeds obtained from auction or sale of the subject matter are placed in escrow where the debtor delivers the subject matter or proceeds thereof to the escrow agency in accordance with law.

Where a subject matter or its proceeds have been placed in escrow, the debtor is deemed to have delivered the subject matter to such extent.

Article 572 After a subject matter is placed in escrow, the debtor shall promptly notify the creditor or the creditor's heirs, estate administrator, guardian, or custodian for his property.

Article 573 After a subject matter is placed in escrow, the risk of destruction, damage, or loss thereof shall be assumed by the creditor. During the period the subject matter is placed in escrow, the accrued proceeds of the subject matter belong to the creditor. The expenses thus incurred are borne by the creditor.

Article 574 A creditor may collect the subject matter placed in escrow at any time, except that where an obligation owed by the creditor to the debtor becomes due, the escrow agency, upon request of the debtor, shall reject the creditor's request for collecting it before the creditor performs such obligation or providing security therefor.

The creditor's right to collect the subject matter placed in escrow is extinguished if such right is not exercised within five years from the date the subject matter is delivered to the escrow agency, and the subject matter shall be escheated to the State after the escrow agency's expenses are deducted. However, where a creditor fails to perform his overdue obligation to the debtor, or where the creditor waives his right to collect the subject matter placed in escrow in writing to the escrow agency, the debtor has the right to take back the subject matter after paying the escrow agency's expenses.

Article 575 Where a creditor exempts part or all of the debtor's obligations, the claims and obligations are terminated in part or in whole, unless the debtor objects within a reasonable period of time.

Article 576 Where a claim and an obligation are merged to be held by the same person, both the claim and the obligation are terminated unless it is detrimental to the interests of a third person.

Chapter Ⅷ Default Liability

Article 577 Where a party fails to perform the contractual obligations or the performance does not conform to the agreement, it shall bear default liability such as continuing to perform the obligations, taking remedial measures, or compensating for losses.

Article 578 Where a party explicitly expresses or indicates by act that it will not perform the contractual obligations, the other party may, prior to expiration of the period of performance, request the former party to bear default liability.

Article 579 Where a party fails to pay the price, remuneration, rent, or interests, or fails to perform another pecuniary obligation, the other party may request for such payment.

Article 580 Where a party fails to perform a non-pecuniary obligation or the performance does not conform to the agreement, the other party may request for such performance unless:

(1) the performance is impossible either *de jure* or *de facto*;

(2) the object of the obligation is not suitable for a compulsory performance or the expenses for the performance are excessively high; or

(3) the creditor fails to request for performance within a reasonable period of time.

Where one of the situations specified in the preceding paragraph exists so that the purpose of the contract cannot be achieved, the people's court or an arbitration institution may terminate the contractual relationship of rights and obligations upon request by a party, but the default liability to be borne is not affected.

Article 581 Where a party fails to perform the obligation or the performance does not conform to the agreement, if the obligation may not be enforced by virtue of its nature, the other party may request such party to bear the expenses of a substitute performance by a third person.

Article 582 Where a party's performance does not conform to the agreement, the party shall bear default liability as agreed in the contract. Where there is no agreement between the parties on the default liability or the relevant agreement is unclear, and if it cannot be determined according to the provisions of Article 510 of this Code, the aggrieved party may, by virtue of the nature of the object and according to the degree of the losses, reasonably request the other party to bear the default liability such as repair, redoing, replacement, return of the subject matter, decrease in price or remuneration, and the like.

Article 583 Where a party fails to perform the contractual obligation or the performance does not conform to the agreement, the party shall make compensation if, after it has performed the obligation or has taken remedial measures, the other party still suffers losses.

Article 584 Where a party fails to perform the contractual obligation or the performance does not conform to the agreement so that the other party suffers losses, the amount of compensation shall be equivalent to the losses caused by the breach of contract, including the benefits expected to be obtained should the contract had been performed, except that it may not exceed such losses that the breaching party foresees or should have foreseen at the time of conclusion of the contract.

Article 585 The parties may agree that, upon default by a party, a certain amount of liquidated damages shall be paid to the other party according to the circumstances of the breach, or the parties may agree on the method of calculating the amount of compensation for the losses arising from the breach.

Where the agreed amount of liquidated damages is lower than the losses caused, the people's court or an arbitration institution may, upon request of a party, increase the amount. Where the agreed amount of liquidated damages is excessively higher than the losses caused, the people's court or an arbitration institution may, upon request of a party, reduce it appropriately.

Where the parties agree on the liquidated damages for delayed performance, the breaching party shall continue to perform the obligation after paying the liquidated damages.

Article 586 The parties may agree that one party provides earnest money with the other party to secure the claim. An earnest money contract is formed upon actual delivery of the earnest money.

The amount of the earnest money shall be agreed by the parties, except that it may not exceed 20% of the value of the object of the principal contract, and any excessive amount does not have the effect of earnest money. Where the amount of the earnest money actually delivered is more or less than the agreed amount, the agreed amount of the earnest money is deemed to have been changed.

Article 587 After a debtor has performed the obligation, the earnest money shall be calculated as part of the price or be refunded. Where a party paying the earnest money fails to perform the obligation or fails to perform it in conformity with the agreement so that the purpose of the contract cannot be achieved, the party is not entitled to request a refund of the earnest money. Where a party receiving the earnest money fails to perform the obligation or fails to perform it in conformity with the agreement so that the purpose of the contract cannot be achieved, the party shall refund twice the amount of the earnest money to the other party.

Article 588 Where the parties agree on both liquidated damages and earnest money, when a party defaults, the other party may choose to apply either the clause on the liquidated damages or the clause on the earnest money.

Where the amount of the earnest money is insufficient to compensate the losses caused by one party's default, the other party may request compensation for the losses in excess of the amount of the earnest money.

Article 589 Where a debtor performs the obligation in accordance with the agreement, and the creditor refuses to accept the performance without just cause, the debtor may request the creditor to compensate for any additional expenses.

The debtor does not need to pay interests for the period of delay in acceptance by the creditor.

Article 590 Where a party is unable to perform the contract due to *force majeure*, it shall be exempted from liability in whole or in part according to the impact of the *force majeure*, unless otherwise provided by law. The party unable to perform the contract due to *force majeure* shall promptly notify the other party to mitigate the losses that may be caused to the other party, and shall provide proof of the *force majeure* within a reasonable period of time.

Where the *force majeure* occurs after a party's delay in performance, such party's default liability may not be exempted.

Article 591　After a party defaults, the other party shall take appropriate measures to prevent further loss. Where no appropriate measures are taken so that the loss is aggravated, no compensation shall be claimed for the aggravated part of the loss.

The reasonable expenses incurred by a party in preventing the aggravation of the loss shall be borne by the breaching party.

Article 592　Where both parties default, each shall bear the corresponding liability.

Where one party's default causes losses to the other party, and the other party's fault contributes to such losses, the amount of compensation may be mitigated accordingly.

Article 593　A party who breaches a contract due to a third person's reason shall bear default liability to the other party in accordance with law. The dispute between the breaching party and the third person shall be handled in accordance with the provisions of law or their agreement.

Article 594　The limitation period for filing a lawsuit or arbitration on a dispute arising from a contract for international sale of goods and a contract for the import and export of technology is four years.

Part Two　Nominate Contracts

Chapter Ⅸ　Sales Contracts

Article 595　A sales contract is a contract under which a seller transfers his ownership over the subject matter to a buyer who pays the price in return.

Article 596　A sales contract generally contains clauses specifying the name, quantity, quality, and price of the subject matter, the period, place, and method of performance, the packaging, the standard and methods for inspection, the means of settlement, the language used in the contract, the validity thereof, and the like.

Article 597 If the ownership of a subject matter is unable to be transferred due to the fact that the seller fails to obtain the right of disposal thereof, the buyer may rescind the contract and request the seller to bear default liability.

Where there are laws or administrative regulations prohibiting or restricting the transfer of a subject matter, such provisions shall be followed.

Article 598 A seller shall perform his obligation of delivering the subject matter or the documents for taking delivery thereof, and transferring the ownership over the subject matter to the buyer.

Article 599 A seller shall deliver to the buyer the relevant certificates and information in addition to the documents for taking delivery of the subject matter in accordance with the contract or the course of dealing.

Article 600 Where a subject matter to be sold involves intellectual property rights, unless otherwise provided by law or agreed by the parties, such intellectual property rights do not belong to the buyer.

Article 601 A seller shall deliver the subject matter at a time as agreed in the contract. Where a period of delivery is agreed in the contract, the seller may deliver the subject matter at any time within such period.

Article 602 Where there is no agreement between the parties on the period of delivery or the relevant agreement is unclear, the provisions of Article 510 and Subparagraph (4) of Article 511 of this Code shall be applied.

Article 603 A seller shall deliver the subject matter at the agreed place of delivery.

Where there is no agreement between the parties on the place of delivery or the relevant agreement is unclear, if it cannot be determined according to the provisions of Article 510 of this Code, the following provisions shall be applied:

(1) where the subject matter needs to be transported, the seller shall consign it to the first carrier for its delivery to the buyer; and

(2) where the subject matter does not need to be transported, if the seller and the buyer know the place where the subject matter is located when they conclude the contract, the seller shall deliver the subject matter at the said place; if the location of the subject matter is unknown, the seller shall deliver the subject matter at the place where the seller's place of business is located at the time the contract is concluded.

Article 604 The risks of destruction, damage, or loss of the subject matter shall be borne by the seller prior to the delivery and by the buyer after the delivery, unless otherwise provided by law or agreed by the parties.

Article 605 Where a subject matter fails to be delivered within the agreed time limit due to the buyer's reason, the buyer shall bear the risks of destruction, damage, or loss of the subject matter from the time he defaults.

Article 606 Where a seller sells a subject matter *en route* that has been consigned to a carrier for transport, unless otherwise agreed by the parties, the risks of destruction, damage, or loss of the subject matter shall be borne by the buyer from the time the contract is formed.

Article 607 A buyer shall bear the risks of destruction, damage, or loss of the subject matter when the seller has transported the subject matter to the place designated by the buyer and delivered to the carrier in accordance with the agreement.

Where there is no agreement between the parties on the place of delivery or the relevant agreement is unclear, if the subject matter needs to be transported according to Subparagraph (1) of the second paragraph of Article 603 of this Code, the buyer shall bear the risks of destruction, damage, or loss of the subject matter when the seller consigns the subject matter to the first carrier for transport.

Article 608 Where a seller has placed the subject matter at the place of delivery in accordance with the agreement or the provisions of Subparagraph (2) of the second paragraph of Article 603 of this Code, if the buyer fails to take delivery in default of the agreement, the risks of destruction, damage, or loss of the subject matter shall be borne by the buyer from the time the buyer defaults.

Article 609 A seller's failure to deliver the documents and information of the subject matter in accordance with the agreement does not affect the shift of the risks of destruction, damage, or loss of the subject matter.

Article 610 Where a subject matter fails to meet the quality requirements so that the purpose of the contract cannot be achieved, the buyer may refuse to accept the subject matter or may rescind the contract. Where the buyer refuses to accept the subject matter or rescind the contract, the risks of destruction, damage, or loss of the subject matter shall be borne by the seller.

Article 611 Where a seller's performance is not in conformity with the agreement, the assumption of the risks of destruction, damage, or loss of the subject matter by the buyer does not affect the buyer's right to request the seller to bear default liability.

Article 612 A seller has an obligation to guarantee that no third person has any right over the subject matter delivered, unless otherwise provided by law.

Article 613 Where, at the time a contract is concluded, the buyer knows or should have known that a third person has a right over the subject matter of the contract, the seller does not assume the obligation provided in the preceding Article.

Article 614 Where a buyer has clear evidence to prove that a third person has a right over the subject matter, he may suspend payment, unless the seller has provided an appropriate security.

Article 615 A seller shall deliver the subject matter in conformity with the quality requirements as agreed by the parties. Where a seller provides quality specifications of the subject matter, the subject matter delivered shall conform to the specified quality requirements.

Article 616 Where there is no agreement between the parties on the quality requirements of the subject matter or the relevant agreement is unclear, if the quality requirements cannot be determined according to the provisions of Article 510 of this Code, the provisions of Subparagraph (1) of Article 511 of this Code shall be applied.

Article 617 Where a subject matter delivered by the seller fails to meet the quality requirements, the buyer may request the seller to bear default liability in accordance with the provisions of Articles 582 through 584 of this Code.

Article 618 Where the parties agree to alleviate or exempt the seller's liability for the defects of the subject matter, if the seller, intentionally or by gross negligence, fails to inform the buyer of the defect of the subject matter, he has no right to claim alleviation or exemption of the liability.

Article 619 A seller shall deliver the subject matter in compliance with the packaging method as agreed in the contract. Where there is no agreement between the parties on the packaging method or the relevant agreement is unclear, if the packaging method cannot be determined according to the provisions of Article 510 of this Code, the subject matter shall be packaged in a general way, or, in the absence of a general way, in a manner sufficient to protect the subject matter and conducive to saving resources and protecting the ecological environment.

Article 620 After a buyer receives the subject matter, inspection shall be conducted within the agreed period of inspection. If there is no agreed period of inspection, the buyer shall inspect it in a timely manner.

Article 621 Where the parties have agreed on a period of inspection, the buyer shall, within such period, notify the seller of any inconformity of the subject matter with the agreed quantity or quality. If notice is not given to the seller owing to the buyer's indolence, the subject matter is deemed to be in conformity with the agreed quantity or quality.

Where the parties have not agreed on a period of inspection, the buyer shall notify the seller of any inconformity of the subject matter with the agreed quantity or quality within a reasonable period of time after he discovers or should have discovered the inconformity. Where the buyer fails to notify the seller within a reasonable period of time or within two years after he takes delivery of the subject matter, the subject matter shall be deemed to be in conformity with the agreed quantity or quality, except that where there is a warranty period within which the quality of the subject matter is guaranteed, the warranty period shall be applied.

Where a seller knows or should have known that the subject matter delivered does not conform to the agreement, the buyer is not subject to the time limit for notification as provided in the preceding two paragraphs.

Article 622 Where a period of inspection agreed by the parties is excessively short, and it is difficult for the buyer to complete a comprehensive inspection within such a period by virtue of the nature of the subject matter and in accordance with the course of dealing, such period shall be deemed only as a period for the buyer to raise objections on the patent defects of the subject matter.

Where an agreed period of inspection or a warranty period for quality guarantee is shorter than the period provided by the relevant laws or administrative regulations, the latter shall prevail.

Article 623 Where the parties have not agreed on a period of inspection, and the buyer has signed a delivery note, confirmation slip, or the like document on which the quantity, model, and specifications of the subject matter are stated, the buyer shall be presumed to have inspected the quantity and the patent defects of the subject matter, unless there is sufficient evidence to overturn such a presumption.

Article 624 Where a seller delivers a subject matter to a third person according to the instructions given by the buyer, if the inspection standard agreed between the seller and the buyer are inconsistent with that agreed between the buyer and the third person, the inspection standard agreed between the seller and the buyer shall prevail.

Article 625 Where, in accordance with the provisions of laws or administrative regulations or as agreed by the parties, the subject matter shall be recycled after expiration of its valid service life, the seller has an obligation to recycle the subject matter on his own or by an authorized third person.

Article 626 A buyer shall make payment in accordance with the agreed amount and method of payment. Where there is no agreement between the parties on the amount of price or the method of payment, or the relevant agreement is unclear, the provisions of Article 510 and Subparagraphs (2) and (5) of Article 511 of this Code shall be applied.

Article 627 A buyer shall make payment at the place agreed in the contract. Where there is no agreement between the parties on the place of payment, or the relevant agreement is unclear, if the place cannot be determined in accordance with the provisions of Article 510 of this Code, the buyer shall make the payment at the seller's place of business, except that payment shall be made at the place where the subject matter or the document for taking delivery thereof is delivered if the payment is conditioned upon the delivery of the subject matter.

Article 628 A buyer shall make payment at the time agreed in the contract. Where there is no agreement between the parties on the time of payment, or the relevant agreement is unclear, if the time of payment cannot be determined according to the provisions of Article 510 of this Code, the buyer shall make payment at the same time as it receives the subject matter or the document for taking delivery thereof.

Article 629 Where the amount of the subject matter delivered by a seller exceeds the agreed amount, the buyer may accept or refuse to accept the excess amount. Where the buyer accepts the excess amount, it shall pay for it at the price agreed in the contract. If the buyer refuses to accept the excess amount, it shall notify the seller in a timely manner.

Article 630 Any proceeds accrued from the subject matter before delivery belong to the seller and any proceeds accrued from the subject matter after delivery belong to the buyer, unless otherwise agreed by the parties.

Article 631 Where a contract is rescinded due to the inconformity of the principal subject matter with the agreed requirements, the effect of the rescission shall be effective against the accessory subject matter. Where a rescission is due to the inconformity of the accessory subject matter with the agreed requirements, the effect of the rescission is not effective against the principal subject matter.

Article 632 Where the object of a contract is composed of several subject matters, if one of the subject matters fails to conform to the requirements agreed in the contract, the buyer may rescind the part of the contract in connection with the said subject matter. However, where separation of the said subject matter from the other subject matters is to markedly harm the value of the subject matters of the contract, the buyer may rescind the contract in connection with the multiple subject matters concerned.

Article 633 Where the subject matters are to be delivered by installment by a seller, if the seller fails to deliver one lot of the subject matters, or has delivered the lot in a manner not in conformity with the agreement, so that the purpose of the contract in connection with the said lot cannot be achieved, the buyer may rescind the part of the contract in connection with the said lot.

Where a seller fails to deliver one lot of the subject matters, or has delivered the lot in a manner not in conformity with the agreement, so that the subsequent delivery of the remaining lots cannot achieve the purpose of the contract, the buyer may rescind the part of the contract in connection with the said lot and the remaining lots.

Where a buyer has rescinded a part of the contract in connection with one lot of the subject matters, if the said lot and any other lot are interdependent on each other, the buyer may rescind the contract in connection with all the lots disregarding whether they have been delivered or not.

Article 634 Where a buyer under an installment contract fails to make payment and the unpaid amount reaches one-fifth of the total price, if the buyer still fails to pay the due installment amount within a reasonable period of time after being demanded, the seller may request the buyer to pay the total sum or he may rescind the contract.

The seller who rescinds the contract may request the buyer to pay a fee for the use of the subject matter.

Article 635 The parties to a sale by sample shall seal up the sample and may make specifications of its quality. The subject matter delivered by the seller shall be identical in quality with the sample and its specifications.

Article 636 Where a buyer to a sale by sample is unaware of the sample's latent defects, even if the subject matter delivered is identical with the sample, the quality of the subject matter delivered by the seller shall still conform to the general standard for the goods in the same category.

Article 637 The parties to a sale on trial use may agree on a period for trial use of the subject matter. Where there is no agreement between the parties on the period for trial use or the relevant agreement is unclear, if the period for trial use cannot be determined according to the provisions of Article 510 of this

Code, it shall be determined by the seller.

Article 638 A buyer to a sale on trial use may purchase or refuse to purchase the subject matter within the period for trial use. Where, upon expiration of the period for trial use, the buyer makes no indication as to whether to purchase it or not, the buyer is deemed to have purchased the subject matter.

If a buyer to a sale on trial use has, within the period for the trial use, already made partial payment or has sold, leased, created a security interest in the subject matter, the buyer is deemed to have agreed to purchase it.

Article 639 Where there is no agreement between the parties to a sale on trial use on the fee for the use of the subject matter, or the relevant agreement is unclear, the seller has no right to request the buyer to pay such fee.

Article 640 The risks of destruction, damage, or loss of the subject matter shall be borne by the seller within the period for the trial use.

Article 641 The parties may agree in a sales contract that the seller retains the ownership of the subject matter if the buyer fails to pay the price or perform other obligations.

The ownership of the subject matter retained by a seller, without being registered, may not be asserted against a *bona fide* third person.

Article 642 Where the parties agree that the seller shall retain the ownership of the subject matter of the contract, unless otherwise agreed by the parties, the seller has the right to take back the subject matter if the buyer falls under any of the following circumstances before such ownership is transferred and if losses are thus caused to the seller:

(1) the buyer fails to make payment in accordance with the contract, and fails to pay it within a reasonable period of time after being demanded;

(2) the buyer fails to fulfill the specific conditions in accordance with the contract; or

(3) the buyer sells, pledges, or otherwise improperly disposes of the subject matter.

The seller may negotiate with the buyer to take back the subject matter. Where such a negotiation fails, the procedures for enforcement of security interests may be applied *mutatis mutandis*.

Article 643 After a seller has taken back the subject matter according to the first paragraph of the preceding Article, the buyer may request to redeem the subject matter if he eliminates the cause for the seller's retrieving of the subject matter within a reasonable period of redemption agreed by the parties or set by the seller.

Where the buyer does not redeem the subject matter within the redemption period, the seller may sell the subject matter to a third person at a reasonable price. After deducting from the sale proceeds the amount unpaid by the buyer and the necessary expenses, any balance shall be returned to the buyer; if the sale proceeds are insufficient to cover the unpaid amount and the other necessary expenses, the deficiency balance shall be paid by the buyer.

Article 644 The rights and obligations of the parties to a sale through bidding, as well as the procedures for the bidding, are governed by the provisions of the relevant laws and administrative regulations.

Article 645 The rights and obligations of the parties to an auction, as well as the procedures of the auction, are governed by the provisions of the relevant laws and administrative regulations.

Article 646 Where there are provisions of laws governing other non-gratuitous contracts, such provisions shall be followed. In the absence of such a provision, the relevant provisions on sales contracts shall be applied *mutatis mutandis*.

Article 647 Where the parties agree to transfer the ownership of the subject matter by barter trade, the relevant provisions on sales contracts shall be applied *mutatis mutandis*.

Chapter X Contracts for the Supply and Consumption of Electricity, Water, Gas, or Heat

Article 648 A contract for the supply and consumption of electricity is a contract under which a supplier provides electricity to the consumer who pays the price in return.

A supplier providing electricity to the public may not refuse a reasonable request of a consumer to conclude such a contract.

Article 649 A contract for the supply and consumption of electricity generally contains clauses specifying the mode, quality and time of the supply, the volume, address of the location, and nature of the consumption, the measuring method, the price, the settlement method of electricity fees, the responsibility for the maintenance of electricity supply and consumption facilities, and the like.

Article 650 The place of performance of a contract for the supply and consumption of electricity shall be agreed by the parties; if there is no agreement between the parties or the relevant agreement is unclear, the place of demarcation of the property rights in the electricity supply facilities is the place of performance.

Article 651 A supplier of electricity shall safely supply electricity in accordance with the quality standard for power supply set by the State and in the agreement. Where a supplier fails to safely supply electricity in accordance with the quality standard for power supply set by the State or in the agreement, thus causing losses to the consumer, the supplier shall bear the liability for compensation.

Article 652 Where a supplier of electricity needs to cut off electricity supply due to scheduled or unscheduled overhauls of the electricity supply facilities, restriction on electricity consumption in accordance with law, or consumer's illegal consumption of the electricity, and the like, the consumer shall be notified in advance in accordance with the relevant regulations of the State. Where a supplier cuts off the electricity supply without notifying the consumer in advance, thus causing losses to the consumer, the supplier shall bear the liability for compensation.

Article 653 A supplier of electricity shall rush to repair without delay in accordance with the relevant regulations of the State whenever the electricity supply is cut off due to such reasons as natural disasters. Where the supplier fails to do so and losses are thus caused to the consumer, the supplier shall bear the liability for compensation.

Article 654 A consumer of electricity shall pay the electricity fees in time in accordance with the relevant regulations of the State and the agreement between the parties. Where a consumer fails to make due payment for the electricity fees, he shall pay the agreed liquidated damages. Where a consumer, after being demanded, still fails to make due payment for the electricity fees and the liquidated damages within a reasonable period of time, the supplier may stop the supply of electricity in accordance with the procedures provided by the State.

Where a supplier stops the supply of electricity in accordance with the provision of the preceding paragraph, it shall notify the consumer in advance.

Article 655 A consumer shall use the electricity in a safe, economical and planned manner in accordance with the relevant regulations of the State and the agreement between the parties. Where a consumer fails to use the electricity in accordance with the relevant regulations of the State or the agreement between the parties, and losses are thus caused to the supplier, the consumer shall bear the liability for compensation.

Article 656 The relevant provisions governing the contracts for the supply and consumption of electricity shall be applied *mutatis mutandis* to contracts for the supply and consumption of water, gas, or heat.

Chapter XI Gift Contracts

Article 657 A gift contract is a contract under which a donor gives his own property to a donee gratuitously and the donee expresses his intent to accept the gift.

Article 658 A donor may revoke the gift prior to the transfer of the rights in the gifted property.

The provisions of the preceding paragraph do not apply to a notarized gift contract, or a gift contract with a purpose of serving a public interest or performing a moral obligation that shall in accordance with law not be revoked, such as a gift contract for disaster-relief, poverty-relief, disability-relief, or the like purposes.

Article 659 A gifted property shall go through registration or other procedures if the law so requires.

Article 660 For a notarized gift contract or a gift contract with a purpose of serving a public interest or performing a moral obligation that shall in accordance with law not be revoked, such as a contract for disaster-relief, poverty-relief, disability-relief, or the like purposes, where the donor does not deliver the gifted property, the donee may request such delivery.

Where the gifted property that shall be delivered in accordance with the preceding paragraph is destructed, damaged, or lost due to the donor's intentional act or by his gross negligence, the donor shall bear the liability for compensation.

Article 661 A gift may be subject to an obligation.

Where a gift is subject to an obligation, the donee shall perform the obligation in accordance with the agreement.

Article 662 A donor is not liable for any defect of the gifted property. Where a gift is subject to an obligation, if the gifted property has defects, the donor shall, to the extent of the attached obligation, bear the same liability as a seller.

Where a donor intentionally fails to notify the donee about the defect of the gifted property or has made a warranty therefor, thus causing losses to the donee, the donor shall bear the liability for compensation.

Article 663 A donor may revoke the gift if the donee has done any of the following acts:

(1) severely infringing upon the lawful rights and interests of the donor or any close relative of the donor;

(2) having an obligation to support the donor but failing to perform that obligation; or

(3) failing to perform the obligation as agreed in the gift contract.

The right to revocation of the donor shall be exercised within one year from the date the donor knows or should have known of the cause for revocation.

Article 664 Where a donee's illegal act leads to the donor's death or loss of capacity for performing civil juristic acts, the donor's heir or legal representative may revoke the gift.

The right to revocation of the donor's heir or his legal representative shall be exercised within six months from the date the heir or the legal representative knows or should have known of the cause for revocation.

Article 665 Upon revocation of a gift, the person having the right to revocation may request the donee to return the gifted property.

Article 666 Where a donor's financial situation markedly deteriorates and his production and operation or family life is thus severely affected, he may cease to perform the obligation of delivering the gift.

Chapter XII Loan Contracts

Article 667 A loan contract is a contract under which a borrower borrows a sum of money from a lender and repays it with interests when the loan becomes due.

Article 668 A loan contract shall be made in writing, unless the loan is between natural persons who agree otherwise.

A loan contract generally contains clauses specifying the category of the loan, the kind of currency, purpose of use, amount, interest rate, term, and the method of repayment, and the like, of the loan.

Article 669 Upon concluding a loan contract, a borrower shall, as required by the lender, provide true information about his business activities and financial conditions related to the borrowing to the lender.

Article 670 The interest on a loan may not be deducted from the principal in advance. Where the interest is deducted from the principal in advance, the loan shall be repaid and the interest shall be calculated according to the actual amount of money provided.

Article 671 A lender who fails to provide the loan at the agreed time and amount and thus causing losses to the borrower shall bear the liability for compensation.

A borrower who fails to take the loan at the agreed time and amount shall pay an interest based on the agreed time and amount.

Article 672 A lender may inspect and supervise the use of the loan in accordance with the agreement. A borrower shall regularly provide the relevant financial and accounting statements or other materials to the lender in accordance with the agreement.

Article 673 Where a borrower fails to use the loan for a purpose in accordance with the contract, the lender may stop providing the loan, recall the loan prior to its due date, or rescind the contract.

Article 674 A borrower shall pay the interest within the agreed time limit. Where there is no agreement between the parties on the time limit for payment of interest or the relevant agreement is unclear, if it cannot be determined according to the provisions of Article 510 of this Code, the interest shall be paid at the time the principal is repaid if the term of the loan is less than one year; the interest shall be paid at the end of each full year if the term of the loan is more than one year, and the interest shall be paid when the principal is repaid if the remaining term is less than one year.

Article 675 A borrower shall repay the loan within the agreed time limit. Where there is no agreement between the parties on the time limit of repayment of the loan, or the relevant agreement is unclear, if it cannot be determined according to the provisions of Article 510 of this Code, the borrower may repay the loan at any time, and the lender may demand the borrower to repay the loan within a reasonable period of time.

Article 676 A borrower who fails to repay the loan within the agreed time limit shall pay an overdue interest in accordance with the agreement or the relevant regulations of the State.

Article 677 Where a borrower makes a prepayment of the loan, unless otherwise agreed by the parties, the interest shall be calculated according to the actual duration of the loan.

Article 678 A borrower may apply to the lender for an extension of the term of the loan before the loan becomes due. The term of the loan may be extended upon consent of the lender.

Article 679 A loan contract between natural persons is formed at the time when the lender provides the loan.

Article 680 Usurious loans are prohibited, and the interest rate for lending may not violate the relevant regulations of the State.

Where there is no agreement on payment of interest in the loan contract, the loan is deemed as bearing no interest.

Where the agreement in a loan contract is unclear on the payment of interest, if the parties are unable to reach a supplementary agreement, the interest shall be determined by taking account of the practices in the local area or between the parties such as the method of transaction, course of dealing, the market interest rate, and the like. Where such a loan is between natural persons, the loan is deemed as bearing no interest.

Chapter XIII Suretyship Contracts

Section 1 General Rules

Article 681 A suretyship contract is a contract under which a surety and a creditor agree, for the purpose of ensuring the enforcement of an underlying claim, that the surety shall perform the obligation or bear the liability when the debtor fails to perform the obligation when it is due or a circumstance as agreed by the parties occurs.

Article 682 A suretyship contract is an accessary contract subordinated to a principal claim-obligation contract. Where the principal contract is invalid, the suretyship contract is invalid, unless otherwise provided by law.

Where a suretyship contract is determined to be invalid, the debtor, surety, or creditor who are at fault shall each bear civil liability in proportion to their respective fault.

Article 683 No State-organ legal person may act as a surety, except that such a State organ may, upon approval of the State Council, act as a surety in re-lending of the loans granted by a foreign government or an international economic organization.

No non-profit legal person established for public interest purposes or unincorporated organization may act as a surety.

Article 684 A suretyship contract generally contains clauses specifying the kind and amount of the principal claim that is secured, the time limit for the debtor to perform the obligation, the mode, scope, and term of the suretyship, and the like.

Article 685 A suretyship contract may be a contract concluded separately in writing or a guarantee clause in a principal claim-obligation contract.

A suretyship contract is formed when a third person unilaterally makes a guarantee in writing to a creditor who accepts it without making an objection.

Article 686 Suretyship consists of general suretyship and suretyship with joint and several liability.

Where there is no agreement in the suretyship contract on the form of the suretyship or the relevant agreement is unclear, the surety shall bear the liability as in the form of a general suretyship.

Article 687 Where the parties agree in a suretyship contract that the surety shall undertake suretyship liability when the debtor is unable to perform his obligation, such a suretyship is a general suretyship.

A surety in a general suretyship may refuse to undertake suretyship liability to the creditor before a dispute arising from the principal contract is adjudicated or arbitrated and the debtor is still unable to fully perform the obligation after his assets have been enforced in accordance with law, unless one of the following circumstances occurs:

(1) the whereabouts of the debtor have been unknown and the debtor has no assets available for enforcement;

(2) the people's court has accepted the debtor's bankruptcy petition;

(3) the creditor has evidence to prove that the debtor's assets are insufficient to perform all of the obligations or the debtor loses his capacity to perform the obligation; or

(4) the surety waives his rights provided in this paragraph in writing.

Article 688 Where the parties agree in a suretyship contract that the surety and the debtor shall be jointly and severally liable for the obligation, such a suretyship is a suretyship with joint and several liability.

Where a debtor under a suretyship with joint and several liability fails to perform his obligation due or when a circumstance agreed by the parties occurs, the creditor may request the debtor to perform his obligation, or request the surety to undertake the suretyship liability within the scope of his suretyship.

Article 689 A surety may request the debtor to provide a counter-security.

Article 690 A surety and a creditor may, through consultation, conclude a contract of maximum suretyship for floating claims to provide guarantee for the creditor's claims which will arise consecutively within a certain period of time and the total amount of which is up to the maximum amount of his claims.

In addition to applying the provisions of this Chapter, the relevant provisions of Book Two of this Code on the maximum mortgage for floating claims shall be applied *mutatis mutandis*.

Section 2 Suretyship Liability

Article 691 The scope of suretyship covers the principal claim and the interest thereof, the liquidated damages, compensatory damages, and the expenses for enforcing the claim, unless otherwise agreed by the parties.

Article 692 The term of suretyship is the period during which the surety undertakes suretyship liability, and such period may not be suspended, interrupted, or extended.

A creditor and a surety may agree on the term of suretyship. However, where the expiration date of the agreed term of suretyship is earlier than or the same as the expiration date of the period of performance of the principal obligation, it is deemed as there is no agreement on the term of suretyship. Where there is no agreement between the parties on the term of suretyship or the relevant agreement is unclear, the term of suretyship shall be six months from the expiration date of the period of performance of the principal obligation.

Where a creditor and a debtor fail to agree on the period of performance of the principal obligation or the relevant agreement is unclear, the term of suretyship shall be counted from the date when the grace period for the creditor to request the debtor to perform the obligation expires.

Article 693 Where a creditor of a general suretyship fails to file a lawsuit or apply for arbitration against the debtor within the term of suretyship, the surety no longer bears the suretyship liability.

Where a creditor of a suretyship with joint and several liability fails to request the surety to undertake his suretyship liability within the term of suretyship, the surety no longer bears the suretyship liability.

Article 694 Where a creditor of a general suretyship files a lawsuit or applies for arbitration against the debtor prior to the expiration of the term of suretyship, the limitation period of the suretyship obligation shall be counted from the date when the surety's right to refuse to undertake the suretyship liability is extinguished.

Where a creditor of a suretyship with joint and several liability requests the surety to undertake his suretyship liability prior to the expiration of the term of suretyship, the limitation period of the suretyship obligation shall be counted from the date when the creditor requests the surety to undertake his suretyship liability.

Article 695 Where a creditor and a debtor, without the surety's consent in writing, agree to alter the content of the principal claim-obligation contract, if the obligation is thus reduced, the surety shall continue to bear the suretyship liability to the extent of the altered obligation; if the obligation is thus increased, the surety does not bear the suretyship liability to the extent of the increased part.

Where a creditor and a debtor alter the period for performance of the principal claim-obligation contract, the term of suretyship is not affected unless upon the surety's written consent.

Article 696 Where a creditor transfers his claim in whole or in part without notifying the surety, such a transfer is not effective against the surety.

Where transfer of a claim is prohibited as agreed between the surety and the creditor, if the creditor transfers its claim without the surety's written consent, the surety shall no longer bear the suretyship liability.

Article 697 Where a creditor, without the surety's written consent, allows the debtor to transfer the obligation in whole or in part, the surety shall no longer bear the suretyship liability to the extent of the obligation transferred without his consent, unless otherwise agreed by the creditor and the surety.

Where a third person joins to be one of the debtors, the surety's liability is not affected.

Article 698 Upon expiration of the period of performance of the principal obligation, if the surety of a general suretyship provides to the creditor true information concerning the debtor's assets available for enforcement, but the creditor waives or is indolent in exercising his right, and thus causing such assets to be unenforceable, the surety shall no longer bear liability to the extent of the value of the said assets the information of which is provided by the surety.

Article 699 Where there are two or more sureties guaranteeing one obligation, the sureties shall undertake the suretyship liability in proportion to their share of suretyship in accordance with the suretyship contract. In the absence of such an agreement, the creditor may request any of the sureties to undertake the suretyship liability within the scope of his liability.

Article 700 After a surety has assumed the suretyship liability, unless otherwise agreed by the parties, the surety has the right to indemnification against the debtor within the scope of his suretyship liability, and may enjoy the right of a creditor against the debtor, provided that the creditor's interests may not be harmed.

Article 701 A surety may claim a defense that the debtor has against the creditor. Where the debtor waives his right of defense, the surety still has the right to claim such defense against the creditor.

Article 702 Where a debtor has the right to offset or the right to revocation against the creditor, the surety may refuse to undertake the suretyship liability to such extent.

Chapter XIV Lease Contracts

Article 703 A lease contract is a contract under which a lessor delivers the leased object to a lessee for use or for obtaining proceeds, for which the lessee pays the rent.

Article 704 A lease contract generally contains clauses specifying the name, quantity, purpose of use of the leased object, the term of the lease, rent, and the period and method of its payment, and the maintenance of the leased object, and the like.

Article 705 The term of a lease may not exceed twenty years. If a lease exceeds twenty years, the part beyond twenty years is void.

Upon expiration of the term of the lease, the parties may renew the lease contract, provided that the renewed term of the lease agreed by the parties may not exceed twenty years from the date of renewal.

Article 706 The parties' failure to register the lease contract in accordance with the provisions of laws or administrative regulations does not affect the validity of the contract.

Article 707 A lease contract with a term exceeding six months shall be made in writing. Where the lease contract between the parties is not in writing, if the term cannot be determined, the lease shall be deemed as a lease with an indefinite term.

Article 708 A lessor shall deliver the leased object to the lessee in accordance with the agreement and keep the leased object fit for the agreed use during the term of the lease.

Article 709 A lessee shall use the leased object in a manner as agreed by the parties. Where there is no agreement between the parties on the manner of use or the relevant agreement is unclear, if it cannot be determined according to the provisions of Article 510 of this Code, the leased object shall be used in line with its nature.

Article 710 Where a lessee uses the leased object in a manner as agreed by the parties or in line with its nature, he is not liable for the wear and tear on the leased object.

Article 711 Where a lessee fails to use the leased object in a manner as agreed by the parties or in line with its nature, thus causing damage to the leased object, the lessor may rescind the contract and request for compensation.

Article 712 A lessor shall perform the duty of maintaining the leased object, unless otherwise agreed by the parties.

Article 713 Where a leased object needs to be maintained or repaired, the lessee may request the lessor to have it maintained or repaired within a reasonable period of time. Where the lessor fails to perform the obligation of maintenance or repair, the lessee may maintain or repair the leased object by himself and the expenses thus incurred shall be borne by the lessor. If the maintenance or repair of the leased object affects the lessee's use of it, the rent shall be reduced or the term of the lease shall be extended accordingly.

Where a leased object needs to be maintained or repaired due to the lessee's fault, the lessor does not bear the obligation of maintenance or repair as provided in the preceding paragraph.

Article 714 A lessee shall properly keep the leased object and shall bear the liability for compensation if the leased object is destructed, damaged, or lost owing to his failing to properly keep it.

Article 715 A lessee may, upon the lessor's consent, improve the leased object or install additions thereto.

Where a lessee improves or installs additions to the leased object without the consent of the lessor, the lessor may request the lessee to restore the leased object to its original status or to compensate for the losses.

Article 716 A lessee may, upon the lessor's consent, sublease the leased object to a third person. The lease contract between the lessee and the lessor shall continue to be valid despite the sublease by the lessee, and if the third person causes losses to the leased object, the lessee shall bear the liability for compensation.

Where a lessee subleases the leased object without the consent of the lessor, the lessor may rescind the contract.

Article 717 Where a lessee, upon consent of the lessor, subleases the leased object to a third person, if the term of the sublease exceeds the remaining term of the original lease, the sublease beyond the term of the original lease is not legally binding on the lessor unless otherwise agreed by the lessor and the lessee.

Article 718 Where a lessor knows or should have known of the sublease made by a lessee but fails to raise any objection within six months, the lessor is deemed to have consented to the sublease.

Article 719 Where a lessee defaults on payment of the rent, the sublessee may pay the rent in arrears and the liquidated damages for the lessee, unless the sublease contract is not legally binding on the lessor.

The rent and liquidated damages paid by the sublessee for the lessee may be used to offset the rent payable by the sublessee to the lessee. If the amount of rent and liquidated damages thus paid by the sublessee exceeds the rent, the sublessee has the right to indemnification against the lessee.

Article 720 Any proceeds accrued from the possession or use of the leased object during the term of the lease shall belong to the lessee, unless otherwise provided by the parties.

Article 721 A lessee shall pay the rent within the period of payment in accordance with the agreement. Where there is no agreement between the parties on the period of payment of the rent or the relevant agreement is unclear, if it cannot be determined according to the provisions of Article 510 of this Code, the rent shall be paid at the time the term of lease expires if the term is less than one year, and, where the term of the lease is more than one year, the rent shall be paid at the end of each full year or at the time the term of lease expires if the remaining term is less than one year.

Article 722 Where a lessee fails to pay the rent or delays a payment of the rent without just cause, the lessor may request the lessee to pay the rent within a reasonable period of time, and may rescind the contract if the lessee fails to pay the rent within such period.

Article 723 Where a lessee is unable to use or to receive benefit from the leased object owing to a claim from a third person, the lessee may request for a reduction of or exemption from the rent.

Where a third person claims his right against the leased object, the lessee shall notify the lessor in a timely manner.

Article 724 A lessee may rescind the contract under any of the following circumstances if the leased object cannot be used due to a reason not attributable to the lessee:

(1) the leased object is sealed up or detained by the judicial authority or administrative authority in accordance with law;

(2) there are disputes over the attribution of rights of the leased object; or

(3) the leased object violates mandatory provisions of laws or administrative regulations in respect of its conditions for use.

Article 725 A change in the ownership of a leased object during the period that a lessee possesses the leased object in accordance with the lease contract does not affect the validity of the lease contract.

Article 726 A lessor intending to sell a leased house shall notify the lessee within a reasonable period of time prior to the sale, and the lessee has the priority right to purchase the house under equivalent conditions, unless the person who is a co-owner by shares exercises his priority right to purchase the house or if the lessor sells it to his close relatives.

Where a lessee fails to explicitly express his intention to purchase the house within 15 days after the lessor has fulfilled his obligation of notification, the lessee is deemed to have waived such priority right.

Article 727 Where a lessor authorizes an auctioneer to sell the leased house through auction, he shall notify the lessee five days prior to the auction. The lessee is deemed to have waived his priority right to purchase it if he fails to participate in the auction.

Article 728 Where a lessor fails to notify the lessee or otherwise hinders the lessee from exercising his priority right to purchase the leased house, the lessee may request the lessor to bear the liability for compensation. Provided, however, that the validity of the contract for sale of the leased house concluded between the lessor and a third person is not affected.

Article 729 Where a leased object is partially or wholly destructed, damaged, or lost due to a cause not attributable to the lessee, the lessee may request a reduction or exemption of the rent, and the lessee may rescind the contract if the purpose of the contract is unable to be achieved owing to such destruction, damage, or loss.

Article 730 Where there is no agreement between the parties on the term of the lease, or the relevant agreement is unclear, if it cannot be determined according to the provisions of Article 510 of this Code, the lease is deemed a lease with an indefinite term. Either party may rescind the contract at any time, provided that the other party is notified within a reasonable period of time in advance.

Article 731 Where a leased object endangers a lessee's safety or health, the lessee may rescind the contract at any time, even if the lessee is clearly aware of the substandard quality of the leased object upon concluding the contract.

Article 732 Where a lessee dies within the term of the lease of a house, a person who lives with or the joint operator of the deceased may lease the house according to the original lease contract.

Article 733 A lessee shall return the leased object upon expiration of the term of the lease. The leased object returned shall be maintained in its after-use state in accordance with the agreement or in line with its nature.

Article 734 Where a lessee continues to use the leased object upon expiration of the term of the lease and the lessor has not raised any objection, the original lease contract continues to be valid, except that the term of the lease becomes indefinite.

Upon expiration of a lease, the lessee of a house has the priority right to lease it under equivalent conditions.

Chapter XV Contracts for Financing Lease

Article 735 A contract for financing lease is a contract under which a lessee selects a leased object and its seller, and a lessor purchases the leased object from the selected seller and provides it to the lessee for use, who pays the rent in return.

Article 736 A contract for financing lease generally contains clauses specifying the name, quantity, specifications, technical performance, and inspection method of the leased object, the term of the lease, the composition of rent, the period, method, and currency of payment of the rent, the ownership over the leased object upon expiration of the term, and the like.

A contract for financing lease shall be made in writing.

Article 737 A contract for financing lease concluded by the parties under which a fictitious thing is to be leased is void.

Article 738 Where the operation or use of a leased object requires an administrative license in accordance with the provision of laws or administrative regulations, the failure of the lessor to obtain such administrative license does not affect the validity of the contract for financing lease.

Article 739 Where a lessor concludes a sales contract based on a lessee's selection of the seller and the leased object, the seller shall deliver the subject matter to the lessee as agreed by the parties, and the lessee shall enjoy the rights of a buyer with regard to the subject matter received.

Article 740 A lessee may refuse to accept the subject matter delivered by the seller where a seller breaches his obligation of delivery of the subject matter to the lessee and either of the following circumstances occurs:

(1) the subject matter is materially inconsistent with the agreement; or

(2) the seller fails to deliver the subject matter as agreed by the parties, and still fails to deliver it within a reasonable period of time after being demanded by the lessee or the lessor.

Where a lessee refuses to take delivery of the subject matter, he shall promptly notify the lessor.

Article 741 The lessor, the seller, and the lessee may agree that, where the seller fails to perform the obligations under the sales contract, the lessee shall exercise the right to claim against the seller. Where the lessee exercises such a right, the lessor shall render assistance.

Article 742 A lessee's exercise of the right to claim against the seller does not affect his performance of the obligation to pay the rent. However, where a lessee has relied upon the lessor's expertise in selecting the leased object or the lessor has intervened with the selection of the leased object, the lessee may request reduction or exemption of the rent accordingly.

Article 743 Where the lessee fails to exercise the right to claim against the seller due to either of the following causes, the lessee has the right to request the lessor to bear the corresponding liability:

(1) the lessor clearly knows that the leased object has quality defects but fails to notify the lessee; or

(2) when the lessee exercises the right to claim, the lessor fails to provide necessary assistance in a timely manner.

Where a right to claim against the seller may only be exercised by the lessor but the lessor fails to exercise such right owing to his indolence, thus causing losses to the lessee, the lessee has the right to request the lessor to bear the liability for compensation.

Article 744 Where a lessor concludes a sales contract based on the lessee's selection of the seller and the leased object, the lessor may not, without the consent of the lessee, modify the content of the contract related to the lessee.

Article 745 The lessor's ownership over the leased object shall, without being registered, not be asserted against a *bona fide* third person.

Article 746 The rent under a contract for financing lease shall, unless otherwise agreed by the parties, be determined according to the whole or major part of the cost for purchasing the leased object plus reasonable profits to be gained by the lessor.

Article 747 Where a leased object does not conform to the agreement or the purpose of its use, the lessor does not bear any liability, unless the lessee has relied upon the lessor's expertise in selecting the leased object or the lessor has intervened with the selection of the leased object.

Article 748 A lessor shall guarantee the lessee's possession and use of the leased object.

A lessee has the right to request the lessor to bear the liability for compensation where the lessor falls under any of the following circumstances:

(1) the lessor takes back the leased object without just cause;

(2) the lessor obstructs or interferes with the lessee's possession and use of the leased object without just cause;

(3) a third person claims a right over the leased object due to a reason attributable to the lessor; or

(4) the lessor otherwise improperly affects the lessee's possession and use of the leased object.

Article 749 Where a leased object causes any personal injury or property damage to a third person during the period it is under the lessee's possession, the lessor does not bear any liability.

Article 750 A lessee shall properly keep and use the leased object.

A lessee shall perform the obligation for the maintenance and repair of the leased object during the period the leased object is under his possession.

Article 751 Where the leased object is destructed, damaged, or lost during the period it is under the possession of the lessee, the lessor has the right to request the lessee to continue to pay the rent, unless otherwise provided by law or agreed by the parties.

Article 752 A lessee shall pay the rent in accordance with the agreement. Where a lessee fails to pay the rent within a reasonable period of time after being demanded, the lessor may request full payment of the rent, or rescind the contract and take back the leased object.

Article 753 Where a lessee transfers, mortgages, pledges, invests and contributes as share, or otherwise disposes of the leased object without the lessor's consent, the lessor may rescind the contract for financing lease.

Article 754 A lessor or a lessee may rescind the contract for financing lease under any of the following circumstances:

(1) the sales contract between the lessor and the seller is rescinded or determined as void or revoked, and the parties fail to conclude a sales contract anew;

(2) the leased object is destructed, damaged, or lost due to a reason not attributable to the parties, and it is impossible to repair the leased object or determine a substitute for it; or

(3) the purpose of the contract for financing lease cannot be achieved due to a reason attributable to the seller.

Article 755 Where a contract for financing lease is rescinded because the sales contract is rescinded, invalidated, or revoked, if the seller and the leased object are selected by the lessee, the lessor has the right to request the lessee to compensate for the corresponding losses, unless the sales contract is rescinded, invalidated, or revoked due to a reason attributable to the lessor.

Where the losses of the lessor have been recovered at the time the sales contract is rescinded, invalidated, or revoked, the lessee no longer bears liability for compensation.

Article 756 Where a contract for financing lease is rescinded due to a reason not attributable to the parties, such as an accidental destruction, damage, or loss of the leased object after it is delivered to the lessee, the lessor may request the lessee to make compensation based on the depreciation of the leased object.

Article 757 A lessor and a lessee may agree on the ownership over the leased object upon expiration of the term of the lease. Where there is no agreement between the parties on the ownership of the leased object or the relevant agreement is unclear, if it cannot be determined according to the provisions of Article 510 of this Code, the ownership of the leased object belongs to the lessor.

Article 758 Where the parties agree that the lessee shall have the ownership over the leased object upon expiration of the term of the lease, if the lessee has paid most of the rent but is unable to pay the remaining part, and the lessor has therefore rescinded the contract and taken back the leased object, the lessee may request the corresponding refund if the value of the leased object taken back exceeds the rent and other expenses in arrears.

Where the parties agree that the lessor shall have the ownership over the leased object upon expiration of the term of the lease, and the lessee is unable to return the leased object due to destruction, damage, or loss of the leased object, or because the leased object has been attached to or mixed with another thing, the lessor has the right to request the lessee to make reasonable compensation.

Article 759 Where the parties agree that the lessee is only required to pay the lessor a symbolic price upon expiration of the term of the lease, the ownership of the leased object is deemed as belonging to the lessee after the lessee has fulfilled his obligation to pay the rent in accordance with the agreement.

Article 760 Where a contract for financing lease is invalid and the parties have agreed on the ownership of the leased object under such a circumstance, such an agreement shall be followed. Where there is no agreement between the parties on the ownership of the leased object or the relevant agreement is unclear, the leased object shall be returned to the lessor. However, where the contract becomes invalid due to a reason attributable to the lessee, if the lessor does not request the return of the leased object or the return of the leased object will significantly reduce the usefulness of it, the ownership of the leased object belongs to the lessee, and the lessee shall make reasonable compensation to the lessor.

Chapter XVI Factoring Contracts

Article 761 A factoring contract is a contract under which a creditor of accounts receivable transfers the existing or after-acquired accounts receivable to a factor who provides services such as accommodation of funds, management or collection of the accounts receivable, guarantee for the payment of a debtor of the accounts receivable, and the like.

Article 762 A factoring contract generally contains clauses specifying the business type, scope of service, term of service, information on the underlying transaction contract and the accounts receivable, the financing funds through factoring, the service remuneration, the methods of payment thereof, and the like.

A factoring contract shall be in writing.

Article 763 Where a creditor and a debtor fabricate an account receivable as the object of transfer and then conclude a factoring contract on it with a factor, the debtor of the fabricated account receivable may not assert a defense against the factor on the ground that the account receivable does not exist, unless the factor clearly knows such fabrication.

Article 764 Where a factor notifies a debtor of an account receivable of the assignment of the account receivable, he shall disclose his identity as a factor and present necessary certifying documents.

Article 765 Where, after a debtor of an account receivable receives the notice of assignment thereof, the creditor and the debtor of the account receivable agree to modify or terminate the underlying contract without just cause, if it has an adverse impact on the factor, such modification or termination is not effective against the factor.

Article 766 Where the parties agree that the factoring is one with the right of recourse, the factor may claim against the creditor of the account receivable for refunding the principal and interest of the financing funds or redemption of the claim on the account receivable, or claim against the debtor of the account receivable. Where a factor claims against the debtor of the account receivable after deducting the principal and interest of the financing funds and the other relevant expenses, any balance shall be returned to the creditor of the account receivable.

Article 767 Where the parties agree that the factoring is one without the right of recourse, the factor shall claim against the debtor of the account receivable, and the factor is not required to return to the creditor of the account receivable the amount he has obtained, which is in excess of the principal and interest of the financing funds and the other relevant expenses.

Article 768 Where a creditor of an account receivable concludes multiple factoring contracts with different factors so that the factors claim their rights against the same account receivable, the account receivable shall be obtained by the factor of a registered factoring contract in priority over the factors of unregistered factoring contracts, or, where all factoring contracts are registered, by the factors in an order of priority according to the time of registration, or, where none of the factoring contracts have been registered, by the factor stated in the transfer notice which has reached the debtor of the account receivable first in time. Where none of the factoring contracts have been registered and no transfer notice has been sent, the account receivable shall be obtained by the factors on a *pro rata* basis on the amount of financing funds each has provided, or the service remuneration each is entitled to.

Article 769 For matters not provided in this Chapter, the relevant provisions of Chapter Ⅵ of this Book on the assignment of claims shall be applied.

Chapter XVII Work Contracts

Article 770 A work contract is a contract under which a contractor, in accordance with the requirements of a client, completes a work and delivers the work product to the client who pays remuneration in return.

A contracted work includes processing, manufacturing on order, repair, reproduction, testing, inspection, and the like.

Article 771 A work contract generally contains clauses specifying the object, quantity, and quality of the work, remuneration of the work, the mode of the work, supply of materials, the period of performance, the standard and method of inspection, and the like.

Article 772 A contractor shall complete the principal part of the work with his own equipment, technology, and labor force, unless otherwise agreed by the parties.

Where a contractor entrusts the major part of the contracted work with a third person, the contractor shall be accountable to his client concerning the work completed by the third person and the client may rescind the contract if he has not consented thereto.

Article 773 A contractor may entrust the accessory part of the contracted work with a third person. Where a contractor entrusts an accessory part of the contracted work to a third person, the contractor shall be accountable to the client concerning the work product completed by the third person.

Article 774 Where a contractor is to provide the materials, he shall select and use the materials in accordance with the agreement and accept the client's inspection.

Article 775 Where a client is to provide the materials, he shall provide the materials in accordance with the agreement. The contractor shall promptly inspect the materials provided by the client, and, if any inconformity is found, the contractor shall promptly request the client to make replacement, make up the shortage, or take other remedial measures.

Without the consent of the client, a contractor may not replace the materials provided by the client nor replace the accessories and parts which do not need repair.

Article 776 A contractor shall promptly notify the client if he finds that the drawings or technical requirements provided by the client are unreasonable. Where losses are caused to the contractor due to the client's indolence in responding or the like reasons, the client shall bear the liability for compensation.

Article 777 Where, in the course of performing a work contract, the client changes his requirements, thus causing losses to the contractor, the client shall bear liability for compensation.

Article 778 Where a contracted work requires assistance from the client, the client has the obligation to provide such assistance. Where the client fails to perform such obligation, thus making the completion of the contracted work impossible, the contractor may demand him to perform his obligation within a reasonable period of time, and may also extend the period of performance accordingly. If the client still fails to fulfill his obligation within the extended period, the contractor may rescind the contract.

Article 779 In the course of his work, a contractor shall accept the client's supervision and inspection that are necessary. The client may not disturb the normal work of the contractor by such supervision and inspection.

Article 780 Upon completion of his work, a contractor shall deliver to the client the work product and provide the client with the necessary technical materials and related quality certificates. The client shall inspect the work product for acceptance.

Article 781 Where the work product delivered by the contractor fails to meet the quality requirements, the client may, in a reasonable manner, request the contractor to bear default liability in forms of repair, reworking, remuneration reduction, or compensation for losses.

Article 782 A client shall pay remuneration within the time limit agreed by the parties. Where there is no agreement between the parties on the time limit for paying remuneration or the relevant agreement is unclear, if it cannot be determined according to the provisions of Article 510 of this Code, the client shall make payment at the time of delivery of the work product, and where part of the work product is delivered, the client shall make the corresponding payment.

Article 783 Where a client fails to pay the remuneration, material fees, or the like, the contractor has the right to retain the work product under lien or to refuse delivery, unless otherwise agreed by the parties.

Article 784 A contractor shall properly keep the materials provided by the client and the completed work product, and shall bear the liability for compensation if such materials or the work product is destructed, damaged, or lost owing to his inappropriate maintenance thereof.

Article 785 A contractor shall keep confidential the relevant information in accordance with the requirements of the client and, without the latter's permission, may not retain copies or technical data thereof.

Article 786 Co-contractors shall bear joint and several liabilities to the client, unless otherwise agreed by the parties.

Article 787 The client may rescind the work contract at any time before the contractor completes his work and shall bear the liability for compensating any loss thus caused to the contractor.

Chapter XVIII Contracts for Construction Project

Article 788 A contract for construction project is a contract under which a contractor carries out the construction of a project and the contract-offering party pays the price in return.

Contracts for construction project consist of contracts for project prospecting, designing, and construction.

Article 789 A contract for construction project shall be made in writing.

Article 790 Bidding for a construction project shall be carried out in an open, fair, and impartial manner in accordance with the provisions of the relevant laws.

Article 791 A contract-offering party may conclude a contract for construction project with a general contractor, or conclude separate contracts for prospecting, designing, and construction with the prospecting, designing, and construction parties respectively. A contract-offering party may not break up one construction project that should be completed by one contractor into several parts and offer them to several contractors.

A general contractor or a prospecting, designing, or construction contractor may, upon consent by the contract-offering party, entrust part of the contracted work with a third person. The third person shall assume joint and several liability with the general contractor or the prospecting, designing, or construction contractor to the contract-offering party on the work product of the third person. A contractor may not delegate the whole of the contracted construction project to a third person or break up the contracted construction project into several parts and delegate them separately to third persons in the name of subcontracting.

A contractor is prohibited from subcontracting the contracted project to any entity without the corresponding qualifications. A subcontractor is prohibited from re-subcontracting the contracted project. The main structure of the construction project must be completed by the contractor itself.

Article 792 Contracts for major construction projects of the State shall be concluded in accordance with the procedures set forth by the State and such documents as investment plans and feasibility study reports approved by the State.

Article 793 Where a contract for construction project is invalid but the construction project has passed the inspection for acceptance, the contractor may be compensated, with reference to the project price agreed in the contract, based on the appraised price of the construction project.

Where a contract for construction project is invalid and the construction project fails to pass the inspection for acceptance, it shall be dealt with in accordance with the following provisions:

(1) where the construction project after being repaired has passed the inspection for acceptance, the contract-offering party may request the contractor to bear the repairing costs; or

(2) where the construction project after being repaired still fails to pass the inspection for acceptance, the contractor has no right to request for payment with reference to the project price agreed in the contract and based on the appraised price of the construction project.

Where a contract-offering party is at fault for the losses caused by the substandard of the construction project, he shall bear corresponding liabilities.

Article 794 A prospecting or designing contract generally contains clauses specifying the time limit for submission of documents relating to the basic materials and budget, quality requirements, expenses and other cooperative conditions, and the like.

Article 795 A construction contract generally contains clauses specifying the scope of the project, the period for construction, the time of commencement and completion of the project to be delivered in midcourse, project quality, costs, delivery time of technical materials, the responsibility for the supply of materials and equipment, fund allocation and settlement, project inspection and acceptance upon its completion, range and period of quality warranty, cooperation, and the like.

Article 796 For any construction project to which a superintendence system is applied, the contract-offering party shall conclude an entrustment contract of superintendence in writing with the entrusted superintendent. The rights and obligations as well as the legal liabilities of the contract-offering party and the superintendent shall be defined in accordance with the provisions on entrustment contracts of this Book as well as the relevant provisions of other laws and administrative regulations.

Article 797 The contract-offering party may, without disturbing the normal operation of the contractor, inspect the progress and quality of the work at any time.

Article 798 Prior to the concealment of a concealed project, the contractor shall notify the contract-offering party to inspect it. If the contract-offering party fails to conduct an inspection in a timely manner, the contractor may extend the period for the completion of the project accordingly, and may request compensation for the losses caused by the work stoppage, the workers' forced idleness, and the like.

Article 799 Upon completion of a construction project, the contract-offering party shall promptly undertake the inspection for acceptance in accordance with the construction drawings and descriptions, as well as the rules of inspection and acceptance of construction projects and the standards for quality inspection issued by the State. Where the project passes the inspection for acceptance, the contract-offering party shall pay the agreed price and take over the construction project.

A construction project may be delivered and put into use only after it has passed the inspection for acceptance upon completion. Without being inspected or failing to pass the inspection, the construction project may not be delivered or put into use.

Article 800 Where losses are caused to a contract-offering party due to the fact that the prospecting or designing does not conform to the quality requirements or that the prospecting or designing documents are not submitted as scheduled, so that the period for construction is delayed, the prospecting or designing party shall continue on perfecting the prospecting or designing, reduce or waive the prospecting or designing fees, and make compensation for the losses.

Article 801 Where the quality of a construction project fails to conform to the contract due to a reason attributable to the constructor, the contract-offering party has the right to request the constructor to repair, rework, or reconstruct the project without further charge within a reasonable period of time. If delivery is delayed because of the repair, reworking, or reconstruction, the constructor shall bear default liability.

Article 802 Where a construction project causes personal injury and property damage within a reasonable period of use of the project due to a reason attributable to the contractor, the contractor shall bear the liability for compensation.

Article 803 Where a contract-offering party fails to provide raw materials, equipment, premises, funds, or technical materials at the agreed time and pursuant to the agreed requirements, the contractor may extend the period of construction accordingly and has the right to request compensation for the losses caused by work stoppage, workers' forced idleness, and the like.

Article 804 If a construction project is stopped or suspended in midcourse due to a reason attributable to the contract-offering party, the contract-offering party shall take measures to make up for or mitigate the loss, and compensate the contractor for any losses caused and any actual expenses incurred by work stoppage, workers' forced idleness, back transportation, transfer of machinery equipment, the backlog of materials and structural components, and the like.

Article 805 Where a contract-offering party alters his plan, provides inaccurate materials, or fails to provide necessary working conditions for prospecting or designing according to the schedule, thus causing the redoing or stoppage of the prospecting or designing work or the revision of the design, the contract-offering party shall pay additional fees according to the amount of work actually undertaken by the prospecting or designing party.

Article 806 Where a contractor delegates or illegally subcontracts the construction project to others, the contract-offering party may rescind the contract.

Where the main construction materials, construction components and accessories, and equipment provided by the contract-offering party fail to conform to the mandatory standard, or the contract-offering party fails to perform the obligation of providing assistance, so that the contractor cannot undertake the construction work, if the contract-offering party still fails to perform the corresponding obligations within a reasonable period of time after being demanded, the contractor may rescind the contract.

Where, after the contract is rescinded, the quality of the completed construction project is found to be up to standard, the contract-offering party shall make corresponding payment for the construction project in accordance with the agreement. If the quality of the completed construction project is found to be substandard, the provisions of Article 793 of this Code shall be applied *mutatis mutandis*.

Article 807 Where a contract-offering party fails to pay the price in accordance with the agreement, the contractor may demand the contract-offering party to make the payment within a reasonable period of time. Where the contract-offering party still fails to pay the price upon expiration of the said period, the contractor may negotiate with the contract-offering party to appraise the construction project, or request the people's court to sell the project through auction in accordance with law, unless the construction project is by its nature unsuitable for appraisal or auction. The payment for the construction of the project shall be satisfied, in priority, from the proceeds obtained from the appraisal or auction of the said project.

Article 808 For matters not provided in this Chapter, the relevant provisions on work contracts shall be applied.

Chapter XIX Transport Contracts

Section 1 General Rules

Article 809 A transport contract is a contract under which a carrier transports a passenger or goods from the place of dispatch to a destination agreed by the parties, and the passenger, consignor, or consignee pays the fare or the freight.

Article 810 A carrier engaged in public transport may not reject an ordinary and reasonable transport request made by a passenger or consignor.

Article 811 A carrier shall safely transport a passenger or goods to a destination as agreed within the agreed or a reasonable period of time.

Article 812 A carrier shall transport a passenger or goods to a destination as agreed *via* an agreed or a usual transport route.

Article 813 A passenger, consignor, or consignee shall pay the fare or the freight. If a carrier does not transport *via* an agreed route or the usual route, thus increasing the fare or the freight, the passenger, consignor, or consignee may refuse to pay the extra fare or freight.

Section 2 Passenger Transport Contracts

Article 814 A passenger transport contract is formed at the time when the carrier issues a ticket to the passenger, unless otherwise provided by the parties or in accordance with the course of dealing.

Article 815 A passenger shall get on board pursuant to the time, the number of runs or flights, and the seat number indicated on the valid ticket. Any passenger who boards without a ticket, beyond the paid distance, in a higher class, or with a discounted ticket while he is unqualified therefor shall pay or make up for the difference in the ticket price, and the carrier may charge an extra fare according to the regulations. Where a passenger refuses to pay the fare accordingly, the carrier may refuse to transport him.

Where a passenger under a real-name passenger transport contract loses his ticket, he may request the carrier to report the loss and reissue a ticket, and the carrier may not re-collect ticket fees or other unreasonable expenses.

Article 816 A passenger who is unable to get on board at the time indicated on the ticket due to his own reason shall, within the period of time agreed by the parties, undergo the procedures for refund or change of the ticket. If the passenger fails to undergo the refund or change procedures within the agreed period of time, the carrier may refuse to refund the ticket, and no longer has the transport obligation.

Article 817 The carry-on baggage of a passenger shall conform to the quantity limit and category requirements in accordance with the agreement. A passenger who carries baggage in excess of the quantity limit or in violation of the requirements for the category shall have the baggage checked in.

Article 818 A passenger may not carry with him or secretly carry in his baggage any inflammable, explosive, toxic, corrosive, or radioactive articles, any other dangerous articles that might endanger the safety of persons and property aboard, or any contraband articles.

Where a passenger violates the provision of the preceding paragraph, the carrier may unload or destroy the dangerous or contraband articles or deliver them to the relevant departments. Where a passenger insists on carrying with him the dangerous articles or the contraband articles or secretly carrying them in his baggage, the carrier shall refuse to transport him.

Article 819 A carrier shall strictly fulfill his obligations of safe transport and timely notify the passengers about matters of attention for a safe transport. A passenger shall actively assist in and be cooperative with the carrier with regard to the reasonable arrangements made for safe transport.

Article 820 A carrier shall transport a passenger at the time and in the number of runs or flights and seat number indicated on the valid ticket. Under circumstances where the transport is delayed or provided out of a normal state, the carrier shall inform and remind the passenger in a timely manner, take necessary measures for arrangement, and, upon the passenger's request, arrange him to take other numbers of runs or flights or refund his ticket. The carrier shall bear the liability for compensation for any loss thus caused to the passenger, unless such loss is not attributable to the carrier.

Article 821 A carrier who unilaterally downgrades the service standard shall, upon the passenger's request, refund his ticket or reduce the fare. A carrier who upgrades the service standard may not charge extra fare.

Article 822 A carrier shall, in the course of transportation, spare no effort to rescue and help a passenger who suffers an emergent disease, commence childbirth, or otherwise in danger.

Article 823 A carrier shall bear the liability for compensation arising from the injury or death of a passenger occurred in the course of transportation, unless the injury or death is a result of the passenger's own health condition, or the carrier can prove that the injury or death is caused by the passenger's intentional or grossly negligent act.

The provision of the preceding paragraph shall apply to any passenger exempted from ticket in accordance with the regulations, holding a complimentary ticket, or permitted by the carrier to travel without a ticket.

Article 824 Where an article that a passenger carries with him is destructed, damaged, or lost in the course of transportation, the carrier shall bear the liability for compensation if the carrier is at fault.

Where a passenger's checked-in baggage is destructed, damaged, or lost, the relevant provisions on the freight transport shall be applied.

Section 3 Freight Transport Contracts

Article 825 A consignor, when consigning goods for transport, shall clearly declare to the carrier the information necessary for freight transport such as the name or entity name of the consignee or the consignee by order, as well as the name, nature, weight and quantity of the goods, and the place of delivery.

If losses are caused to the carrier due to the consignor's untrue declaration or omission of substantial information in the declaration, the consignor shall bear the liability for compensation.

Article 826 Where a freight transport is subject to approval or inspection, the consignor shall submit to the carrier the documents showing the completion of the relevant formalities.

Article 827 A consignor shall package the goods in a manner as agreed by the parties. Where there is no agreement by the parties on the packaging methods or the relevant agreement is unclear, the provisions of Article 619 of this Code shall be applied.

Where a consignor violates the provision of the preceding paragraph, the carrier may refuse to conduct the transportation.

Article 828 Where a consignor consigns for transportation such dangerous goods as inflammable, explosive, toxic, corrosive, or radioactive articles, the consignor shall, in accordance with the regulations of the State on the transport of dangerous goods, properly package the dangerous goods, affix warning signs and labels thereto, and submit to the carrier written documents concerning the name, nature, and precautionary measures relevant to the dangerous goods.

Where a consignor violates the provision of the preceding paragraph, the carrier may refuse to conduct the transport, or may take appropriate measures to prevent losses, and the expenses thus incurred shall be borne by the consignor.

Article 829 Before a carrier delivers the goods to the consignee, the consignor may ask the carrier to stop transportation, return the goods, change the place of destination, or deliver the goods to another consignee, provided that the consignor shall compensate for the losses thus caused to the carrier.

Article 830 After the goods are transported to the place of destination, where the carrier knows who is the consignee, the carrier shall promptly notify the consignee and the consignee shall promptly take delivery of the goods. Where the consignee delays in taking delivery of the goods, the consignee shall pay the storage and other fees to the carrier.

Article 831 Upon taking delivery of the goods, a consignee shall inspect the goods within the time limit as agreed by the parties. Where there is no agreement between the parties on the time limit for inspection of the goods or the relevant agreement is unclear, if it cannot be determined according to the provisions of Article 510 of this Code, the consignee shall inspect the goods within a reasonable period of time. Where the consignee does not raise any objection on the quantity, destruction, damage, or loss of the goods within the agreed time limit or a reasonable period of time, the silence is deemed as preliminary evidence that the carrier has delivered the goods in accordance with the transport documents.

Article 832 A carrier shall bear the liability for compensation for any destruction, damage, or loss of the goods occurring in the course of transport. Provided, however, that the carrier does not bear the liability for compensation if the carrier proves that the destruction, damage, or loss of the goods is caused by *force majeure*, the inherent nature of the goods, or reasonable wear and tear, or is caused by the negligence of the consignor or the consignee.

Article 833 The amount of compensation for the destruction, damage, or loss of the goods shall be in accordance with the agreement between the parties if there is such an agreement. Where the agreement on the amount of compensation is unclear, if it cannot be determined according to the provisions of Article 510 of this Code, the amount of compensation shall be calculated based on the market price of the goods at the place of delivery at the time when the goods are delivered or should have been delivered. If there are laws or administrative regulations providing otherwise concerning the calculation method and the limit of the compensation amount, such provisions shall be followed.

Article 834 Where two or more carriers engage in a connected transport of the same mode, the carrier who concludes the contract with the consignor shall be responsible for the entire transport. If a loss occurs at one section of the transportation, the carrier who concludes the contract with the consignor and the carrier in the said section shall assume joint and several liability.

Article 835 Where the goods are lost in the course of transport due to *force majeure*, unless otherwise provided by law, the carrier may not request the payment of the freight if the freight has not yet been paid, and the consignor may request for a refund if the freight has already been paid.

Article 836 If a consignor or consignee fails to pay freight, storage fee, or other expenses, the carrier has the right to retain the goods under a lien, unless otherwise agreed by the parties.

Article 837 Where a consignee is unknown or the consignee refuses to take delivery of the goods without just cause, the carrier may have the goods placed in escrow in accordance with law.

Section 4 Multi-modal Transport Contracts

Article 838 An operator of multi-modal transport is responsible for performing or organizing the performance of a multi-modal transport contract, and enjoys the rights and assumes the obligations of a carrier throughout the entire transport.

Article 839 An operator of multi-modal transport may agree with the carriers of the different sections of the multi-modal transport on their respective responsibilities for transport in each section under the multi-modal transport contract, except that such an agreement does not affect the obligations of the operator for the entire transport.

Article 840 An operator of multi-modal transport shall, upon receipt of the goods consigned for transport by the consignor, issue multi-modal transport documents. The multi-modal transport documents may be negotiable or non-negotiable, as requested by the consignor.

Article 841 Where losses are caused to an operator of multi-modal transport due to the fault of a consignor at the time of consigning the goods for transport, the consignor shall bear the liability for compensation even if the consignor has transferred the multi-modal transport documents.

Article 842 Where destruction, damage, or loss of goods occurs in one section of the multi-modal transport, the provisions of the relevant laws regulating the transport modes of the section shall apply to the liability for compensation to be assumed by the operator of multi-modal transport and the limit of the liability. Where the section of transport in which such destruction, damage, or loss has occurred cannot be determined, liability for compensation shall be borne in accordance with the provisions of this Chapter.

Chapter XX Technology Contracts

Section 1 General Rules

Article 843 A technology contract is a contract concluded by the parties to establish their rights and obligations for technology development, transfer, licensing, consultation, or service.

Article 844 The conclusion of a technology contract shall be conducive to the protection of intellectual property rights and the advance of science and technology, and shall promote the research and development, transformation, application, and dissemination of the achievements in science and technology.

Article 845 A technology contract generally contains clauses specifying the name of the project, the content, scope, and requirements of the object, the plan, place, and manner of performance, the confidentiality of technological information and materials, the ownership over the technological achievements and the method of proceeds distribution, the criteria and method of the inspection for acceptance, interpretation of terminologies, and the like.

Materials such as technological background information, the feasibility studies and technological evaluation reports, the project task paper and plans, technology standards, technology norms, original design and technical documents, as well as other technical documents which are relevant to the performance of the contract may, as agreed by the parties, be component parts of the contract.

Where a technology contract involves a patent, it shall indicate the designation of the invention, the applicant and the patentee thereof, the date of application, the application number, the patent number, and the term of the patent rights.

Article 846 The method of payment for the price, remuneration, or royalty shall be agreed by the parties in a technology contract, and the payment may be made in a lump-sum or by installment based on one-time calculation, or based on the method of commission payment or such payment plus an upfront fee.

Where the parties agree to adopt a method of commission payment, the commission may be drawn at a specific percentage from the price of the product, the newly-increased output value and profits attained from the exploitation of patents and the utilization of technological know-how, or the sales revenue of the product, or be calculated by other methods as agreed by the parties. The said percentage may be a fixed percentage, or one that increases or decreases year by year.

Where the parties agree to adopt commission payment, they may specify the method for examining the relevant accounting books.

Article 847 Where a right to use or transfer a work for hire belongs to a legal person or an unincorporated organization, the legal person or unincorporated organization may conclude a technology contract on the work for hire. Where the legal person or unincorporated organization concludes a technology contract to transfer the work for hire, the creator of the work for hire has a priority right to acquire it on equivalent conditions.

A work for hire is a technological achievement that is accomplished as a result of performing the tasks assigned by a legal person or unincorporated organization or that is accomplished mainly by using the materials and technological resources of the said legal person or unincorporated organization.

Article 848 The right to use or transfer a technological work product other than a work for hire belongs to its creator who may conclude a technology contract on such work product.

Article 849 An individual person who has accomplished a technological work product has the right to indicate on the relevant documents of the technological work product that he is the creator thereof, and to receive certificate of honor and rewards.

Article 850 A technology contract that illegally monopolies technologies or infringes upon other's technological work product is void.

Section 2 Technology Development Contracts

Article 851 A technology development contract is a contract concluded by the parties concerning the research and development of a new technology, product, technique, variety, or material, as well as the system thereof.

Technology development contracts consist of commissioned development contracts and cooperative development contracts.

A technology development contract shall be in writing.

The relevant provisions on the technology development contracts shall be applied *mutatis mutandis* to a contract concluded by the parties on the application and transformation of a technological product with a value for practical use.

Article 852 A client of a commissioned development contract shall pay for the research and development fees and the remunerations in accordance with the agreement, provide technological materials, make proposals for research and development, complete his tasks in the cooperative work, and accept the work product of the research and development.

Article 853 A researcher-developer of a commissioned development contract shall work out and implement a research and development plan in accordance with the contract, make reasonable use of the research and development funds, complete the research and development work as scheduled, deliver the work product of research and development, provide relevant technological materials and necessary technological guidance so as to help the client comprehend the work product of the research and development.

Article 854 Where a party to a commissioned development contract defaults, thus causing the stoppage, delay, or failure of the research and development work, the party shall bear default liability.

Article 855 The parties to a cooperative development contract shall make investments in a form agreed by the parties, including contribution of the technology in investment, participation in the research and development work by performing their respective duties, and cooperation in the research and development.

Article 856 Where a party to a cooperative development contract defaults, thus causing the stoppage, delay, or failure of the research and development work, the party shall bear default liability.

Article 857 Where a technology which is the object of a technology development contract is revealed to the public by others, thus rendering the performance of the contract meaningless, the parties may rescind the contract.

Article 858 The parties to a technology development contract shall agree on the allocation of risks of insurmountable technological difficulties arising in the performance of the contract which causes total or partial failure of the research and development. Where there is no such an agreement between the parties or the relevant agreement is unclear, if it cannot be determined according to the provisions of Article 510 of this Code, the parties shall share the risks in a reasonable way.

Where a party finds that a situation specified in the preceding paragraph exists which may cause total or partial failure of the research and development, the party shall promptly notify the other party and take appropriate measures to mitigate the loss. Where the party fails to promptly inform the other party and take appropriate measures so that the loss is aggravated, it shall be liable for the aggravated part of the loss.

Article 859 Where an invention is accomplished through commissioned development, the right to apply for patent on the invention belongs to the researcher-developer, unless otherwise provided by law or agreed by the parties. Where the researcher-developer has obtained the patent right, the client may exploit the patent in accordance with law.

Where a researcher-developer is to transfer his patent application right, the client has a priority right to acquire the right on equivalent conditions.

Article 860 Where an invention is accomplished through cooperative development, the right to apply for patent thereon jointly belongs to all parties to the cooperative development. Where one party is to transfer the part of the joint patent application right he owns, the other party or parties shall have a priority right to acquire the right on equivalent conditions, unless otherwise agreed by the parties.

Where a party to a cooperative development waives the part of patent application right he owns, unless otherwise agreed by the parties, the other party may make the application, or the other parties may jointly make the application, as the case may be. Where an applicant acquires the patent right, the party who has waived the right to application of the patent may exploit the patent free of charge.

Where one party to a cooperative development does not agree to apply for patent, the other party or parties may not file such an application.

Article 861 The right to use and the right to transfer a work product containing technological know-how accomplished through commissioned development or cooperative development, as well as the method for distributing the proceeds thereof, shall be agreed by the parties. Where there is no such an agreement between the parties or the relevant agreement is unclear, if it cannot be determined according to the provisions of Article 510 of this Code, all the parties have the right to use and transfer the said work product, as long as no patent right has been granted on a same technological solution. Provided, however, that a researcher-developer of a commissioned development may not transfer the work product to a third person before he delivers it to the client.

Section 3 Technology Transfer Contracts and Technology Licensing Contracts

Article 862 A technology transfer contract is a contract under which a lawful right holder of a technology assigns to another person the relevant rights in respect of a specific patent, application for a patent, or technological know-how.

A technology licensing contract is a contract under which a lawful right holder of a technology authorizes another person to exercise the relevant rights to apply and exploit a specific patent or technological know-how.

The agreement in a technology transfer contract or a technology licensing contract on the provision of special equipment and raw materials for application of the technology or on the provision of the relevant technology consultation and technology service is a component part of the contract.

Article 863 Technology transfer contracts include the contracts for the transfer of patent right, the contracts for transfer of the patent application right, the contracts for transfer of technological know-how, and the like.

Technology licensing contracts include the patent exploitation licensing contracts, technological know-how licensing contracts, and the like.

Technology transfer contracts and technology licensing contracts shall be in writing.

Article 864 A technology transfer contract or a technology licensing contract may specify the scope to exploit the patent or to use the technological know-how, but may not restrict competition or development of the technologies.

Article 865 A patent exploitation licensing contract is valid only within the period during which the patent is valid. Where the term of the patent right expires or the patent right is declared invalid, the patentee may not conclude a patent exploitation licensing contract relating to the said patent with another person.

Article 866 A licensor under a patent exploitation licensing contract shall permit the licensee to exploit the patent, deliver the technological materials related to the patent exploitation, and provide necessary technological guidance in accordance with the agreement.

Article 867 A licensee under a patent exploitation licensing contract shall exploit the patent in accordance with the agreement, may not allow a third person outside the contract to exploit the patent, and shall pay the agreed royalties.

Article 868 A transferor under a technological know-how transfer contract or a licensor under a technological know-how licensing contract shall, in accordance with the agreement, provide technological materials, give technological guidance, guarantee the practical applicability and reliability of the technology, and perform confidentiality obligations.

The confidentiality obligations provided in the preceding paragraph may not restrict the licensor's ability to file an application for a patent, unless otherwise agreed by the parties.

Article 869 A transferee under a technological know-how transfer contract or a licensee under a technological know-how licensing contract shall, in accordance with the agreement, exploit the technology, pay the transfer fee and royalties, and perform the confidentiality obligations.

Article 870 A transferor under a technological transfer contract or a licensor under a technological know-how licensing contract shall guarantee that he is the lawful owner of the technology provided therein, and guarantee that the technology provided is complete, errorless, effective, and capable of achieving the goal as agreed by the parties.

Article 871 A transferee under a technology transfer contract or a licensee under a technological know-how licensing contract shall, in accordance with the scope and time limit agreed by the parties, perform the confidentiality obligation regarding the part of the technology provided by the transferor or licensor that has not been disclosed to the public.

Article 872 A licensor who fails to license the technology in accordance with the agreement shall refund the royalties in part or in full and bear default liability. A licensor who exploits a patent or technological know-how beyond the agreed scope, or, without authorization, allows a third person to exploit the patent or utilize the technological know-how in breach of the agreement shall stop his breaching act and bear default liability. A licensor who breaches the agreed confidentiality obligation shall bear default liability.

Where a transferor is liable for breach of contract, the provisions of the preceding paragraph shall be applied *mutatis mutandis*.

Article 873 A licensee who fails to pay royalties in accordance with the agreement shall make up for the payment and pay the liquidated damages according to the agreement. A licensee who fails to make up for the payment of royalties and pay the liquidated damages shall stop exploitation of the patent or utilization of the technological know-how, return the technological materials, and bear default liability. A licensee who exploits the patent or utilizes the technological know-how beyond the agreed scope, or, without authorization of the licensor, allows a third person to exploit the patent or to utilize the technological know-how, shall stop the breaching act and bear default liability. The licensee who breaches the agreed confidentiality obligation shall bear default liability.

The provisions of the preceding paragraph shall be applied *mutatis mutandis* to a transferee who shall bear default liability.

Article 874 Where exploitation of a patent or utilization of a technological know-how by the transferee or the licensee in accordance with the agreement infringes upon the lawful rights and interests of another person, the transferor or the licensor shall bear the liability, unless otherwise agreed by the parties.

Article 875 The parties may, in compliance with the principle of mutual benefit, agree in the contract the method for sharing any subsequently improved technological product obtained in exploitation of the patent or utilization of the technological know-how. Where there is no agreement on such method or the relevant agreement is unclear, if it cannot be determined according to the provisions of Article 510 of this Code, the subsequently improved technological product made by one party may not be shared by any other party.

Article 876 The relevant provisions of this Section shall be applied *mutatis mutandis* to the transfer and licensing of the exclusive rights to layout-designs of integrated circuits, rights to new plant varieties, computer software copyrights, and other intellectual property rights.

Article 877 Where there are laws or administrative regulations providing otherwise on contracts for technology import and export, or on contracts for patents and application of patents, the relevant provisions shall be followed.

Section 4 Technology Consultation Contracts and Technology Service Contracts

Article 878 A technology consultation contract is a contract under which one party uses technological knowledge to provide the other party with the feasibility study, technological forecast, special technological investigation, and analysis and evaluation report on a specific technological project.

A technology service contract is a contract under which one party uses his technological knowledge to solve specific technological problems for the other party. Technology service contracts does not include work contracts or contracts for construction project.

Article 879 A client in a technology consultation contract shall, in accordance with the agreement, clarify the issues for consultation, provide technological background information and the related materials, accept the work product of the entrusted person, and pay remuneration.

Article 880 The entrusted person in a technology consultation contract shall complete the consultation report or resolve the issues within the agreed time limit, and the consultation report submitted shall meet the requirements as agreed by the parties.

Article 881 Where a client in a technology consultation contract fails to provide the necessary materials in accordance with the agreement thus affecting the progress and quality of the work, or if the client fails to accept the work product or delays the acceptance, he may not request refund for the paid remuneration and shall pay any unpaid remuneration.

An entrusted person in a technology consultation contract who fails to submit the consultation report as scheduled or submits a report failing to meet the requirements as agreed by the parties shall bear default liability in form of reduction or waiver of its remuneration, and the like.

Where a client in a technology consultation contract makes a decision in reliance upon the entrusted person's consultation report and advice that meet the requirements as agreed by the parties, any loss thus caused shall be borne by the client, unless otherwise agreed by the parties.

Article 882 A client in a technology service contract shall, in accordance with the agreement, provide working conditions, perform the cooperative work, accept the work product, and pay remuneration.

Article 883 An entrusted person in a technology service contract shall, in accordance with the agreement, complete the services, solve the technological issues, guarantee the quality of the work, and impart the knowledge for solving the technological problems.

Article 884 Where a client to a technology service contract fails to perform the contractual obligations or performs the obligations in a manner inconsistent with the contract, thus affecting the progress and quality of the work, or fails to accept the work product or delays the acceptance, the client may not request for refund of the paid remuneration, and shall pay any unpaid remuneration.

An entrusted person in a technology service contract who fails to complete the service work in accordance with the agreement shall bear default liability in such form as waiver of remuneration, and the like.

Article 885 Unless otherwise agreed by the parties, in the course of performance of a technology consultation contract or a technology service contract, the new technological product made by the entrusted person with technological materials and working conditions provided by the client belongs to the entrusted person, and the new technological product made by the client based on the work product of the entrusted person belongs to the client.

Article 886 Where there is no agreement in a technology consultation contract or a technology service contract on the bearing of the necessary expenses for the entrusted person to carry out the normal work, or the relevant agreement is unclear, the said expenses shall be borne by the entrusted person.

Article 887 Where there are laws or administrative regulations providing otherwise on technology intermediary contracts and technology training contracts, the relevant provisions shall be followed.

Chapter XXI Contracts for Custody of Property

Article 888 A contract for custody of property is a contract under which a custodian keeps an article delivered by a depositor and returns the said article.

Where a depositor conducts shopping, dining, lodging, or other activities in the custodian's place and deposits an article at a designated area, the article is deemed to be placed under the custodian's custody unless otherwise agreed by the parties or required by the course of dealing.

Article 889 A depositor shall pay the safekeeping fee to the custodian in accordance with the agreement.

Where there is no agreement between the parties on the safekeeping fee or the relevant agreement is unclear, if it cannot be determined according to the provisions of Article 510 of this Code, the article is deemed to be placed in a gratuitous custody.

Article 890 A contract for custody of property is formed upon delivery of the article to be placed under custody, unless otherwise agreed by the parties.

Article 891 Where a depositor delivers to a custodian an article to be kept under his custody, the custodian shall issue a safekeeping certificate, unless otherwise required by the course of dealing.

Article 892 A custodian shall properly keep the article under his custody.

The parties may agree on the place and method of safekeeping. Except in case of emergency or in the interests of the depositor, the place and method of safekeeping may not be changed without the other party's consent.

Article 893 Where an article delivered by the depositor to be kept under custody has defects or needs special safekeeping measures based on its nature, the depositor shall inform the custodian of the relevant information. Where the depositor fails to do so, if damage is thus caused to the article, the custodian does not bear the liability for compensation, and if losses are thus caused to the custodian, the depositor shall be liable for compensation unless the custodian knows or should have known the situation but fails to take remedial measures.

Article 894 A custodian may not re-deposit an article under his custody to a third person for safekeeping, unless otherwise agreed by the parties.

A custodian who re-deposits the article under his custody to a third person for safekeeping in violation of the preceding paragraph thus causing damage to the article shall bear the liability for compensation.

Article 895 A custodian may not use or permit a third person to use the article under his custody, unless otherwise agreed by the parties.

Article 896 Where a third person claims against an article under custody, the custodian shall perform the obligation of returning the article to the depositor, unless the said article is put under preservation or enforcement in accordance with law.

Where a third person files a lawsuit against the custodian or applies for detention of the article under custody, the custodian shall promptly notify the depositor.

Article 897 Where an article under custody is destructed, damaged, or lost due to improper safekeeping by the custodian during the period the article is under his custody, the custodian shall bear the liability for compensation. Provided, however, that a custodian who keeps the deposited article free of charge does not bear the liability for compensation if he can prove that the destruction, damage, or loss of the article is not caused by his intentional or grossly negligent act.

Article 898 A depositor shall declare to the custodian if he places money, negotiable securities, or other valuable articles under custody, and the custodian shall examine them for acceptance or seal them; where the depositor fails to make such a declaration, if the said article is destructed, damaged, or lost, the custodian may make compensation based on a rate for ordinary articles.

Article 899 A depositor may collect the article he places under custody at any time.

Where there is no agreement between the parties on the period for custody or the relevant agreement is unclear, the custodian may, at any time, request the depositor to collect the article under his custody. Where there is an agreement on the period for custody, without special cause, the custodian may not request the depositor to collect the article before such period expires.

Article 900 Upon expiration of the period for custody or where the depositor collects the article he places under custody before expiration of such period, the custodian shall return the article and the proceeds accrued thereof to the depositor.

Article 901 Where money is placed under custody, the custodian may return the money in the same currency and amount. Where other fungible goods are placed under custody, the custodian may return the goods of the same kind, quality, and quantity in accordance with the agreement.

Article 902 Under a contract for non-gratuitous custody, the depositor shall pay the safekeeping fee to the custodian at a time agreed by the parties.

Where there is no agreement between the parties on the time limit for payment of the safekeeping fee or the relevant agreement is unclear, if it cannot be determined according to the provisions of Article 510 of this Code, the payment shall be made at the time the article under custody is collected.

Article 903 Where a depositor fails to pay the safekeeping fee or the other expenses, the custodian has the right to retain the article under his custody under a lien, unless otherwise agreed by the parties.

Chapter XXII Warehousing Contracts

Article 904 A warehousing contract is a contract under which a warehouser stores the goods delivered by a depositor for which the depositor pays the warehousing fee.

Article 905 A warehousing contract is formed when there is a consensus of expression of intent between the warehouser and the depositor.

Article 906 Where dangerous goods such as inflammable, explosive, toxic, corrosive, or radioactive articles, or perishable articles are to be stored, the depositor shall state the nature of the said goods and provide relevant information thereof to the warehouser.

Where a depositor violates the provision of the preceding paragraph, the warehouser may refuse to accept the goods for storage, or take appropriate measures to avoid losses, and the expenses thus incurred shall be borne by the depositor.

A warehouser that stores dangerous goods such as inflammable, explosive, toxic, corrosive, or radioactive articles shall have the corresponding warehousing qualifications.

Article 907 A warehouser shall, in accordance with the agreement, examine the goods before accepting them. Where a warehouser, upon examining the goods, finds that the goods to be stored are inconsistent with the agreement, he shall promptly notify the depositor. A warehouser shall bear the liability for compensation if, after he has examined and accepted the stored goods, the goods are not in conformity with the agreement in terms of the type, quantity, or quality.

Article 908 Upon delivery of the goods for storage by a depositor, the warehouser shall issue a document such as a warehouse receipt or entry.

Article 909 A warehouser shall sign or stamp on a warehouse receipt. A warehouse receipt shall contain the following particulars:

(1) the name or entity name and domicile of the depositor;

(2) the type, quantity, quality, package, the number of pieces, and marks of the stored goods;

(3) the standard for damage and spoilage of the stored goods;

(4) the warehousing site;

(5) the warehousing period;

(6) the warehousing fee;

(7) the insured amount, term of insurance, and the entity name of the insurer if the goods to be stored have been insured; and

(8) the name of the issuer and the place and date of issuance.

Article 910 A warehouse receipt is a proof for collecting the stored goods. Where a warehouse receipt is endorsed by the depositor or a holder of the receipt, and is signed or stamped by the warehouser, the right to collect the stored goods may be assigned to another person.

Article 911 A warehouser shall, upon request of the depositor or the holder of the warehouse receipt, allow the depositor or the holder to examine the stored goods or to take samples of the goods.

Article 912 Where a warehouser finds that the stored goods deteriorate or suffer from other damage, the warehouser shall promptly notify the depositor or the holder of the warehouse receipt.

Article 913 Where a warehouser finds that the stored goods deteriorate or suffer from other damage, which endangers the safety and the normal warehousing of the other stored goods, he shall demand the depositor or the holder of the warehouse receipt to dispose of the goods when necessary. In case of emergency, a warehouser may make necessary disposal, but afterwards shall promptly notify the depositor or the holder of the warehouse receipt about the situation.

Article 914 Where there is no agreement between the parties on the warehousing period or the relevant agreement is unclear, the depositor or the holder of the warehouse receipt may collect the stored goods at any time, and the warehouser may, at any time, request the depositor to collect the stored goods, provided that a reasonable period of time necessary for preparations shall be given.

Article 915 Upon expiration of the warehousing period, the depositor or the holder of the warehouse receipt shall collect the stored goods by presenting the warehouse receipt, warehouse entry, or the like. Additional warehousing fees shall be charged if the depositor or the holder of the warehouse receipt delays in collecting the stored goods, whereas the warehousing fees may not be reduced if the goods are collected before expiration of the warehousing period.

Article 916 Where a depositor or a holder of the warehouse receipt fails to collect the stored goods upon expiration of the warehousing period, the warehouser may demand the depositor or the holder of the warehouse receipt to collect the goods within a reasonable period of time; if the depositor or the holder still fails to collect the goods beyond the reasonable period, the warehouser may have the warehoused goods placed in escrow.

Article 917 If within the warehousing period, the stored goods are destructed, damaged, or lost due to improper warehousing, the warehouser shall bear the liability for compensation. Where the deterioration or damage of the stored goods is due to the inherent nature of the goods, or because the goods are not packaged in accordance with the agreement, or because they are stored beyond a valid storage period, the warehouser is not liable for compensation.

Article 918 For matters not provided in this Chapter, the relevant provisions on the contracts for custody of property shall be applied.

Chapter XVIII Entrustment Contracts

Article 919 An entrustment contract is a contract under which a principal and an agent agree that the agent shall handle the matters for the principal.

Article 920 A principal may specifically entrust an agent to handle one or several matters, and may also generally entrust an agent to handle all matters of his.

Article 921 A principal shall pay in advance the expenses for handling the entrusted matter. Where an agent pays for the principal the necessary expenses in handling an entrusted matter, the principal shall reimburse the expenses with interest.

Article 922 An agent shall handle the entrusted matter in accordance with the instructions given by the principal. Where it is necessary to modify such instructions, the modification shall be consented to by the principal; where the situation is emergent and it is difficult to obtain the principal's consent, the agent shall properly handle the entrusted matter, and shall, afterwards, promptly inform the principal of the situation.

Article 923 An agent shall handle the entrusted matter in person. With the consent of the principal, an agent may sub-entrust it to a third person. Where the sub-entrustment is consented to or ratified by the principal, the principal may directly instruct the sub-entrusted third person on an entrusted matter, and the agent shall only be liable for the selection of the third person and for the instructions given by himself to the third person. If the sub-entrustment is not consented to or ratified by the principal, the agent shall be liable for an act done by the sub-entrusted third person, unless the sub-entrustment is for protecting the interests of the principal in case of emergency.

Article 924 An agent shall, upon request of the principal, report on the situation of the entrusted matter. Upon termination of the entrustment contract, an agent shall report on the result of the entrusted matter.

Article 925 Where an agent, acting within the scope of authority granted by the principal, concludes a contract with a third person in his own name, if the third person is aware of the agency relationship between the agent and the principal, the said contract shall directly bind the principal and the third person, unless there is clear evidence establishing that the said contract binds only the agent and the third person.

Article 926 Where a contract is concluded by an agent in his own name with a third person who is not aware of the agency relationship between the agent and the principal, if the agent fails to perform his obligations owed to the principal due to a reason attributable to the third person, the agent shall disclose the third person to the principal, and the principal may then exercise the right of the agent against the third person, unless the third person would not have concluded the contract had he been aware of the existence of the principal at the time of concluding the contract.

Where an agent fails to perform his obligations owed to a third person due to a reason attributable to the principal, the agent shall disclose the principal to the third person, and the third person may then claim his rights against either the agent or the principal as a counterparty, except that he may not change the counterparty once he has made the selection.

Where a principal exercises the right of the agent against the third person, the third person may claim the defenses he has against the agent against the principal. Where the third person elects the principal as the counterparty, the principal may claim against the third person the defenses he has against the agent, as well as the agent's defenses against the third person.

Article 927 An agent shall hand over to the principal any property acquired in handling the entrusted matter.

Article 928 When an agent has accomplished the entrusted matter, the principal shall pay remuneration to the agent in accordance with the agreement.

Where an entrustment contract is rescinded or the entrusted matter cannot be accomplished due to a cause not attributable to the agent, the principal shall pay corresponding remuneration to the agent, unless otherwise agreed by the parties.

Article 929 Under a non-gratuitous entrustment contract, where losses are caused to the principal due to the agent's fault, the principal may request compensation. Under a gratuitous entrustment contract, where losses are caused to the principal by the agent's intentional act or by his gross negligence, the principal may request for compensation.

Where an agent acts *ultra vires* thus causing losses to the principal, the agent shall make compensation.

Article 930 Where an agent suffers a loss in handling the entrusted matter due to a cause not attributable to himself, he may request compensation from the principal.

Article 931 A principal may, with consent of the agent, authorize a third person other than the agent to handle the entrusted matter. If a loss is thus caused to the agent, the agent may request compensation from the principal.

Article 932 Where two or more agents jointly handle an entrusted matter, they shall bear joint and several liabilities to the principal.

Article 933 A principal or an agent may rescind the entrustment contract at any time. Where rescission of the contract by a party causes losses to the other party, the party rescinding a gratuitous entrustment contract shall compensate for the direct loss caused by the rescission at an improper time, and the party rescinding a non-gratuitous entrustment contract shall compensate for the direct loss and the expected profit obtainable had the contract been performed, unless the loss is incurred by a cause not attributable to the rescinding party.

Article 934 An entrustment contract is terminated where the principal dies or is terminated, or if the agent dies, loses capacity for performing civil juristic acts, or is terminated, unless otherwise agreed by the parties or it is inappropriate to terminate the contract based on the nature of the entrusted matter.

Article 935 Where termination of an entrustment contract resulting from the death, declared bankruptcy, or declared dissolution of the principal is to harm the interests of the principal, the agent shall continue to handle the entrusted matter until the heirs, administrator of estate, or the liquidator of the principal takes it over.

Article 936 Where an entrustment contract is terminated owing to the death, loss of capacity for performing civil juristic acts, declared bankruptcy or dissolution of the agent, the heirs, administrator of estate, legal representative, or liquidator of the agent shall promptly notify the principal. Where termination of the entrustment contract is to harm the interests of the principal, the heirs, administrator of estate, legal representative, or liquidator of the agent shall take necessary measures before the principal takes remedial measures.

Chapter XXIV Contracts for Property Management Service

Article 937 A contract for property management service is a contract under which a property management service provider provides the property owners with property management services within the service area, such as repair and maintenance of buildings and the auxiliary facilities thereof, the management and maintenance of the environmental hygiene, keeping the order, and the like, and the property owners pay property management fees in return.

Property management service providers include property management service enterprises and other managers.

Article 938 A property management service contract generally contains clauses specifying the contents of the services, the service quality, the rates and the collection methods of the service fee, the use of the maintenance funds, the management and use of the service premises, the term of service, the service handover, and the like.

A commitment of service made publicly by a property management service provider in favor of the property owners shall be a component part of the property management service contract.

A property management service contract shall be in writing.

Article 939 A preliminary property management service contract concluded between a developer and a property management service provider in accordance with law, or a property management service contract concluded by an owners' committee and a property management service provider selected and hired in the owners' assembly in accordance with law are legally binding on the owners.

Article 940 Where a contract for property management service concluded by the owners' committee or the owners with a new property management service provider becomes effective prior to expiration of the service term as agreed in a preliminary contract for property management service concluded between the developer and the old property management service provider in accordance with law, the preliminary contract for property management service is terminated.

Article 941 Where a property management service provider authorizes a specialized service entity or any other third person to handle some specialized services in the property management service area, the property management service provider shall be responsible to the owners in terms of the specialized services.

A property management service provider may not delegate to a third person all the property management services it is obligated to provide, or divide the property management services and delegate each to a third person.

Article 942 A property management service provider shall, in accordance with the contract and the nature of the use of the property, properly repair, maintain, clean, grow plants in, and manage the common space of the property management service area co-owned by the owners, maintain the basic order in the property management service area, and take reasonable measures to protect the owners' personal and property safety.

For any violation of the relevant laws or regulations on public security, environmental protection, fire protection, and the like in the property management service area, the property management service provider shall, in a timely manner, take reasonable measures to stop the violation, make a report to the competent department, and render assistance to the department in handling the violation.

Article 943 A property management service provider shall, in a reasonable manner, regularly disclose to the owners and report to the owners' assembly and the owners' committee on its services, the responsible personnel, the quality requirements, the items that a fee is charged, the rate of the fee, the performance of obligations, use of the maintenance funds, and the management and income generated from using the common space co-owned by the owners, and the like.

Article 944 An owner shall pay property management fees to the property management service provider in accordance with the agreement. Where a property management service provider has provided services in accordance with the agreement and the relevant regulations, an owner may not refuse to pay the property management fees on the ground that he has not accepted or need not accept the relevant property management service.

Where an owner fails to pay the property management fees within the agreed period in breach of the agreement, the property management service provider may demand the payment be made within a reasonable period of time; if the owner still fails to make payment within the said period, the property management service provider may file a lawsuit or apply for arbitration.

The property management service provider may not collect the property management fees by such means as shutting off power, water, heat, or gas.

Article 945 Where an owner decorates or remodels the unit he owns in a building, he shall notify the property management service provider in advance, follow the reasonable rules provided by the property management service provider, and cooperate with the property management service provider in the necessary onsite inspection.

If an owner transfers or leases the unit exclusively owned by him within a building, creates a right of habitation therein, or changes the use of the common space in accordance with law, he shall timely inform the property management service provider of the relevant situation.

Article 946 Where the owners jointly decide to dismiss the property management service provider in accordance with the statutory procedure, they may rescind the contract for property management service. In such a case, the property management service provider shall be notified in writing 60 days in advance, unless otherwise agreed by the parties.

If rescission of the contract in accordance with the preceding paragraph causes losses to the property management service provider, the owners shall compensate for the losses, unless the losses are incurred by a cause not attributable to the owners.

Article 947 Prior to expiration of the service term of a property management service provider, where the owners jointly decide to continue employing it, they shall renew the contract with it before expiration of the term of the original contract.

Prior to expiration of the service term, where the property management service provider does not consent to continued employment, it shall notify the owners or the owners' committee in writing 90 days before expiration of the term of the contract, unless a time limit for the notice is otherwise agreed in the contract.

Article 948 Where, upon expiration of the property management service term, the owners fail to make a decision in accordance with law to continue employing the original service provider or to employ another service provider, if the property management service provider continues to provide property management services, the original contract for property management service shall continue to be valid, except that it becomes one with an indefinite term.

Either party may rescind such a contract for property management service at any time, provided that the other party shall be notified in writing 60 days in advance.

Article 949 Upon termination of a contract for property management service, the original property management service provider shall vacate the property management service area within the agreed time or a reasonable period of time, surrender the property service premises, the related facilities, and the relevant materials necessary for property management service, and the like, to the owners' committee, the owners who decide to exercise management themselves, or the person designated by them, cooperate with the new property management service provider in effectively handing over the work, and truthfully disclose the information regarding the use and management of the property.

The original property management service provider who violates the provisions of the preceding paragraph may not request the owners to pay the property management fee after the termination of the contract for property management service, and shall bear the liability for compensation if any loss is caused to the owners.

Article 950 After a contract for property management service is terminated and before the handover to the new property management service provider selected by the owners or the owners' assembly or to the owners who decide to exercise management by themselves, the original property management service provider shall continue to provide property management services, and may request the owners to pay the property management fee during this period.

Chapter XXV Brokerage Contracts

Article 951 A brokerage contract is a contract under which a broker in his own name engages in trade activities for a client who pays remuneration in return.

Article 952 The expenses incurred by a broker in handling the entrusted matters shall be borne by the broker, unless otherwise agreed by the parties.

Article 953 A broker who possesses the commissioned article shall properly keep it.

Article 954 If the commissioned article has a defect at the time when it is delivered to a broker, or if it is perishable, the broker may dispose of the article upon the client's consent; if the broker is unable to make prompt contact with the client, the broker may dispose of the article in a proper manner.

Article 955 Where a broker sells an article at a price lower than the price set by the client, or buys an article at a price higher than the price set by the client, the broker shall obtain the consent of the client; where such a deal is made without the consent of the client and the broker makes up for the price difference, the said deal is binding on the client.

Where a broker sells an article at a price higher than the price set by the client or buys an article at a price lower than the price set by the client, remuneration may be increased in accordance with the agreement. Where there is no such an agreement or the relevant agreement is unclear, if it cannot be determined according to the provisions of Article 510 of this Code, the benefit shall belong to the client.

Where a client has given a special instruction on the price of an article, the broker may not sell or buy it contrary to the said instruction.

Article 956 Where a broker buys or sells a commodity which has a market price, unless otherwise indicated by the client, the broker himself may serve as the buyer or the seller.

Despite the situation provided in the preceding paragraph, the broker may still request the client to pay remuneration.

Article 957 Where a broker buys a commissioned article in accordance with the contract, the client shall accept the article in a timely manner. Where, after being demanded by the broker, the client refuses to accept the article without just cause, the broker may have the commissioned article placed in escrow in accordance with law.

Where a commissioned article cannot be sold or the client withdraws from the commissioned sale, if the client, after being demanded by the broker, fails to take back or dispose of the said article, the broker may have the commissioned article placed in escrow in accordance with law.

Article 958 A broker who concludes a contract with a third person shall directly enjoy the rights and assume the obligations under the said contract.

Where a third person fails to fulfill the contractual obligation thus causing losses to the client, the broker shall bear the liability for compensation, unless otherwise agreed by the broker and the client.

Article 959 Where a broker has accomplished the entrusted matter in full or in part, the client shall pay remuneration accordingly. Where a client fails to pay remuneration as scheduled, the broker has the right to retain the commissioned article under a lien unless otherwise agreed by the parties.

Article 960 For matters not provided in this Chapter, the relevant provisions on entrustment contracts shall be applied *mutatis mutandis*.

Chapter XXVI Intermediary Contracts

Article 961 An intermediary contract is a contract under which a middle-man reports to the client the opportunity for concluding a contract or provides intermediary services for the conclusion of a contract, for which the client pays remuneration.

Article 962 The middleman shall truthfully report to the client matters related to the conclusion of the contract.

Where a middleman intentionally conceals important facts in relation to the conclusion of the contract or provides untrue information thereof, thus harming the interests of the client, he may not request for remuneration and shall bear the liability for compensation.

Article 963 Where a middleman contributes to the conclusion of a contract, the client shall pay remuneration in accordance with the agreement. Where there is no agreement between the parties on the remuneration for the middleman or the relevant agreement is unclear, if it cannot be determined according to the provisions of Article 510 of this Code, the remuneration shall be reasonably determined in accordance with the middleman's services. Where the intermediary services provided by the middleman facilitate the conclusion of a contract, the parties to the said contract shall equally share the disbursement of the remuneration to the middleman.

In facilitating the conclusion of a contract, the expenses incurred in the intermediary activities shall be borne by the middleman.

Article 964 A middleman who fails to facilitate the conclusion of a contract may not request the payment of remuneration, but may request the client to pay for the necessary expenses incurred in the intermediary activities in accordance with the agreement.

Article 965 Where a client, after accepting the services of the middleman, uses the trading opportunity or intermediary services provided by the middleman to bypass the middleman and directly concludes a contract with another person, the client shall pay remuneration to the middleman.

Article 966 For matters not provided in this Chapter, the relevant provisions on entrustment contracts shall be applied *mutatis mutandis*.

Chapter XXVII Partnership Contracts

Article 967 A partnership contract is an agreement between two or more partners to share benefits and assume risks for a joint enterprise.

Article 968 A partner shall fulfill the obligation to contribute capital in accordance with the method, amount, and schedule for payment in accordance with the agreement.

Article 969 The capital contributions made by the partners and the proceeds thereof and other property acquired in accordance with law in the course of the partnership business are partnership property.

A partner may not request partition of the partnership property prior to the termination of the partnership contract.

Article 970 When partners make a decision on the partnership businesses, unless otherwise agreed in the partnership contract, unanimous consent of all partners shall be obtained.

The partnership businesses shall be jointly managed by all partners. One or more partners may be authorized to manage the partnership business in accordance with the partnership contract or the decision made by all partners; and the other partners shall cease to manage the partnership business, except that they have the right to supervise the management.

Where the partners manage the partnership business separately, the managing partner may raise objections on a matter managed by the other partners, in which case, the other partners shall suspend the management of such matter.

Article 971 A partner may not request remuneration for management of the partnership business, unless otherwise agreed in the partnership contract.

Article 972 The sharing of the profits and allocation of losses of a partnership shall be in accordance with the partnership contract; where there is no such an agreement in the partnership contract or the relevant agreement is unclear, the partners shall make a decision through consultation. Where such consultation fails, the partners shall share the profits and assume the losses in proportion to their paid-in capital, or in equal share if the proportions of their paid-in capital cannot be determined.

Article 973 The partners shall bear joint and several liabilities for the partnership obligations. A partner who has performed the partnership obligations in excess of his share has the right to contribution against the other partners.

Article 974 Unless otherwise agreed in the partnership contract, a partner who transfers all or part of his share of property to a person other than a partner shall obtain unanimous consent of the other partners.

Article 975 A creditor of a partner may not subrogate and exercise any right of the partner provided in this Chapter and the partnership contract, except that a creditor may subrogate and exercise the partner's claim against the partnership for distribution of the benefits.

Article 976 Where there is no agreement between or among the partners on the term of the partnership, or the relevant agreement is unclear, if the term cannot be determined according to the provisions of Article 510 of this Code, the partnership is deemed as a partnership with an indefinite term.

If a partner continues to manage the partnership business upon expiration of the term of the partnership, and the other partners fail to raise any objection, the original partnership contract continues to be valid, but with an indefinite term.

A partner may rescind a partnership contract with an indefinite term at any time, but the other partners shall be notified within a reasonable period of time in advance.

Article 977 Where a partner dies, loses capacity for performing civil juristic acts, or is terminated, the partnership contract is terminated, unless otherwise provided in the partnership contract or it is inappropriate to terminate the contract due to the nature of the partnership affairs.

Article 978 Upon termination of a partnership contract, after paying the expenses for termination and discharging the partnership debts, the residual assets of the partnership property, if any, shall be distributed in accordance with the provisions of Article 972 of this Code.

Part Three Quasi-contracts

Chapter XXVIII *Negotiorum Gestio*

Article 979 Where a person who has neither a statutory nor a contractual obligation acts as a custodian to manage another person's affairs in order to prevent the latter from suffering a loss of interests, the said person may request the beneficiary to reimburse the necessary expenses thus incurred. Where such a custodian suffers losses when managing another person's affairs, the custodian may request the beneficiary to make appropriate compensation.

Where the management of another person's affairs is contrary to the true will of the beneficiary, the custodian does not have the right provided in the preceding paragraph, unless the true will of the beneficiary is in violation of law or against the public order or good morals.

Article 980 Where the management by a custodian of another person's affairs does not fall within the circumstances provided in the preceding Article, but the beneficiary has enjoyed the benefit of the management, the beneficiary shall be subject to the obligations provided in the first paragraph of the preceding Article to the custodian to the extent of the benefit thus gained by him.

Article 981 A custodian shall manage another person's affairs in the best interest of the beneficiary. Where suspension of management is to put the beneficiary at a disadvantageous position, the management may not be suspended without just cause.

Article 982 A custodian who manages another person's affairs shall promptly notify the beneficiary if he is able to do so. Where a matter does not need urgent management, the custodian shall wait for the beneficiary's instruction.

Article 983 Upon termination of the management, a custodian shall report the management of the affairs to the beneficiary. The property obtained by the custodian in the management of the affairs shall be surrendered to the beneficiary in a timely manner.

Article 984 Where the management of another person's affairs by a custodian is subsequently ratified by the beneficiary, the provisions on entrustment contracts shall be applied to the management from the commencement of the management, unless the custodian expresses his intention otherwise.

Chapter XXIX Unjust Enrichment

Article 985 Where a person is unjustly enriched without a legal basis, the person who thus suffers losses is entitled to request the enriched person to return the benefit, unless under any of the following circumstances:

(1) the payment is made for performing a moral obligation;

(2) the payment is made to satisfy an obligation not yet due; or

(3) the payment is made to discharge an obligation by the person knowing that there is no obligation to pay.

Article 986 Where a person enriched does not know or should not have known that the enrichment is without a legal basis, and if the enrichment no longer exists, the person has no obligation to return the benefit thus received.

Article 987 Where a person enriched knows or should have known that the enrichment is without a legal basis, the aggrieved person may request the enriched person to return the benefit thus received and make compensation for the losses in accordance with law.

Article 988 Where a person enriched has gratuitously transferred the benefit received to a third person, the aggrieved person may request the third person to assume the obligation to return the benefit to the corresponding extent.

Book Four Personality Rights

Chapter Ⅰ General Rules

Article 989 This Book regulates the civil-law relations arising from the enjoyment and protection of personality rights.

Article 990 Personality rights are the rights enjoyed by persons of the civil law, such as the right to life, the right to corporeal integrity, the right to health, the right to name, the right to entity name, the right to likeness, the right to reputation, the right to honor, the right to privacy, and the like.

In addition to the personality rights provided in the preceding paragraph, a natural person enjoys other personality rights and interests arising from personal liberty and human dignity.

Article 991 The personality rights of persons of the civil law are protected by law and free from infringement by any organization or individual.

Article 992 Personality rights may not be waived, transferred, or inherited.

Article 993 The name, entity name, likeness, or the like of a person of the civil law may be used by others upon authorization, unless the authorization of use is not allowed by law or based on the nature of the right.

Article 994 Where the name, likeness, reputation, honor, privacy, remains, or the like of the deceased is harmed, the spouse, children, and parents of the deceased have the right to request the actor to bear civil liability in accordance with law. Where the deceased has no spouse or children, and the parents of the deceased have already died, other close relatives of the deceased have the right to request the actor to bear civil liability in accordance with law.

Article 995 A person whose personality rights are infringed upon has the right to request the actor to bear civil liability in accordance with the provisions of this Code and the other laws. Where a person exercises his right to request the actor to stop the infringement, remove the nuisance, eliminate the danger, eliminate the adverse effects, rehabilitate his reputation, or extend apologies, the provisions on limitation periods do not apply.

Article 996 Where the personality rights of a party are harmed by the other party's breach of contract and the injured party thus suffers severe mental distress, if the injured party elects to request the other party to bear liability based on breach of contract, his right to claim for compensation for mental distress is not affected.

Article 997 Where a person of the civil law has evidence to prove that an actor is committing or is about to commit an illegal act that infringes upon his personality rights, and that failure to timely stop the act will cause irreparable harm to his lawful rights and interests, the person has the right, in accordance with law, to request the people's court to order the actor to stop the act.

Article 998 In determining the civil liability an actor is to bear for infringing upon other's personality rights, other than the right to life, the right to corporeal integrity, or the right to health, consideration shall be given to the occupations of the actor and the injured person, the scope of impact of the act, the degree of fault, as well as the factors such as the purposes, methods, and consequences of the act.

Article 999 The name, entity name, likeness, personal information, and the like of a person of the civil law may be reasonably used by those engaged in news reporting, supervision of public opinions, or the like for public interests, except that civil liability shall be borne in accordance with law where the use unreasonably harms the personality rights of the person.

Article 1000 Where an actor shall bear civil liability such as elimination of adverse effects, rehabilitation of reputation, or extension of apologies for infringing upon other's personality rights, the civil liability to be borne shall be commensurate with the specific way the act is done and the scope of its impact.

Where an actor refuses to bear civil liability as provided in the preceding paragraph, the people's court may take such measures as making an announcement, publishing the final judgment, or the like, through media, such as newspapers, periodicals, or online websites, and any expenses thus incurred shall be borne by the actor.

Article 1001 The relevant provisions of Book One and Book Five of this Code and the other laws shall apply to the protection of a natural person's relation-based rights such as a right arising from a marital and familial relationship; in the absence of such provisions, the relevant provisions of this Book on the protection of personality rights shall, based on the nature of the right, be applied *mutatis mutandis*.

Chapter II Rights to Life, Rights to Corporeal Integrity, and Rights to Health

Article 1002 A natural person enjoys the right to life. A natural person's life safety and dignity are protected by law and free from infringement by any organization or individual.

Article 1003 A natural person enjoys the right to corporeal integrity. A natural person's corporeal integrity and freedom of movement are protected by law and free from infringement by any organization or individual.

Article 1004 A natural person enjoys the right to health. A natural person's physical and mental health are protected by law and free from infringement by any organization or individual.

Article 1005 Where a natural person's right to life, right to corporeal integrity, or right to health is infringed upon or otherwise in peril, the organization or individual who is legally obligated to aid shall promptly extend rescue.

Article 1006 A person with full capacity for performing civil juristic acts has the right to make a voluntary decision in accordance with law to donate his cells, tissues, organs, and remains. No organization or individual may force, deceive, or induce the person to make such a donation.

The consent of a person with full capacity for performing civil juristic acts to make such a donation in accordance with the provisions of the preceding paragraph shall be made in writing or through a will.

Where a natural person, during his life, has not disagreed to make such a donation after he dies, his spouse, adult children, and parents may, upon his death, jointly decide to make the donation, and such a decision shall be made in writing.

Article 1007 Any form of purchase or sale of human cells, tissues, organs, or remains is prohibited.

Any purchase or sale in violation of the preceding paragraph is void.

Article 1008 Where a clinical trial is needed for developing new drugs and medical devices or developing new prevention and treatment methods, upon approval of the relevant competent authorities and the examination and approval of the ethics committee in accordance with law, the participants or their guardians shall be informed of the details including the purposes, methods, and the possible risks of the trial, and their written consent must be obtained.

When conducting a clinical trial, no fees may be collected from the participants of the trial.

Article 1009 A medical and scientific research activity related to human genes, embryos, or the like shall be done in accordance with the relevant provisions of laws, administrative regulations, and the regulations of the State, and may not endanger human health, offend ethics and morals, or harm public interests.

Article 1010 A person who has been sexually harassed against his will by another person through oral words, written languages, images, physical acts, or the like has the right to request the actor to bear civil liability in accordance with law.

The State organs, enterprises, schools, and other organizations shall take reasonable precautions, accept and hear complaints, investigate and handle cases, and take other like measures to prevent and stop sexual harassment conducted by a person through taking advantage of his position and power or a superior-subordinate relationship, and the like.

Article 1011 A person, whose freedom of movement has been deprived of or restricted by illegal detention or the like measures, or whose body has been illegally searched, has the right to request the actor to bear civil liability in accordance with law.

Chapter Ⅲ Rights to Name and Rights to Entity Name

Article 1012 A natural person enjoys the right to name and is entitled to determine, use, change, or allow others to use his name in accordance with law, provided that public order and good morals are not offended.

Article 1013 A legal person or an unincorporated organization enjoys the right to entity name and is entitled to decide, use, change, transfer, or allow others to use its entity name in accordance with law.

Article 1014 No organization or individual may infringe upon other's rights to name or rights to entity name by means such as interference, misappropriation, impersonation, or the like.

Article 1015 A natural person shall take the surname of either his father or mother, and may take a surname other than his father's or mother's under any of the following circumstances:

(1) taking the surname of a senior lineal relative by blood;

(2) taking the surname of a foster parent, other than the legal care provider, who provides care to him; and

(3) taking a surname with other legitimate reasons that do not offend public order or good morals.

Natural persons of ethnic minorities may take a surname in compliance with their cultural traditions and local customs.

Article 1016 A natural person who decides to take or change his name, or a legal person or an unincorporated organization who decides to take, change, or transfer its entity name, shall file registration with the relevant authorities in accordance with law, unless otherwise provided by law.

For a person of the civil law who changes the name or entity name, the civil juristic acts performed by the person before the name change is legally binding on the person.

Article 1017 With regard to a pseudonym, stage name, screen name, translated name, trade name, abbreviation of a name or entity name of a social popularity, where the use of which by others will suffice to cause public confusion, the relevant provisions on protection of the rights to name and the rights to entity name shall be applied *mutatis mutandis*.

Chapter Ⅳ Rights to Likeness

Article 1018 A natural person enjoys the right to likeness and is entitled to make, use, publicize, or authorize others to use his image in accordance with law.

The likeness is an external image of a specific natural person reflected in video recordings, sculptures, drawings, or on other media by which the person can be identified.

Article 1019 No organization or individual may infringe upon other's rights to likeness by vilifying or defacing the image thereof, or through other ways such as falsifying other's image by utilizing information technology. Unless otherwise provided by law, no one may make, use, or publicize the image of the right holder without his consent.

Without the consent of the person holding the right to likeness, a person holding a right in the works of the image of the former person may not use or publicize the said image by ways such as publishing, duplicating, distributing, leasing, or exhibiting it.

Article 1020 The following acts, if done in a reasonable way, may be performed without the consent of the person holding the right to likeness:

(1) using a publicly available image of the person holding the right to likeness to the extent necessary for personal study, art appreciation, classroom teaching, or scientific research;

(2) making, using, or publicizing an image of the person holding the right to likeness, which is inevitable for conducting news reporting;

(3) making, using, or publicizing an image of the person holding the right to likeness to the extent necessary for a State organ to perform its responsibilities in accordance with law;

(4) making, using, or publicizing an image of the person holding the right to likeness, which is inevitable for demonstrating a specific public environment; and

(5) performing other acts of making, using, or publicizing an image of the person holding the right to likeness for protecting the public interests and the lawful rights and interests of the said person.

Article 1021 Where the parties have a dispute on a clause relating to the use of an image in a contract authorizing the use of the image, interpretations shall be made in favor of the person holding the right to likeness over his image.

Article 1022 Where the parties have not agreed on the term of authorized use of an image, or the relevant agreement is unclear, either party may rescind the contract authorizing the use of the image at any time, provided that the other party shall be notified within a reasonable period of time.

Where the parties have expressly agreed on the term of authorized use of the image, the person holding the right to likeness over the image may rescind the contract authorizing such use if with just cause, provided that the other party shall be notified within a reasonable period of time. Where rescission of the contract causes losses to the other party, unless the losses are caused by a reason not attributable to the person holding the right to likeness over the image, compensation shall be paid.

Article 1023 For an authorized use of another person's name or the like, the relevant provisions on the authorized use of other's images shall be applied *mutatis mutandis*.

For the protection of a natural person's voice, the relevant provisions on the protection of the right to likeness shall be applied *mutatis mutandis*.

Chapter V Rights to Reputation and Rights to Honor

Article 1024 A person of the civil law enjoys the right to reputation. No organization or individual may infringe upon other's right to reputation by insultation, defamation, or the like.

Reputation is a social evaluation of the moral character, prestige, talent, and credit of a person of the civil law.

Article 1025 A person whose act adversely affects another person's reputation when reporting news or supervising public opinions or the like for public interest purposes does not bear civil liability except where one of the following situations exists:

(1) he has fabricated or distorted the facts;

(2) he has failed to fulfill the obligation to reasonably verify the seriously misrepresentative information provided by others; or

(3) he has used insulting words and the like to degrade the other's reputation.

Article 1026 To determine whether an actor has fulfilled the obligation to reasonably verify the information as provided in Subparagraph (2) of the preceding Article, the following factors shall be considered:

(1) the credibility of the source of the information;

(2) whether the information that is clearly controversial has been fully investigated;

(3) the timeliness of the information;

(4) the relevance of the information with public order and good morals;

(5) the likelihood that the victim's reputation would be degraded; and

(6) his ability to verify and the cost for the verification of the information.

Article 1027 Where a literary or artistic work published by an actor depicts real people and real events or a specific person with insulting or defamatory content and thus infringes upon another person's right to reputation, the person whose right is infringed upon has the right to request the actor to bear civil liability in accordance with law.

Where a literary or artistic work published by an actor does not depict a specific person, but only some patterns of the story are similar to the situation of such person, the actor does not bear civil liability.

Article 1028 Where a person of the civil law has evidence to prove that the content reported by a media, such as a newspaper, a periodical, or an online website, is inaccurate and thus infringes upon his reputation, he has the right to request the media to take necessary measures including making correction of or deleting the content in a timely manner.

Article 1029 A person of the civil law may check his own credit report in accordance with law, and has the right to raise an objection and request correction, deletion, or other necessary measures to be taken where he discovers that the credit report is incorrect. The evaluators of the credit standing shall examine the report and take necessary measures in a timely manner if it is verified to be false.

Article 1030 The provisions of this Book on the protection of personal information and the relevant provisions of other laws and administrative regulations shall be applied to the relationship between a person of the civil law and a credit information processor such as a credit reporting agency.

Article 1031 A person of the civil law enjoys the right to honor. No organization or individual may unlawfully deprive others of their honorary titles or defame or degrade their honors.

Where an awarded honorary title of a person of the civil law should have been recorded, the person may request that it be so recorded. Where such an awarded honorary title is incorrectly recorded, the person may request that it be corrected.

Chapter Ⅵ Rights to Privacy and Protection of Personal Information

Article 1032 A natural person enjoys the right to privacy. No organization or individual may infringe upon the other's right to privacy by prying into, intruding upon, disclosing, or publicizing other's private matters.

Privacy is the undisturbed private life of a natural person and his private space, private activities, and private information that he does not want to be known to others.

Article 1033 Unless otherwise provided by law or expressly consented to by the right holder, no organization or individual shall do the following acts:

(1) intruding upon another person's private life through making phone calls, sending text messages, using instant messaging tools, sending emails and flyers, and the like means;

(2) entering into, taking photographs of, or peeping into other's private spaces such as the residence or hotel room of another person;

(3) taking photographs of, peeping into, eavesdropping, or disclosing the private activities of another person;

(4) taking photographs of or peeping at the private parts of another person's body;

(5) processing another person's private information; and

(6) infringing upon another person's privacy through other means.

Article 1034 A natural person's personal information is protected by law.

Personal information is the information recorded electronically or in other ways that can be used, by itself or in combination with other information, to identify a natural person, including his name, date of birth, identification number, biometric information, residential address, telephone number, email address, health information, whereabouts, and the like.

The provisions on the right to privacy, or, in the absence of which, the provisions on the protection of personal information, shall be applied to the private personal information.

Article 1035 The processing of personal information shall be in compliance with the principles of lawfulness, justification, and within a necessary limit, and may not be excessively processed; meanwhile, the following conditions shall be satisfied;

(1) consent has been obtained from the natural person or his guardian, unless otherwise provided by laws or administrative regulations;

(2) the rules for processing information are publicized;

(3) the purpose, method, and scope of the information processing are clearly

indicated; and

(4) it is not in violation of laws or administrative regulations or in breach of the agreement between both parties.

The processing of personal information includes the collection, storage, use, process, transmission, provision, disclosure, and the like of the personal information.

Article 1036 When processing personal information, an actor does not bear civil liability under any of the following circumstances:

(1) the actor reasonably performs the act to the extent that the natural person or his guardian consents to;

(2) the actor reasonably processes the information disclosed by the natural person himself or the other information that has already been legally disclosed, unless the said person explicitly refuses or the processing of the information infringes upon a significant interest of the person; and

(3) the actor reasonably performs the other acts to protect the public interests or the lawful rights and interests of the person.

Article 1037 A natural person may retrieve or make copies of his personal information from the information processers in accordance with law. Where the person discovers that the information is incorrect, he has the right to raise an objection and request corrections or other necessary measures to be taken in a timely manner.

Where a natural person discovers that an information processer has violated the provisions of laws or administrative regulations or breached the agreement between both parties while processing his personal information, he has the right to request the information processor to delete it in a timely manner.

Article 1038 An information processor may not disclose or tamper with the personal information he collects and stores, and may not illegally provide to others the personal information of a natural person without the latter's consent, unless the information, after being processed, cannot be used to identify any specific individual and cannot be restored to its original status.

An information processor shall take technical measures and other necessary measures to ensure the security of the personal information he collects and stores, and prevent the information from being leaked, tampered with, or lost. Where a person's personal information has been or is likely to be leaked, tampered with, or lost, the information processor shall take remedial measures in a timely manner, notify the natural person concerned in accordance with the regulations, and report to the relevant competent authorities.

Article 1039 State organs and the chartered institutions assuming administrative functions as well as their staff shall keep confidential the privacy and the personal information of natural persons known to them during the performance of their responsibilities, and may not disclose or illegally provide it to others.

Book Five Marriage and Family

Chapter Ⅰ General Rules

Article 1040 This Book regulates the civil-law relations arising from marriage or family.

Article 1041 Marriage and family are protected by the State.

A marriage system based on freedom of marriage, monogamy, and equality between men and women is implemented.

The lawful rights and interests of women, minors, the elderly, and persons with disabilities are protected.

Article 1042 Arranged marriages, mercenary marriages, and other acts interfering with the freedom of marriage are prohibited. The exaction of money or other property by way of marriage is prohibited.

Bigamy is prohibited. No one who has a spouse may cohabit with another person.

Domestic violence is prohibited. Maltreatment or desertion of family members is prohibited.

Article 1043 Families shall establish good family values, promote family virtues, and enhance family civility.

Husband and wife shall be loyal to each other, respect each other, and care for each other. Family members shall respect the elderly, take care of the young, help each other, and maintain a marital and familial relationship of equality, harmony, and civility.

Article 1044 Adoption shall be in compliance with the principle of acting in the best interest of the adoptee, and the lawful rights and interests of both the adoptee and the adopter shall be protected.

Trafficking minors in the name of adoption is prohibited.

Article 1045 Relatives include spouses, relatives by blood, and relatives by marriage.

Spouses, parents, children, siblings, paternal and maternal grandparents, and paternal and maternal grandchildren are close relatives.

Spouses, parents, children, and other close relatives living together are family members.

Chapter Ⅱ Entering into Marriage

Article 1046 A man and a woman shall enter into marriage freely and voluntarily. Neither party may compel the other party to enter into marriage against his will, and no organization or individual may interfere with the freedom of marriage.

Article 1047 To enter into a marriage, a man shall reach the age of twenty-two, and a woman shall reach the age of twenty.

Article 1048 Persons who are lineal relatives by blood, or collateral relatives by blood up to the third degree of kinship are prohibited from being married.

Article 1049 Both the man and the woman intending to enter into a marriage shall file registration of the marriage in person with a marriage registration authority. If the proposed marriage is found to conform to the provisions of this Code, the marriage shall be registered and a marriage certificate shall be issued. A marital relationship is established upon completion of the marriage registration. The couple who has failed to file a marriage registration shall complete the registration.

Article 1050 After a marriage has been registered, by mutual consent, the woman may become a member of the man's family or vice versa.

Article 1051 A marriage is void under any of the following circumstances:

(1) either party to the marriage commits bigamy;

(2) the parties to the marriage fall within the relative relations prohibited by law from marrying each other; or

(3) either party to the marriage is under the statutory marriageable age.

Article 1052 If a marriage is entered into as a result of coercion, the coerced party may apply to the people's court to annul the marriage.

Such an application to annul the marriage shall be made within one year from the date the coercive act ceases.

Where the coerced party whose personal freedom is illegally restricted wishes to annul the marriage, the application to annul the marriage shall be made within one year from the date when the party's personal freedom is restored.

Article 1053 If one of the parties suffers from a serious disease, he shall truthfully inform the other party of such disease prior to marriage registration; where such information is not truthfully provided, the other party may apply to the people's court to annul the marriage.

The application to annul a marriage shall be made within one year from the date when the party knows or should have known of the cause for the annulment.

Article 1054 A void or annulled marriage has no legal effect *ab initio*, and neither party to such a marriage shall have any rights or duties arising from the marital relationship. Property acquired during the cohabitation period shall be disposed of by mutual agreement. Where the parties fail to reach such an agreement, the people's court shall adjudicate the case in compliance with the principle of favoring the no-fault party. When disposing of the property acquired during a marriage which has been voided due to bigamy, the proprietary rights and interests of the parties to the lawful marriage may not be infringed upon. The provisions of this Code on parents and children shall apply to the children born by the parties to a void or annulled marriage.

Where a marriage is void or annulled, the no-fault party has the right to request for damages.

Chapter Ⅲ Domestic Relations

Section 1 Spousal Relationship

Article 1055 Husband and wife are equal in marriage and family.

Article 1056 Both spouses have the right to retain their own surname and given name.

Article 1057 Both spouses are free to engage in production and other work, and to study and to participate in social activities. Neither party may restrain or interfere with such freedom of the other party.

Article 1058 Both spouses have equal rights and joint duties to raise, educate, and protect their minor children.

Article 1059 Both spouses have the duty to support each other.

The party in need of spousal support is entitled to claim such payments against the other party who has failed to fulfill the duty of spousal support.

Article 1060 A civil juristic act performed by one of the spouses to meet the daily needs of the family is binding on both spouses unless otherwise agreed between the third person and the spouse performing the act.

Restrictions imposed by the spouses on the scope of civil juristic acts that may be performed by one of the spouses may not be asserted against a *bona fide* counterparty.

Article 1061 Husband and wife have the right to inherit the estates of each other.

Article 1062 The following property acquired by the spouses during their marriage constitutes community property and is jointly owned by the spouses:

(1) salaries and wages as well as bonuses and other remunerations received from services rendered;

(2) proceeds obtained from production, business operation, and investment;

(3) proceeds arising from intellectual property rights;

(4) except as otherwise provided in Subparagraph (3) of Article 1063 of this Code, property acquired from inheritance or given as a gift; and

(5) other property that shall be jointly owned by the spouses.

Husband and wife have equal rights when disposing of the community property.

Article 1063 The following property constitutes separate property of one of the spouses:

(1) premarital property of one spouse;

(2) compensation or indemnification received by one spouse for injury inflicted upon him;

(3) property that belongs to only one spouse as specified in a will or gift contract;

(4) articles exclusively used by one spouse for daily life; and

(5) other property that shall be owned by one spouse.

Article 1064 Debts incurred according to the common expression of intent of both spouses, such as a debt jointly signed by both spouses and a debt signed by one spouse and subsequently ratified by the other spouse, and debts incurred by one of the spouses in his own name during the marriage to meet the daily needs of the family, constitute community debts.

A debt incurred by one of the spouses in his own name during the marriage in excess of the daily needs of the family is not a community debt, unless the creditor can prove that such debt is incurred for the purpose of providing for both spouses' daily life or for the production and operation jointly conducted by both spouses, or such debt is incurred according to the common expression of intent of both spouses.

Article 1065 The spouses or a man and a woman in anticipation of marriage may agree that their premarital property and the property to be acquired by them during their marriage may be owned by them separately or jointly, or partially owned separately and partially owned jointly. The agreement shall be in writing. Where there is no agreement or the relevant agreement is unclear, Articles 1062 and 1063 of this Code shall apply.

The agreement on their premarital property and the property acquired during the marriage is legally binding on both parties to the marriage.

Where the spouses agree that the property acquired during the marriage is to be owned by them separately, a debt incurred by one of the spouses shall be paid off with his separate property to the extent that the third person concerned is aware of such an agreement.

Article 1066 During the marriage, either spouse may apply to the people's court for partition of their community property under any of the following circumstances:

(1) the other spouse has concealed, transferred, sold, destructed or damaged, or squandered the community property, created a false community debt, or committed other acts that seriously infringe upon the interests of the community property; or

(2) a person, whom one of the spouses has a statutory obligation to support, is suffering from a serious disease and needs medical treatment, but the other spouse does not agree to pay the relevant medical expenses.

Section 2 Relationship Between Parents and Children, and Relationship Among Other Close Relatives

Article 1067 Where parents fail to fulfill their duty to raise their children, a minor child or an adult child who is incapable of supporting himself has the right to claim child support payments against his parents.

Where an adult child fails to fulfill the duty to support his parents, his parents who lack the capacity to work or are in financial hardship have the right to claim support payments against the adult child.

Article 1068 Parents have the right and duty to educate and protect their minor children. Where a minor causes damage to others, his parents shall bear civil liability in accordance with law.

Article 1069 Children shall respect their parents' right to marriage and may not interfere with their parents' divorce, remarriage, or their marital life thereafter. Children's duty to support their parents does not end with the change of their parents' marital relationship.

Article 1070 Parents have the right to inherit their children's estates, and vice versa.

Article 1071 Children born out of wedlock have equal rights as children born in wedlock, and no organization or individual may harm or discriminate against them.

A natural parent who does not have physical custody of his out-of-wedlock child shall pay child support for such child who is a minor or who is an adult but incapable of supporting himself.

Article 1072 Stepparents may not maltreat or discriminate against a step-child, and vice versa.

Provisions of this Code governing the parents-children relationship shall apply to the rights and duties between a stepmother or a stepfather and a stepchild who has been raised and educated by such stepfather or stepmother.

Article 1073 Where a parent challenges maternity or paternity with just cause, either parent may file a lawsuit with the people's court for affirmation or denial of such maternity or paternity.

Where an adult child challenges maternity or paternity with just cause, he may file a lawsuit with the people's court for affirmation of such maternity or paternity.

Article 1074 Paternal or maternal grandparents, if financially capable, have the duty to raise their minor grandchildren whose parents are deceased or are incapable of such raising.

Paternal or maternal grandchildren, if financially capable, have the duty to support their grandparents whose children are deceased or are incapable of providing such support.

Article 1075 Elder brothers or sisters, if financially capable, have the duty to raise their minor siblings whose parents are deceased or are incapable of such raising.

Younger brothers or sisters who have been brought up by their elder siblings and who are financially capable have the duty to support such elder siblings who lack both the capacity to work and the means to support themselves.

Chapter Ⅳ Divorce

Article 1076 Where the husband and the wife both agree to divorce, they shall enter into a divorce agreement in writing and file divorce registration in person with the marriage registration authority.

A divorce agreement shall include expression of intent of both parties to voluntarily divorce and their mutual agreement on such matters as child support, property division, and allocation of debts.

Article 1077 Where either party is unwilling to divorce, he may withdraw the divorce registration application within 30 days after such an application is received by the marriage registration authority.

Within 30 days after expiration of the period provided in the preceding paragraph, both parties shall personally visit the marriage registration authority to apply for issuance of a divorce certificate, and failing to do so will cause the divorce registration application to be deemed as withdrawn.

Article 1078 Upon ascertaining that the divorce is voluntarily intended and that the two parties have reached agreement on such matters as child support, property division, and allocation of debts, the marriage registration authority shall register the divorce and issue a divorce certificate.

Article 1079 Where the husband or the wife unilaterally petitions for divorce, a relevant organization may offer mediation, or such person may file for divorce directly with the people's court.

The people's court shall, during the divorce trial, offer a mediation, and grant divorce if mutual affection no longer exists between the two parties and the mediation fails.

A divorce shall be granted where any of the following circumstances exists and the mediation fails:

(1) one spouse commits bigamy or cohabitates with another person;

(2) one spouse commits domestic violence or maltreats or deserts a family member;

(3) one spouse habitually commits acts such as gambling, drug abuse, or the like, and refuses to correct such behavior despite of repeated warnings;

(4) the spouses have been separated for no less than two years due to marital discord; or

(5) there exists any other circumstance under which mutual affection no longer exists between the spouses.

Where one spouse is declared to be missing and the other spouse files for divorce, such divorce shall be granted.

Where, after a judgment has been made against divorce and the spouses have been separated for one more year, such divorce shall be granted where one of the spouses files again for divorce with the people's court.

Article 1080 A marital relationship is dissolved upon completion of registration of divorce or when a judgment of divorce or mediation paper of divorce comes into effect.

Article 1081 Where the spouse of a military personnel on active service requests for divorce, the consent of the spouse who is military personnel on active service shall be obtained unless he is at serious fault.

Article 1082 A husband may not file for divorce during his wife's pregnancy, within one year after his wife delivers, or within six months after termination of her pregnancy, unless the wife applies for divorce, or the people's court deems it necessary to hear the divorce request made by the husband.

Article 1083 Where, after divorce, both the man and the woman intend to resume their marital relationship, they shall file for re-registration of marriage at a marriage registration authority.

Article 1084 The parents-children relationship is not dissolved upon divorce of the parents. Whether a child is under the physical custody of the father or the mother, he remains to be the child of both parents.

After divorce, parents continue to have the rights and duties to raise, educate, and protect their children.

As a matter of principle, a mother shall, upon divorce, have physical custody of her child under the age of two. Where parents fail to reach an agreement on the physical custody of their child over the age of two, the people's court shall adjudicate it in compliance with the principle of acting in the best interest of the minor child and in light of the actual situations of both parents. Where the minor child has attained the age of eight, the child's true will shall be respected.

Article 1085 After divorce, where a parent has the physical custody of his child, the other parent shall pay for the child support in part or in whole. The amount and duration of such payment shall be determined by both parents through agreement, or, where no such an agreement is reached, adjudicated by the people's court through making a judgment.

The agreement or judgment provided in the preceding paragraph may not preclude the child, when necessary, from making reasonable demand of payment on either parent in excess of the amount specified in the agreement or judgment.

Article 1086 After divorce, a parent who does not have the physical custody of his child has the right to visit the child, and the other parent is obligated to facilitate the visit.

The manner and schedule for exercising the right to visitation shall be determined by both parents through agreement, or, where no such an agreement is reached, adjudicated by the people's court.

If a parent's visit to a child is detrimental to the child's physical or mental health, the visit shall be suspended by the people's court in accordance with law, and the visit shall be resumed when the cause for such suspension no longer exists.

Article 1087 Upon divorce, the community property of the spouses shall be partitioned by them through agreement, or, where no such an agreement is reached, adjudicated by the people's court in light of the actual state of the property and in compliance with the principle of favoring the rights and interests of their children, the wife, and the no-fault party.

The rights and interests of the husband or wife arising from the contractual management of land based on the household shall be protected in accordance with law.

Article 1088 Where one spouse is burdened with additional duties for raising children, looking after the elderly, or assisting the other spouse in his work, the said spouse has the right to request for compensation upon divorce against the other party, and the other party shall make due compensation. The specific arrangements for making such compensation shall be determined by the spouses through agreement, or adjudicated by the people's court where no such an agreement is reached.

Article 1089 Upon divorce, the husband and wife shall jointly pay off their community debts. Where the community property is insufficient to pay off the debts, or the property is owned by each spouse separately, such debts shall be paid off by the spouses through agreement, or adjudicated by the people's court where no such an agreement is reached.

Article 1090 Where one party is in financial hardship upon divorce, the other party, if financially capable, shall render appropriate assistance. The specific arrangements shall be determined by the spouses through agreement, or adjudicated by the people's court where no such an agreement is reached.

Article 1091 A no-fault spouse has the right to claim compensation where divorce is caused by one of the following acts done by the other spouse:

(1) has committed bigamy;

(2) has cohabitated with another person;

(3) has committed domestic violence;

(4) has maltreated or deserted a family member; or

(5) has acted with other serious faults.

Article 1092 Any spouse who conceals, transfers, sells off, destructs or damages, or squanders the community property, or fabricates a false community debt in an attempt to unlawfully seize the property of the other spouse may be awarded a smaller percentage of or no property upon partition of the community property during the divorce proceedings. Where one of the aforementioned acts committed by one spouse is found after divorce, the other party may file a lawsuit with the people's court for re-partition of the community property.

Chapter V Adoption

Section 1 Establishment of an Adoptive Relationship

Article 1093 The following minors may be adopted:

(1) an orphan bereaved of parents;

(2) a minor whose natural parents cannot be traced; or

(3) a minor whose natural parents are incapable of raising him due to unusual difficulties.

Article 1094 The following individuals and organizations may place a minor for adoption:

(1) the guardian of an orphan;

(2) a children's welfare institution; or

(3) a minor's natural parents who are incapable of raising him due to unusual difficulties.

Article 1095 Where neither of the parents of a minor has full capacity for performing civil juristic acts, and where they may seriously harm the minor, the guardian of the minor may place such minor for adoption.

Article 1096 Where a guardian intends to place an orphan under his guardianship for adoption, he shall obtain the consent of the person who has the duty to raise the orphan. Where the person with the duty to raise the orphan does not consent to the adoption and the guardian is unwilling to continue exercising the duties of guardian, a successive guardian shall be appointed in accordance with the provisions of Book One of this Code.

Article 1097 Where the natural parents intend to place their child for adoption, they shall act in concert. Where one of the natural parents is unknown or cannot be traced, the other parent may place the child for adoption by himself.

Article 1098 A prospective adopter shall meet all the following conditions:

(1) having no children or having only one child;

(2) being capable of raising, educating, and protecting the adoptee;

(3) not suffering from any disease that is deemed medically unfit to be an adopter;

(4) having no criminal record unfavorable to the healthy growth of the adoptee; and

(5) having reached the age of thirty.

Article 1099 Adoption of a child from one's collateral relatives by blood of the same generation and up to the third degree of kinship may be exempted from the restrictions provided in Subparagraph (3) of Article 1093, Subparagraph (3) of Article 1094, and Article 1102 of this Code.

Adoption of a child by an overseas Chinese from his collateral relatives by blood of the same generation and up to the third degree of kinship may also be exempted from the restrictions provided in Subparagraph (1) of Article 1098 of this Code.

Article 1100 A childless adopter may adopt two children, and an adopter with one child may adopt only one more child.

Adoption of an orphan, a minor with disabilities, or a minor in a children's welfare institution whose natural parents cannot be traced may be exempted from the restrictions provided in the preceding paragraph and Subparagraph (1) of Article 1098 of this Code.

Article 1101 Where a person with a spouse intends to adopt a child, the person and his spouse shall jointly adopt the child.

Article 1102 Where a person without a spouse intends to adopt a child of a different gender, the prospective adopter shall be at least 40 years older than the adoptee.

Article 1103 A stepparent may, with the consent of the natural parents of the stepchild, adopt the stepchild, and such adoption may be exempted from the restrictions provided in Subparagraph (3) of Article 1093, Subparagraph (3) of Article 1094, Article 1098, and Subparagraph (1) of Article 1100 of this Code.

Article 1104 Both adoption and placing for adoption shall be based on mutual consent. Where a minor adoptee is aged eight or above, his consent shall be obtained.

Article 1105 Adoption shall be registered with the civil affairs department of the people's government at or above the county level. The adoptive relationship is established upon registration.

In the case of adopting a minor whose parents cannot be traced, the civil affairs department for adoption registration shall make public notice prior to the registration.

The parties to an adoptive relationship may enter into an adoption agreement on a voluntary basis.

Upon request of both parties or one of the parties to an adoptive relationship, an adoption shall be notarized.

The civil affairs department of the people's government at or above the county level shall evaluate the adoption in accordance with law.

Article 1106 Upon establishment of an adoptive relationship, the public security department shall facilitate household registration for the adoptee in accordance with the relevant regulations of the State.

Article 1107 An orphan or a child whose natural parents are incapable of raising him may be raised by the relatives or friends of his natural parents. The provisions of this Chapter do not apply to such a relationship between two persons one of whom is raised by the other.

Article 1108 Where one spouse is deceased and the surviving spouse intends to place their minor child for adoption, the parents of the deceased spouse shall have priority in raising the child.

Article 1109 Foreign nationals may adopt children in the People's Republic of China in accordance with law.

The adoption of a child by a foreign national in the People's Republic of China shall be subject to the review and approval of the competent authorities of the foreign national's country of residence in accordance with the law of that country. The foreign adopter shall submit documents issued by the competent authorities of his country of residence certifying such personal information as his age, marital status, occupation, financial situation, physical condition, and whether he has criminal record. The foreign adopter shall conclude a written agreement with the person who places the child for adoption and register the adoption in person with the civil affairs department of the people's government at the level of provinces, autonomous regions, or municipalities directly under the State Council.

The certifying documents provided in the preceding paragraph shall be authenticated by the diplomatic authorities of the country in which the foreign national resides or by an agency authorized by the said diplomatic authorities, and then authenticated by the embassy or consulate of the People's Republic of China in the said country unless otherwise provided by the State.

Article 1110 Where an adopter or a party placing a child for adoption requires that the adoption be kept confidential, the other persons shall respect their will and may not disclose it.

Section 2 Effect of Adoption

Article 1111 Upon establishment of an adoptive relationship, the provisions of this Code governing the parents-children relationship shall apply to the rights and duties between the adoptive parents and the adopted children. The provisions of this Code governing the relationship between children and the close relatives of their parents shall apply to the rights and duties between the adopted children and the close relatives of their adoptive parents.

Upon establishment of an adoptive relationship, the rights and duties arising between the adoptee and his natural parents as well as the latter's other close relatives shall be terminated.

Article 1112 An adopted child may take the surname of his adoptive father or mother, or may retain his original surname upon consent of all the parties to the adoption.

Article 1113 An adoption shall be void when it constitutes a void civil juristic act as provided in Book One of this Code or violates the provisions provided in this Book.

A void adoption has no legal effect *ab initio*.

Section 3 Dissolution of an Adoptive Relationship

Article 1114 No adopter may dissolve an adoptive relationship before the adoptee has reached the majority age unless there is an agreement between the adopter and the party who places the child for adoption to dissolve such relationship. Where an adoptee is aged eight or above, his own consent shall be obtained.

Where an adopter fails to perform the duty to raise the adoptee or commits maltreatment, desertion, or other acts infringing upon the lawful rights and interests of the minor adoptee, the person who has placed the child for adoption has the right to request that the adoptive relationship be dissolved. Where an adopter and a party who has placed a child for adoption fail to reach an agreement for dissolution of the adoptive relationship, either party may file a lawsuit with the people's court.

Article 1115 Where the relationship between the adoptive parents and the adopted child who has become an adult so deteriorates that they are unable to live together, the adoption may be dissolved by agreement. Where the parties fail to reach such an agreement, either party may file a lawsuit with the people's court.

Article 1116 Where the parties agree to dissolve an adoptive relationship, they shall register the dissolution with the civil affairs department.

Article 1117 Upon dissolution of an adoptive relationship, the rights and duties between an adoptee and his adoptive parents as well as the latter's other close relatives shall be terminated, and the rights and duties between the adoptee and his natural parents as well as the latter's other close relatives shall be automatically restored. However, while an adopted child has become an adult, whether the rights and duties between such an adoptee and his natural parents as well as the latter's other close relatives are to be restored may be decided through consultation.

Article 1118 After dissolution of an adoptive relationship, an adoptee who has been raised up by the adoptive parents and now become an adult shall provide living expenses to his adoptive parents who lack both the capacity to work and the means to support themselves. Where an adoptive relationship is dissolved because the adopted child maltreats or deserts his adoptive parents after the adopted child has become an adult, the adoptive parents may request the adoptee to compensate for the expenses incurred to raise the adoptee during the adoption period.

Where dissolution of an adoptive relationship is required by the natural parents of the adoptee, the adoptive parents may request the natural parents of the adoptee to appropriately compensate for the expenses incurred to raise the adoptee during the adoption period, unless the adoptive relationship is dissolved because the adoptive parents maltreat or desert the adoptee.

Book Six Succession

Chapter I General Rules

Article 1119 This Book regulates the civil-law relations arising from succession.

Article 1120 The State protects a natural person's right to inheritance.

Article 1121 Succession begins upon the death of a decedent.

Where two or more persons with the right to inherit each other's estate die in the same incident and it is difficult to determine the time of each person's death, the person without any other successor is presumed to have predeceased those with other successor(s). Where the aforementioned deceased persons are from different generations and all of them have other successor(s), the person of the elder generation is presumed to have predeceased those of the younger generation; or, where the deceased are in the same generation, they are presumed to have died simultaneously and no succession occurs between or among them.

Article 1122 An estate refers to the property lawfully owned by a natural person upon death.

An estate not inheritable according to the provisions of law or based on the nature of the estate may not be inherited.

Article 1123 After succession opens, it shall be processed as an intestate succession, or where there is a will, as a testate succession by the successor(s) or donee(s)-by-will; or be processed in accordance with the agreement on testamentary gift for *inter vivos* support, where there is such an agreement.

Article 1124 A successor who, after the opening of succession, disclaims an inheritance shall manifest his decision in writing before the estate is disposed of. In the absence of such a manifestation, he is deemed to have accepted the inheritance.

A donee-by-will shall, within 60 days after he learns of the testamentary gift, manifest his decision to accept or disclaim it. In the absence of such a manifestation within the specified period, he is deemed to have disclaimed the gift.

Article 1125 A successor is disinherited if he has committed any of the following acts:

(1) intentionally killing the now decedent;

(2) killing any other successor in fighting over the estate;

(3) abandoning the now decedent, or maltreating him and the circumstances are serious;

(4) forging, tampering with, concealing, or destroying the will, and the circumstances are serious; or

(5) through fraud or duress, compelling the testator to write, alter, or revoke a will or interfering with such acts, and the circumstances are serious.

A successor who had committed one of the acts listed in Subparagraphs (3) through (5) of the preceding paragraph may not be disinherited if he truly repented and mended his ways, and was forgiven by the now decedent or was thereafter appointed as one of the successors in the decedent's will.

A donee-by-will who has committed the act listed in the first paragraph of this Article loses his right to receive the testamentary gift.

Chapter II Intestate Succession

Article 1126 Men and women are equal in their right to inheritance.

Article 1127 The estate of a decedent shall be succeeded in the following order:

(1) first in order: spouse, children, and parents;

(2) second in order: siblings, paternal grandparents, and maternal grandparents.

When succession opens, the successor(s) first in order shall inherit to the exclusion of the successor(s) second in order. The successor(s) second in order shall inherit the estate in default of any successor first in order.

"Children" referred to in this Book include children born in or out of wedlock, and adopted children, as well as stepchildren who were raised up by the decedent.

"Parents" referred to in this Book include natural parents and adoptive parents, as well as stepparents who raised up the decedent.

"Siblings" referred to in this Book include siblings of whole blood and half blood, and adopted siblings, as well as stepsiblings who supported or were supported by the decedent.

Article 1128 Where a decedent is predeceased by a child of his, the lineal descendants of the predeceased child shall inherit in subrogation.

Where a decedent is predeceased by a sibling of his, the children of the predeceased sibling shall inherit in subrogation.

Successors who inherit in subrogation generally may only take the share of the estate *per stirpes*.

Article 1129 Widowed daughters-in-law or sons-in-law who have made predominant contributions in supporting their parents-in-law shall, in relationship to their parents-in-law, be regarded as successors first in order.

Article 1130 Successors same in order shall, in general, inherit share and share alike.

When distributing an estate, due consideration shall be given to a successor who has special financial difficulties and is unable to work.

When distributing an estate, a successor who has made predominant contributions in supporting the now decedent, or who has been living with the now decedent may be given a larger share.

When distributing an estate, a successor who had the ability and was in a position to support the now decedent but failed to fulfill the duty of support shall be given no or a smaller share.

Successors may take unequal shares upon agreement among them.

Article 1131 An appropriate share of the estate may be given to a person, other than a successor, who has been a dependent of the now decedent, or to a person, other than a successor, who has made considerable contributions in supporting the now decedent.

Article 1132 Any issue arising from succession shall be dealt with through consultation by and among the successors in the spirit of amity, unity, mutual understanding, and accommodation. The time and mode for partitioning the estate and the shares to be distributed shall be determined by the successors through consultation. Where no agreement is reached through consultation, they may apply to a people's mediation committee for mediation or file a lawsuit with the people's court.

Chapter Ⅲ Testate Succession and Testamentary Gift

Article 1133 A natural person may, by making a will in accordance with the provisions of this Code, dispose of his estate and may appoint an executor in the will.

A natural person may, by making a will, designate one or more of his statutory successors to inherit his estate.

A natural person may, by making a will, donate his estate to the State or a collective, or an organization or individual other than his statutory successor.

A natural person may, in accordance with law, create a testamentary trust.

Article 1134 A holographic will is one written by the testator's hand and signed by him, specifying the year, month, and day of its making.

Article 1135 A will written on behalf of a testator shall be attested by two or more witnesses, of whom one writes the will, specifying the year, month, and day of its making, and signs it along with the other witness(es) and with the testator.

Article 1136 A will in printed form shall be attested by two or more witnesses. The testator and the witnesses shall sign and specify the year, month, and day on each page.

Article 1137 A will made in the form of an audio or video recording shall be attested by two or more witnesses. The testator and the witnesses shall record their names or likeness in the recording and specify the year, month, and day of its making.

Article 1138 A testator may, when facing imminent danger, make a nuncupative will. A nuncupative will shall be attested by two or more witnesses. When the imminent danger is removed and where the testator is able to make a will in writing or in the form of an audio or video recording, the nuncupative will thus made becomes invalid.

Article 1139 A notarized will is one made by a testator through a notary agency.

Article 1140 None of the following persons is eligible to act as a witness to a will:

(1) a person with no or limited capacity for performing civil juristic acts, or a person otherwise incompetent to attest a will;

(2) a successor or a donee-by-will; or

(3) a person having an interest with a successor or a donee-by-will.

Article 1141 Reservation of a necessary portion of an estate shall be made in a will for a successor who has neither the ability to work nor the source of income.

Article 1142 A testator may revoke or alter a will he has made.

Where a testator who, after making a will, acts inconsistently with the content of his will, the pertinent part of the will is deemed to be revoked.

Where several wills have been made and their contents are inconsistent, the will made last in time shall prevail.

Article 1143 A will made by a person with no or limited capacity for performing civil juristic acts is void.

A will must manifest the genuine intention of the testator, and a will made under fraud or duress is void.

A forged will is void.

Where a will has been tampered with, the affected part of the will is void.

Article 1144 Where a testate succession or a testamentary gift is conditioned upon performance of an obligation, the successor or donee-by-will shall perform the obligation. Where a successor or donee-by-will fails to perform such an obligation without just cause, the people's court may, upon request by an interested person or a relevant organization, deprive him of the right to inherit the portion of the estate to which performance of the obligation is attached.

Chapter Ⅳ Disposition of Estates

Article 1145 Upon opening of a succession, the executor of the will is the administrator of the estate; where no executor is designated in the will, the successors shall elect an administrator in a timely manner. Where the successors fail to do so, all of the successors are co-administrators. Where there is no successor or where all of the successors disclaim the inheritance, the civil affairs department or the villagers' committee in the place where the decedent was domiciled at the time of his death shall serve as the administrator.

Article 1146 Where a dispute arises over the determination of an administrator of the estate, any interested person may request the people's court to appoint an administrator.

Article 1147 An administrator of an estate shall perform the following duties:

(1) verifying and making an inventory of the estate;

(2) reporting to the successors about the inventory of the estate;

(3) taking necessary measures to prevent the estate from being destructed, damaged, or lost;

(4) clearing the decedent's claims and debts;

(5) partitioning the estate in accordance with the will, or in accordance with law; and

(6) performing any other act necessary for managing the estate.

Article 1148 An administrator of an estate shall perform his duties in accordance with law, and shall bear civil liability if any successor, donee-by-will, or creditor of the decedent suffers damage caused by his intentional act or gross negligence.

Article 1149 An administrator of an estate may receive remuneration in accordance with law or based upon agreement.

Article 1150 Upon opening of the succession, a successor who has knowledge of the death of the decedent shall notify the other successors and the executor of the will in a timely manner. Where none of the successors knows about the death of the decedent or is able to make the notification upon learning of the death of the decedent, the organization to which the decedent was employed at the time of his death, or the urban residents' committee or the villagers' committee in the place where the decedent was domiciled at the time of his death shall make the notification.

Article 1151 Anyone who has in his possession the property of a decedent shall properly keep such property, and no organization or individual may misappropriate or contend for it.

Article 1152 Where, after a succession opens, a successor who has not disclaimed the inheritance dies before the estate is partitioned, the share that he should have inherited shall be inherited by his successors, unless otherwise provided in the will.

Article 1153 When partitioning an estate, where community property of husband and wife is involved, unless otherwise agreed upon, half of the community property shall be allocated first to the surviving spouse as separate property, while the remaining property shall be part of the decedent's estate.

When partitioning an estate, where the decedent's estate is a portion of common property of the family, the portion of the property belonging to the other family members shall first be separated from the decedent's estate.

Article 1154 Under any of the following circumstances, the affected portion of an estate shall be disposed of as in an intestate succession:

(1) where a successor designated in a will or a donee-by-will disclaims the inheritance or gift;

(2) where a testamentary successor is disinherited or a donee-by-will is disqualified as such;

(3) where a testamentary successor predeceases the testator, or a donee-by-will predeceases the testator or is terminated prior to the decedent's death;

(4) where a part of a will affecting a portion of the estate is invalidated; or

(5) where a portion of the estate is not disposed of by the will.

Article 1155 When partitioning an estate, a share shall be reserved for a fetus. If the fetus is stillborn, the reserved share shall be disposed of as in an intestate succession.

Article 1156 The partitioning of a decedent's estate shall be conducted in a way beneficial to production and people's livelihood, and without diminishing its efficacy.

If an estate is unsuitable for partitioning, it may be disposed of by such means as appraisal, appropriate compensation, or co-ownership.

Article 1157 A surviving spouse who remarries is entitled to disposing of the property he has inherited, free from interference by any organization or individual.

Article 1158 A natural person may enter into an agreement on testamentary gift for *inter vivos* support with an organization or individual other than a successor. Such organization or individual assumes, in accordance with the agreement, a duty to support the said person during his lifetime, and attends to his interment after death, in return for the right to receive the testamentary gift under the agreement.

Article 1159 Upon partitioning an estate, the taxes and debts payable or owed by the decedent in accordance with law shall be paid out of the estate, provided that a necessary portion of the estate is preserved for any successor who has neither the ability to work nor the source of income.

Article 1160 An estate with neither a successor nor a donee-by-will shall be escheated to the State for public interest purposes. Where the decedent was a member of a collective organization at the time of his death, the estate shall be escheated to the collective organization.

Article 1161 A successor shall pay the taxes and debts legally payable or owed by the decedent to the extent of the actual value of the portion of the estate he inherits, unless the successor pays voluntarily in excess of such limit.

A successor who disclaims an inheritance assumes no responsibility for the payment of taxes and debts legally payable or owed by the decedent.

Article 1162 The execution of a testamentary gift may not affect the payment of taxes and debts legally payable or owed by the donor-by-will.

Article 1163 Where intestate succession, testate succession, and testamentary gift concurrently exist, the taxes and debts legally payable or owed by the decedent shall be paid by the intestate successor(s); such taxes and debts in excess of the actual value of the portion of the estate inherited by the intestate successor(s) shall be paid by the testamentary successor(s) and donee(s)-by-will in proportion to the shares of the estate each of them has received.

Book Seven　Tort Liability

Chapter Ⅰ　General Rules

Article 1164　This Book regulates the civil-law relations arising from the infringement of the civil-law rights and interests.

Article 1165　An actor who through his fault infringes upon another person's civil-law rights and interests shall bear tort liability.

Where an actor is presumed to be at fault according to the provisions of law and is unable to prove that he is not at fault, the actor shall bear tort liability.

Article 1166　Where an actor harms the civil-law rights and interests of another person, if the law provides that tort liability shall be borne by such an actor disregarding whether or not the actor is at fault, such provisions shall be followed.

Article 1167　Where a tortious act endangers another person's personal or property safety, the infringed person has the right to request the tortfeasor to bear tort liability such as cessation of the infringement, removal of the nuisance, or elimination of the danger.

Article 1168　Where two or more persons jointly commit a tortious act causing damage to another person, they shall bear joint and several liability.

Article 1169　A person who aids or abets an actor in the commission of a tortious act shall assume joint and several liability with the actor.

A person who aids or abets an actor with no or limited capacity for performing civil juristic acts in the commission of a tortious act shall assume tort liability, and the guardian of the actor with no or limited capacity for performing civil juristic acts shall assume corresponding liability to the extent he fails to fulfill the duties of guardian.

Article 1170 Where two or more persons commit acts that endanger another person's personal or property safety and the damage is caused only by acts of one or several of them, if the specific tortfeasor (s) can be identified, the tortfeasor(s) shall bear liability, and if the specific tortfeasor (s) cannot be identified, all of the actors shall assume joint and several liability.

Article 1171 Where the tortious acts separately committed by two or more persons cause the same damage to another person, and each act is sufficient to independently cause the entire damage, the actors shall assume joint and several liability.

Article 1172 Where the tortious acts separately committed by two or more persons cause the same damage to another person, each of them shall bear the liability in proportion to their respective share of fault if it can be determined, or in equal share if it cannot be determined.

Article 1173 Where an infringed person is also at fault for the occurrence or aggravation of the same damage to himself, the liability of the tortfeasor may be mitigated.

Article 1174 An actor does not assume liability for any damage intentionally caused by the victim.

Article 1175 Where a damage is caused by a third person, the third person shall bear tort liability.

Article 1176 Where a person voluntarily participates in a recreational or sports activity with certain inherent risks and thus suffers damage due to another participant's act, he may not request the other participant to bear tort liability unless the damage is caused by the latter's intentional act or gross negligence.

The liability of an organizer of such an activity is governed by the provisions of Articles 1198 through 1201 of this Code.

Article 1177 Where a person's lawful rights and interests are infringed upon and he may suffer irreparable harm if actions are not immediately taken because the situation is urgent and no protection from the State organ is immediately available, he may take reasonable measures such as seizing the property of the tortfeasor to the extent necessary for protecting his lawful rights and interests, provided that he shall immediately thereafter request the relevant State organ to handle it.

A victim who has taken an improper measure so that damage is caused to another person shall bear tort liability.

Article 1178 Where this Code or other laws provide otherwise on the circumstances under which an actor bears no or mitigated liability, such provisions shall be followed.

Chapter II Damages

Article 1179 Where a person suffers personal injury as a result of an infringement by another person, compensation shall be made for medical expenses, nursing expenses, transportation expenses, nutrition expenses, food allowances for hospitalization, and other reasonable expenses for treatment and rehabilitation, as well as lost earnings due to missed work. Where a person is disabled as a result of an infringement by another person, compensation shall also include the costs of auxiliary equipment and disability compensation. Where a person dies as a result of an infringement by another person, compensation shall also include his funeral expenses and death compensation.

Article 1180 Where a same tortious act causes multiple deaths, the same amount of death compensation may be applied to all of the victims.

Article 1181 Where an infringed person dies, his close relatives have the right to request the tortfeasor to bear tort liability. Where the infringed is an organization and the organization is thereafter split into or merged with other organization(s), the organization succeeding to the right thereof is entitled to request the tortfeasor to bear tort liability.

Where an infringed person dies, the person who has paid for his medical expenses, funeral expenses, and other reasonable expenses has the right to request the tortfeasor to compensate the expenses, except for those expenses already paid by the tortfeasor.

Article 1182 Where an infringement upon the personal rights and interests of a person causes property damage, compensation shall be made according to the damage suffered by the infringed person or the interests gained by the tortfeasor. Where it is difficult to determine the damage suffered by the infringed person and the interests gained by the tortfeasor, and where the infringed person cannot agree with the tortfeasor on the amount of compensation and thus files a lawsuit with the people's court, the people's court shall determine the amount of compensation according to the actual situation.

Article 1183 Where an infringement upon the personal rights and interests of a natural person causes serious mental distress, the infringed person has the right to request compensation for mental distress.

Where, owing to an actor's intentional or grossly negligent act, a specific object of personal significance of a natural person is infringed upon, which causes serious mental distress to the person, the infringed person has the right to request compensation for mental distress.

Article 1184 In case of an infringement upon another person's property, property damage shall be calculated according to the market price at the time the damage occurs or by other reasonable methods.

Article 1185 In case of an intentional infringement of another person's intellectual property rights, where the circumstances are serious, the infringed person has the right to request for corresponding punitive damages.

Article 1186 Where neither the victim nor the actor is at fault for the occurrence of the damage, the losses shall be shared by both parties in accordance with the provisions of law.

Article 1187 After damage has been caused, the parties may negotiate the method of payment of the compensation. Where they fail to reach an agreement, compensation shall be paid in a lump sum, or may be paid in installments where it is truly difficult for the tortfeasor to make a lump-sum payment, except that the infringed person has the right to request the tortfeasor to provide a corresponding security.

Chapter Ⅲ Special Provisions on Assumption of Liability

Article 1188 Where a person with no or limited capacity for performing civil juristic acts causes damage to another person, the guardian of the said person shall assume tort liability. The guardian's tort liability may be mitigated if the guardian has fulfilled his duties of guardian.

Where a person, who has assets but has no or limited capacity for performing civil juristic acts, causes damage to another person, compensation shall be paid out of his own assets and any deficiency balance shall be paid by the guardian.

Article 1189 Where a person with no or limited capacity for performing civil juristic acts causes damage to another person and his guardian has delegated the duties of guardian to someone else, the guardian shall assume tort liability, and the delegated person who is at fault shall assume corresponding liability.

Article 1190 Where a person with full capacity for performing civil juristic acts is at fault for causing damage to another person due to temporary loss of consciousness or loss of control, he shall bear tort liability. Where he is not at fault, he shall make appropriate compensation to the victim according to his financial situation.

Where a person with full capacity for performing civil juristic acts causes damage to another person due to temporary loss of consciousness or loss of control as a result of intoxication or abuse of narcotic or psychotropic drugs, he shall bear tort liability.

Article 1191 Where an employee causes damage to another person in connection with the performance of his work, his employer shall assume tort liability. The employer may, after assuming the tort liability, claim indemnification against the employee who acts intentionally or with gross negligence.

Where, during the period of labor dispatch, a dispatched employee causes damage to another person in connection with the performance of his work, the employer receiving the dispatched employee shall assume tort liability. If the employer dispatching the employee is at fault, it shall assume the corresponding liability.

Article 1192 Where, in a labor relationship formed between individuals, the party providing labor services causes damage to another person in connection with the labor services, the party receiving labor services shall assume tort liability. The service-receiving party may, after assuming the tort liability, claim indemnification against the service-providing party who acts intentionally or with gross negligence. Where the service-providing party suffers damage in connection with the labor services, both parties shall assume corresponding liabilities according to their respective faults.

Where an act of a third person causes damage to the service-providing party when such services are provided, the service-providing party has the right to request the third person to bear tort liability, or to request the service-receiving party to make compensation. The service-receiving party may, after making the compensation, claim indemnification against the third person.

Article 1193 Where a contractor causes damage to a third person or to himself while completing the contracted work, the ordering party does not assume tort liability, except that the ordering party shall assume corresponding liability where he is at fault in placing the order, making the instructions, or selecting the contractor.

Article 1194 Network users and network service providers who, through the network, infringes upon the civil-law rights and interests of another person shall bear tort liability, unless otherwise provided by law.

Article 1195 Where a network user commits a tortious act through using the network service, the right holder is entitled to notify the network service provider to take such necessary measures as deletion, block, or disconnection. The notice shall include the preliminary evidence establishing the tort and the real identity information of the right holder.

After receiving the notice, the network service provider shall timely forward the notice to the relevant network user and take necessary measures based on the preliminary evidence establishing the tort and the type of service complained about. Where it fails to take necessary measures in time, it shall assume joint and several liability for the aggravated part of the damage with the network user.

The right holder who causes damage to the network user or network service provider due to erroneous notification shall bear tort liability, unless otherwise provided by law.

Article 1196 After receiving the forwarded notice, the network user may submit a declaration of non-infringement to the network service provider, which shall include the preliminary evidence of non-infringement and the real identity information of the network user.

After receiving the declaration, the network service provider shall forward it to the right holder who issues the notice, and inform him that he may file a complaint to the relevant department or file a lawsuit with the people's court. The network service provider shall timely terminate the measures taken where, within a reasonable period of time after the forwarded declaration reaches the right holder, it fails to receive notice that the right holder has filed a complaint or a lawsuit.

Article 1197 A network service provider, who knows or should have known that a network user has infringed upon the civil-law rights and interests of another person by using its network services but fails to take necessary measures, shall assume joint and several liability with the network user.

Article 1198 The operators or managers of business or public premises such as hotels, shopping malls, banks, bus or train stations, airports, stadiums, and places of entertainment, or the organizers of public activities shall bear tort liability where they fail to fulfill the duty of maintaining safety and thus cause damage to another person.

Where the damage to another person is caused by a third person, the third person shall bear tort liability, and the operator, manager, or organizer who fails to fulfill the duty of maintaining safety shall assume the corresponding supplementary liability. After assuming the supplementary liability, the operator, manager, or organizer may claim indemnification against the third person.

Article 1199 Where a person with no capacity for performing civil juristic acts suffers personal injury while studying or living in a kindergarten, school, or any other educational institution, the said kindergarten, school, or educational institution shall assume tort liability, except that the kindergarten, school, or educational institution does not assume tort liability if it can prove that it has fulfilled its responsibilities in education and management.

Article 1200 Where a person with limited capacity for performing civil juristic acts suffers personal injury while studying or living in a school or any other educational institution, the school or educational institution shall assume tort liability if it fails to fulfill its responsibilities in education and management.

Article 1201 Where a person with no or limited capacity for performing civil juristic acts, while studying or living in a kindergarten, school, or any other educational institution, suffers personal injury caused by a third person other than the kindergarten, school, or the educational institution, the third person shall bear tort liability, and the kindergarten, school, or the educational institution shall assume the corresponding supplementary liability if it fails to fulfill its responsibilities in management. After assuming the supplementary liability, the kindergarten, school, or the educational institution may claim indemnification against the third person.

Chapter Ⅳ Product Liability

Article 1202 Where a defect of a product causes damage to another person, the manufacturer of the product shall bear tort liability.

Article 1203 Where a defect of a product causes damage to another person, the infringed person may claim compensation against the manufacturer or the seller of the product.

Where a defect is caused by the manufacturer, the seller who has paid compensation has the right to indemnification against the manufacturer. Where a defect is caused by the fault of the seller, the manufacturer who has paid compensation has the right to indemnification against the seller.

Article 1204 Where the damage is caused by a defect of a product due to the fault of a third person, such as a transporter or a warehouser, the manufacturer or seller of the product who has paid compensation has the right to indemnification against the third person.

Article 1205 Where a defect of a product endangers the personal or property safety of another person, the infringed person has the right to request the manufacturer or seller of the product to bear tort liability in forms of cessation of the infringement, removal of the nuisance, elimination of the danger, or the like.

Article 1206 Where a defect of a product is discovered after the product is put into circulation, the manufacturer or seller of the product shall take remedial measures such as stopping sales, providing warnings, or recalling the product in a timely manner. The manufacturer or seller, who fails to take remedial measures in a timely manner or take ineffective measures so that the damage is aggravated, shall be liable also for the aggravated part of the damage.

Where a product is recalled in accordance with the preceding paragraph, the manufacturer or seller of the product shall bear the necessary expenses incurred to the infringed person.

Article 1207 Where a manufacturer or seller manufactures or sells a product knowing that the product is defective, or failing to take remedial measures in accordance with the provisions of the preceding Article, so that death or serious physical harm is caused to another person, the infringed person has the right to request for the corresponding punitive damages.

Chapter V Liability for Motor Vehicle Traffic Accidents

Article 1208 Where a motor vehicle is involved in a traffic accident which causes damage, the liability for compensation shall be assumed in accordance with the relevant provisions of the laws on road traffic safety and this Code.

Article 1209 Where the owner, manager, or user of a motor vehicle are not the same person in leasing, borrowing, or the other like situations, and a traffic accident occurs and causes damage to another person, the user of the motor vehicle shall bear the liability for compensation if the liability is attributed to the motor vehicle driver, and the owner or manager of the vehicle who is at fault shall assume the corresponding liability for compensation.

Article 1210 Where a party has transferred and delivered a motor vehicle by way of sale or other means but fails to file for registration, the transferee of the motor vehicle shall bear the liability for compensation if damage is caused as a result of a traffic accident and the liability is attributed to the motor vehicle driver.

Article 1211 Where a person uses his motor vehicle in association with an entity to engage in the business of road transportation, if damage is caused as a result of a traffic accident and the liability is attributed to the motor vehicle driver, the person and the entity shall assume joint and several liability for compensation.

Article 1212 Where a person drives another person's motor vehicle without authorization, the user of the motor vehicle shall bear the liability for compensation if damage is caused as a result of a traffic accident and the liability is attributed to the motor vehicle driver; the owner or manager of the motor vehicle shall bear the liability for compensation if he has fault which contributes to the damage, unless otherwise provided in this Chapter.

Article 1213 Where damage is caused to another person as a result of a traffic accident and the liability is attributed to the motor vehicle driver, compensation shall be made first by the insurer that underwrites the compulsory motor vehicle insurance within the limit of the insured liability. The deficiencies shall be paid by the insurer that underwrites the commercial motor vehicle insurance in accordance with the stipulations of the insurance contract. Any remaining balance or the part not covered by any commercial motor vehicle insurance shall be paid by the tortfeasor.

Article 1214 Where damage is caused as a result of a traffic accident involving a motor vehicle that has been illegally assembled or has reached the end-of-life standard which is transferred by way of sale or by other means, the transferor and the transferee shall assume joint and several liability.

Article 1215 Where damage is caused as a result of a traffic accident involving a motor vehicle that has been stolen, robbed, or snatched, the thief, robber, or snatcher shall bear the liability for compensation. Where the aforementioned motor vehicle is used by a person other than the thief, robber, or snatcher and causes damage in a traffic accident, if the liability is attributed to the motor vehicle driver, the thief, robber, or snatcher shall assume joint and several liability with the user.

Where an insurer pays the expenses for rescue within the limits of the compulsory insurance liability for motor vehicles, it has the right to indemnification against the person who is liable for the traffic accident.

Article 1216 In a hit-and-run accident, if the motor vehicle is insured by a compulsory insurance, compensation shall be paid by the insurer within the limit of the insured liability. Where the motor vehicle cannot be located, is not covered by the compulsory insurance, or the rescue expenses exceed the limit of liability of the compulsory motor vehicle insurance, and payment needs to be made against the rescue, funeral, and other expenses incurred as a result of the death or bodily injury of the infringed person, such payment shall be paid from the Social Assistance Fund for Road Traffic Accidents. After the Social Assistance Fund for Road Traffic Accidents makes the payment, its administrative agency has the right to indemnification against the person who is liable for the traffic accident.

Article 1217 Where a motor vehicle not engaged in operation of business causes damage in a traffic accident to a guest passenger who is on the ride for free, if the liability is attributed to the motor vehicle driver, the liability of the user of the motor vehicle for compensation shall be mitigated unless he acts intentionally or with gross negligence.

Chapter Ⅵ Liability for Medical Malpractice

Article 1218 Where a patient suffers damage during diagnosis and treatment, and the medical institution or its medical staff is at fault, the medical institution shall assume the liability for compensation.

Article 1219 The medical staff shall explain the medical conditions and treatment measures to the patient when diagnosing and treating him. Where a surgery, a special examination, or a special treatment is needed, the medical staff shall explain to the patient the medical risks, alternative treatment plans, and other information in a timely manner and obtain his express consent. Where it is impossible or inappropriate to do so, the medical staff shall explain it to the patient's close relatives and get their express consent.

Where the medical staff fail to fulfill the obligations as provided in the preceding paragraph and thus cause damage to the patient, the medical institution shall assume the liability for compensation.

Article 1220 In the case of rescuing a terminally ill patient or in another emergency situation, where consent of the patient or his close relatives cannot be obtained, upon the approval of the person in charge of the medical institution or an authorized person in charge, the corresponding medical measures may be taken forthwith.

Article 1221 Where the medical staff fail to fulfill the duty of diagnosing and treating the patient up to the then current appropriate medical level, and thus causes damage to the patient, the medical institution shall assume the liability for compensation.

Article 1222 A medical institution shall be presumed to be at fault where damage is caused to a patient during diagnosis and treatment under any of the following circumstances:

(1) there is a violation of the provisions of laws, administrative regulations,

rules, or other relevant guidelines for diagnosis and treatment;

(2) the medical records are concealed or the request for provision thereof is refused; or

(3) the medical records are lost, forged, tempered with, or illegally destroyed.

Article 1223 Where damage is caused to a patient due to a defect in a drug, disinfection product, or medical instrument, or due to the transfusion of substandard blood, the patient may claim compensation against the drug marketing license holder or the manufacturer of the drug, or the blood supply institution, or against the medical institution. Where the patient claims compensation against a medical institution, the medical institution, after paying compensation, has the right to indemnification against the responsible drug marketing license holder or manufacturer of the drug, or the blood supplier.

Article 1224 Under any of the following circumstances, a medical institution does not assume liability for compensation for any damage caused to a patient during diagnosis and treatment:

(1) the patient or his close relative does not cooperate with the medical institution to go through diagnosis and treatment which is in compliance with the guidelines for diagnosis and treatment;

(2) the medical staff have fulfilled their duty of providing reasonable diagnosis and treatment in an emergent situation, such as rescuing a terminally ill patient; or

(3) it is difficult to diagnose and treat a patient due to the restriction of the then current medical level.

Under the circumstance specified in Subparagraph (1) of the preceding paragraph, the medical institution or its medical staff shall assume corresponding liability for compensation where they are also at fault.

Article 1225 Medical institutions and their medical staff shall properly enter and maintain medical records such as hospitalization logs, medical orders, test reports, surgical and anesthesia records, pathological data, and nursing records in accordance with the regulations.

Where a patient requests to retrieve or make copies of their medical records as provided in the preceding paragraph, the medical institution shall provide the records in a timely manner.

Article 1226 Medical institutions and their medical staff shall keep their patients' private information and personal information confidential. Anyone who divulges the private information or personal information of a patient or discloses his medical records without the patient's consent shall bear tort liability.

Article 1227 Medical institutions and their medical staff may not conduct unnecessary examinations for the patients in violation of the guidelines for diagnosis and treatment.

Article 1228 The lawful rights and interests of a medical institution and its medical staff are protected by law.

Anyone, who interferes with the order of a medical institution, obstructs the work or life of the medical staff, or infringes upon the lawful rights and interests of the medical staff, shall bear liability in accordance with law.

Chapter Ⅶ Liability for Environmental Pollution and Ecological Damage

Article 1229 A tortfeasor who has polluted the environment or harmed the ecological system and thus causes damage to others shall bear tort liability.

Article 1230 Where any dispute arises from environmental pollution or ecological damage, the actor shall bear the burden to prove that he should not be liable or that his liability could be mitigated as provided by law, and that there is no causation between his act and the damage.

Article 1231 Where environmental pollution or ecological damage is caused by two or more tortfeasors, the extent of liability of each tortfeasor shall be determined according to the factors such as the type, concentration, and quantity of discharge of the pollutants, the way, scope, and degree of damage to the ecological system, and the impact of the act on the consequences of damage.

Article 1232 Where a tortfeasor intentionally pollutes the environment or harms the ecological system in violation of the provisions of law resulting in serious consequences, the infringed person has the right to request for the corresponding punitive damages.

Article 1233 Where environmental pollution or ecological damage is caused owing to the fault of a third person, the infringed person may claim compensation against either the tortfeasor or the third person. After making compensation, the tortfeasor has the right to indemnification against the third person.

Article 1234 Where a tortfeasor causes damage to the ecological environment in violation of the State regulations and if restoration is possible, the State authorized agencies or the organizations authorized by law have the right to request the tortfeasor to bear the responsibility for restoration within a reasonable period of time. Where the tortfeasor fails to restore it within the time limit, the State authorized agencies or the organizations authorized by law may initiate the restoration on its own or entrust it with others, and any expenses thus incurred shall be borne by the tortfeasor.

Article 1235 Where ecological damage is caused in violation of the State regulations, the State authorized agencies or the organizations authorized by law have the right to request the tortfeasor to compensate the following losses and expenses:

(1) losses caused by loss of service function from the time the ecological environment is damaged to the time the restoration is completed;

(2) losses caused by permanent damage to the function of the ecological environment;

(3) expenses for investigation, appraisal, and assessment of the damage to the ecological environment;

(4) expenses for cleaning-up the pollution and restoring the ecological environment; and

(5) other reasonable expenses incurred to prevent the occurrence or aggravation of the damage.

Chapter Ⅷ Liability for Ultra-hazardous Activities

Article 1236 A person who engages in ultra-hazardous operations and thus causes damage to another person shall bear tort liability.

Article 1237 Where a nuclear accident occurs at a civil nuclear facility or when nuclear materials are transported into or out of a civil nuclear facility and damage is thus caused to another person, the operator of the facility shall bear tort liability, except that the operator does not assume such liability if it can be proven that the damage is caused by a war, an armed conflict, a riot, or under other like circumstances, or the damage is intentionally caused by the victim.

Article 1238 Where a civil aircraft causes damage to another person, the operator of the aircraft shall bear tort liability, except that the operator does not assume any liability if it can be proven that the damage is intentionally caused by the victim.

Article 1239 Where the possession or use of flammable, explosive, highly toxic, highly radioactive, strongly corrosive, highly pathogenic, or other ultra-hazardous things causes damage to another person, the possessor or user thereof shall bear tort liability, except that such a possessor or user does not assume any liability if it can be proven that the damage was intentionally caused by the victim or caused by *force majeure*. Where the infringed person is grossly negligent for the occurrence of the damage, the liability of the possessor or user may be mitigated.

Article 1240 Where damage is caused to another person by a person engaging in work at a height, high voltage, or underground excavation activities, or by using high-speed rail transport vehicles, the operator shall bear tort liability, except that the operator does not assume any liability if it can be proven that the damage was intentionally caused by the victim or caused by *force majeure*. Where the infringed person is grossly negligent for the occurrence of the damage, the liability of the operator may be mitigated.

Article 1241 Where damage is caused to another person by an ultra-hazardous thing that is lost or abandoned, the owner of the ultra-hazardous thing shall bear tort liability. Where the owner has delivered the ultra-hazardous thing to another person for management, the manager shall bear tort liability, and the owner shall assume joint and several liability with the manager where he is at fault.

Article 1242 Where damage is caused to another person by an ultra-hazardous thing that is illegally possessed, the illegal possessor of the ultra-hazardous thing shall bear tort liability. The owner or manager of the thing shall assume joint and several liability with the illegal possessor if he cannot prove that he has fulfilled a high duty of care to prevent the illegal possession.

Article 1243 Where a person, without authorization, enters into an area where ultra-hazardous activities are conducted or ultra-hazardous things are stored therein and is thus injured, the liability of the manager of the area may be mitigated or eliminated if it can be proven that he has taken sufficient security measures and fulfilled the duty of sufficient warning.

Article 1244 Where there are provisions of law providing for a limit of compensation for liability incurred as a result of an ultra-hazardous activity, such provisions shall be followed unless the damage is caused by the actor intentionally or with gross negligence.

Chapter IX Liability for Damage Caused by Domesticated Animals

Article 1245 Where a domesticated animal causes damage to another person, the keeper or custodian of the animal shall bear tort liability, except that his liability may be mitigated or eliminated if it can be proven that the damage is caused by the infringed person intentionally or by gross negligence.

Article 1246 A keeper or custodian of an animal who, in violation of the rules of management, fails to take safety measures on the animal and thus causes damage to another person shall bear tort liability, except that his liability may be mitigated if it can be proven that the damage is intentionally caused by the infringed person.

Article 1247 Where damage is caused to another person by a dangerous animal that is prohibited from being kept, such as a fierce dog, the keeper or custodian of the animal shall bear tort liability.

Article 1248 Where an animal of a zoo causes damage to another person, the zoo shall bear tort liability unless it can be proven that it has fulfilled its duties of management.

Article 1249 Where an abandoned or escaped animal causes damage to another person during the period of being abandoned or on the run, the original keeper or custodian of the animal shall bear tort liability.

Article 1250 Where an animal causes damage to another person due to a third person's fault, the infringed person may claim compensation against the keeper or custodian of the animal, or against the third person. The keeper or custodian of the animal who has paid compensation has the right to indemnification against the third person.

Article 1251 Anyone who keeps an animal shall abide by laws and regulations, respect social morality, and may not disturb the life of others.

Chapter X Liability for Damage Caused by Buildings and Objects

Article 1252 Where a building, structure, or another type of facility collapses or subsides and causes damage to another person, the project owner and the constructor shall assume joint and several liability unless they can prove that there is no quality defect. Where the damage is due to the fault of another responsible person, the project owner or constructor who has made compensation has the right to indemnification against the responsible person.

Where a building, structure, or another type of facility collapses or subsides, and damage is thus caused to another person due to the fault of the owner, manager, user, or a third person, the owner, manager, user, or the third person shall bear tort liability.

Article 1253 Where a building, structure, or another type of facility, or any object laid or hanged thereon, comes loose or falls down and thus causes damage to another person, the owner, manager, or user shall bear tort liability if it cannot be proven that he is not at fault. Where the damage is due to the fault of another responsible person, the owner, manager, or user who has paid compensation has the right to indemnification against the responsible person.

Article 1254 Throwing objects from within a building is prohibited. Where an object thrown from within a building or falling off a building causes damage to another person, the tortfeasor shall bear tort liability in accordance with law. Where it is difficult to identify the specific tortfeasor upon investigation, any user of the building who may have caused the damage shall make compensation, unless he can prove that he is not the tortfeasor. A user of the building who has paid compensation has the right to indemnification against the tortfeasor.

The manager of a building such as the property management service enterprise shall take necessary security measures to prevent the occurrence of the incident specified in the preceding paragraph. Where no necessary security measures are taken, it shall bear tort liability for failure to perform the obligation of providing security measures in accordance with law.

Where an incident as specified in the first paragraph of this Article occurs, the relevant authorities, such as the public security department, shall timely conduct investigation in accordance with law and identify the responsible person(s).

Article 1255 Where a stack of objects collapses, rolls down, or slips down, and causes damage to another person, the person who piles up the stack shall bear tort liability if he cannot prove that he is not at fault.

Article 1256 Where damage is caused to another person due to an object stacked, dumped, or left on public road so that the road is obstructed, the actor shall bear tort liability. The public road manager shall assume the corresponding liability if he cannot prove that he has fulfilled his duties such as the duty of clean-up, protection, and warning.

Article 1257 Where a breaking or falling tree or a falling fruit causes damage to another person, the owner or manager of the tree shall bear tort liability if he cannot prove that he is not at fault.

Article 1258 Where excavation of the ground or repair or installation of underground facilities is conducted in a public place or on a public road, which causes damage to another person, the constructor shall bear tort liability if he cannot prove that he has posted an obvious warning sign and taken safety measures.

Where an underground facility, such as a utility access manhole, causes damage to another person, the manager shall bear tort liability if he cannot prove that he has fulfilled his management responsibilities.

Supplementary Provisions

Article 1259 In the civil law, the terms "not less than", "not more than", "within" and "expiration/expire on" include the given figure; the terms "less than", "more than" and "beyond" do not include the given figure.

Article 1260 This Code shall come into force on January 1, 2021. The Marriage Law of the People's Republic of China, the Succession Law of the People's Republic of China, the General Principles of Civil Law of the People's Republic of China, the Adoption Law of the People's Republic of China, the Security Law of the People's Republic of China, the Contract Law of the People's Republic of China, the Real Right Law of the People's Republic of China, the Tort Liability Law of the People's Republic of China, and the General Provisions of Civil Law of the People's Republic of China shall be repealed at the same time.

中华人民共和国民法典

中华人民共和国主席令

第四十五号

《中华人民共和国民法典》已由中华人民共和国第十三届全国人民代表大会第三次会议于2020年5月28日通过,现予公布,自2021年1月1日起施行。

中华人民共和国主席　**习近平**

2020年5月28日

中华人民共和国民法典

（2020 年 5 月 28 日第十三届全国人民代表大会第三次会议通过）

目　录

第一编　总　　则

第一章　基本规定

第一条　为了保护民事主体的合法权益,调整民事关系,维护社会和经济秩序,适应中国特色社会主义发展要求,弘扬社会主义核心价值观,根据宪法,制定本法。

第二条　民法调整平等主体的自然人、法人和非法人组织之间的人身关系和财产关系。

第三条　民事主体的人身权利、财产权利以及其他合法权益受法律保护,任何组织或者个人不得侵犯。

第四条　民事主体在民事活动中的法律地位一律平等。

第五条　民事主体从事民事活动,应当遵循自愿原则,按照自己的意思设立、变更、终止民事法律关系。

第六条　民事主体从事民事活动,应当遵循公平原则,合理确定各方的权利和义务。

第七条　民事主体从事民事活动,应当遵循诚信原则,秉持诚实,恪守承诺。

第八条　民事主体从事民事活动,不得违反法律,不得违背公序良俗。

第九条　民事主体从事民事活动,应当有利于节约资源、保护生态环境。

第十条　处理民事纠纷,应当依照法律;法律没有规定的,可以适用习惯,但是不得违背公序良俗。

第十一条　其他法律对民事关系有特别规定的,依照其规定。

第十二条　中华人民共和国领域内的民事活动,适用中华人民共和国法律。法律另有规定的，依照其规定。

第二章　自　然　人

第一节　民事权利能力和民事行为能力

第十三条　自然人从出生时起到死亡时止，具有民事权利能力，依法享有民事权利，承担民事义务。

第十四条　自然人的民事权利能力一律平等。

第十五条　自然人的出生时间和死亡时间，以出生证明、死亡证明记载的时间为准；没有出生证明、死亡证明的，以户籍登记或者其他有效身份登记记载的时间为准。有其他证据足以推翻以上记载时间的，以该证据证明的时间为准。

第十六条　涉及遗产继承、接受赠与等胎儿利益保护的，胎儿视为具有民事权利能力。但是，胎儿娩出时为死体的，其民事权利能力自始不存在。

第十七条　十八周岁以上的自然人为成年人。不满十八周岁的自然人为未成年人。

第十八条　成年人为完全民事行为能力人，可以独立实施民事法律行为。

十六周岁以上的未成年人，以自己的劳动收入为主要生活来源的，视为完全民事行为能力人。

第十九条　八周岁以上的未成年人为限制民事行为能力人，实施民事法律行为由其法定代理人代理或者经其法定代理人同意、追认；但是，可以独立实施纯获利益的民事法律行为或者与其年龄、智力相适应的民事法律行为。

第二十条　不满八周岁的未成年人为无民事行为能力人，由其法定代理人代理实施民事法律行为。

第二十一条　不能辨认自己行为的成年人为无民事行为能力人，由其法定代理人代理实施民事法律行为。

八周岁以上的未成年人不能辨认自己行为的,适用前款规定。

第二十二条 不能完全辨认自己行为的成年人为限制民事行为能力人,实施民事法律行为由其法定代理人代理或者经其法定代理人同意、追认;但是,可以独立实施纯获利益的民事法律行为或者与其智力、精神健康状况相适应的民事法律行为。

第二十三条 无民事行为能力人、限制民事行为能力人的监护人是其法定代理人。

第二十四条 不能辨认或者不能完全辨认自己行为的成年人,其利害关系人或者有关组织,可以向人民法院申请认定该成年人为无民事行为能力人或者限制民事行为能力人。

被人民法院认定为无民事行为能力人或者限制民事行为能力人的,经本人、利害关系人或者有关组织申请,人民法院可以根据其智力、精神健康恢复的状况,认定该成年人恢复为限制民事行为能力人或者完全民事行为能力人。

本条规定的有关组织包括:居民委员会、村民委员会、学校、医疗机构、妇女联合会、残疾人联合会、依法设立的老年人组织、民政部门等。

第二十五条 自然人以户籍登记或者其他有效身份登记记载的居所为住所;经常居所与住所不一致的,经常居所视为住所。

第二节 监 护

第二十六条 父母对未成年子女负有抚养、教育和保护的义务。

成年子女对父母负有赡养、扶助和保护的义务。

第二十七条 父母是未成年子女的监护人。

未成年人的父母已经死亡或者没有监护能力的,由下列有监护能力的人按顺序担任监护人:

(一)祖父母、外祖父母;

(二)兄、姐;

(三)其他愿意担任监护人的个人或者组织,但是须经未成年人住所地的居民委员会、村民委员会或者民政部门同意。

第二十八条 无民事行为能力或者限制民事行为能力的成年人，由下列有监护能力的人按顺序担任监护人：

（一）配偶；

（二）父母、子女；

（三）其他近亲属；

（四）其他愿意担任监护人的个人或者组织，但是须经被监护人住所地的居民委员会、村民委员会或者民政部门同意。

第二十九条 被监护人的父母担任监护人的，可以通过遗嘱指定监护人。

第三十条 依法具有监护资格的人之间可以协议确定监护人。协议确定监护人应当尊重被监护人的真实意愿。

第三十一条 对监护人的确定有争议的，由被监护人住所地的居民委员会、村民委员会或者民政部门指定监护人，有关当事人对指定不服的，可以向人民法院申请指定监护人；有关当事人也可以直接向人民法院申请指定监护人。

居民委员会、村民委员会、民政部门或者人民法院应当尊重被监护人的真实意愿，按照最有利于被监护人的原则在依法具有监护资格的人中指定监护人。

依据本条第一款规定指定监护人前，被监护人的人身权利、财产权利以及其他合法权益处于无人保护状态的，由被监护人住所地的居民委员会、村民委员会、法律规定的有关组织或者民政部门担任临时监护人。

监护人被指定后，不得擅自变更；擅自变更的，不免除被指定的监护人的责任。

第三十二条 没有依法具有监护资格的人的，监护人由民政部门担任，也可以由具备履行监护职责条件的被监护人住所地的居民委员会、村民委员会担任。

第三十三条 具有完全民事行为能力的成年人，可以与其近亲属、其他愿意担任监护人的个人或者组织事先协商,以书面形式确定自己的监护人,在自己丧失或者部分丧失民事行为能力时,由该监护人履行监护职责。

第三十四条 监护人的职责是代理被监护人实施民事法律行为,保护被监护人的人身权利、财产权利以及其他合法权益等。

监护人依法履行监护职责产生的权利,受法律保护。

监护人不履行监护职责或者侵害被监护人合法权益的,应当承担法律责任。

因发生突发事件等紧急情况,监护人暂时无法履行监护职责,被监护人的生活处于无人照料状态的,被监护人住所地的居民委员会、村民委员会或者民政部门应当为被监护人安排必要的临时生活照料措施。

第三十五条 监护人应当按照最有利于被监护人的原则履行监护职责。监护人除为维护被监护人利益外,不得处分被监护人的财产。

未成年人的监护人履行监护职责,在作出与被监护人利益有关的决定时,应当根据被监护人的年龄和智力状况,尊重被监护人的真实意愿。

成年人的监护人履行监护职责,应当最大程度地尊重被监护人的真实意愿,保障并协助被监护人实施与其智力、精神健康状况相适应的民事法律行为。对被监护人有能力独立处理的事务,监护人不得干涉。

第三十六条 监护人有下列情形之一的,人民法院根据有关个人或者组织的申请,撤销其监护人资格,安排必要的临时监护措施,并按照最有利于被监护人的原则依法指定监护人:

(一)实施严重损害被监护人身心健康的行为;

(二)怠于履行监护职责,或者无法履行监护职责且拒绝将监护职责部分或者全部委托给他人,导致被监护人处于危困状态;

(三)实施严重侵害被监护人合法权益的其他行为。

本条规定的有关个人、组织包括:其他依法具有监护资格的人,居民委员会、村民委员会、学校、医疗机构、妇女联合会、残疾人联合会、未成年人保护组织、依法设立的老年人组织、民政部门等。

前款规定的个人和民政部门以外的组织未及时向人民法院申请撤销监

护人资格的，民政部门应当向人民法院申请。

第三十七条 依法负担被监护人抚养费、赡养费、扶养费的父母、子女、配偶等，被人民法院撤销监护人资格后，应当继续履行负担的义务。

第三十八条 被监护人的父母或者子女被人民法院撤销监护人资格后，除对被监护人实施故意犯罪的外，确有悔改表现的，经其申请，人民法院可以在尊重被监护人真实意愿的前提下，视情况恢复其监护人资格，人民法院指定的监护人与被监护人的监护关系同时终止。

第三十九条 有下列情形之一的，监护关系终止：

（一）被监护人取得或者恢复完全民事行为能力；

（二）监护人丧失监护能力；

（三）被监护人或者监护人死亡；

（四）人民法院认定监护关系终止的其他情形。

监护关系终止后，被监护人仍然需要监护的，应当依法另行确定监护人。

第三节 宣告失踪和宣告死亡

第四十条 自然人下落不明满二年的，利害关系人可以向人民法院申请宣告该自然人为失踪人。

第四十一条 自然人下落不明的时间自其失去音讯之日起计算。战争期间下落不明的，下落不明的时间自战争结束之日或者有关机关确定的下落不明之日起计算。

第四十二条 失踪人的财产由其配偶、成年子女、父母或者其他愿意担任财产代管人的人代管。

代管有争议，没有前款规定的人，或者前款规定的人无代管能力的，由人民法院指定的人代管。

第四十三条 财产代管人应当妥善管理失踪人的财产，维护其财产权益。

失踪人所欠税款、债务和应付的其他费用，由财产代管人从失踪人的财产中支付。

财产代管人因故意或者重大过失造成失踪人财产损失的,应当承担赔偿责任。

第四十四条 财产代管人不履行代管职责、侵害失踪人财产权益或者丧失代管能力的,失踪人的利害关系人可以向人民法院申请变更财产代管人。

财产代管人有正当理由的,可以向人民法院申请变更财产代管人。

人民法院变更财产代管人的,变更后的财产代管人有权请求原财产代管人及时移交有关财产并报告财产代管情况。

第四十五条 失踪人重新出现,经本人或者利害关系人申请,人民法院应当撤销失踪宣告。

失踪人重新出现,有权请求财产代管人及时移交有关财产并报告财产代管情况。

第四十六条 自然人有下列情形之一的,利害关系人可以向人民法院申请宣告该自然人死亡:

(一)下落不明满四年;

(二)因意外事件,下落不明满二年。

因意外事件下落不明,经有关机关证明该自然人不可能生存的,申请宣告死亡不受二年时间的限制。

第四十七条 对同一自然人,有的利害关系人申请宣告死亡,有的利害关系人申请宣告失踪,符合本法规定的宣告死亡条件的,人民法院应当宣告死亡。

第四十八条 被宣告死亡的人,人民法院宣告死亡的判决作出之日视为其死亡的日期;因意外事件下落不明宣告死亡的,意外事件发生之日视为其死亡的日期。

第四十九条 自然人被宣告死亡但是并未死亡的,不影响该自然人在被宣告死亡期间实施的民事法律行为的效力。

第五十条 被宣告死亡的人重新出现,经本人或者利害关系人申请,人民法院应当撤销死亡宣告。

第五十一条 被宣告死亡的人的婚姻关系,自死亡宣告之日起消除。死亡宣告被撤销的,婚姻关系自撤销死亡宣告之日起自行恢复。但是,其配偶再婚或者向婚姻登记机关书面声明不愿意恢复的除外。

第五十二条 被宣告死亡的人在被宣告死亡期间,其子女被他人依法收养的,在死亡宣告被撤销后,不得以未经本人同意为由主张收养行为无效。

第五十三条 被撤销死亡宣告的人有权请求依照本法第六编取得其财产的民事主体返还财产;无法返还的,应当给予适当补偿。

利害关系人隐瞒真实情况,致使他人被宣告死亡而取得其财产的,除应当返还财产外,还应当对由此造成的损失承担赔偿责任。

第四节 个体工商户和农村承包经营户

第五十四条 自然人从事工商业经营,经依法登记,为个体工商户。个体工商户可以起字号。

第五十五条 农村集体经济组织的成员,依法取得农村土地承包经营权,从事家庭承包经营的,为农村承包经营户。

第五十六条 个体工商户的债务,个人经营的,以个人财产承担;家庭经营的,以家庭财产承担;无法区分的,以家庭财产承担。

农村承包经营户的债务,以从事农村土地承包经营的农户财产承担;事实上由农户部分成员经营的,以该部分成员的财产承担。

第三章 法 人

第一节 一般规定

第五十七条 法人是具有民事权利能力和民事行为能力,依法独立享有民事权利和承担民事义务的组织。

第五十八条 法人应当依法成立。

法人应当有自己的名称、组织机构、住所、财产或者经费。法人成立的具体条件和程序,依照法律、行政法规的规定。

设立法人,法律、行政法规规定须经有关机关批准的,依照其规定。

第五十九条 法人的民事权利能力和民事行为能力,从法人成立时产生,到法人终止时消灭。

第六十条 法人以其全部财产独立承担民事责任。

第六十一条 依照法律或者法人章程的规定,代表法人从事民事活动的负责人,为法人的法定代表人。

法定代表人以法人名义从事的民事活动,其法律后果由法人承受。

法人章程或者法人权力机构对法定代表人代表权的限制,不得对抗善意相对人。

第六十二条 法定代表人因执行职务造成他人损害的,由法人承担民事责任。

法人承担民事责任后,依照法律或者法人章程的规定,可以向有过错的法定代表人追偿。

第六十三条 法人以其主要办事机构所在地为住所。依法需要办理法人登记的,应当将主要办事机构所在地登记为住所。

第六十四条 法人存续期间登记事项发生变化的,应当依法向登记机关申请变更登记。

第六十五条 法人的实际情况与登记的事项不一致的,不得对抗善意相对人。

第六十六条 登记机关应当依法及时公示法人登记的有关信息。

第六十七条 法人合并的,其权利和义务由合并后的法人享有和承担。

法人分立的,其权利和义务由分立后的法人享有连带债权,承担连带债务,但是债权人和债务人另有约定的除外。

第六十八条 有下列原因之一并依法完成清算、注销登记的,法人终止:

(一)法人解散;

（二）法人被宣告破产；

（三）法律规定的其他原因。

法人终止，法律、行政法规规定须经有关机关批准的，依照其规定。

第六十九条 有下列情形之一的，法人解散：

（一）法人章程规定的存续期间届满或者法人章程规定的其他解散事由出现；

（二）法人的权力机构决议解散；

（三）因法人合并或者分立需要解散；

（四）法人依法被吊销营业执照、登记证书，被责令关闭或者被撤销；

（五）法律规定的其他情形。

第七十条 法人解散的，除合并或者分立的情形外，清算义务人应当及时组成清算组进行清算。

法人的董事、理事等执行机构或者决策机构的成员为清算义务人。法律、行政法规另有规定的，依照其规定。

清算义务人未及时履行清算义务，造成损害的，应当承担民事责任；主管机关或者利害关系人可以申请人民法院指定有关人员组成清算组进行清算。

第七十一条 法人的清算程序和清算组职权，依照有关法律的规定；没有规定的，参照适用公司法律的有关规定。

第七十二条 清算期间法人存续，但是不得从事与清算无关的活动。

法人清算后的剩余财产，按照法人章程的规定或者法人权力机构的决议处理。法律另有规定的，依照其规定。

清算结束并完成法人注销登记时，法人终止；依法不需要办理法人登记的，清算结束时，法人终止。

第七十三条 法人被宣告破产的，依法进行破产清算并完成法人注销登记时，法人终止。

第七十四条 法人可以依法设立分支机构。法律、行政法规规定分支机构应当登记的，依照其规定。

分支机构以自己的名义从事民事活动,产生的民事责任由法人承担;也可以先以该分支机构管理的财产承担,不足以承担的,由法人承担。

第七十五条 设立人为设立法人从事的民事活动,其法律后果由法人承受;法人未成立的,其法律后果由设立人承受,设立人为二人以上的,享有连带债权,承担连带债务。

设立人为设立法人以自己的名义从事民事活动产生的民事责任,第三人有权选择请求法人或者设立人承担。

第二节 营利法人

第七十六条 以取得利润并分配给股东等出资人为目的成立的法人,为营利法人。

营利法人包括有限责任公司、股份有限公司和其他企业法人等。

第七十七条 营利法人经依法登记成立。

第七十八条 依法设立的营利法人,由登记机关发给营利法人营业执照。营业执照签发日期为营利法人的成立日期。

第七十九条 设立营利法人应当依法制定法人章程。

第八十条 营利法人应当设权力机构。

权力机构行使修改法人章程,选举或者更换执行机构、监督机构成员,以及法人章程规定的其他职权。

第八十一条 营利法人应当设执行机构。

执行机构行使召集权力机构会议,决定法人的经营计划和投资方案,决定法人内部管理机构的设置,以及法人章程规定的其他职权。

执行机构为董事会或者执行董事的,董事长、执行董事或者经理按照法人章程的规定担任法定代表人;未设董事会或者执行董事的,法人章程规定的主要负责人为其执行机构和法定代表人。

第八十二条 营利法人设监事会或者监事等监督机构的,监督机构依法行使检查法人财务,监督执行机构成员、高级管理人员执行法人职务的行为,以及法人章程规定的其他职权。

第八十三条　营利法人的出资人不得滥用出资人权利损害法人或者其他出资人的利益;滥用出资人权利造成法人或者其他出资人损失的,应当依法承担民事责任。

营利法人的出资人不得滥用法人独立地位和出资人有限责任损害法人债权人的利益;滥用法人独立地位和出资人有限责任,逃避债务,严重损害法人债权人的利益的,应当对法人债务承担连带责任。

第八十四条　营利法人的控股出资人、实际控制人、董事、监事、高级管理人员不得利用其关联关系损害法人的利益;利用关联关系造成法人损失的,应当承担赔偿责任。

第八十五条　营利法人的权力机构、执行机构作出决议的会议召集程序、表决方式违反法律、行政法规、法人章程,或者决议内容违反法人章程的,营利法人的出资人可以请求人民法院撤销该决议。但是,营利法人依据该决议与善意相对人形成的民事法律关系不受影响。

第八十六条　营利法人从事经营活动,应当遵守商业道德,维护交易安全,接受政府和社会的监督,承担社会责任。

第三节　非营利法人

第八十七条　为公益目的或者其他非营利目的成立,不向出资人、设立人或者会员分配所取得利润的法人,为非营利法人。

非营利法人包括事业单位、社会团体、基金会、社会服务机构等。

第八十八条　具备法人条件,为适应经济社会发展需要,提供公益服务设立的事业单位,经依法登记成立,取得事业单位法人资格;依法不需要办理法人登记的,从成立之日起,具有事业单位法人资格。

第八十九条　事业单位法人设理事会的,除法律另有规定外,理事会为其决策机构。事业单位法人的法定代表人依照法律、行政法规或者法人章程的规定产生。

第九十条　具备法人条件,基于会员共同意愿,为公益目的或者会员共同利益等非营利目的设立的社会团体,经依法登记成立,取得社会团体法人资格;依法不需要办理法人登记的,从成立之日起,具有社会团体法人资格。

第九十一条 设立社会团体法人应当依法制定法人章程。

社会团体法人应当设会员大会或者会员代表大会等权力机构。

社会团体法人应当设理事会等执行机构。理事长或者会长等负责人按照法人章程的规定担任法定代表人。

第九十二条 具备法人条件,为公益目的以捐助财产设立的基金会、社会服务机构等,经依法登记成立,取得捐助法人资格。

依法设立的宗教活动场所,具备法人条件的,可以申请法人登记,取得捐助法人资格。法律、行政法规对宗教活动场所有规定的,依照其规定。

第九十三条 设立捐助法人应当依法制定法人章程。

捐助法人应当设理事会、民主管理组织等决策机构,并设执行机构。理事长等负责人按照法人章程的规定担任法定代表人。

捐助法人应当设监事会等监督机构。

第九十四条 捐助人有权向捐助法人查询捐助财产的使用、管理情况,并提出意见和建议,捐助法人应当及时、如实答复。

捐助法人的决策机构、执行机构或者法定代表人作出决定的程序违反法律、行政法规、法人章程,或者决定内容违反法人章程的,捐助人等利害关系人或者主管机关可以请求人民法院撤销该决定。但是,捐助法人依据该决定与善意相对人形成的民事法律关系不受影响。

第九十五条 为公益目的成立的非营利法人终止时,不得向出资人、设立人或者会员分配剩余财产。剩余财产应当按照法人章程的规定或者权力机构的决议用于公益目的;无法按照法人章程的规定或者权力机构的决议处理的,由主管机关主持转给宗旨相同或者相近的法人,并向社会公告。

第四节 特 别 法 人

第九十六条 本节规定的机关法人、农村集体经济组织法人、城镇农村的合作经济组织法人、基层群众性自治组织法人,为特别法人。

第九十七条 有独立经费的机关和承担行政职能的法定机构从成立之

日起，具有机关法人资格，可以从事为履行职能所需要的民事活动。

第九十八条 机关法人被撤销的，法人终止，其民事权利和义务由继任的机关法人享有和承担；没有继任的机关法人的，由作出撤销决定的机关法人享有和承担。

第九十九条 农村集体经济组织依法取得法人资格。

法律、行政法规对农村集体经济组织有规定的，依照其规定。

第一百条 城镇农村的合作经济组织依法取得法人资格。

法律、行政法规对城镇农村的合作经济组织有规定的，依照其规定。

第一百零一条 居民委员会、村民委员会具有基层群众性自治组织法人资格，可以从事为履行职能所需要的民事活动。

未设立村集体经济组织的，村民委员会可以依法代行村集体经济组织的职能。

第四章 非法人组织

第一百零二条 非法人组织是不具有法人资格，但是能够依法以自己的名义从事民事活动的组织。

非法人组织包括个人独资企业、合伙企业、不具有法人资格的专业服务机构等。

第一百零三条 非法人组织应当依照法律的规定登记。

设立非法人组织，法律、行政法规规定须经有关机关批准的，依照其规定。

第一百零四条 非法人组织的财产不足以清偿债务的，其出资人或者设立人承担无限责任。法律另有规定的，依照其规定。

第一百零五条 非法人组织可以确定一人或者数人代表该组织从事民事活动。

第一百零六条 有下列情形之一的，非法人组织解散：

（一）章程规定的存续期间届满或者章程规定的其他解散事由出现；

（二）出资人或者设立人决定解散；

(三)法律规定的其他情形。

第一百零七条 非法人组织解散的,应当依法进行清算。

第一百零八条 非法人组织除适用本章规定外,参照适用本编第三章第一节的有关规定。

第五章 民事权利

第一百零九条 自然人的人身自由、人格尊严受法律保护。

第一百一十条 自然人享有生命权、身体权、健康权、姓名权、肖像权、名誉权、荣誉权、隐私权、婚姻自主权等权利。

法人、非法人组织享有名称权、名誉权和荣誉权。

第一百一十一条 自然人的个人信息受法律保护。任何组织或者个人需要获取他人个人信息的,应当依法取得并确保信息安全,不得非法收集、使用、加工、传输他人个人信息,不得非法买卖、提供或者公开他人个人信息。

第一百一十二条 自然人因婚姻家庭关系等产生的人身权利受法律保护。

第一百一十三条 民事主体的财产权利受法律平等保护。

第一百一十四条 民事主体依法享有物权。

物权是权利人依法对特定的物享有直接支配和排他的权利,包括所有权、用益物权和担保物权。

第一百一十五条 物包括不动产和动产。法律规定权利作为物权客体的,依照其规定。

第一百一十六条 物权的种类和内容,由法律规定。

第一百一十七条 为了公共利益的需要,依照法律规定的权限和程序征收、征用不动产或者动产的,应当给予公平、合理的补偿。

第一百一十八条 民事主体依法享有债权。

债权是因合同、侵权行为、无因管理、不当得利以及法律的其他规定,权利人请求特定义务人为或者不为一定行为的权利。

第一百一十九条　依法成立的合同，对当事人具有法律约束力。

第一百二十条　民事权益受到侵害的，被侵权人有权请求侵权人承担侵权责任。

第一百二十一条　没有法定的或者约定的义务，为避免他人利益受损失而进行管理的人，有权请求受益人偿还由此支出的必要费用。

第一百二十二条　因他人没有法律根据，取得不当利益，受损失的人有权请求其返还不当利益。

第一百二十三条　民事主体依法享有知识产权。

知识产权是权利人依法就下列客体享有的专有的权利：

（一）作品；

（二）发明、实用新型、外观设计；

（三）商标；

（四）地理标志；

（五）商业秘密；

（六）集成电路布图设计；

（七）植物新品种；

（八）法律规定的其他客体。

第一百二十四条　自然人依法享有继承权。

自然人合法的私有财产，可以依法继承。

第一百二十五条　民事主体依法享有股权和其他投资性权利。

第一百二十六条　民事主体享有法律规定的其他民事权利和利益。

第一百二十七条　法律对数据、网络虚拟财产的保护有规定的，依照其规定。

第一百二十八条　法律对未成年人、老年人、残疾人、妇女、消费者等的民事权利保护有特别规定的，依照其规定。

第一百二十九条　民事权利可以依据民事法律行为、事实行为、法律规定的事件或者法律规定的其他方式取得。

第一百三十条　民事主体按照自己的意愿依法行使民事权利，不受干涉。

第一百三十一条 民事主体行使权利时,应当履行法律规定的和当事人约定的义务。

第一百三十二条 民事主体不得滥用民事权利损害国家利益、社会公共利益或者他人合法权益。

第六章 民事法律行为

第一节 一般规定

第一百三十三条 民事法律行为是民事主体通过意思表示设立、变更、终止民事法律关系的行为。

第一百三十四条 民事法律行为可以基于双方或者多方的意思表示一致成立,也可以基于单方的意思表示成立。

法人、非法人组织依照法律或者章程规定的议事方式和表决程序作出决议的,该决议行为成立。

第一百三十五条 民事法律行为可以采用书面形式、口头形式或者其他形式;法律、行政法规规定或者当事人约定采用特定形式的,应当采用特定形式。

第一百三十六条 民事法律行为自成立时生效,但是法律另有规定或者当事人另有约定的除外。

行为人非依法律规定或者未经对方同意,不得擅自变更或者解除民事法律行为。

第二节 意思表示

第一百三十七条 以对话方式作出的意思表示,相对人知道其内容时生效。

以非对话方式作出的意思表示,到达相对人时生效。以非对话方式作出的采用数据电文形式的意思表示,相对人指定特定系统接收数据电文的,该数据电文进入该特定系统时生效;未指定特定系统的,相对人知道或者应当知道该数据电文进入其系统时生效。当事人对采用数据电文形式的意思表示的生效时间另有约定的,按照其约定。

第一百三十八条 无相对人的意思表示,表示完成时生效。法律另有规定的,依照其规定。

第一百三十九条 以公告方式作出的意思表示,公告发布时生效。

第一百四十条 行为人可以明示或者默示作出意思表示。

沉默只有在有法律规定、当事人约定或者符合当事人之间的交易习惯时,才可以视为意思表示。

第一百四十一条 行为人可以撤回意思表示。撤回意思表示的通知应当在意思表示到达相对人前或者与意思表示同时到达相对人。

第一百四十二条 有相对人的意思表示的解释,应当按照所使用的词句,结合相关条款、行为的性质和目的、习惯以及诚信原则,确定意思表示的含义。

无相对人的意思表示的解释,不能完全拘泥于所使用的词句,而应当结合相关条款、行为的性质和目的、习惯以及诚信原则,确定行为人的真实意思。

第三节 民事法律行为的效力

第一百四十三条 具备下列条件的民事法律行为有效:

(一)行为人具有相应的民事行为能力;

(二)意思表示真实;

(三)不违反法律、行政法规的强制性规定,不违背公序良俗。

第一百四十四条 无民事行为能力人实施的民事法律行为无效。

第一百四十五条 限制民事行为能力人实施的纯获利益的民事法律行为或者与其年龄、智力、精神健康状况相适应的民事法律行为有效;实施的其他民事法律行为经法定代理人同意或者追认后有效。

相对人可以催告法定代理人自收到通知之日起三十日内予以追认。法定代理人未作表示的,视为拒绝追认。民事法律行为被追认前,善意相对人有撤销的权利。撤销应当以通知的方式作出。

第一百四十六条 行为人与相对人以虚假的意思表示实施的民事法律行为无效。

以虚假的意思表示隐藏的民事法律行为的效力,依照有关法律规定处理。

第一百四十七条 基于重大误解实施的民事法律行为,行为人有权请求人民法院或者仲裁机构予以撤销。

第一百四十八条 一方以欺诈手段,使对方在违背真实意思的情况下实施的民事法律行为,受欺诈方有权请求人民法院或者仲裁机构予以撤销。

第一百四十九条 第三人实施欺诈行为,使一方在违背真实意思的情况下实施的民事法律行为,对方知道或者应当知道该欺诈行为的,受欺诈方有权请求人民法院或者仲裁机构予以撤销。

第一百五十条 一方或者第三人以胁迫手段,使对方在违背真实意思的情况下实施的民事法律行为,受胁迫方有权请求人民法院或者仲裁机构予以撤销。

第一百五十一条 一方利用对方处于危困状态、缺乏判断能力等情形,致使民事法律行为成立时显失公平的,受损害方有权请求人民法院或者仲裁机构予以撤销。

第一百五十二条 有下列情形之一的,撤销权消灭:

(一)当事人自知道或者应当知道撤销事由之日起一年内、重大误解的当事人自知道或者应当知道撤销事由之日起九十日内没有行使撤销权;

(二)当事人受胁迫,自胁迫行为终止之日起一年内没有行使撤销权;

(三)当事人知道撤销事由后明确表示或者以自己的行为表明放弃撤销权。

当事人自民事法律行为发生之日起五年内没有行使撤销权的,撤销权消灭。

第一百五十三条 违反法律、行政法规的强制性规定的民事法律行为无效。但是,该强制性规定不导致该民事法律行为无效的除外。

违背公序良俗的民事法律行为无效。

第一百五十四条 行为人与相对人恶意串通，损害他人合法权益的民事法律行为无效。

第一百五十五条 无效的或者被撤销的民事法律行为自始没有法律约束力。

第一百五十六条 民事法律行为部分无效，不影响其他部分效力的，其他部分仍然有效。

第一百五十七条 民事法律行为无效、被撤销或者确定不发生效力后，行为人因该行为取得的财产，应当予以返还；不能返还或者没有必要返还的，应当折价补偿。有过错的一方应当赔偿对方由此所受到的损失；各方都有过错的，应当各自承担相应的责任。法律另有规定的，依照其规定。

第四节 民事法律行为的附条件和附期限

第一百五十八条 民事法律行为可以附条件，但是根据其性质不得附条件的除外。附生效条件的民事法律行为，自条件成就时生效。附解除条件的民事法律行为，自条件成就时失效。

第一百五十九条 附条件的民事法律行为，当事人为自己的利益不正当地阻止条件成就的，视为条件已经成就；不正当地促成条件成就的，视为条件不成就。

第一百六十条 民事法律行为可以附期限，但是根据其性质不得附期限的除外。附生效期限的民事法律行为，自期限届至时生效。附终止期限的民事法律行为，自期限届满时失效。

第七章 代 理

第一节 一般规定

第一百六十一条 民事主体可以通过代理人实施民事法律行为。

依照法律规定、当事人约定或者民事法律行为的性质，应当由本人亲自实施的民事法律行为,不得代理。

第一百六十二条 代理人在代理权限内,以被代理人名义实施的民事法律行为,对被代理人发生效力。

第一百六十三条 代理包括委托代理和法定代理。

委托代理人按照被代理人的委托行使代理权。法定代理人依照法律的规定行使代理权。

第一百六十四条 代理人不履行或者不完全履行职责,造成被代理人损害的,应当承担民事责任。

代理人和相对人恶意串通,损害被代理人合法权益的,代理人和相对人应当承担连带责任。

第二节 委托代理

第一百六十五条 委托代理授权采用书面形式的,授权委托书应当载明代理人的姓名或者名称、代理事项、权限和期限,并由被代理人签名或者盖章。

第一百六十六条 数人为同一代理事项的代理人的,应当共同行使代理权,但是当事人另有约定的除外。

第一百六十七条 代理人知道或者应当知道代理事项违法仍然实施代理行为,或者被代理人知道或者应当知道代理人的代理行为违法未作反对表示的,被代理人和代理人应当承担连带责任。

第一百六十八条 代理人不得以被代理人的名义与自己实施民事法律行为,但是被代理人同意或者追认的除外。

代理人不得以被代理人的名义与自己同时代理的其他人实施民事法律行为,但是被代理的双方同意或者追认的除外。

第一百六十九条 代理人需要转委托第三人代理的,应当取得被代理人的同意或者追认。

转委托代理经被代理人同意或者追认的,被代理人可以就代理事务直接指示转委托的第三人,代理人仅就第三人的选任以及对第三人的指示承担责任。

转委托代理未经被代理人同意或者追认的，代理人应当对转委托的第三人的行为承担责任；但是，在紧急情况下代理人为了维护被代理人的利益需要转委托第三人代理的除外。

第一百七十条　执行法人或者非法人组织工作任务的人员，就其职权范围内的事项，以法人或者非法人组织的名义实施的民事法律行为，对法人或者非法人组织发生效力。

法人或者非法人组织对执行其工作任务的人员职权范围的限制，不得对抗善意相对人。

第一百七十一条　行为人没有代理权、超越代理权或者代理权终止后，仍然实施代理行为，未经被代理人追认的，对被代理人不发生效力。

相对人可以催告被代理人自收到通知之日起三十日内予以追认。被代理人未作表示的，视为拒绝追认。行为人实施的行为被追认前，善意相对人有撤销的权利。撤销应当以通知的方式作出。

行为人实施的行为未被追认的，善意相对人有权请求行为人履行债务或者就其受到的损害请求行为人赔偿。但是，赔偿的范围不得超过被代理人追认时相对人所能获得的利益。

相对人知道或者应当知道行为人无权代理的，相对人和行为人按照各自的过错承担责任。

第一百七十二条　行为人没有代理权、超越代理权或者代理权终止后，仍然实施代理行为，相对人有理由相信行为人有代理权的，代理行为有效。

第三节　代理终止

第一百七十三条　有下列情形之一的，委托代理终止：

（一）代理期限届满或者代理事务完成；

（二）被代理人取消委托或者代理人辞去委托；

（三）代理人丧失民事行为能力；

(四)代理人或者被代理人死亡;

(五)作为代理人或者被代理人的法人、非法人组织终止。

第一百七十四条 被代理人死亡后,有下列情形之一的,委托代理人实施的代理行为有效:

(一)代理人不知道且不应当知道被代理人死亡;

(二)被代理人的继承人予以承认;

(三)授权中明确代理权在代理事务完成时终止;

(四)被代理人死亡前已经实施,为了被代理人的继承人的利益继续代理。

作为被代理人的法人、非法人组织终止的,参照适用前款规定。

第一百七十五条 有下列情形之一的,法定代理终止:

(一)被代理人取得或者恢复完全民事行为能力;

(二)代理人丧失民事行为能力;

(三)代理人或者被代理人死亡;

(四)法律规定的其他情形。

第八章 民事责任

第一百七十六条 民事主体依照法律规定或者按照当事人约定,履行民事义务,承担民事责任。

第一百七十七条 二人以上依法承担按份责任,能够确定责任大小的,各自承担相应的责任;难以确定责任大小的,平均承担责任。

第一百七十八条 二人以上依法承担连带责任的,权利人有权请求部分或者全部连带责任人承担责任。

连带责任人的责任份额根据各自责任大小确定;难以确定责任大小的,平均承担责任。实际承担责任超过自己责任份额的连带责任人,有权向其他连带责任人追偿。

连带责任,由法律规定或者当事人约定。

第一百七十九条 承担民事责任的方式主要有:

（一）停止侵害；
（二）排除妨碍；
（三）消除危险；
（四）返还财产；
（五）恢复原状；
（六）修理、重作、更换；
（七）继续履行；
（八）赔偿损失；
（九）支付违约金；
（十）消除影响、恢复名誉；
（十一）赔礼道歉。

法律规定惩罚性赔偿的，依照其规定。

本条规定的承担民事责任的方式，可以单独适用，也可以合并适用。

第一百八十条 因不可抗力不能履行民事义务的，不承担民事责任。法律另有规定的，依照其规定。

不可抗力是不能预见、不能避免且不能克服的客观情况。

第一百八十一条 因正当防卫造成损害的，不承担民事责任。

正当防卫超过必要的限度，造成不应有的损害的，正当防卫人应当承担适当的民事责任。

第一百八十二条 因紧急避险造成损害的，由引起险情发生的人承担民事责任。

危险由自然原因引起的，紧急避险人不承担民事责任，可以给予适当补偿。

紧急避险采取措施不当或者超过必要的限度，造成不应有的损害的，紧急避险人应当承担适当的民事责任。

第一百八十三条 因保护他人民事权益使自己受到损害的，由侵权人承担民事责任，受益人可以给予适当补偿。没有侵权人、侵权人逃逸或者无力承担民事责任，受害人请求补偿的，受益人应当给予适当补偿。

第一百八十四条 因自愿实施紧急救助行为造成受助人损害的,救助人不承担民事责任。

第一百八十五条 侵害英雄烈士等的姓名、肖像、名誉、荣誉,损害社会公共利益的,应当承担民事责任。

第一百八十六条 因当事人一方的违约行为,损害对方人身权益、财产权益的,受损害方有权选择请求其承担违约责任或者侵权责任。

第一百八十七条 民事主体因同一行为应当承担民事责任、行政责任和刑事责任的,承担行政责任或者刑事责任不影响承担民事责任;民事主体的财产不足以支付的,优先用于承担民事责任。

第九章 诉讼时效

第一百八十八条 向人民法院请求保护民事权利的诉讼时效期间为三年。法律另有规定的,依照其规定。

诉讼时效期间自权利人知道或者应当知道权利受到损害以及义务人之日起计算。法律另有规定的,依照其规定。但是,自权利受到损害之日起超过二十年的,人民法院不予保护,有特殊情况的,人民法院可以根据权利人的申请决定延长。

第一百八十九条 当事人约定同一债务分期履行的,诉讼时效期间自最后一期履行期限届满之日起计算。

第一百九十条 无民事行为能力人或者限制民事行为能力人对其法定代理人的请求权的诉讼时效期间,自该法定代理终止之日起计算。

第一百九十一条 未成年人遭受性侵害的损害赔偿请求权的诉讼时效期间,自受害人年满十八周岁之日起计算。

第一百九十二条 诉讼时效期间届满的,义务人可以提出不履行义务的抗辩。

诉讼时效期间届满后,义务人同意履行的,不得以诉讼时效期间届满为由抗辩;义务人已经自愿履行的,不得请求返还。

第一百九十三条 人民法院不得主动适用诉讼时效的规定。

第一百九十四条　在诉讼时效期间的最后六个月内,因下列障碍,不能行使请求权的,诉讼时效中止:

(一)不可抗力;

(二)无民事行为能力人或者限制民事行为能力人没有法定代理人,或者法定代理人死亡、丧失民事行为能力、丧失代理权;

(三)继承开始后未确定继承人或者遗产管理人;

(四)权利人被义务人或者其他人控制;

(五)其他导致权利人不能行使请求权的障碍。

自中止时效的原因消除之日起满六个月,诉讼时效期间届满。

第一百九十五条　有下列情形之一的,诉讼时效中断,从中断、有关程序终结时起,诉讼时效期间重新计算:

(一)权利人向义务人提出履行请求;

(二)义务人同意履行义务;

(三)权利人提起诉讼或者申请仲裁;

(四)与提起诉讼或者申请仲裁具有同等效力的其他情形。

第一百九十六条　下列请求权不适用诉讼时效的规定:

(一)请求停止侵害、排除妨碍、消除危险;

(二)不动产物权和登记的动产物权的权利人请求返还财产;

(三)请求支付抚养费、赡养费或者扶养费;

(四)依法不适用诉讼时效的其他请求权。

第一百九十七条　诉讼时效的期间、计算方法以及中止、中断的事由由法律规定,当事人约定无效。

当事人对诉讼时效利益的预先放弃无效。

第一百九十八条　法律对仲裁时效有规定的,依照其规定;没有规定的,适用诉讼时效的规定。

第一百九十九条　法律规定或者当事人约定的撤销权、解除权等权利的存续期间,除法律另有规定外,自权利人知道或者应当知道权利产生之日起计算,不适用有关诉讼时效中止、中断和延长的规定。存续期间届满,撤销权、解除权等权利消灭。

第十章　期间计算

第二百条　民法所称的期间按照公历年、月、日、小时计算。

第二百零一条　按照年、月、日计算期间的,开始的当日不计入,自下一日开始计算。

按照小时计算期间的,自法律规定或者当事人约定的时间开始计算。

第二百零二条　按照年、月计算期间的,到期月的对应日为期间的最后一日;没有对应日的,月末日为期间的最后一日。

第二百零三条　期间的最后一日是法定休假日的,以法定休假日结束的次日为期间的最后一日。

期间的最后一日的截止时间为二十四时;有业务时间的,停止业务活动的时间为截止时间。

第二百零四条　期间的计算方法依照本法的规定,但是法律另有规定或者当事人另有约定的除外。

第二编　物　　权

第一分编　通　　则

第一章　一般规定

第二百零五条　本编调整因物的归属和利用产生的民事关系。

第二百零六条　国家坚持和完善公有制为主体、多种所有制经济共同发展，按劳分配为主体、多种分配方式并存，社会主义市场经济体制等社会主义基本经济制度。

国家巩固和发展公有制经济，鼓励、支持和引导非公有制经济的发展。

国家实行社会主义市场经济，保障一切市场主体的平等法律地位和发展权利。

第二百零七条　国家、集体、私人的物权和其他权利人的物权受法律平等保护，任何组织或者个人不得侵犯。

第二百零八条　不动产物权的设立、变更、转让和消灭，应当依照法律规定登记。动产物权的设立和转让，应当依照法律规定交付。

第二章　物权的设立、变更、转让和消灭

第一节　不动产登记

第二百零九条　不动产物权的设立、变更、转让和消灭，经依法登记，发生效力；未经登记，不发生效力，但是法律另有规定的除外。

依法属于国家所有的自然资源，所有权可以不登记。

第二百一十条　不动产登记，由不动产所在地的登记机构办理。

国家对不动产实行统一登记制度。统一登记的范围、登记机构和登记

办法,由法律、行政法规规定。

第二百一十一条 当事人申请登记,应当根据不同登记事项提供权属证明和不动产界址、面积等必要材料。

第二百一十二条 登记机构应当履行下列职责:

(一)查验申请人提供的权属证明和其他必要材料;

(二)就有关登记事项询问申请人;

(三)如实、及时登记有关事项;

(四)法律、行政法规规定的其他职责。

申请登记的不动产的有关情况需要进一步证明的,登记机构可以要求申请人补充材料,必要时可以实地查看。

第二百一十三条 登记机构不得有下列行为:

(一)要求对不动产进行评估;

(二)以年检等名义进行重复登记;

(三)超出登记职责范围的其他行为。

第二百一十四条 不动产物权的设立、变更、转让和消灭,依照法律规定应当登记的,自记载于不动产登记簿时发生效力。

第二百一十五条 当事人之间订立有关设立、变更、转让和消灭不动产物权的合同,除法律另有规定或者当事人另有约定外,自合同成立时生效;未办理物权登记的,不影响合同效力。

第二百一十六条 不动产登记簿是物权归属和内容的根据。

不动产登记簿由登记机构管理。

第二百一十七条 不动产权属证书是权利人享有该不动产物权的证明。不动产权属证书记载的事项,应当与不动产登记簿一致;记载不一致的,除有证据证明不动产登记簿确有错误外,以不动产登记簿为准。

第二百一十八条 权利人、利害关系人可以申请查询、复制不动产登记资料,登记机构应当提供。

第二百一十九条 利害关系人不得公开、非法使用权利人的不动产登记资料。

第二百二十条 权利人、利害关系人认为不动产登记簿记载的事项错误的,可以申请更正登记。不动产登记簿记载的权利人书面同意更正或者有证据证明登记确有错误的,登记机构应当予以更正。

不动产登记簿记载的权利人不同意更正的,利害关系人可以申请异议登记。登记机构予以异议登记,申请人自异议登记之日起十五日内不提起诉讼的,异议登记失效。异议登记不当,造成权利人损害的,权利人可以向申请人请求损害赔偿。

第二百二十一条 当事人签订买卖房屋的协议或者签订其他不动产物权的协议,为保障将来实现物权,按照约定可以向登记机构申请预告登记。预告登记后,未经预告登记的权利人同意,处分该不动产的,不发生物权效力。

预告登记后,债权消灭或者自能够进行不动产登记之日起九十日内未申请登记的,预告登记失效。

第二百二十二条 当事人提供虚假材料申请登记,造成他人损害的,应当承担赔偿责任。

因登记错误,造成他人损害的,登记机构应当承担赔偿责任。登记机构赔偿后,可以向造成登记错误的人追偿。

第二百二十三条 不动产登记费按件收取,不得按照不动产的面积、体积或者价款的比例收取。

第二节 动产交付

第二百二十四条 动产物权的设立和转让,自交付时发生效力,但是法律另有规定的除外。

第二百二十五条 船舶、航空器和机动车等的物权的设立、变更、转让和消灭,未经登记,不得对抗善意第三人。

第二百二十六条 动产物权设立和转让前,权利人已经占有该动产的,物权自民事法律行为生效时发生效力。

第二百二十七条 动产物权设立和转让前,第三人占有该动产的,负有交付义务的人可以通过转让请求第三人返还原物的权利代替交付。

第二百二十八条 动产物权转让时,当事人又约定由出让人继续占有该动产的,物权自该约定生效时发生效力。

第三节 其他规定

第二百二十九条 因人民法院、仲裁机构的法律文书或者人民政府的征收决定等,导致物权设立、变更、转让或者消灭的,自法律文书或者征收决定等生效时发生效力。

第二百三十条 因继承取得物权的,自继承开始时发生效力。

第二百三十一条 因合法建造、拆除房屋等事实行为设立或者消灭物权的,自事实行为成就时发生效力。

第二百三十二条 处分依照本节规定享有的不动产物权,依照法律规定需要办理登记的,未经登记,不发生物权效力。

第三章 物权的保护

第二百三十三条 物权受到侵害的,权利人可以通过和解、调解、仲裁、诉讼等途径解决。

第二百三十四条 因物权的归属、内容发生争议的,利害关系人可以请求确认权利。

第二百三十五条 无权占有不动产或者动产的,权利人可以请求返还原物。

第二百三十六条 妨害物权或者可能妨害物权的,权利人可以请求排除妨害或者消除危险。

第二百三十七条 造成不动产或者动产毁损的,权利人可以依法请求修理、重作、更换或者恢复原状。

第二百三十八条 侵害物权,造成权利人损害的,权利人可以依法请求损害赔偿,也可以依法请求承担其他民事责任。

第二百三十九条 本章规定的物权保护方式,可以单独适用,也可以根据权利被侵害的情形合并适用。

第二分编 所 有 权

第四章 一 般 规 定

第二百四十条 所有权人对自己的不动产或者动产,依法享有占有、使用、收益和处分的权利。

第二百四十一条 所有权人有权在自己的不动产或者动产上设立用益物权和担保物权。用益物权人、担保物权人行使权利,不得损害所有权人的权益。

第二百四十二条 法律规定专属于国家所有的不动产和动产,任何组织或者个人不能取得所有权。

第二百四十三条 为了公共利益的需要,依照法律规定的权限和程序可以征收集体所有的土地和组织、个人的房屋以及其他不动产。

征收集体所有的土地,应当依法及时足额支付土地补偿费、安置补助费以及农村村民住宅、其他地上附着物和青苗等的补偿费用,并安排被征地农民的社会保障费用,保障被征地农民的生活,维护被征地农民的合法权益。

征收组织、个人的房屋以及其他不动产,应当依法给予征收补偿,维护被征收人的合法权益;征收个人住宅的,还应当保障被征收人的居住条件。

任何组织或者个人不得贪污、挪用、私分、截留、拖欠征收补偿费等费用。

第二百四十四条 国家对耕地实行特殊保护,严格限制农用地转为建设用地,控制建设用地总量。不得违反法律规定的权限和程序征收集体所有的土地。

第二百四十五条 因抢险救灾、疫情防控等紧急需要,依照法律规定的权限和程序可以征用组织、个人的不动产或者动产。被征用的不动产或者动产使用后,应当返还被征用人。组织、个人的不动产或者动产被征用或者征用后毁损、灭失的,应当给予补偿。

第五章 国家所有权和集体所有权、私人所有权

第二百四十六条 法律规定属于国家所有的财产,属于国家所有即全民所有。

国有财产由国务院代表国家行使所有权。法律另有规定的,依照其规定。

第二百四十七条 矿藏、水流、海域属于国家所有。

第二百四十八条 无居民海岛属于国家所有,国务院代表国家行使无居民海岛所有权。

第二百四十九条 城市的土地,属于国家所有。法律规定属于国家所有的农村和城市郊区的土地,属于国家所有。

第二百五十条 森林、山岭、草原、荒地、滩涂等自然资源,属于国家所有,但是法律规定属于集体所有的除外。

第二百五十一条 法律规定属于国家所有的野生动植物资源,属于国家所有。

第二百五十二条 无线电频谱资源属于国家所有。

第二百五十三条 法律规定属于国家所有的文物,属于国家所有。

第二百五十四条 国防资产属于国家所有。

铁路、公路、电力设施、电信设施和油气管道等基础设施,依照法律规定为国家所有的,属于国家所有。

第二百五十五条 国家机关对其直接支配的不动产和动产,享有占有、使用以及依照法律和国务院的有关规定处分的权利。

第二百五十六条 国家举办的事业单位对其直接支配的不动产和动产,享有占有、使用以及依照法律和国务院的有关规定收益、处分的权利。

第二百五十七条 国家出资的企业,由国务院、地方人民政府依照法律、行政法规规定分别代表国家履行出资人职责,享有出资人权益。

第二百五十八条 国家所有的财产受法律保护,禁止任何组织或者个人侵占、哄抢、私分、截留、破坏。

第二百五十九条 履行国有财产管理、监督职责的机构及其工作人员，应当依法加强对国有财产的管理、监督，促进国有财产保值增值，防止国有财产损失；滥用职权，玩忽职守，造成国有财产损失的，应当依法承担法律责任。

违反国有财产管理规定，在企业改制、合并分立、关联交易等过程中，低价转让、合谋私分、擅自担保或者以其他方式造成国有财产损失的，应当依法承担法律责任。

第二百六十条 集体所有的不动产和动产包括：

（一）法律规定属于集体所有的土地和森林、山岭、草原、荒地、滩涂；

（二）集体所有的建筑物、生产设施、农田水利设施；

（三）集体所有的教育、科学、文化、卫生、体育等设施；

（四）集体所有的其他不动产和动产。

第二百六十一条 农民集体所有的不动产和动产，属于本集体成员集体所有。

下列事项应当依照法定程序经本集体成员决定：

（一）土地承包方案以及将土地发包给本集体以外的组织或者个人承包；

（二）个别土地承包经营权人之间承包地的调整；

（三）土地补偿费等费用的使用、分配办法；

（四）集体出资的企业的所有权变动等事项；

（五）法律规定的其他事项。

第二百六十二条 对于集体所有的土地和森林、山岭、草原、荒地、滩涂等，依照下列规定行使所有权：

（一）属于村农民集体所有的，由村集体经济组织或者村民委员会依法代表集体行使所有权；

（二）分别属于村内两个以上农民集体所有的，由村内各该集体经济组织或者村民小组依法代表集体行使所有权；

（三）属于乡镇农民集体所有的，由乡镇集体经济组织代表集体行使所有权。

第二百六十三条 城镇集体所有的不动产和动产,依照法律、行政法规的规定由本集体享有占有、使用、收益和处分的权利。

第二百六十四条 农村集体经济组织或者村民委员会、村民小组应当依照法律、行政法规以及章程、村规民约向本集体成员公布集体财产的状况。集体成员有权查阅、复制相关资料。

第二百六十五条 集体所有的财产受法律保护,禁止任何组织或者个人侵占、哄抢、私分、破坏。

农村集体经济组织、村民委员会或者其负责人作出的决定侵害集体成员合法权益的,受侵害的集体成员可以请求人民法院予以撤销。

第二百六十六条 私人对其合法的收入、房屋、生活用品、生产工具、原材料等不动产和动产享有所有权。

第二百六十七条 私人的合法财产受法律保护,禁止任何组织或者个人侵占、哄抢、破坏。

第二百六十八条 国家、集体和私人依法可以出资设立有限责任公司、股份有限公司或者其他企业。国家、集体和私人所有的不动产或者动产投到企业的,由出资人按照约定或者出资比例享有资产收益、重大决策以及选择经营管理者等权利并履行义务。

第二百六十九条 营利法人对其不动产和动产依照法律、行政法规以及章程享有占有、使用、收益和处分的权利。

营利法人以外的法人,对其不动产和动产的权利,适用有关法律、行政法规以及章程的规定。

第二百七十条 社会团体法人、捐助法人依法所有的不动产和动产,受法律保护。

第六章 业主的建筑物区分所有权

第二百七十一条 业主对建筑物内的住宅、经营性用房等专有部分享有所有权,对专有部分以外的共有部分享有共有和共同管理的权利。

第二百七十二条 业主对其建筑物专有部分享有占有、使用、收益和处分的权利。业主行使权利不得危及建筑物的安全,不得损害其他业主的合法权益。

第二百七十三条 业主对建筑物专有部分以外的共有部分,享有权利,承担义务;不得以放弃权利为由不履行义务。

业主转让建筑物内的住宅、经营性用房,其对共有部分享有的共有和共同管理的权利一并转让。

第二百七十四条 建筑区划内的道路,属于业主共有,但是属于城镇公共道路的除外。建筑区划内的绿地,属于业主共有,但是属于城镇公共绿地或者明示属于个人的除外。建筑区划内的其他公共场所、公用设施和物业服务用房,属于业主共有。

第二百七十五条 建筑区划内,规划用于停放汽车的车位、车库的归属,由当事人通过出售、附赠或者出租等方式约定。

占用业主共有的道路或者其他场地用于停放汽车的车位,属于业主共有。

第二百七十六条 建筑区划内,规划用于停放汽车的车位、车库应当首先满足业主的需要。

第二百七十七条 业主可以设立业主大会,选举业主委员会。业主大会、业主委员会成立的具体条件和程序,依照法律、法规的规定。

地方人民政府有关部门、居民委员会应当对设立业主大会和选举业主委员会给予指导和协助。

第二百七十八条 下列事项由业主共同决定:

(一)制定和修改业主大会议事规则;

(二)制定和修改管理规约;

(三)选举业主委员会或者更换业主委员会成员;

(四)选聘和解聘物业服务企业或者其他管理人;

(五)使用建筑物及其附属设施的维修资金;

(六)筹集建筑物及其附属设施的维修资金;

(七)改建、重建建筑物及其附属设施;

(八)改变共有部分的用途或者利用共有部分从事经营活动;

(九)有关共有和共同管理权利的其他重大事项。

业主共同决定事项,应当由专有部分面积占比三分之二以上的业主且人数占比三分之二以上的业主参与表决。决定前款第六项至第八项规定的事项,应当经参与表决专有部分面积四分之三以上的业主且参与表决人数四分之三以上的业主同意。决定前款其他事项,应当经参与表决专有部分面积过半数的业主且参与表决人数过半数的业主同意。

第二百七十九条 业主不得违反法律、法规以及管理规约,将住宅改变为经营性用房。业主将住宅改变为经营性用房的,除遵守法律、法规以及管理规约外,应当经有利害关系的业主一致同意。

第二百八十条 业主大会或者业主委员会的决定,对业主具有法律约束力。

业主大会或者业主委员会作出的决定侵害业主合法权益的,受侵害的业主可以请求人民法院予以撤销。

第二百八十一条 建筑物及其附属设施的维修资金,属于业主共有。经业主共同决定,可以用于电梯、屋顶、外墙、无障碍设施等共有部分的维修、更新和改造。建筑物及其附属设施的维修资金的筹集、使用情况应当定期公布。

紧急情况下需要维修建筑物及其附属设施的,业主大会或者业主委员会可以依法申请使用建筑物及其附属设施的维修资金。

第二百八十二条 建设单位、物业服务企业或者其他管理人等利用业主的共有部分产生的收入,在扣除合理成本之后,属于业主共有。

第二百八十三条 建筑物及其附属设施的费用分摊、收益分配等事项,有约定的,按照约定;没有约定或者约定不明确的,按照业主专有部分面积所占比例确定。

第二百八十四条 业主可以自行管理建筑物及其附属设施,也可以委托物业服务企业或者其他管理人管理。

对建设单位聘请的物业服务企业或者其他管理人，业主有权依法更换。

第二百八十五条　物业服务企业或者其他管理人根据业主的委托，依照本法第三编有关物业服务合同的规定管理建筑区划内的建筑物及其附属设施，接受业主的监督，并及时答复业主对物业服务情况提出的询问。

物业服务企业或者其他管理人应当执行政府依法实施的应急处置措施和其他管理措施，积极配合开展相关工作。

第二百八十六条　业主应当遵守法律、法规以及管理规约，相关行为应当符合节约资源、保护生态环境的要求。对于物业服务企业或者其他管理人执行政府依法实施的应急处置措施和其他管理措施，业主应当依法予以配合。

业主大会或者业主委员会，对任意弃置垃圾、排放污染物或者噪声、违反规定饲养动物、违章搭建、侵占通道、拒付物业费等损害他人合法权益的行为，有权依照法律、法规以及管理规约，请求行为人停止侵害、排除妨碍、消除危险、恢复原状、赔偿损失。

业主或者其他行为人拒不履行相关义务的，有关当事人可以向有关行政主管部门报告或者投诉，有关行政主管部门应当依法处理。

第二百八十七条　业主对建设单位、物业服务企业或者其他管理人以及其他业主侵害自己合法权益的行为，有权请求其承担民事责任。

第七章　相邻关系

第二百八十八条　不动产的相邻权利人应当按照有利生产、方便生活、团结互助、公平合理的原则，正确处理相邻关系。

第二百八十九条　法律、法规对处理相邻关系有规定的，依照其规定；法律、法规没有规定的，可以按照当地习惯。

第二百九十条　不动产权利人应当为相邻权利人用水、排水提供必要的便利。

对自然流水的利用，应当在不动产的相邻权利人之间合理分配。对自然流水的排放，应当尊重自然流向。

第二百九十一条 不动产权利人对相邻权利人因通行等必须利用其土地的,应当提供必要的便利。

第二百九十二条 不动产权利人因建造、修缮建筑物以及铺设电线、电缆、水管、暖气和燃气管线等必须利用相邻土地、建筑物的,该土地、建筑物的权利人应当提供必要的便利。

第二百九十三条 建造建筑物,不得违反国家有关工程建设标准,不得妨碍相邻建筑物的通风、采光和日照。

第二百九十四条 不动产权利人不得违反国家规定弃置固体废物,排放大气污染物、水污染物、土壤污染物、噪声、光辐射、电磁辐射等有害物质。

第二百九十五条 不动产权利人挖掘土地、建造建筑物、铺设管线以及安装设备等,不得危及相邻不动产的安全。

第二百九十六条 不动产权利人因用水、排水、通行、铺设管线等利用相邻不动产的,应当尽量避免对相邻的不动产权利人造成损害。

第八章 共　　有

第二百九十七条 不动产或者动产可以由两个以上组织、个人共有。共有包括按份共有和共同共有。

第二百九十八条 按份共有人对共有的不动产或者动产按照其份额享有所有权。

第二百九十九条 共同共有人对共有的不动产或者动产共同享有所有权。

第三百条 共有人按照约定管理共有的不动产或者动产;没有约定或者约定不明确的,各共有人都有管理的权利和义务。

第三百零一条 处分共有的不动产或者动产以及对共有的不动产或者动产作重大修缮、变更性质或者用途的,应当经占份额三分之二以上的按份共有人或者全体共同共有人同意,但是共有人之间另有约定的除外。

第三百零二条 共有人对共有物的管理费用以及其他负担,有约定的,按照其约定;没有约定或者约定不明确的,按份共有人按照其份额负担,共同共有人共同负担。

第三百零三条 共有人约定不得分割共有的不动产或者动产，以维持共有关系的，应当按照约定，但是共有人有重大理由需要分割的，可以请求分割；没有约定或者约定不明确的，按份共有人可以随时请求分割，共同共有人在共有的基础丧失或者有重大理由需要分割时可以请求分割。因分割造成其他共有人损害的，应当给予赔偿。

第三百零四条 共有人可以协商确定分割方式。达不成协议，共有的不动产或者动产可以分割且不会因分割减损价值的，应当对实物予以分割；难以分割或者因分割会减损价值的，应当对折价或者拍卖、变卖取得的价款予以分割。

共有人分割所得的不动产或者动产有瑕疵的，其他共有人应当分担损失。

第三百零五条 按份共有人可以转让其享有的共有的不动产或者动产份额。其他共有人在同等条件下享有优先购买的权利。

第三百零六条 按份共有人转让其享有的共有的不动产或者动产份额的，应当将转让条件及时通知其他共有人。其他共有人应当在合理期限内行使优先购买权。

两个以上其他共有人主张行使优先购买权的，协商确定各自的购买比例；协商不成的，按照转让时各自的共有份额比例行使优先购买权。

第三百零七条 因共有的不动产或者动产产生的债权债务，在对外关系上，共有人享有连带债权、承担连带债务，但是法律另有规定或者第三人知道共有人不具有连带债权债务关系的除外；在共有人内部关系上，除共有人另有约定外，按份共有人按照份额享有债权、承担债务，共同共有人共同享有债权、承担债务。偿还债务超过自己应当承担份额的按份共有人，有权向其他共有人追偿。

第三百零八条 共有人对共有的不动产或者动产没有约定为按份共有或者共同共有，或者约定不明确的，除共有人具有家庭关系等外，视为按份共有。

第三百零九条 按份共有人对共有的不动产或者动产享有的份额，没有约定或者约定不明确的,按照出资额确定;不能确定出资额的,视为等额享有。

第三百一十条 两个以上组织、个人共同享有用益物权、担保物权的,参照适用本章的有关规定。

第九章 所有权取得的特别规定

第三百一十一条 无处分权人将不动产或者动产转让给受让人的,所有权人有权追回;除法律另有规定外,符合下列情形的,受让人取得该不动产或者动产的所有权:

(一)受让人受让该不动产或者动产时是善意;

(二)以合理的价格转让;

(三)转让的不动产或者动产依照法律规定应当登记的已经登记,不需要登记的已经交付给受让人。

受让人依据前款规定取得不动产或者动产的所有权的,原所有权人有权向无处分权人请求损害赔偿。

当事人善意取得其他物权的,参照适用前两款规定。

第三百一十二条 所有权人或者其他权利人有权追回遗失物。该遗失物通过转让被他人占有的,权利人有权向无处分权人请求损害赔偿,或者自知道或者应当知道受让人之日起二年内向受让人请求返还原物;但是,受让人通过拍卖或者向具有经营资格的经营者购得该遗失物的,权利人请求返还原物时应当支付受让人所付的费用。权利人向受让人支付所付费用后,有权向无处分权人追偿。

第三百一十三条 善意受让人取得动产后,该动产上的原有权利消灭。但是,善意受让人在受让时知道或者应当知道该权利的除外。

第三百一十四条 拾得遗失物,应当返还权利人。拾得人应当及时通知权利人领取,或者送交公安等有关部门。

第三百一十五条 有关部门收到遗失物,知道权利人的,应当及时通知其领取;不知道的,应当及时发布招领公告。

第三百一十六条　拾得人在遗失物送交有关部门前，有关部门在遗失物被领取前，应当妥善保管遗失物。因故意或者重大过失致使遗失物毁损、灭失的，应当承担民事责任。

第三百一十七条　权利人领取遗失物时，应当向拾得人或者有关部门支付保管遗失物等支出的必要费用。

权利人悬赏寻找遗失物的，领取遗失物时应当按照承诺履行义务。

拾得人侵占遗失物的，无权请求保管遗失物等支出的费用，也无权请求权利人按照承诺履行义务。

第三百一十八条　遗失物自发布招领公告之日起一年内无人认领的，归国家所有。

第三百一十九条　拾得漂流物、发现埋藏物或者隐藏物的，参照适用拾得遗失物的有关规定。法律另有规定的，依照其规定。

第三百二十条　主物转让的，从物随主物转让，但是当事人另有约定的除外。

第三百二十一条　天然孳息，由所有权人取得；既有所有权人又有用益物权人的，由用益物权人取得。当事人另有约定的，按照其约定。

法定孳息，当事人有约定的，按照约定取得；没有约定或者约定不明确的，按照交易习惯取得。

第三百二十二条　因加工、附合、混合而产生的物的归属，有约定的，按照约定；没有约定或者约定不明确的，依照法律规定；法律没有规定的，按照充分发挥物的效用以及保护无过错当事人的原则确定。因一方当事人的过错或者确定物的归属造成另一方当事人损害的，应当给予赔偿或者补偿。

第三分编　用益物权

第十章　一般规定

第三百二十三条　用益物权人对他人所有的不动产或者动产，依法享有占有、使用和收益的权利。

第三百二十四条 国家所有或者国家所有由集体使用以及法律规定属于集体所有的自然资源,组织、个人依法可以占有、使用和收益。

第三百二十五条 国家实行自然资源有偿使用制度,但是法律另有规定的除外。

第三百二十六条 用益物权人行使权利,应当遵守法律有关保护和合理开发利用资源、保护生态环境的规定。所有权人不得干涉用益物权人行使权利。

第三百二十七条 因不动产或者动产被征收、征用致使用益物权消灭或者影响用益物权行使的,用益物权人有权依据本法第二百四十三条、第二百四十五条的规定获得相应补偿。

第三百二十八条 依法取得的海域使用权受法律保护。

第三百二十九条 依法取得的探矿权、采矿权、取水权和使用水域、滩涂从事养殖、捕捞的权利受法律保护。

第十一章　土地承包经营权

第三百三十条 农村集体经济组织实行家庭承包经营为基础、统分结合的双层经营体制。

农民集体所有和国家所有由农民集体使用的耕地、林地、草地以及其他用于农业的土地,依法实行土地承包经营制度。

第三百三十一条 土地承包经营权人依法对其承包经营的耕地、林地、草地等享有占有、使用和收益的权利,有权从事种植业、林业、畜牧业等农业生产。

第三百三十二条 耕地的承包期为三十年。草地的承包期为三十年至五十年。林地的承包期为三十年至七十年。

前款规定的承包期限届满,由土地承包经营权人依照农村土地承包的法律规定继续承包。

第三百三十三条 土地承包经营权自土地承包经营权合同生效时设立。

登记机构应当向土地承包经营权人发放土地承包经营权证、林权证等证书,并登记造册,确认土地承包经营权。

第三百三十四条 土地承包经营权人依照法律规定,有权将土地承包经营权互换、转让。未经依法批准,不得将承包地用于非农建设。

第三百三十五条 土地承包经营权互换、转让的,当事人可以向登记机构申请登记;未经登记,不得对抗善意第三人。

第三百三十六条 承包期内发包人不得调整承包地。

因自然灾害严重毁损承包地等特殊情形,需要适当调整承包的耕地和草地的,应当依照农村土地承包的法律规定办理。

第三百三十七条 承包期内发包人不得收回承包地。法律另有规定的,依照其规定。

第三百三十八条 承包地被征收的,土地承包经营权人有权依据本法第二百四十三条的规定获得相应补偿。

第三百三十九条 土地承包经营权人可以自主决定依法采取出租、入股或者其他方式向他人流转土地经营权。

第三百四十条 土地经营权人有权在合同约定的期限内占有农村土地,自主开展农业生产经营并取得收益。

第三百四十一条 流转期限为五年以上的土地经营权,自流转合同生效时设立。当事人可以向登记机构申请土地经营权登记;未经登记,不得对抗善意第三人。

第三百四十二条 通过招标、拍卖、公开协商等方式承包农村土地,经依法登记取得权属证书的,可以依法采取出租、入股、抵押或者其他方式流转土地经营权。

第三百四十三条 国家所有的农用地实行承包经营的,参照适用本编的有关规定。

第十二章 建设用地使用权

第三百四十四条 建设用地使用权人依法对国家所有的土地享有占

有、使用和收益的权利,有权利用该土地建造建筑物、构筑物及其附属设施。

第三百四十五条 建设用地使用权可以在土地的地表、地上或者地下分别设立。

第三百四十六条 设立建设用地使用权,应当符合节约资源、保护生态环境的要求,遵守法律、行政法规关于土地用途的规定,不得损害已经设立的用益物权。

第三百四十七条 设立建设用地使用权,可以采取出让或者划拨等方式。

工业、商业、旅游、娱乐和商品住宅等经营性用地以及同一土地有两个以上意向用地者的,应当采取招标、拍卖等公开竞价的方式出让。

严格限制以划拨方式设立建设用地使用权。

第三百四十八条 通过招标、拍卖、协议等出让方式设立建设用地使用权的,当事人应当采用书面形式订立建设用地使用权出让合同。

建设用地使用权出让合同一般包括下列条款:

(一)当事人的名称和住所;

(二)土地界址、面积等;

(三)建筑物、构筑物及其附属设施占用的空间;

(四)土地用途、规划条件;

(五)建设用地使用权期限;

(六)出让金等费用及其支付方式;

(七)解决争议的方法。

第三百四十九条 设立建设用地使用权的,应当向登记机构申请建设用地使用权登记。建设用地使用权自登记时设立。登记机构应当向建设用地使用权人发放权属证书。

第三百五十条 建设用地使用权人应当合理利用土地,不得改变土地用途;需要改变土地用途的,应当依法经有关行政主管部门批准。

第三百五十一条 建设用地使用权人应当依照法律规定以及合同约定支付出让金等费用。

第三百五十二条　建设用地使用权人建造的建筑物、构筑物及其附属设施的所有权属于建设用地使用权人，但是有相反证据证明的除外。

第三百五十三条　建设用地使用权人有权将建设用地使用权转让、互换、出资、赠与或者抵押，但是法律另有规定的除外。

第三百五十四条　建设用地使用权转让、互换、出资、赠与或者抵押的，当事人应当采用书面形式订立相应的合同。使用期限由当事人约定，但是不得超过建设用地使用权的剩余期限。

第三百五十五条　建设用地使用权转让、互换、出资或者赠与的，应当向登记机构申请变更登记。

第三百五十六条　建设用地使用权转让、互换、出资或者赠与的，附着于该土地上的建筑物、构筑物及其附属设施一并处分。

第三百五十七条　建筑物、构筑物及其附属设施转让、互换、出资或者赠与的，该建筑物、构筑物及其附属设施占用范围内的建设用地使用权一并处分。

第三百五十八条　建设用地使用权期限届满前，因公共利益需要提前收回该土地的，应当依据本法第二百四十三条的规定对该土地上的房屋以及其他不动产给予补偿，并退还相应的出让金。

第三百五十九条　住宅建设用地使用权期限届满的，自动续期。续期费用的缴纳或者减免，依照法律、行政法规的规定办理。

非住宅建设用地使用权期限届满后的续期，依照法律规定办理。该土地上的房屋以及其他不动产的归属，有约定的，按照约定；没有约定或者约定不明确的，依照法律、行政法规的规定办理。

第三百六十条　建设用地使用权消灭的，出让人应当及时办理注销登记。登记机构应当收回权属证书。

第三百六十一条　集体所有的土地作为建设用地的，应当依照土地管理的法律规定办理。

第十三章　宅基地使用权

第三百六十二条　宅基地使用权人依法对集体所有的土地享有占有和

使用的权利,有权依法利用该土地建造住宅及其附属设施。

第三百六十三条 宅基地使用权的取得、行使和转让,适用土地管理的法律和国家有关规定。

第三百六十四条 宅基地因自然灾害等原因灭失的,宅基地使用权消灭。对失去宅基地的村民,应当依法重新分配宅基地。

第三百六十五条 已经登记的宅基地使用权转让或者消灭的,应当及时办理变更登记或者注销登记。

第十四章　居　住　权

第三百六十六条 居住权人有权按照合同约定,对他人的住宅享有占有、使用的用益物权,以满足生活居住的需要。

第三百六十七条 设立居住权,当事人应当采用书面形式订立居住权合同。

居住权合同一般包括下列条款:

(一)当事人的姓名或者名称和住所;

(二)住宅的位置;

(三)居住的条件和要求;

(四)居住权期限;

(五)解决争议的方法。

第三百六十八条 居住权无偿设立,但是当事人另有约定的除外。设立居住权的,应当向登记机构申请居住权登记。居住权自登记时设立。

第三百六十九条 居住权不得转让、继承。设立居住权的住宅不得出租,但是当事人另有约定的除外。

第三百七十条 居住权期限届满或者居住权人死亡的,居住权消灭。居住权消灭的,应当及时办理注销登记。

第三百七十一条 以遗嘱方式设立居住权的,参照适用本章的有关规定。

第十五章 地 役 权

第三百七十二条 地役权人有权按照合同约定，利用他人的不动产，以提高自己的不动产的效益。

前款所称他人的不动产为供役地，自己的不动产为需役地。

第三百七十三条 设立地役权，当事人应当采用书面形式订立地役权合同。

地役权合同一般包括下列条款：

（一）当事人的姓名或者名称和住所；

（二）供役地和需役地的位置；

（三）利用目的和方法；

（四）地役权期限；

（五）费用及其支付方式；

（六）解决争议的方法。

第三百七十四条 地役权自地役权合同生效时设立。当事人要求登记的，可以向登记机构申请地役权登记；未经登记，不得对抗善意第三人。

第三百七十五条 供役地权利人应当按照合同约定，允许地役权人利用其不动产，不得妨害地役权人行使权利。

第三百七十六条 地役权人应当按照合同约定的利用目的和方法利用供役地，尽量减少对供役地权利人物权的限制。

第三百七十七条 地役权期限由当事人约定；但是，不得超过土地承包经营权、建设用地使用权等用益物权的剩余期限。

第三百七十八条 土地所有权人享有地役权或者负担地役权的，设立土地承包经营权、宅基地使用权等用益物权时，该用益物权人继续享有或者负担已经设立的地役权。

第三百七十九条 土地上已经设立土地承包经营权、建设用地使用权、宅基地使用权等用益物权的，未经用益物权人同意，土地所有权人不得设立地役权。

第三百八十条 地役权不得单独转让。土地承包经营权、建设用地使用权等转让的,地役权一并转让,但是合同另有约定的除外。

第三百八十一条 地役权不得单独抵押。土地经营权、建设用地使用权等抵押的,在实现抵押权时,地役权一并转让。

第三百八十二条 需役地以及需役地上的土地承包经营权、建设用地使用权等部分转让时,转让部分涉及地役权的,受让人同时享有地役权。

第三百八十三条 供役地以及供役地上的土地承包经营权、建设用地使用权等部分转让时,转让部分涉及地役权的,地役权对受让人具有法律约束力。

第三百八十四条 地役权人有下列情形之一的,供役地权利人有权解除地役权合同,地役权消灭:

(一)违反法律规定或者合同约定,滥用地役权;

(二)有偿利用供役地,约定的付款期限届满后在合理期限内经两次催告未支付费用。

第三百八十五条 已经登记的地役权变更、转让或者消灭的,应当及时办理变更登记或者注销登记。

第四分编 担保物权

第十六章 一般规定

第三百八十六条 担保物权人在债务人不履行到期债务或者发生当事人约定的实现担保物权的情形,依法享有就担保财产优先受偿的权利,但是法律另有规定的除外。

第三百八十七条 债权人在借贷、买卖等民事活动中,为保障实现其债权,需要担保的,可以依照本法和其他法律的规定设立担保物权。

第三人为债务人向债权人提供担保的,可以要求债务人提供反担保。反担保适用本法和其他法律的规定。

第三百八十八条 设立担保物权,应当依照本法和其他法律的规定订立担保合同。担保合同包括抵押合同、质押合同和其他具有担保功能的合同。担保合同是主债权债务合同的从合同。主债权债务合同无效的，担保合同无效，但是法律另有规定的除外。

担保合同被确认无效后，债务人、担保人、债权人有过错的，应当根据其过错各自承担相应的民事责任。

第三百八十九条 担保物权的担保范围包括主债权及其利息、违约金、损害赔偿金、保管担保财产和实现担保物权的费用。当事人另有约定的，按照其约定。

第三百九十条 担保期间，担保财产毁损、灭失或者被征收等，担保物权人可以就获得的保险金、赔偿金或者补偿金等优先受偿。被担保债权的履行期限未届满的，也可以提存该保险金、赔偿金或者补偿金等。

第三百九十一条 第三人提供担保，未经其书面同意，债权人允许债务人转移全部或者部分债务的，担保人不再承担相应的担保责任。

第三百九十二条 被担保的债权既有物的担保又有人的担保的，债务人不履行到期债务或者发生当事人约定的实现担保物权的情形，债权人应当按照约定实现债权；没有约定或者约定不明确，债务人自己提供物的担保的，债权人应当先就该物的担保实现债权；第三人提供物的担保的，债权人可以就物的担保实现债权，也可以请求保证人承担保证责任。提供担保的第三人承担担保责任后，有权向债务人追偿。

第三百九十三条 有下列情形之一的，担保物权消灭：

（一）主债权消灭；

（二）担保物权实现；

（三）债权人放弃担保物权；

（四）法律规定担保物权消灭的其他情形。

第十七章 抵 押 权

第一节 一般抵押权

第三百九十四条 为担保债务的履行，债务人或者第三人不转移财产的占有,将该财产抵押给债权人的,债务人不履行到期债务或者发生当事人约定的实现抵押权的情形,债权人有权就该财产优先受偿。

前款规定的债务人或者第三人为抵押人,债权人为抵押权人,提供担保的财产为抵押财产。

第三百九十五条 债务人或者第三人有权处分的下列财产可以抵押:

(一)建筑物和其他土地附着物;

(二)建设用地使用权;

(三)海域使用权;

(四)生产设备、原材料、半成品、产品;

(五)正在建造的建筑物、船舶、航空器;

(六)交通运输工具;

(七)法律、行政法规未禁止抵押的其他财产。

抵押人可以将前款所列财产一并抵押。

第三百九十六条 企业、个体工商户、农业生产经营者可以将现有的以及将有的生产设备、原材料、半成品、产品抵押,债务人不履行到期债务或者发生当事人约定的实现抵押权的情形,债权人有权就抵押财产确定时的动产优先受偿。

第三百九十七条 以建筑物抵押的,该建筑物占用范围内的建设用地使用权一并抵押。以建设用地使用权抵押的,该土地上的建筑物一并抵押。

抵押人未依据前款规定一并抵押的,未抵押的财产视为一并抵押。

第三百九十八条 乡镇、村企业的建设用地使用权不得单独抵押。以乡镇、村企业的厂房等建筑物抵押的,其占用范围内的建设用地使用权一并抵押。

第三百九十九条 下列财产不得抵押:

(一)土地所有权;

(二)宅基地、自留地、自留山等集体所有土地的使用权,但是法律规定可以抵押的除外;

(三)学校、幼儿园、医疗机构等为公益目的成立的非营利法人的教育设施、医疗卫生设施和其他公益设施；

（四）所有权、使用权不明或者有争议的财产；

（五）依法被查封、扣押、监管的财产；

（六）法律、行政法规规定不得抵押的其他财产。

第四百条 设立抵押权，当事人应当采用书面形式订立抵押合同。

抵押合同一般包括下列条款：

（一）被担保债权的种类和数额；

（二）债务人履行债务的期限；

（三）抵押财产的名称、数量等情况；

（四）担保的范围。

第四百零一条 抵押权人在债务履行期限届满前，与抵押人约定债务人不履行到期债务时抵押财产归债权人所有的，只能依法就抵押财产优先受偿。

第四百零二条 以本法第三百九十五条第一款第一项至第三项规定的财产或者第五项规定的正在建造的建筑物抵押的，应当办理抵押登记。抵押权自登记时设立。

第四百零三条 以动产抵押的，抵押权自抵押合同生效时设立；未经登记，不得对抗善意第三人。

第四百零四条 以动产抵押的，不得对抗正常经营活动中已经支付合理价款并取得抵押财产的买受人。

第四百零五条 抵押权设立前，抵押财产已经出租并转移占有的，原租赁关系不受该抵押权的影响。

第四百零六条 抵押期间，抵押人可以转让抵押财产。当事人另有约定的，按照其约定。抵押财产转让的，抵押权不受影响。

抵押人转让抵押财产的，应当及时通知抵押权人。抵押权人能够证明抵押财产转让可能损害抵押权的，可以请求抵押人将转让所得的价款向抵押权人提前清偿债务或者提存。转让的价款超过债权数额的部分归抵押人所有，不足部分由债务人清偿。

第四百零七条 抵押权不得与债权分离而单独转让或者作为其他债权的担保。债权转让的,担保该债权的抵押权一并转让,但是法律另有规定或者当事人另有约定的除外。

第四百零八条 抵押人的行为足以使抵押财产价值减少的,抵押权人有权请求抵押人停止其行为;抵押财产价值减少的,抵押权人有权请求恢复抵押财产的价值,或者提供与减少的价值相应的担保。抵押人不恢复抵押财产的价值,也不提供担保的,抵押权人有权请求债务人提前清偿债务。

第四百零九条 抵押权人可以放弃抵押权或者抵押权的顺位。抵押权人与抵押人可以协议变更抵押权顺位以及被担保的债权数额等内容。但是,抵押权的变更未经其他抵押权人书面同意的,不得对其他抵押权人产生不利影响。

债务人以自己的财产设定抵押,抵押权人放弃该抵押权、抵押权顺位或者变更抵押权的,其他担保人在抵押权人丧失优先受偿权益的范围内免除担保责任,但是其他担保人承诺仍然提供担保的除外。

第四百一十条 债务人不履行到期债务或者发生当事人约定的实现抵押权的情形,抵押权人可以与抵押人协议以抵押财产折价或者以拍卖、变卖该抵押财产所得的价款优先受偿。协议损害其他债权人利益的,其他债权人可以请求人民法院撤销该协议。

抵押权人与抵押人未就抵押权实现方式达成协议的,抵押权人可以请求人民法院拍卖、变卖抵押财产。

抵押财产折价或者变卖的,应当参照市场价格。

第四百一十一条 依据本法第三百九十六条规定设定抵押的,抵押财产自下列情形之一发生时确定:

(一)债务履行期限届满,债权未实现;

(二)抵押人被宣告破产或者解散;

(三)当事人约定的实现抵押权的情形;

(四)严重影响债权实现的其他情形。

第四百一十二条 债务人不履行到期债务或者发生当事人约定的实现

抵押权的情形，致使抵押财产被人民法院依法扣押的，自扣押之日起，抵押权人有权收取该抵押财产的天然孳息或者法定孳息，但是抵押权人未通知应当清偿法定孳息义务人的除外。

前款规定的孳息应当先充抵收取孳息的费用。

第四百一十三条　抵押财产折价或者拍卖、变卖后，其价款超过债权数额的部分归抵押人所有，不足部分由债务人清偿。

第四百一十四条　同一财产向两个以上债权人抵押的，拍卖、变卖抵押财产所得的价款依照下列规定清偿：

（一）抵押权已经登记的，按照登记的时间先后确定清偿顺序；

（二）抵押权已经登记的先于未登记的受偿；

（三）抵押权未登记的，按照债权比例清偿。

其他可以登记的担保物权，清偿顺序参照适用前款规定。

第四百一十五条　同一财产既设立抵押权又设立质权的，拍卖、变卖该财产所得的价款按照登记、交付的时间先后确定清偿顺序。

第四百一十六条　动产抵押担保的主债权是抵押物的价款，标的物交付后十日内办理抵押登记的，该抵押权人优先于抵押物买受人的其他担保物权人受偿，但是留置权人除外。

第四百一十七条　建设用地使用权抵押后，该土地上新增的建筑物不属于抵押财产。该建设用地使用权实现抵押权时，应当将该土地上新增的建筑物与建设用地使用权一并处分。但是，新增建筑物所得的价款，抵押权人无权优先受偿。

第四百一十八条　以集体所有土地的使用权依法抵押的，实现抵押权后，未经法定程序，不得改变土地所有权的性质和土地用途。

第四百一十九条　抵押权人应当在主债权诉讼时效期间行使抵押权；未行使的，人民法院不予保护。

第二节　最高额抵押权

第四百二十条　为担保债务的履行，债务人或者第三人对一定期间内将要连续发生的债权提供担保财产的,债务人不履行到期债务或者发生当事人约定的实现抵押权的情形,抵押权人有权在最高债权额限度内就该担保财产优先受偿。

最高额抵押权设立前已经存在的债权,经当事人同意,可以转入最高额抵押担保的债权范围。

第四百二十一条 最高额抵押担保的债权确定前,部分债权转让的,最高额抵押权不得转让,但是当事人另有约定的除外。

第四百二十二条 最高额抵押担保的债权确定前,抵押权人与抵押人可以通过协议变更债权确定的期间、债权范围以及最高债权额。但是,变更的内容不得对其他抵押权人产生不利影响。

第四百二十三条 有下列情形之一的,抵押权人的债权确定:

(一)约定的债权确定期间届满;

(二)没有约定债权确定期间或者约定不明确,抵押权人或者抵押人自最高额抵押权设立之日起满二年后请求确定债权;

(三)新的债权不可能发生;

(四)抵押权人知道或者应当知道抵押财产被查封、扣押;

(五)债务人、抵押人被宣告破产或者解散;

(六)法律规定债权确定的其他情形。

第四百二十四条 最高额抵押权除适用本节规定外,适用本章第一节的有关规定。

第十八章 质 权

第一节 动产质权

第四百二十五条 为担保债务的履行,债务人或者第三人将其动产出质给债权人占有的,债务人不履行到期债务或者发生当事人约定的实现质权的情形,债权人有权就该动产优先受偿。

前款规定的债务人或者第三人为出质人,债权人为质权人,交付的动产为质押财产。

第四百二十六条 法律、行政法规禁止转让的动产不得出质。

第四百二十七条 设立质权,当事人应当采用书面形式订立质押合同。

质押合同一般包括下列条款:

(一)被担保债权的种类和数额;

(二)债务人履行债务的期限;

(三)质押财产的名称、数量等情况;

(四)担保的范围;

(五)质押财产交付的时间、方式。

第四百二十八条 质权人在债务履行期限届满前,与出质人约定债务人不履行到期债务时质押财产归债权人所有的,只能依法就质押财产优先受偿。

第四百二十九条 质权自出质人交付质押财产时设立。

第四百三十条 质权人有权收取质押财产的孳息,但是合同另有约定的除外。

前款规定的孳息应当先充抵收取孳息的费用。

第四百三十一条 质权人在质权存续期间,未经出质人同意,擅自使用、处分质押财产,造成出质人损害的,应当承担赔偿责任。

第四百三十二条 质权人负有妥善保管质押财产的义务;因保管不善致使质押财产毁损、灭失的,应当承担赔偿责任。

质权人的行为可能使质押财产毁损、灭失的,出质人可以请求质权人将质押财产提存,或者请求提前清偿债务并返还质押财产。

第四百三十三条 因不可归责于质权人的事由可能使质押财产毁损或者价值明显减少,足以危害质权人权利的,质权人有权请求出质人提供相应的担保;出质人不提供的,质权人可以拍卖、变卖质押财产,并与出质人协议将拍卖、变卖所得的价款提前清偿债务或者提存。

第四百三十四条 质权人在质权存续期间,未经出质人同意转质,造成质押财产毁损、灭失的,应当承担赔偿责任。

第四百三十五条 质权人可以放弃质权。债务人以自己的财产出质,质权人放弃该质权的,其他担保人在质权人丧失优先受偿权益的范围内免除担保责任,但是其他担保人承诺仍然提供担保的除外。

第四百三十六条 债务人履行债务或者出质人提前清偿所担保的债权的,质权人应当返还质押财产。

债务人不履行到期债务或者发生当事人约定的实现质权的情形,质权人可以与出质人协议以质押财产折价,也可以就拍卖、变卖质押财产所得的价款优先受偿。

质押财产折价或者变卖的,应当参照市场价格。

第四百三十七条 出质人可以请求质权人在债务履行期限届满后及时行使质权;质权人不行使的,出质人可以请求人民法院拍卖、变卖质押财产。

出质人请求质权人及时行使质权,因质权人怠于行使权利造成出质人损害的,由质权人承担赔偿责任。

第四百三十八条 质押财产折价或者拍卖、变卖后,其价款超过债权数额的部分归出质人所有,不足部分由债务人清偿。

第四百三十九条 出质人与质权人可以协议设立最高额质权。

最高额质权除适用本节有关规定外,参照适用本编第十七章第二节的有关规定。

第二节 权利质权

第四百四十条 债务人或者第三人有权处分的下列权利可以出质:

(一)汇票、本票、支票;

(二)债券、存款单;

(三)仓单、提单;

(四)可以转让的基金份额、股权;

(五)可以转让的注册商标专用权、专利权、著作权等知识产权中的财产权;

(六)现有的以及将有的应收账款;

（七）法律、行政法规规定可以出质的其他财产权利。

第四百四十一条 以汇票、本票、支票、债券、存款单、仓单、提单出质的，质权自权利凭证交付质权人时设立；没有权利凭证的，质权自办理出质登记时设立。法律另有规定的，依照其规定。

第四百四十二条 汇票、本票、支票、债券、存款单、仓单、提单的兑现日期或者提货日期先于主债权到期的，质权人可以兑现或者提货，并与出质人协议将兑现的价款或者提取的货物提前清偿债务或者提存。

第四百四十三条 以基金份额、股权出质的，质权自办理出质登记时设立。

基金份额、股权出质后，不得转让，但是出质人与质权人协商同意的除外。出质人转让基金份额、股权所得的价款，应当向质权人提前清偿债务或者提存。

第四百四十四条 以注册商标专用权、专利权、著作权等知识产权中的财产权出质的，质权自办理出质登记时设立。

知识产权中的财产权出质后，出质人不得转让或者许可他人使用，但是出质人与质权人协商同意的除外。出质人转让或者许可他人使用出质的知识产权中的财产权所得的价款，应当向质权人提前清偿债务或者提存。

第四百四十五条 以应收账款出质的，质权自办理出质登记时设立。

应收账款出质后，不得转让，但是出质人与质权人协商同意的除外。出质人转让应收账款所得的价款，应当向质权人提前清偿债务或者提存。

第四百四十六条 权利质权除适用本节规定外，适用本章第一节的有关规定。

第十九章 留 置 权

第四百四十七条 债务人不履行到期债务，债权人可以留置已经合法占有的债务人的动产，并有权就该动产优先受偿。

前款规定的债权人为留置权人，占有的动产为留置财产。

第四百四十八条 债权人留置的动产，应当与债权属于同一法律关系,但是企业之间留置的除外。

第四百四十九条 法律规定或者当事人约定不得留置的动产,不得留置。

第四百五十条 留置财产为可分物的,留置财产的价值应当相当于债务的金额。

第四百五十一条 留置权人负有妥善保管留置财产的义务;因保管不善致使留置财产毁损、灭失的,应当承担赔偿责任。

第四百五十二条 留置权人有权收取留置财产的孳息。

前款规定的孳息应当先充抵收取孳息的费用。

第四百五十三条 留置权人与债务人应当约定留置财产后的债务履行期限;没有约定或者约定不明确的,留置权人应当给债务人六十日以上履行债务的期限,但是鲜活易腐等不易保管的动产除外。债务人逾期未履行的,留置权人可以与债务人协议以留置财产折价,也可以就拍卖、变卖留置财产所得的价款优先受偿。

留置财产折价或者变卖的,应当参照市场价格。

第四百五十四条 债务人可以请求留置权人在债务履行期限届满后行使留置权;留置权人不行使的,债务人可以请求人民法院拍卖、变卖留置财产。

第四百五十五条 留置财产折价或者拍卖、变卖后,其价款超过债权数额的部分归债务人所有,不足部分由债务人清偿。

第四百五十六条 同一动产上已经设立抵押权或者质权,该动产又被留置的,留置权人优先受偿。

第四百五十七条 留置权人对留置财产丧失占有或者留置权人接受债务人另行提供担保的,留置权消灭。

第五分编 占　　有

第二十章 占　　有

第四百五十八条 基于合同关系等产生的占有,有关不动产或者动产的使用、收益、违约责任等，按照合同约定；合同没有约定或者约定不明确的，依照有关法律规定。

第四百五十九条　占有人因使用占有的不动产或者动产，致使该不动产或者动产受到损害的，恶意占有人应当承担赔偿责任。

第四百六十条　不动产或者动产被占有人占有的，权利人可以请求返还原物及其孳息；但是，应当支付善意占有人因维护该不动产或者动产支出的必要费用。

第四百六十一条　占有的不动产或者动产毁损、灭失，该不动产或者动产的权利人请求赔偿的，占有人应当将因毁损、灭失取得的保险金、赔偿金或者补偿金等返还给权利人；权利人的损害未得到足够弥补的，恶意占有人还应当赔偿损失。

第四百六十二条　占有的不动产或者动产被侵占的，占有人有权请求返还原物；对妨害占有的行为，占有人有权请求排除妨害或者消除危险；因侵占或者妨害造成损害的，占有人有权依法请求损害赔偿。

占有人返还原物的请求权，自侵占发生之日起一年内未行使的，该请求权消灭。

第三编 合　　同

第一分编 通　　则

第一章 一般规定

第四百六十三条 本编调整因合同产生的民事关系。

第四百六十四条 合同是民事主体之间设立、变更、终止民事法律关系的协议。

婚姻、收养、监护等有关身份关系的协议，适用有关该身份关系的法律规定；没有规定的，可以根据其性质参照适用本编规定。

第四百六十五条 依法成立的合同，受法律保护。

依法成立的合同，仅对当事人具有法律约束力，但是法律另有规定的除外。

第四百六十六条 当事人对合同条款的理解有争议的，应当依据本法第一百四十二条第一款的规定，确定争议条款的含义。

合同文本采用两种以上文字订立并约定具有同等效力的，对各文本使用的词句推定具有相同含义。各文本使用的词句不一致的，应当根据合同的相关条款、性质、目的以及诚信原则等予以解释。

第四百六十七条 本法或者其他法律没有明文规定的合同，适用本编通则的规定，并可以参照适用本编或者其他法律最相类似合同的规定。

在中华人民共和国境内履行的中外合资经营企业合同、中外合作经营企业合同、中外合作勘探开发自然资源合同，适用中华人民共和国法律。

第四百六十八条 非因合同产生的债权债务关系，适用有关该债权债务关系的法律规定；没有规定的，适用本编通则的有关规定，但是根据其性质不能适用的除外。

第二章　合同的订立

第四百六十九条　当事人订立合同，可以采用书面形式、口头形式或者其他形式。

书面形式是合同书、信件、电报、电传、传真等可以有形地表现所载内容的形式。

以电子数据交换、电子邮件等方式能够有形地表现所载内容，并可以随时调取查用的数据电文，视为书面形式。

第四百七十条　合同的内容由当事人约定，一般包括下列条款：

（一）当事人的姓名或者名称和住所；

（二）标的；

（三）数量；

（四）质量；

（五）价款或者报酬；

（六）履行期限、地点和方式；

（七）违约责任；

（八）解决争议的方法。

当事人可以参照各类合同的示范文本订立合同。

第四百七十一条　当事人订立合同，可以采取要约、承诺方式或者其他方式。

第四百七十二条　要约是希望与他人订立合同的意思表示，该意思表示应当符合下列条件：

（一）内容具体确定；

（二）表明经受要约人承诺，要约人即受该意思表示约束。

第四百七十三条　要约邀请是希望他人向自己发出要约的表示。拍卖公告、招标公告、招股说明书、债券募集办法、基金招募说明书、商业广告和宣传、寄送的价目表等为要约邀请。

商业广告和宣传的内容符合要约条件的，构成要约。

第四百七十四条 要约生效的时间适用本法第一百三十七条的规定。

第四百七十五条 要约可以撤回。要约的撤回适用本法第一百四十一条的规定。

第四百七十六条 要约可以撤销,但是有下列情形之一的除外:

(一)要约人以确定承诺期限或者其他形式明示要约不可撤销;

(二)受要约人有理由认为要约是不可撤销的,并已经为履行合同做了合理准备工作。

第四百七十七条 撤销要约的意思表示以对话方式作出的,该意思表示的内容应当在受要约人作出承诺之前为受要约人所知道;撤销要约的意思表示以非对话方式作出的,应当在受要约人作出承诺之前到达受要约人。

第四百七十八条 有下列情形之一的,要约失效:

(一)要约被拒绝;

(二)要约被依法撤销;

(三)承诺期限届满,受要约人未作出承诺;

(四)受要约人对要约的内容作出实质性变更。

第四百七十九条 承诺是受要约人同意要约的意思表示。

第四百八十条 承诺应当以通知的方式作出;但是,根据交易习惯或者要约表明可以通过行为作出承诺的除外。

第四百八十一条 承诺应当在要约确定的期限内到达要约人。

要约没有确定承诺期限的,承诺应当依照下列规定到达:

(一)要约以对话方式作出的,应当即时作出承诺;

(二)要约以非对话方式作出的,承诺应当在合理期限内到达。

第四百八十二条 要约以信件或者电报作出的,承诺期限自信件载明的日期或者电报交发之日开始计算。信件未载明日期的,自投寄该信件的邮戳日期开始计算。要约以电话、传真、电子邮件等快速通讯方式作出的,承诺期限自要约到达受要约人时开始计算。

第四百八十三条 承诺生效时合同成立,但是法律另有规定或者当事人另有约定的除外。

第四百八十四条 以通知方式作出的承诺，生效的时间适用本法第一百三十七条的规定。

承诺不需要通知的，根据交易习惯或者要约的要求作出承诺的行为时生效。

第四百八十五条 承诺可以撤回。承诺的撤回适用本法第一百四十一条的规定。

第四百八十六条 受要约人超过承诺期限发出承诺，或者在承诺期限内发出承诺，按照通常情形不能及时到达要约人的，为新要约；但是，要约人及时通知受要约人该承诺有效的除外。

第四百八十七条 受要约人在承诺期限内发出承诺，按照通常情形能够及时到达要约人，但是因其他原因致使承诺到达要约人时超过承诺期限的，除要约人及时通知受要约人因承诺超过期限不接受该承诺外，该承诺有效。

第四百八十八条 承诺的内容应当与要约的内容一致。受要约人对要约的内容作出实质性变更的，为新要约。有关合同标的、数量、质量、价款或者报酬、履行期限、履行地点和方式、违约责任和解决争议方法等的变更，是对要约内容的实质性变更。

第四百八十九条 承诺对要约的内容作出非实质性变更的，除要约人及时表示反对或者要约表明承诺不得对要约的内容作出任何变更外，该承诺有效，合同的内容以承诺的内容为准。

第四百九十条 当事人采用合同书形式订立合同的，自当事人均签名、盖章或者按指印时合同成立。在签名、盖章或者按指印之前，当事人一方已经履行主要义务，对方接受时，该合同成立。

法律、行政法规规定或者当事人约定合同应当采用书面形式订立，当事人未采用书面形式但是一方已经履行主要义务，对方接受时，该合同成立。

第四百九十一条 当事人采用信件、数据电文等形式订立合同要求签订确认书的，签订确认书时合同成立。

当事人一方通过互联网等信息网络发布的商品或者服务信息符合要约

条件的,对方选择该商品或者服务并提交订单成功时合同成立,但是当事人另有约定的除外。

第四百九十二条 承诺生效的地点为合同成立的地点。

采用数据电文形式订立合同的,收件人的主营业地为合同成立的地点;没有主营业地的,其住所地为合同成立的地点。当事人另有约定的,按照其约定。

第四百九十三条 当事人采用合同书形式订立合同的,最后签名、盖章或者按指印的地点为合同成立的地点,但是当事人另有约定的除外。

第四百九十四条 国家根据抢险救灾、疫情防控或者其他需要下达国家订货任务、指令性任务的,有关民事主体之间应当依照有关法律、行政法规规定的权利和义务订立合同。

依照法律、行政法规的规定负有发出要约义务的当事人,应当及时发出合理的要约。

依照法律、行政法规的规定负有作出承诺义务的当事人,不得拒绝对方合理的订立合同要求。

第四百九十五条 当事人约定在将来一定期限内订立合同的认购书、订购书、预订书等,构成预约合同。

当事人一方不履行预约合同约定的订立合同义务的,对方可以请求其承担预约合同的违约责任。

第四百九十六条 格式条款是当事人为了重复使用而预先拟定,并在订立合同时未与对方协商的条款。

采用格式条款订立合同的,提供格式条款的一方应当遵循公平原则确定当事人之间的权利和义务,并采取合理的方式提示对方注意免除或者减轻其责任等与对方有重大利害关系的条款,按照对方的要求,对该条款予以说明。提供格式条款的一方未履行提示或者说明义务,致使对方没有注意或者理解与其有重大利害关系的条款的,对方可以主张该条款不成为合同的内容。

第四百九十七条 有下列情形之一的,该格式条款无效:

(一)具有本法第一编第六章第三节和本法第五百零六条规定的无效情形;

(二)提供格式条款一方不合理地免除或者减轻其责任、加重对方责任、限制对方主要权利;

(三)提供格式条款一方排除对方主要权利。

第四百九十八条 对格式条款的理解发生争议的,应当按照通常理解予以解释。对格式条款有两种以上解释的,应当作出不利于提供格式条款一方的解释。格式条款和非格式条款不一致的,应当采用非格式条款。

第四百九十九条 悬赏人以公开方式声明对完成特定行为的人支付报酬的,完成该行为的人可以请求其支付。

第五百条 当事人在订立合同过程中有下列情形之一,造成对方损失的,应当承担赔偿责任:

(一)假借订立合同,恶意进行磋商;

(二)故意隐瞒与订立合同有关的重要事实或者提供虚假情况;

(三)有其他违背诚信原则的行为。

第五百零一条 当事人在订立合同过程中知悉的商业秘密或者其他应当保密的信息,无论合同是否成立,不得泄露或者不正当地使用;泄露、不正当地使用该商业秘密或者信息,造成对方损失的,应当承担赔偿责任。

第三章 合同的效力

第五百零二条 依法成立的合同,自成立时生效,但是法律另有规定或者当事人另有约定的除外。

依照法律、行政法规的规定,合同应当办理批准等手续的,依照其规定。未办理批准等手续影响合同生效的,不影响合同中履行报批等义务条款以及相关条款的效力。应当办理申请批准等手续的当事人未履行义务的,对方可以请求其承担违反该义务的责任。

依照法律、行政法规的规定,合同的变更、转让、解除等情形应当办理批准等手续的,适用前款规定。

第五百零三条 无权代理人以被代理人的名义订立合同,被代理人已经开始履行合同义务或者接受相对人履行的,视为对合同的追认。

第五百零四条 法人的法定代表人或者非法人组织的负责人超越权限订立的合同,除相对人知道或者应当知道其超越权限外,该代表行为有效,订立的合同对法人或者非法人组织发生效力。

第五百零五条 当事人超越经营范围订立的合同的效力,应当依照本法第一编第六章第三节和本编的有关规定确定,不得仅以超越经营范围确认合同无效。

第五百零六条 合同中的下列免责条款无效:

(一)造成对方人身损害的;

(二)因故意或者重大过失造成对方财产损失的。

第五百零七条 合同不生效、无效、被撤销或者终止的,不影响合同中有关解决争议方法的条款的效力。

第五百零八条 本编对合同的效力没有规定的,适用本法第一编第六章的有关规定。

第四章 合同的履行

第五百零九条 当事人应当按照约定全面履行自己的义务。

当事人应当遵循诚信原则,根据合同的性质、目的和交易习惯履行通知、协助、保密等义务。

当事人在履行合同过程中,应当避免浪费资源、污染环境和破坏生态。

第五百一十条 合同生效后,当事人就质量、价款或者报酬、履行地点等内容没有约定或者约定不明确的,可以协议补充;不能达成补充协议的,按照合同相关条款或者交易习惯确定。

第五百一十一条 当事人就有关合同内容约定不明确,依据前条规定仍不能确定的,适用下列规定:

(一)质量要求不明确的,按照强制性国家标准履行;没有强制性国家标准的,按照推荐性国家标准履行;没有推荐性国家标准的,按照行业标准履行；没有国家标准、行业标准的，按照通常标准或者符合合同目的的特定标准履行。

（二）价款或者报酬不明确的，按照订立合同时履行地的市场价格履行；依法应当执行政府定价或者政府指导价的，依照规定履行。

（三）履行地点不明确，给付货币的，在接受货币一方所在地履行；交付不动产的，在不动产所在地履行；其他标的，在履行义务一方所在地履行。

（四）履行期限不明确的，债务人可以随时履行，债权人也可以随时请求履行，但是应当给对方必要的准备时间。

（五）履行方式不明确的，按照有利于实现合同目的的方式履行。

（六）履行费用的负担不明确的，由履行义务一方负担；因债权人原因增加的履行费用，由债权人负担。

第五百一十二条　通过互联网等信息网络订立的电子合同的标的为交付商品并采用快递物流方式交付的，收货人的签收时间为交付时间。电子合同的标的为提供服务的，生成的电子凭证或者实物凭证中载明的时间为提供服务时间；前述凭证没有载明时间或者载明时间与实际提供服务时间不一致的，以实际提供服务的时间为准。

电子合同的标的物为采用在线传输方式交付的，合同标的物进入对方当事人指定的特定系统且能够检索识别的时间为交付时间。

电子合同当事人对交付商品或者提供服务的方式、时间另有约定的，按照其约定。

第五百一十三条　执行政府定价或者政府指导价的，在合同约定的交付期限内政府价格调整时，按照交付时的价格计价。逾期交付标的物的，遇价格上涨时，按照原价格执行；价格下降时，按照新价格执行。逾期提取标的物或者逾期付款的，遇价格上涨时，按照新价格执行；价格下降时，按照原价格执行。

第五百一十四条　以支付金钱为内容的债，除法律另有规定或者当事人另有约定外，债权人可以请求债务人以实际履行地的法定货币履行。

第五百一十五条　标的有多项而债务人只需履行其中一项的，债务人享有选择权;但是,法律另有规定、当事人另有约定或者另有交易习惯的除外。

享有选择权的当事人在约定期限内或者履行期限届满未作选择,经催告后在合理期限内仍未选择的,选择权转移至对方。

第五百一十六条 当事人行使选择权应当及时通知对方,通知到达对方时,标的确定。标的确定后不得变更,但是经对方同意的除外。

可选择的标的发生不能履行情形的,享有选择权的当事人不得选择不能履行的标的,但是该不能履行的情形是由对方造成的除外。

第五百一十七条 债权人为二人以上,标的可分,按照份额各自享有债权的,为按份债权;债务人为二人以上,标的可分,按照份额各自负担债务的,为按份债务。

按份债权人或者按份债务人的份额难以确定的,视为份额相同。

第五百一十八条 债权人为二人以上,部分或者全部债权人均可以请求债务人履行债务的,为连带债权;债务人为二人以上,债权人可以请求部分或者全部债务人履行全部债务的,为连带债务。

连带债权或者连带债务,由法律规定或者当事人约定。

第五百一十九条 连带债务人之间的份额难以确定的,视为份额相同。

实际承担债务超过自己份额的连带债务人,有权就超出部分在其他连带债务人未履行的份额范围内向其追偿,并相应地享有债权人的权利,但是不得损害债权人的利益。其他连带债务人对债权人的抗辩,可以向该债务人主张。

被追偿的连带债务人不能履行其应分担份额的,其他连带债务人应当在相应范围内按比例分担。

第五百二十条 部分连带债务人履行、抵销债务或者提存标的物的,其他债务人对债权人的债务在相应范围内消灭;该债务人可以依据前条规定向其他债务人追偿。

部分连带债务人的债务被债权人免除的,在该连带债务人应当承担的份额范围内,其他债务人对债权人的债务消灭。

部分连带债务人的债务与债权人的债权同归于一人的，在扣除该债务人应当承担的份额后，债权人对其他债务人的债权继续存在。

债权人对部分连带债务人的给付受领迟延的，对其他连带债务人发生效力。

第五百二十一条 连带债权人之间的份额难以确定的，视为份额相同。

实际受领债权的连带债权人，应当按比例向其他连带债权人返还。

连带债权参照适用本章连带债务的有关规定。

第五百二十二条 当事人约定由债务人向第三人履行债务，债务人未向第三人履行债务或者履行债务不符合约定的，应当向债权人承担违约责任。

法律规定或者当事人约定第三人可以直接请求债务人向其履行债务，第三人未在合理期限内明确拒绝，债务人未向第三人履行债务或者履行债务不符合约定的，第三人可以请求债务人承担违约责任；债务人对债权人的抗辩，可以向第三人主张。

第五百二十三条 当事人约定由第三人向债权人履行债务，第三人不履行债务或者履行债务不符合约定的，债务人应当向债权人承担违约责任。

第五百二十四条 债务人不履行债务，第三人对履行该债务具有合法利益的，第三人有权向债权人代为履行；但是，根据债务性质、按照当事人约定或者依照法律规定只能由债务人履行的除外。

债权人接受第三人履行后，其对债务人的债权转让给第三人，但是债务人和第三人另有约定的除外。

第五百二十五条 当事人互负债务，没有先后履行顺序的，应当同时履行。一方在对方履行之前有权拒绝其履行请求。一方在对方履行债务不符合约定时，有权拒绝其相应的履行请求。

第五百二十六条 当事人互负债务，有先后履行顺序，应当先履行债务一方未履行的，后履行一方有权拒绝其履行请求。先履行一方履行债务不符合约定的，后履行一方有权拒绝其相应的履行请求。

第五百二十七条 应当先履行债务的当事人，有确切证据证明对方有

下列情形之一的,可以中止履行:

(一)经营状况严重恶化;

(二)转移财产、抽逃资金,以逃避债务;

(三)丧失商业信誉;

(四)有丧失或者可能丧失履行债务能力的其他情形。

当事人没有确切证据中止履行的,应当承担违约责任。

第五百二十八条 当事人依据前条规定中止履行的,应当及时通知对方。对方提供适当担保的,应当恢复履行。中止履行后,对方在合理期限内未恢复履行能力且未提供适当担保的,视为以自己的行为表明不履行主要债务,中止履行的一方可以解除合同并可以请求对方承担违约责任。

第五百二十九条 债权人分立、合并或者变更住所没有通知债务人,致使履行债务发生困难的,债务人可以中止履行或者将标的物提存。

第五百三十条 债权人可以拒绝债务人提前履行债务,但是提前履行不损害债权人利益的除外。

债务人提前履行债务给债权人增加的费用,由债务人负担。

第五百三十一条 债权人可以拒绝债务人部分履行债务,但是部分履行不损害债权人利益的除外。

债务人部分履行债务给债权人增加的费用,由债务人负担。

第五百三十二条 合同生效后,当事人不得因姓名、名称的变更或者法定代表人、负责人、承办人的变动而不履行合同义务。

第五百三十三条 合同成立后,合同的基础条件发生了当事人在订立合同时无法预见的、不属于商业风险的重大变化,继续履行合同对于当事人一方明显不公平的,受不利影响的当事人可以与对方重新协商;在合理期限内协商不成的,当事人可以请求人民法院或者仲裁机构变更或者解除合同。

人民法院或者仲裁机构应当结合案件的实际情况,根据公平原则变更或者解除合同。

第五百三十四条 对当事人利用合同实施危害国家利益、社会公共利益行为的,市场监督管理和其他有关行政主管部门依照法律、行政法规的规定负责监督处理。

第五章 合同的保全

第五百三十五条 因债务人怠于行使其债权或者与该债权有关的从权利,影响债权人的到期债权实现的,债权人可以向人民法院请求以自己的名义代位行使债务人对相对人的权利,但是该权利专属于债务人自身的除外。

代位权的行使范围以债权人的到期债权为限。债权人行使代位权的必要费用,由债务人负担。

相对人对债务人的抗辩,可以向债权人主张。

第五百三十六条 债权人的债权到期前,债务人的债权或者与该债权有关的从权利存在诉讼时效期间即将届满或者未及时申报破产债权等情形,影响债权人的债权实现的,债权人可以代位向债务人的相对人请求其向债务人履行、向破产管理人申报或者作出其他必要的行为。

第五百三十七条 人民法院认定代位权成立的,由债务人的相对人向债权人履行义务,债权人接受履行后,债权人与债务人、债务人与相对人之间相应的权利义务终止。债务人对相对人的债权或者与该债权有关的从权利被采取保全、执行措施,或者债务人破产的,依照相关法律的规定处理。

第五百三十八条 债务人以放弃其债权、放弃债权担保、无偿转让财产等方式无偿处分财产权益,或者恶意延长其到期债权的履行期限,影响债权人的债权实现的,债权人可以请求人民法院撤销债务人的行为。

第五百三十九条 债务人以明显不合理的低价转让财产、以明显不合理的高价受让他人财产或者为他人的债务提供担保,影响债权人的债权实现,债务人的相对人知道或者应当知道该情形的,债权人可以请求人民法院撤销债务人的行为。

第五百四十条 撤销权的行使范围以债权人的债权为限。债权人行使撤销权的必要费用,由债务人负担。

第五百四十一条 撤销权自债权人知道或者应当知道撤销事由之日起一年内行使。自债务人的行为发生之日起五年内没有行使撤销权的,该撤销权消灭。

第五百四十二条 债务人影响债权人的债权实现的行为被撤销的,自始没有法律约束力。

第六章 合同的变更和转让

第五百四十三条 当事人协商一致,可以变更合同。

第五百四十四条 当事人对合同变更的内容约定不明确的,推定为未变更。

第五百四十五条 债权人可以将债权的全部或者部分转让给第三人,但是有下列情形之一的除外:

(一)根据债权性质不得转让;

(二)按照当事人约定不得转让;

(三)依照法律规定不得转让。

当事人约定非金钱债权不得转让的,不得对抗善意第三人。当事人约定金钱债权不得转让的,不得对抗第三人。

第五百四十六条 债权人转让债权,未通知债务人的,该转让对债务人不发生效力。

债权转让的通知不得撤销,但是经受让人同意的除外。

第五百四十七条 债权人转让债权的,受让人取得与债权有关的从权利,但是该从权利专属于债权人自身的除外。

受让人取得从权利不因该从权利未办理转移登记手续或者未转移占有而受到影响。

第五百四十八条 债务人接到债权转让通知后,债务人对让与人的抗辩,可以向受让人主张。

第五百四十九条 有下列情形之一的,债务人可以向受让人主张抵销:

(一)债务人接到债权转让通知时,债务人对让与人享有债权,且债务人的债权先于转让的债权到期或者同时到期;

(二)债务人的债权与转让的债权是基于同一合同产生。

第五百五十条　因债权转让增加的履行费用,由让与人负担。

第五百五十一条　债务人将债务的全部或者部分转移给第三人的,应当经债权人同意。

债务人或者第三人可以催告债权人在合理期限内予以同意,债权人未作表示的,视为不同意。

第五百五十二条　第三人与债务人约定加入债务并通知债权人,或者第三人向债权人表示愿意加入债务,债权人未在合理期限内明确拒绝的,债权人可以请求第三人在其愿意承担的债务范围内和债务人承担连带债务。

第五百五十三条　债务人转移债务的,新债务人可以主张原债务人对债权人的抗辩;原债务人对债权人享有债权的,新债务人不得向债权人主张抵销。

第五百五十四条　债务人转移债务的,新债务人应当承担与主债务有关的从债务,但是该从债务专属于原债务人自身的除外。

第五百五十五条　当事人一方经对方同意,可以将自己在合同中的权利和义务一并转让给第三人。

第五百五十六条　合同的权利和义务一并转让的,适用债权转让、债务转移的有关规定。

第七章　合同的权利义务终止

第五百五十七条　有下列情形之一的,债权债务终止:

(一)债务已经履行;

(二)债务相互抵销;

(三)债务人依法将标的物提存;

(四)债权人免除债务;

(五)债权债务同归于一人;

(六)法律规定或者当事人约定终止的其他情形。

合同解除的,该合同的权利义务关系终止。

第五百五十八条　债权债务终止后,当事人应当遵循诚信等原则,根据交易习惯履行通知、协助、保密、旧物回收等义务。

第五百五十九条 债权债务终止时,债权的从权利同时消灭,但是法律另有规定或者当事人另有约定的除外。

第五百六十条 债务人对同一债权人负担的数项债务种类相同,债务人的给付不足以清偿全部债务的,除当事人另有约定外,由债务人在清偿时指定其履行的债务。

债务人未作指定的,应当优先履行已经到期的债务;数项债务均到期的,优先履行对债权人缺乏担保或者担保最少的债务;均无担保或者担保相等的,优先履行债务人负担较重的债务;负担相同的,按照债务到期的先后顺序履行;到期时间相同的,按照债务比例履行。

第五百六十一条 债务人在履行主债务外还应当支付利息和实现债权的有关费用,其给付不足以清偿全部债务的,除当事人另有约定外,应当按照下列顺序履行:

(一)实现债权的有关费用;

(二)利息;

(三)主债务。

第五百六十二条 当事人协商一致,可以解除合同。

当事人可以约定一方解除合同的事由。解除合同的事由发生时,解除权人可以解除合同。

第五百六十三条 有下列情形之一的,当事人可以解除合同:

(一)因不可抗力致使不能实现合同目的;

(二)在履行期限届满前,当事人一方明确表示或者以自己的行为表明不履行主要债务;

(三)当事人一方迟延履行主要债务,经催告后在合理期限内仍未履行;

(四)当事人一方迟延履行债务或者有其他违约行为致使不能实现合同目的;

(五)法律规定的其他情形。

以持续履行的债务为内容的不定期合同,当事人可以随时解除合同,但是应当在合理期限之前通知对方。

第五百六十四条　法律规定或者当事人约定解除权行使期限，期限届满当事人不行使的，该权利消灭。

法律没有规定或者当事人没有约定解除权行使期限，自解除权人知道或者应当知道解除事由之日起一年内不行使，或者经对方催告后在合理期限内不行使的，该权利消灭。

第五百六十五条　当事人一方依法主张解除合同的，应当通知对方。合同自通知到达对方时解除；通知载明债务人在一定期限内不履行债务则合同自动解除，债务人在该期限内未履行债务的，合同自通知载明的期限届满时解除。对方对解除合同有异议的，任何一方当事人均可以请求人民法院或者仲裁机构确认解除行为的效力。

当事人一方未通知对方，直接以提起诉讼或者申请仲裁的方式依法主张解除合同，人民法院或者仲裁机构确认该主张的，合同自起诉状副本或者仲裁申请书副本送达对方时解除。

第五百六十六条　合同解除后，尚未履行的，终止履行；已经履行的，根据履行情况和合同性质，当事人可以请求恢复原状或者采取其他补救措施，并有权请求赔偿损失。

合同因违约解除的，解除权人可以请求违约方承担违约责任，但是当事人另有约定的除外。

主合同解除后，担保人对债务人应当承担的民事责任仍应当承担担保责任，但是担保合同另有约定的除外。

第五百六十七条　合同的权利义务关系终止，不影响合同中结算和清理条款的效力。

第五百六十八条　当事人互负债务，该债务的标的物种类、品质相同的，任何一方可以将自己的债务与对方的到期债务抵销；但是，根据债务性质、按照当事人约定或者依照法律规定不得抵销的除外。

当事人主张抵销的，应当通知对方。通知自到达对方时生效。抵销不得附条件或者附期限。

第五百六十九条 当事人互负债务,标的物种类、品质不相同的,经协商一致,也可以抵销。

第五百七十条 有下列情形之一,难以履行债务的,债务人可以将标的物提存:

(一)债权人无正当理由拒绝受领;

(二)债权人下落不明;

(三)债权人死亡未确定继承人、遗产管理人,或者丧失民事行为能力未确定监护人;

(四)法律规定的其他情形。

标的物不适于提存或者提存费用过高的,债务人依法可以拍卖或者变卖标的物,提存所得的价款。

第五百七十一条 债务人将标的物或者将标的物依法拍卖、变卖所得价款交付提存部门时,提存成立。

提存成立的,视为债务人在其提存范围内已经交付标的物。

第五百七十二条 标的物提存后,债务人应当及时通知债权人或者债权人的继承人、遗产管理人、监护人、财产代管人。

第五百七十三条 标的物提存后,毁损、灭失的风险由债权人承担。提存期间,标的物的孳息归债权人所有。提存费用由债权人负担。

第五百七十四条 债权人可以随时领取提存物。但是,债权人对债务人负有到期债务的,在债权人未履行债务或者提供担保之前,提存部门根据债务人的要求应当拒绝其领取提存物。

债权人领取提存物的权利,自提存之日起五年内不行使而消灭,提存物扣除提存费用后归国家所有。但是,债权人未履行对债务人的到期债务,或者债权人向提存部门书面表示放弃领取提存物权利的,债务人负担提存费用后有权取回提存物。

第五百七十五条 债权人免除债务人部分或者全部债务的,债权债务部分或者全部终止,但是债务人在合理期限内拒绝的除外。

第五百七十六条 债权和债务同归于一人的,债权债务终止,但是损害第三人利益的除外。

第八章 违约责任

第五百七十七条 当事人一方不履行合同义务或者履行合同义务不符合约定的，应当承担继续履行、采取补救措施或者赔偿损失等违约责任。

第五百七十八条 当事人一方明确表示或者以自己的行为表明不履行合同义务的，对方可以在履行期限届满前请求其承担违约责任。

第五百七十九条 当事人一方未支付价款、报酬、租金、利息，或者不履行其他金钱债务的，对方可以请求其支付。

第五百八十条 当事人一方不履行非金钱债务或者履行非金钱债务不符合约定的，对方可以请求履行，但是有下列情形之一的除外：

（一）法律上或者事实上不能履行；

（二）债务的标的不适于强制履行或者履行费用过高；

（三）债权人在合理期限内未请求履行。

有前款规定的除外情形之一，致使不能实现合同目的的，人民法院或者仲裁机构可以根据当事人的请求终止合同权利义务关系，但是不影响违约责任的承担。

第五百八十一条 当事人一方不履行债务或者履行债务不符合约定，根据债务的性质不得强制履行的，对方可以请求其负担由第三人替代履行的费用。

第五百八十二条 履行不符合约定的，应当按照当事人的约定承担违约责任。对违约责任没有约定或者约定不明确，依据本法第五百一十条的规定仍不能确定的，受损害方根据标的的性质以及损失的大小，可以合理选择请求对方承担修理、重作、更换、退货、减少价款或者报酬等违约责任。

第五百八十三条 当事人一方不履行合同义务或者履行合同义务不符合约定的，在履行义务或者采取补救措施后，对方还有其他损失的，应当赔偿损失。

第五百八十四条 当事人一方不履行合同义务或者履行合同义务不符

合约定,造成对方损失的,损失赔偿额应当相当于因违约所造成的损失,包括合同履行后可以获得的利益;但是,不得超过违约一方订立合同时预见到或者应当预见到的因违约可能造成的损失。

第五百八十五条　当事人可以约定一方违约时应当根据违约情况向对方支付一定数额的违约金,也可以约定因违约产生的损失赔偿额的计算方法。

约定的违约金低于造成的损失的,人民法院或者仲裁机构可以根据当事人的请求予以增加;约定的违约金过分高于造成的损失的,人民法院或者仲裁机构可以根据当事人的请求予以适当减少。

当事人就迟延履行约定违约金的,违约方支付违约金后,还应当履行债务。

第五百八十六条　当事人可以约定一方向对方给付定金作为债权的担保。定金合同自实际交付定金时成立。

定金的数额由当事人约定;但是,不得超过主合同标的额的百分之二十,超过部分不产生定金的效力。实际交付的定金数额多于或者少于约定数额的,视为变更约定的定金数额。

第五百八十七条　债务人履行债务的,定金应当抵作价款或者收回。给付定金的一方不履行债务或者履行债务不符合约定,致使不能实现合同目的的,无权请求返还定金;收受定金的一方不履行债务或者履行债务不符合约定,致使不能实现合同目的的,应当双倍返还定金。

第五百八十八条　当事人既约定违约金,又约定定金的,一方违约时,对方可以选择适用违约金或者定金条款。

定金不足以弥补一方违约造成的损失的,对方可以请求赔偿超过定金数额的损失。

第五百八十九条　债务人按照约定履行债务,债权人无正当理由拒绝受领的,债务人可以请求债权人赔偿增加的费用。

在债权人受领迟延期间,债务人无须支付利息。

第五百九十条　当事人一方因不可抗力不能履行合同的,根据不可抗力的影响,部分或者全部免除责任,但是法律另有规定的除外。因不可抗力不能履行合同的,应当及时通知对方,以减轻可能给对方造成的损失,并应当在合理期限内提供证明。

当事人迟延履行后发生不可抗力的,不免除其违约责任。

第五百九十一条　当事人一方违约后,对方应当采取适当措施防止损失的扩大;没有采取适当措施致使损失扩大的,不得就扩大的损失请求赔偿。

当事人因防止损失扩大而支出的合理费用,由违约方负担。

第五百九十二条　当事人都违反合同的,应当各自承担相应的责任。

当事人一方违约造成对方损失,对方对损失的发生有过错的,可以减少相应的损失赔偿额。

第五百九十三条　当事人一方因第三人的原因造成违约的,应当依法向对方承担违约责任。当事人一方和第三人之间的纠纷,依照法律规定或者按照约定处理。

第五百九十四条　因国际货物买卖合同和技术进出口合同争议提起诉讼或者申请仲裁的时效期间为四年。

第二分编　典型合同

第九章　买卖合同

第五百九十五条　买卖合同是出卖人转移标的物的所有权于买受人,买受人支付价款的合同。

第五百九十六条　买卖合同的内容一般包括标的物的名称、数量、质量、价款、履行期限、履行地点和方式、包装方式、检验标准和方法、结算方式、合同使用的文字及其效力等条款。

第五百九十七条　因出卖人未取得处分权致使标的物所有权不能转移的,买受人可以解除合同并请求出卖人承担违约责任。

法律、行政法规禁止或者限制转让的标的物,依照其规定。

第五百九十八条 出卖人应当履行向买受人交付标的物或者交付提取标的物的单证，并转移标的物所有权的义务。

第五百九十九条 出卖人应当按照约定或者交易习惯向买受人交付提取标的物单证以外的有关单证和资料。

第六百条 出卖具有知识产权的标的物的，除法律另有规定或者当事人另有约定外，该标的物的知识产权不属于买受人。

第六百零一条 出卖人应当按照约定的时间交付标的物。约定交付期限的，出卖人可以在该交付期限内的任何时间交付。

第六百零二条 当事人没有约定标的物的交付期限或者约定不明确的，适用本法第五百一十条、第五百一十一条第四项的规定。

第六百零三条 出卖人应当按照约定的地点交付标的物。

当事人没有约定交付地点或者约定不明确，依据本法第五百一十条的规定仍不能确定的，适用下列规定：

（一）标的物需要运输的，出卖人应当将标的物交付给第一承运人以运交给买受人；

（二）标的物不需要运输，出卖人和买受人订立合同时知道标的物在某一地点的，出卖人应当在该地点交付标的物；不知道标的物在某一地点的，应当在出卖人订立合同时的营业地交付标的物。

第六百零四条 标的物毁损、灭失的风险，在标的物交付之前由出卖人承担，交付之后由买受人承担，但是法律另有规定或者当事人另有约定的除外。

第六百零五条 因买受人的原因致使标的物未按照约定的期限交付的，买受人应当自违反约定时起承担标的物毁损、灭失的风险。

第六百零六条 出卖人出卖交由承运人运输的在途标的物，除当事人另有约定外，毁损、灭失的风险自合同成立时起由买受人承担。

第六百零七条 出卖人按照约定将标的物运送至买受人指定地点并交付给承运人后，标的物毁损、灭失的风险由买受人承担。

当事人没有约定交付地点或者约定不明确，依据本法第六百零三条第二款第一项的规定标的物需要运输的，出卖人将标的物交付给第一承运人后，标的物毁损、灭失的风险由买受人承担。

第六百零八条　出卖人按照约定或者依据本法第六百零三条第二款第二项的规定将标的物置于交付地点，买受人违反约定没有收取的，标的物毁损、灭失的风险自违反约定时起由买受人承担。

第六百零九条　出卖人按照约定未交付有关标的物的单证和资料的，不影响标的物毁损、灭失风险的转移。

第六百一十条　因标的物不符合质量要求，致使不能实现合同目的的，买受人可以拒绝接受标的物或者解除合同。买受人拒绝接受标的物或者解除合同的，标的物毁损、灭失的风险由出卖人承担。

第六百一十一条　标的物毁损、灭失的风险由买受人承担的，不影响因出卖人履行义务不符合约定，买受人请求其承担违约责任的权利。

第六百一十二条　出卖人就交付的标的物，负有保证第三人对该标的物不享有任何权利的义务，但是法律另有规定的除外。

第六百一十三条　买受人订立合同时知道或者应当知道第三人对买卖的标的物享有权利的，出卖人不承担前条规定的义务。

第六百一十四条　买受人有确切证据证明第三人对标的物享有权利的，可以中止支付相应的价款，但是出卖人提供适当担保的除外。

第六百一十五条　出卖人应当按照约定的质量要求交付标的物。出卖人提供有关标的物质量说明的，交付的标的物应当符合该说明的质量要求。

第六百一十六条　当事人对标的物的质量要求没有约定或者约定不明确，依据本法第五百一十条的规定仍不能确定的，适用本法第五百一十一条第一项的规定。

第六百一十七条　出卖人交付的标的物不符合质量要求的，买受人可以依据本法第五百八十二条至第五百八十四条的规定请求承担违约责任。

第六百一十八条　当事人约定减轻或者免除出卖人对标的物瑕疵承担的责任，因出卖人故意或者重大过失不告知买受人标的物瑕疵的，出卖人无权主张减轻或者免除责任。

第六百一十九条 出卖人应当按照约定的包装方式交付标的物。对包装方式没有约定或者约定不明确,依据本法第五百一十条的规定仍不能确定的,应当按照通用的方式包装;没有通用方式的,应当采取足以保护标的物且有利于节约资源、保护生态环境的包装方式。

第六百二十条 买受人收到标的物时应当在约定的检验期限内检验。没有约定检验期限的,应当及时检验。

第六百二十一条 当事人约定检验期限的,买受人应当在检验期限内将标的物的数量或者质量不符合约定的情形通知出卖人。买受人怠于通知的,视为标的物的数量或者质量符合约定。

当事人没有约定检验期限的,买受人应当在发现或者应当发现标的物的数量或者质量不符合约定的合理期限内通知出卖人。买受人在合理期限内未通知或者自收到标的物之日起二年内未通知出卖人的,视为标的物的数量或者质量符合约定;但是,对标的物有质量保证期的,适用质量保证期,不适用该二年的规定。

出卖人知道或者应当知道提供的标的物不符合约定的,买受人不受前两款规定的通知时间的限制。

第六百二十二条 当事人约定的检验期限过短,根据标的物的性质和交易习惯,买受人在检验期限内难以完成全面检验的,该期限仅视为买受人对标的物的外观瑕疵提出异议的期限。

约定的检验期限或者质量保证期短于法律、行政法规规定期限的,应当以法律、行政法规规定的期限为准。

第六百二十三条 当事人对检验期限未作约定,买受人签收的送货单、确认单等载明标的物数量、型号、规格的,推定买受人已经对数量和外观瑕疵进行检验,但是有相关证据足以推翻的除外。

第六百二十四条 出卖人依照买受人的指示向第三人交付标的物,出卖人和买受人约定的检验标准与买受人和第三人约定的检验标准不一致的,以出卖人和买受人约定的检验标准为准。

第六百二十五条 依照法律、行政法规的规定或者按照当事人的约定，标的物在有效使用年限届满后应予回收的，出卖人负有自行或者委托第三人对标的物予以回收的义务。

第六百二十六条 买受人应当按照约定的数额和支付方式支付价款。对价款的数额和支付方式没有约定或者约定不明确的，适用本法第五百一十条、第五百一十一条第二项和第五项的规定。

第六百二十七条 买受人应当按照约定的地点支付价款。对支付地点没有约定或者约定不明确，依据本法第五百一十条的规定仍不能确定的，买受人应当在出卖人的营业地支付；但是，约定支付价款以交付标的物或者交付提取标的物单证为条件的，在交付标的物或者交付提取标的物单证的所在地支付。

第六百二十八条 买受人应当按照约定的时间支付价款。对支付时间没有约定或者约定不明确，依据本法第五百一十条的规定仍不能确定的，买受人应当在收到标的物或者提取标的物单证的同时支付。

第六百二十九条 出卖人多交标的物的，买受人可以接收或者拒绝接收多交的部分。买受人接收多交部分的，按照约定的价格支付价款；买受人拒绝接收多交部分的，应当及时通知出卖人。

第六百三十条 标的物在交付之前产生的孳息，归出卖人所有；交付之后产生的孳息，归买受人所有。但是，当事人另有约定的除外。

第六百三十一条 因标的物的主物不符合约定而解除合同的，解除合同的效力及于从物。因标的物的从物不符合约定被解除的，解除的效力不及于主物。

第六百三十二条 标的物为数物，其中一物不符合约定的，买受人可以就该物解除。但是，该物与他物分离使标的物的价值显受损害的，买受人可以就数物解除合同。

第六百三十三条 出卖人分批交付标的物的，出卖人对其中一批标的物不交付或者交付不符合约定，致使该批标的物不能实现合同目的的，买受人可以就该批标的物解除。

出卖人不交付其中一批标的物或者交付不符合约定，致使之后其他各批标的物的交付不能实现合同目的的,买受人可以就该批以及之后其他各批标的物解除。

买受人如果就其中一批标的物解除,该批标的物与其他各批标的物相互依存的,可以就已经交付和未交付的各批标的物解除。

第六百三十四条 分期付款的买受人未支付到期价款的数额达到全部价款的五分之一,经催告后在合理期限内仍未支付到期价款的,出卖人可以请求买受人支付全部价款或者解除合同。

出卖人解除合同的,可以向买受人请求支付该标的物的使用费。

第六百三十五条 凭样品买卖的当事人应当封存样品,并可以对样品质量予以说明。出卖人交付的标的物应当与样品及其说明的质量相同。

第六百三十六条 凭样品买卖的买受人不知道样品有隐蔽瑕疵的,即使交付的标的物与样品相同,出卖人交付的标的物的质量仍然应当符合同种物的通常标准。

第六百三十七条 试用买卖的当事人可以约定标的物的试用期限。对试用期限没有约定或者约定不明确,依据本法第五百一十条的规定仍不能确定的,由出卖人确定。

第六百三十八条 试用买卖的买受人在试用期内可以购买标的物,也可以拒绝购买。试用期限届满,买受人对是否购买标的物未作表示的,视为购买。

试用买卖的买受人在试用期内已经支付部分价款或者对标的物实施出卖、出租、设立担保物权等行为的,视为同意购买。

第六百三十九条 试用买卖的当事人对标的物使用费没有约定或者约定不明确的,出卖人无权请求买受人支付。

第六百四十条 标的物在试用期内毁损、灭失的风险由出卖人承担。

第六百四十一条 当事人可以在买卖合同中约定买受人未履行支付价款或者其他义务的,标的物的所有权属于出卖人。

出卖人对标的物保留的所有权,未经登记,不得对抗善意第三人。

第六百四十二条 当事人约定出卖人保留合同标的物的所有权,在标的物所有权转移前，买受人有下列情形之一，造成出卖人损害的，除当事人另有约定外，出卖人有权取回标的物：

（一）未按照约定支付价款，经催告后在合理期限内仍未支付；

（二）未按照约定完成特定条件；

（三）将标的物出卖、出质或者作出其他不当处分。

出卖人可以与买受人协商取回标的物；协商不成的，可以参照适用担保物权的实现程序。

第六百四十三条　出卖人依据前条第一款的规定取回标的物后，买受人在双方约定或者出卖人指定的合理回赎期限内，消除出卖人取回标的物的事由的，可以请求回赎标的物。

买受人在回赎期限内没有回赎标的物，出卖人可以以合理价格将标的物出卖给第三人，出卖所得价款扣除买受人未支付的价款以及必要费用后仍有剩余的，应当返还买受人；不足部分由买受人清偿。

第六百四十四条　招标投标买卖的当事人的权利和义务以及招标投标程序等，依照有关法律、行政法规的规定。

第六百四十五条　拍卖的当事人的权利和义务以及拍卖程序等，依照有关法律、行政法规的规定。

第六百四十六条　法律对其他有偿合同有规定的，依照其规定；没有规定的，参照适用买卖合同的有关规定。

第六百四十七条　当事人约定易货交易，转移标的物的所有权的，参照适用买卖合同的有关规定。

第十章　供用电、水、气、热力合同

第六百四十八条　供用电合同是供电人向用电人供电，用电人支付电费的合同。

向社会公众供电的供电人，不得拒绝用电人合理的订立合同要求。

第六百四十九条　供用电合同的内容一般包括供电的方式、质量、时间，用电容量、地址、性质，计量方式，电价、电费的结算方式，供用电设施的维护责任等条款。

第六百五十条 供用电合同的履行地点,按照当事人约定;当事人没有约定或者约定不明确的,供电设施的产权分界处为履行地点。

第六百五十一条 供电人应当按照国家规定的供电质量标准和约定安全供电。供电人未按照国家规定的供电质量标准和约定安全供电,造成用电人损失的,应当承担赔偿责任。

第六百五十二条 供电人因供电设施计划检修、临时检修、依法限电或者用电人违法用电等原因,需要中断供电时,应当按照国家有关规定事先通知用电人;未事先通知用电人中断供电,造成用电人损失的,应当承担赔偿责任。

第六百五十三条 因自然灾害等原因断电,供电人应当按照国家有关规定及时抢修;未及时抢修,造成用电人损失的,应当承担赔偿责任。

第六百五十四条 用电人应当按照国家有关规定和当事人的约定及时支付电费。用电人逾期不支付电费的,应当按照约定支付违约金。经催告用电人在合理期限内仍不支付电费和违约金的,供电人可以按照国家规定的程序中止供电。

供电人依据前款规定中止供电的,应当事先通知用电人。

第六百五十五条 用电人应当按照国家有关规定和当事人的约定安全、节约和计划用电。用电人未按照国家有关规定和当事人的约定用电,造成供电人损失的,应当承担赔偿责任。

第六百五十六条 供用水、供用气、供用热力合同,参照适用供用电合同的有关规定。

第十一章 赠与合同

第六百五十七条 赠与合同是赠与人将自己的财产无偿给予受赠人,受赠人表示接受赠与的合同。

第六百五十八条 赠与人在赠与财产的权利转移之前可以撤销赠与。

经过公证的赠与合同或者依法不得撤销的具有救灾、扶贫、助残等公益、道德义务性质的赠与合同，不适用前款规定。

第六百五十九条　赠与的财产依法需要办理登记或者其他手续的，应当办理有关手续。

第六百六十条　经过公证的赠与合同或者依法不得撤销的具有救灾、扶贫、助残等公益、道德义务性质的赠与合同，赠与人不交付赠与财产的，受赠人可以请求交付。

依据前款规定应当交付的赠与财产因赠与人故意或者重大过失致使毁损、灭失的，赠与人应当承担赔偿责任。

第六百六十一条　赠与可以附义务。

赠与附义务的，受赠人应当按照约定履行义务。

第六百六十二条　赠与的财产有瑕疵的，赠与人不承担责任。附义务的赠与，赠与的财产有瑕疵的，赠与人在附义务的限度内承担与出卖人相同的责任。

赠与人故意不告知瑕疵或者保证无瑕疵，造成受赠人损失的，应当承担赔偿责任。

第六百六十三条　受赠人有下列情形之一的，赠与人可以撤销赠与：

（一）严重侵害赠与人或者赠与人近亲属的合法权益；

（二）对赠与人有扶养义务而不履行；

（三）不履行赠与合同约定的义务。

赠与人的撤销权，自知道或者应当知道撤销事由之日起一年内行使。

第六百六十四条　因受赠人的违法行为致使赠与人死亡或者丧失民事行为能力的，赠与人的继承人或者法定代理人可以撤销赠与。

赠与人的继承人或者法定代理人的撤销权，自知道或者应当知道撤销事由之日起六个月内行使。

第六百六十五条　撤销权人撤销赠与的，可以向受赠人请求返还赠与的财产。

第六百六十六条　赠与人的经济状况显著恶化，严重影响其生产经营或者家庭生活的，可以不再履行赠与义务。

第十二章 借款合同

第六百六十七条 借款合同是借款人向贷款人借款,到期返还借款并支付利息的合同。

第六百六十八条 借款合同应当采用书面形式,但是自然人之间借款另有约定的除外。

借款合同的内容一般包括借款种类、币种、用途、数额、利率、期限和还款方式等条款。

第六百六十九条 订立借款合同,借款人应当按照贷款人的要求提供与借款有关的业务活动和财务状况的真实情况。

第六百七十条 借款的利息不得预先在本金中扣除。利息预先在本金中扣除的,应当按照实际借款数额返还借款并计算利息。

第六百七十一条 贷款人未按照约定的日期、数额提供借款,造成借款人损失的,应当赔偿损失。

借款人未按照约定的日期、数额收取借款的,应当按照约定的日期、数额支付利息。

第六百七十二条 贷款人按照约定可以检查、监督借款的使用情况。借款人应当按照约定向贷款人定期提供有关财务会计报表或者其他资料。

第六百七十三条 借款人未按照约定的借款用途使用借款的,贷款人可以停止发放借款、提前收回借款或者解除合同。

第六百七十四条 借款人应当按照约定的期限支付利息。对支付利息的期限没有约定或者约定不明确,依据本法第五百一十条的规定仍不能确定,借款期间不满一年的,应当在返还借款时一并支付;借款期间一年以上的,应当在每届满一年时支付,剩余期间不满一年的,应当在返还借款时一并支付。

第六百七十五条 借款人应当按照约定的期限返还借款。对借款期限没有约定或者约定不明确,依据本法第五百一十条的规定仍不能确定的,借款人可以随时返还;贷款人可以催告借款人在合理期限内返还。

第六百七十六条 借款人未按照约定的期限返还借款的,应当按照约定或者国家有关规定支付逾期利息。

第六百七十七条 借款人提前返还借款的,除当事人另有约定外,应当按照实际借款的期间计算利息。

第六百七十八条 借款人可以在还款期限届满前向贷款人申请展期;贷款人同意的,可以展期。

第六百七十九条 自然人之间的借款合同,自贷款人提供借款时成立。

第六百八十条 禁止高利放贷,借款的利率不得违反国家有关规定。

借款合同对支付利息没有约定的,视为没有利息。

借款合同对支付利息约定不明确,当事人不能达成补充协议的,按照当地或者当事人的交易方式、交易习惯、市场利率等因素确定利息;自然人之间借款的,视为没有利息。

第十三章 保证合同

第一节 一般规定

第六百八十一条 保证合同是为保障债权的实现,保证人和债权人约定,当债务人不履行到期债务或者发生当事人约定的情形时,保证人履行债务或者承担责任的合同。

第六百八十二条 保证合同是主债权债务合同的从合同。主债权债务合同无效的,保证合同无效,但是法律另有规定的除外。

保证合同被确认无效后,债务人、保证人、债权人有过错的,应当根据其过错各自承担相应的民事责任。

第六百八十三条 机关法人不得为保证人,但是经国务院批准为使用外国政府或者国际经济组织贷款进行转贷的除外。

以公益为目的的非营利法人、非法人组织不得为保证人。

第六百八十四条 保证合同的内容一般包括被保证的主债权的种类、数额,债务人履行债务的期限,保证的方式、范围和期间等条款。

第六百八十五条 保证合同可以是单独订立的书面合同,也可以是主债权债务合同中的保证条款。

第三人单方以书面形式向债权人作出保证,债权人接收且未提出异议的,保证合同成立。

第六百八十六条 保证的方式包括一般保证和连带责任保证。

当事人在保证合同中对保证方式没有约定或者约定不明确的,按照一般保证承担保证责任。

第六百八十七条 当事人在保证合同中约定,债务人不能履行债务时,由保证人承担保证责任的,为一般保证。

一般保证的保证人在主合同纠纷未经审判或者仲裁,并就债务人财产依法强制执行仍不能履行债务前,有权拒绝向债权人承担保证责任,但是有下列情形之一的除外:

(一)债务人下落不明,且无财产可供执行;

(二)人民法院已经受理债务人破产案件;

(三)债权人有证据证明债务人的财产不足以履行全部债务或者丧失履行债务能力;

(四)保证人书面表示放弃本款规定的权利。

第六百八十八条 当事人在保证合同中约定保证人和债务人对债务承担连带责任的,为连带责任保证。

连带责任保证的债务人不履行到期债务或者发生当事人约定的情形时,债权人可以请求债务人履行债务,也可以请求保证人在其保证范围内承担保证责任。

第六百八十九条 保证人可以要求债务人提供反担保。

第六百九十条 保证人与债权人可以协商订立最高额保证的合同,约定在最高债权额限度内就一定期间连续发生的债权提供保证。

最高额保证除适用本章规定外,参照适用本法第二编最高额抵押权的有关规定。

第二节 保证责任

第六百九十一条 保证的范围包括主债权及其利息、违约金、损害赔偿金和实现债权的费用。当事人另有约定的,按照其约定。

第六百九十二条 保证期间是确定保证人承担保证责任的期间,不发生中止、中断和延长。

债权人与保证人可以约定保证期间,但是约定的保证期间早于主债务履行期限或者与主债务履行期限同时届满的,视为没有约定;没有约定或者约定不明确的,保证期间为主债务履行期限届满之日起六个月。

债权人与债务人对主债务履行期限没有约定或者约定不明确的,保证期间自债权人请求债务人履行债务的宽限期届满之日起计算。

第六百九十三条 一般保证的债权人未在保证期间对债务人提起诉讼或者申请仲裁的,保证人不再承担保证责任。

连带责任保证的债权人未在保证期间请求保证人承担保证责任的,保证人不再承担保证责任。

第六百九十四条 一般保证的债权人在保证期间届满前对债务人提起诉讼或者申请仲裁的,从保证人拒绝承担保证责任的权利消灭之日起,开始计算保证债务的诉讼时效。

连带责任保证的债权人在保证期间届满前请求保证人承担保证责任的,从债权人请求保证人承担保证责任之日起,开始计算保证债务的诉讼时效。

第六百九十五条 债权人和债务人未经保证人书面同意,协商变更主债权债务合同内容,减轻债务的,保证人仍对变更后的债务承担保证责任;加重债务的,保证人对加重的部分不承担保证责任。

债权人和债务人变更主债权债务合同的履行期限,未经保证人书面同意的,保证期间不受影响。

第六百九十六条 债权人转让全部或者部分债权,未通知保证人的,该转让对保证人不发生效力。

保证人与债权人约定禁止债权转让,债权人未经保证人书面同意转让债权的,保证人对受让人不再承担保证责任。

第六百九十七条 债权人未经保证人书面同意,允许债务人转移全部或者部分债务,保证人对未经其同意转移的债务不再承担保证责任,但是债权人和保证人另有约定的除外。

第三人加入债务的,保证人的保证责任不受影响。

第六百九十八条 一般保证的保证人在主债务履行期限届满后,向债权人提供债务人可供执行财产的真实情况,债权人放弃或者怠于行使权利致使该财产不能被执行的,保证人在其提供可供执行财产的价值范围内不再承担保证责任。

第六百九十九条 同一债务有两个以上保证人的,保证人应当按照保证合同约定的保证份额,承担保证责任;没有约定保证份额的,债权人可以请求任何一个保证人在其保证范围内承担保证责任。

第七百条 保证人承担保证责任后,除当事人另有约定外,有权在其承担保证责任的范围内向债务人追偿,享有债权人对债务人的权利,但是不得损害债权人的利益。

第七百零一条 保证人可以主张债务人对债权人的抗辩。债务人放弃抗辩的,保证人仍有权向债权人主张抗辩。

第七百零二条 债务人对债权人享有抵销权或者撤销权的,保证人可以在相应范围内拒绝承担保证责任。

第十四章 租 赁 合 同

第七百零三条 租赁合同是出租人将租赁物交付承租人使用、收益,承租人支付租金的合同。

第七百零四条 租赁合同的内容一般包括租赁物的名称、数量、用途、租赁期限、租金及其支付期限和方式、租赁物维修等条款。

第七百零五条 租赁期限不得超过二十年。超过二十年的,超过部分无效。

租赁期限届满，当事人可以续订租赁合同；但是，约定的租赁期限自续订之日起不得超过二十年。

第七百零六条 当事人未依照法律、行政法规规定办理租赁合同登记备案手续的，不影响合同的效力。

第七百零七条 租赁期限六个月以上的，应当采用书面形式。当事人未采用书面形式，无法确定租赁期限的，视为不定期租赁。

第七百零八条 出租人应当按照约定将租赁物交付承租人，并在租赁期限内保持租赁物符合约定的用途。

第七百零九条 承租人应当按照约定的方法使用租赁物。对租赁物的使用方法没有约定或者约定不明确，依据本法第五百一十条的规定仍不能确定的，应当根据租赁物的性质使用。

第七百一十条 承租人按照约定的方法或者根据租赁物的性质使用租赁物，致使租赁物受到损耗的，不承担赔偿责任。

第七百一十一条 承租人未按照约定的方法或者未根据租赁物的性质使用租赁物，致使租赁物受到损失的，出租人可以解除合同并请求赔偿损失。

第七百一十二条 出租人应当履行租赁物的维修义务，但是当事人另有约定的除外。

第七百一十三条 承租人在租赁物需要维修时可以请求出租人在合理期限内维修。出租人未履行维修义务的，承租人可以自行维修，维修费用由出租人负担。因维修租赁物影响承租人使用的，应当相应减少租金或者延长租期。

因承租人的过错致使租赁物需要维修的，出租人不承担前款规定的维修义务。

第七百一十四条 承租人应当妥善保管租赁物，因保管不善造成租赁物毁损、灭失的，应当承担赔偿责任。

第七百一十五条 承租人经出租人同意，可以对租赁物进行改善或者增设他物。

承租人未经出租人同意,对租赁物进行改善或者增设他物的,出租人可以请求承租人恢复原状或者赔偿损失。

第七百一十六条　承租人经出租人同意,可以将租赁物转租给第三人。承租人转租的,承租人与出租人之间的租赁合同继续有效;第三人造成租赁物损失的,承租人应当赔偿损失。

承租人未经出租人同意转租的,出租人可以解除合同。

第七百一十七条　承租人经出租人同意将租赁物转租给第三人,转租期限超过承租人剩余租赁期限的,超过部分的约定对出租人不具有法律约束力,但是出租人与承租人另有约定的除外。

第七百一十八条　出租人知道或者应当知道承租人转租,但是在六个月内未提出异议的,视为出租人同意转租。

第七百一十九条　承租人拖欠租金的,次承租人可以代承租人支付其欠付的租金和违约金,但是转租合同对出租人不具有法律约束力的除外。

次承租人代为支付的租金和违约金,可以充抵次承租人应当向承租人支付的租金;超出其应付的租金数额的,可以向承租人追偿。

第七百二十条　在租赁期限内因占有、使用租赁物获得的收益,归承租人所有,但是当事人另有约定的除外。

第七百二十一条　承租人应当按照约定的期限支付租金。对支付租金的期限没有约定或者约定不明确,依据本法第五百一十条的规定仍不能确定,租赁期限不满一年的,应当在租赁期限届满时支付;租赁期限一年以上的,应当在每届满一年时支付,剩余期限不满一年的,应当在租赁期限届满时支付。

第七百二十二条　承租人无正当理由未支付或者迟延支付租金的,出租人可以请求承租人在合理期限内支付;承租人逾期不支付的,出租人可以解除合同。

第七百二十三条　因第三人主张权利,致使承租人不能对租赁物使用、收益的,承租人可以请求减少租金或者不支付租金。

第三人主张权利的,承租人应当及时通知出租人。

第七百二十四条　有下列情形之一，非因承租人原因致使租赁物无法使用的，承租人可以解除合同：

（一）租赁物被司法机关或者行政机关依法查封、扣押；

（二）租赁物权属有争议；

（三）租赁物具有违反法律、行政法规关于使用条件的强制性规定情形。

第七百二十五条　租赁物在承租人按照租赁合同占有期限内发生所有权变动的，不影响租赁合同的效力。

第七百二十六条　出租人出卖租赁房屋的，应当在出卖之前的合理期限内通知承租人，承租人享有以同等条件优先购买的权利；但是，房屋按份共有人行使优先购买权或者出租人将房屋出卖给近亲属的除外。

出租人履行通知义务后，承租人在十五日内未明确表示购买的，视为承租人放弃优先购买权。

第七百二十七条　出租人委托拍卖人拍卖租赁房屋的，应当在拍卖五日前通知承租人。承租人未参加拍卖的，视为放弃优先购买权。

第七百二十八条　出租人未通知承租人或者有其他妨害承租人行使优先购买权情形的，承租人可以请求出租人承担赔偿责任。但是，出租人与第三人订立的房屋买卖合同的效力不受影响。

第七百二十九条　因不可归责于承租人的事由，致使租赁物部分或者全部毁损、灭失的，承租人可以请求减少租金或者不支付租金；因租赁物部分或者全部毁损、灭失，致使不能实现合同目的的，承租人可以解除合同。

第七百三十条　当事人对租赁期限没有约定或者约定不明确，依据本法第五百一十条的规定仍不能确定的，视为不定期租赁；当事人可以随时解除合同，但是应当在合理期限之前通知对方。

第七百三十一条　租赁物危及承租人的安全或者健康的，即使承租人订立合同时明知该租赁物质量不合格，承租人仍然可以随时解除合同。

第七百三十二条　承租人在房屋租赁期限内死亡的，与其生前共同居住的人或者共同经营人可以按照原租赁合同租赁该房屋。

第七百三十三条　租赁期限届满，承租人应当返还租赁物。返还的租赁物应当符合按照约定或者根据租赁物的性质使用后的状态。

第七百三十四条　租赁期限届满,承租人继续使用租赁物,出租人没有提出异议的,原租赁合同继续有效,但是租赁期限为不定期。

租赁期限届满,房屋承租人享有以同等条件优先承租的权利。

第十五章　融资租赁合同

第七百三十五条　融资租赁合同是出租人根据承租人对出卖人、租赁物的选择,向出卖人购买租赁物,提供给承租人使用,承租人支付租金的合同。

第七百三十六条　融资租赁合同的内容一般包括租赁物的名称、数量、规格、技术性能、检验方法,租赁期限,租金构成及其支付期限和方式、币种,租赁期限届满租赁物的归属等条款。

融资租赁合同应当采用书面形式。

第七百三十七条　当事人以虚构租赁物方式订立的融资租赁合同无效。

第七百三十八条　依照法律、行政法规的规定,对于租赁物的经营使用应当取得行政许可的,出租人未取得行政许可不影响融资租赁合同的效力。

第七百三十九条　出租人根据承租人对出卖人、租赁物的选择订立的买卖合同,出卖人应当按照约定向承租人交付标的物,承租人享有与受领标的物有关的买受人的权利。

第七百四十条　出卖人违反向承租人交付标的物的义务,有下列情形之一的,承租人可以拒绝受领出卖人向其交付的标的物:

(一)标的物严重不符合约定;

(二)未按照约定交付标的物,经承租人或者出租人催告后在合理期限内仍未交付。

承租人拒绝受领标的物的,应当及时通知出租人。

第七百四十一条　出租人、出卖人、承租人可以约定,出卖人不履行买卖合同义务的,由承租人行使索赔的权利。承租人行使索赔权利的,出租人应当协助。

第七百四十二条 承租人对出卖人行使索赔权利，不影响其履行支付租金的义务。但是，承租人依赖出租人的技能确定租赁物或者出租人干预选择租赁物的，承租人可以请求减免相应租金。

第七百四十三条 出租人有下列情形之一，致使承租人对出卖人行使索赔权利失败的，承租人有权请求出租人承担相应的责任：

（一）明知租赁物有质量瑕疵而不告知承租人；

（二）承租人行使索赔权利时，未及时提供必要协助。

出租人怠于行使只能由其对出卖人行使的索赔权利，造成承租人损失的，承租人有权请求出租人承担赔偿责任。

第七百四十四条 出租人根据承租人对出卖人、租赁物的选择订立的买卖合同，未经承租人同意，出租人不得变更与承租人有关的合同内容。

第七百四十五条 出租人对租赁物享有的所有权，未经登记，不得对抗善意第三人。

第七百四十六条 融资租赁合同的租金，除当事人另有约定外，应当根据购买租赁物的大部分或者全部成本以及出租人的合理利润确定。

第七百四十七条 租赁物不符合约定或者不符合使用目的的，出租人不承担责任。但是，承租人依赖出租人的技能确定租赁物或者出租人干预选择租赁物的除外。

第七百四十八条 出租人应当保证承租人对租赁物的占有和使用。

出租人有下列情形之一的，承租人有权请求其赔偿损失：

（一）无正当理由收回租赁物；

（二）无正当理由妨碍、干扰承租人对租赁物的占有和使用；

（三）因出租人的原因致使第三人对租赁物主张权利；

（四）不当影响承租人对租赁物占有和使用的其他情形。

第七百四十九条 承租人占有租赁物期间，租赁物造成第三人人身损害或者财产损失的，出租人不承担责任。

第七百五十条 承租人应当妥善保管、使用租赁物。

承租人应当履行占有租赁物期间的维修义务。

第七百五十一条 承租人占有租赁物期间,租赁物毁损、灭失的,出租人有权请求承租人继续支付租金,但是法律另有规定或者当事人另有约定的除外。

第七百五十二条 承租人应当按照约定支付租金。承租人经催告后在合理期限内仍不支付租金的,出租人可以请求支付全部租金;也可以解除合同,收回租赁物。

第七百五十三条 承租人未经出租人同意,将租赁物转让、抵押、质押、投资入股或者以其他方式处分的,出租人可以解除融资租赁合同。

第七百五十四条 有下列情形之一的,出租人或者承租人可以解除融资租赁合同:

(一)出租人与出卖人订立的买卖合同解除、被确认无效或者被撤销,且未能重新订立买卖合同;

(二)租赁物因不可归责于当事人的原因毁损、灭失,且不能修复或者确定替代物;

(三)因出卖人的原因致使融资租赁合同的目的不能实现。

第七百五十五条 融资租赁合同因买卖合同解除、被确认无效或者被撤销而解除,出卖人、租赁物系由承租人选择的,出租人有权请求承租人赔偿相应损失;但是,因出租人原因致使买卖合同解除、被确认无效或者被撤销的除外。

出租人的损失已经在买卖合同解除、被确认无效或者被撤销时获得赔偿的,承租人不再承担相应的赔偿责任。

第七百五十六条 融资租赁合同因租赁物交付承租人后意外毁损、灭失等不可归责于当事人的原因解除的,出租人可以请求承租人按照租赁物折旧情况给予补偿。

第七百五十七条 出租人和承租人可以约定租赁期限届满租赁物的归属;对租赁物的归属没有约定或者约定不明确,依据本法第五百一十条的规定仍不能确定的,租赁物的所有权归出租人。

第七百五十八条 当事人约定租赁期限届满租赁物归承租人所有，承租人已经支付大部分租金，但是无力支付剩余租金，出租人因此解除合同收回租赁物，收回的租赁物的价值超过承租人欠付的租金以及其他费用的，承租人可以请求相应返还。

当事人约定租赁期限届满租赁物归出租人所有，因租赁物毁损、灭失或者附合、混合于他物致使承租人不能返还的，出租人有权请求承租人给予合理补偿。

第七百五十九条 当事人约定租赁期限届满，承租人仅需向出租人支付象征性价款的，视为约定的租金义务履行完毕后租赁物的所有权归承租人。

第七百六十条 融资租赁合同无效，当事人就该情形下租赁物的归属有约定的，按照其约定；没有约定或者约定不明确的，租赁物应当返还出租人。但是，因承租人原因致使合同无效，出租人不请求返还或者返还后会显著降低租赁物效用的，租赁物的所有权归承租人，由承租人给予出租人合理补偿。

第十六章 保理合同

第七百六十一条 保理合同是应收账款债权人将现有的或者将有的应收账款转让给保理人，保理人提供资金融通、应收账款管理或者催收、应收账款债务人付款担保等服务的合同。

第七百六十二条 保理合同的内容一般包括业务类型、服务范围、服务期限、基础交易合同情况、应收账款信息、保理融资款或者服务报酬及其支付方式等条款。

保理合同应当采用书面形式。

第七百六十三条 应收账款债权人与债务人虚构应收账款作为转让标的，与保理人订立保理合同的，应收账款债务人不得以应收账款不存在为由对抗保理人，但是保理人明知虚构的除外。

第七百六十四条 保理人向应收账款债务人发出应收账款转让通知

的,应当表明保理人身份并附有必要凭证。

第七百六十五条 应收账款债务人接到应收账款转让通知后,应收账款债权人与债务人无正当理由协商变更或者终止基础交易合同,对保理人产生不利影响的,对保理人不发生效力。

第七百六十六条 当事人约定有追索权保理的,保理人可以向应收账款债权人主张返还保理融资款本息或者回购应收账款债权,也可以向应收账款债务人主张应收账款债权。保理人向应收账款债务人主张应收账款债权,在扣除保理融资款本息和相关费用后有剩余的,剩余部分应当返还给应收账款债权人。

第七百六十七条 当事人约定无追索权保理的,保理人应当向应收账款债务人主张应收账款债权,保理人取得超过保理融资款本息和相关费用的部分,无需向应收账款债权人返还。

第七百六十八条 应收账款债权人就同一应收账款订立多个保理合同,致使多个保理人主张权利的,已经登记的先于未登记的取得应收账款;均已经登记的,按照登记时间的先后顺序取得应收账款;均未登记的,由最先到达应收账款债务人的转让通知中载明的保理人取得应收账款;既未登记也未通知的,按照保理融资款或者服务报酬的比例取得应收账款。

第七百六十九条 本章没有规定的,适用本编第六章债权转让的有关规定。

第十七章 承揽合同

第七百七十条 承揽合同是承揽人按照定作人的要求完成工作,交付工作成果,定作人支付报酬的合同。

承揽包括加工、定作、修理、复制、测试、检验等工作。

第七百七十一条 承揽合同的内容一般包括承揽的标的、数量、质量、报酬,承揽方式,材料的提供,履行期限,验收标准和方法等条款。

第七百七十二条 承揽人应当以自己的设备、技术和劳力,完成主要工作,但是当事人另有约定的除外。

承揽人将其承揽的主要工作交由第三人完成的,应当就该第三人完成的工作成果向定作人负责;未经定作人同意的,定作人也可以解除合同。

第七百七十三条　承揽人可以将其承揽的辅助工作交由第三人完成。承揽人将其承揽的辅助工作交由第三人完成的,应当就该第三人完成的工作成果向定作人负责。

第七百七十四条　承揽人提供材料的,应当按照约定选用材料,并接受定作人检验。

第七百七十五条　定作人提供材料的,应当按照约定提供材料。承揽人对定作人提供的材料应当及时检验,发现不符合约定时,应当及时通知定作人更换、补齐或者采取其他补救措施。

承揽人不得擅自更换定作人提供的材料,不得更换不需要修理的零部件。

第七百七十六条　承揽人发现定作人提供的图纸或者技术要求不合理的,应当及时通知定作人。因定作人怠于答复等原因造成承揽人损失的,应当赔偿损失。

第七百七十七条　定作人中途变更承揽工作的要求,造成承揽人损失的,应当赔偿损失。

第七百七十八条　承揽工作需要定作人协助的,定作人有协助的义务。定作人不履行协助义务致使承揽工作不能完成的,承揽人可以催告定作人在合理期限内履行义务,并可以顺延履行期限;定作人逾期不履行的,承揽人可以解除合同。

第七百七十九条　承揽人在工作期间,应当接受定作人必要的监督检验。定作人不得因监督检验妨碍承揽人的正常工作。

第七百八十条　承揽人完成工作的,应当向定作人交付工作成果,并提交必要的技术资料和有关质量证明。定作人应当验收该工作成果。

第七百八十一条　承揽人交付的工作成果不符合质量要求的,定作人可以合理选择请求承揽人承担修理、重作、减少报酬、赔偿损失等违约责任。

第七百八十二条　定作人应当按照约定的期限支付报酬。对支付报酬的期限没有约定或者约定不明确,依据本法第五百一十条的规定仍不能确定的,定作人应当在承揽人交付工作成果时支付;工作成果部分交付的,定作人应当相应支付。

第七百八十三条 定作人未向承揽人支付报酬或者材料费等价款的,承揽人对完成的工作成果享有留置权或者有权拒绝交付,但是当事人另有约定的除外。

第七百八十四条 承揽人应当妥善保管定作人提供的材料以及完成的工作成果,因保管不善造成毁损、灭失的,应当承担赔偿责任。

第七百八十五条 承揽人应当按照定作人的要求保守秘密,未经定作人许可,不得留存复制品或者技术资料。

第七百八十六条 共同承揽人对定作人承担连带责任,但是当事人另有约定的除外。

第七百八十七条 定作人在承揽人完成工作前可以随时解除合同,造成承揽人损失的,应当赔偿损失。

第十八章 建设工程合同

第七百八十八条 建设工程合同是承包人进行工程建设,发包人支付价款的合同。

建设工程合同包括工程勘察、设计、施工合同。

第七百八十九条 建设工程合同应当采用书面形式。

第七百九十条 建设工程的招标投标活动,应当依照有关法律的规定公开、公平、公正进行。

第七百九十一条 发包人可以与总承包人订立建设工程合同,也可以分别与勘察人、设计人、施工人订立勘察、设计、施工承包合同。发包人不得将应当由一个承包人完成的建设工程支解成若干部分发包给数个承包人。

总承包人或者勘察、设计、施工承包人经发包人同意,可以将自己承包的部分工作交由第三人完成。第三人就其完成的工作成果与总承包人或者勘察、设计、施工承包人向发包人承担连带责任。承包人不得将其承包的全部建设工程转包给第三人或者将其承包的全部建设工程支解以后以分包的名义分别转包给第三人。

禁止承包人将工程分包给不具备相应资质条件的单位。禁止分包单位将其承包的工程再分包。建设工程主体结构的施工必须由承包人自行完成。

第七百九十二条 国家重大建设工程合同，应当按照国家规定的程序和国家批准的投资计划、可行性研究报告等文件订立。

第七百九十三条 建设工程施工合同无效，但是建设工程经验收合格的，可以参照合同关于工程价款的约定折价补偿承包人。

建设工程施工合同无效，且建设工程经验收不合格的，按照以下情形处理：

（一）修复后的建设工程经验收合格的，发包人可以请求承包人承担修复费用；

（二）修复后的建设工程经验收不合格的，承包人无权请求参照合同关于工程价款的约定折价补偿。

发包人对因建设工程不合格造成的损失有过错的，应当承担相应的责任。

第七百九十四条 勘察、设计合同的内容一般包括提交有关基础资料和概预算等文件的期限、质量要求、费用以及其他协作条件等条款。

第七百九十五条 施工合同的内容一般包括工程范围、建设工期、中间交工工程的开工和竣工时间、工程质量、工程造价、技术资料交付时间、材料和设备供应责任、拨款和结算、竣工验收、质量保修范围和质量保证期、相互协作等条款。

第七百九十六条 建设工程实行监理的，发包人应当与监理人采用书面形式订立委托监理合同。发包人与监理人的权利和义务以及法律责任，应当依照本编委托合同以及其他有关法律、行政法规的规定。

第七百九十七条 发包人在不妨碍承包人正常作业的情况下，可以随时对作业进度、质量进行检查。

第七百九十八条 隐蔽工程在隐蔽以前,承包人应当通知发包人检查。发包人没有及时检查的,承包人可以顺延工程日期,并有权请求赔偿停工、窝工等损失。

第七百九十九条 建设工程竣工后,发包人应当根据施工图纸及说明书、国家颁发的施工验收规范和质量检验标准及时进行验收。验收合格的,发包人应当按照约定支付价款,并接收该建设工程。

建设工程竣工经验收合格后,方可交付使用;未经验收或者验收不合格的,不得交付使用。

第八百条 勘察、设计的质量不符合要求或者未按照期限提交勘察、设计文件拖延工期,造成发包人损失的,勘察人、设计人应当继续完善勘察、设计,减收或者免收勘察、设计费并赔偿损失。

第八百零一条 因施工人的原因致使建设工程质量不符合约定的,发包人有权请求施工人在合理期限内无偿修理或者返工、改建。经过修理或者返工、改建后,造成逾期交付的,施工人应当承担违约责任。

第八百零二条 因承包人的原因致使建设工程在合理使用期限内造成人身损害和财产损失的,承包人应当承担赔偿责任。

第八百零三条 发包人未按照约定的时间和要求提供原材料、设备、场地、资金、技术资料的,承包人可以顺延工程日期,并有权请求赔偿停工、窝工等损失。

第八百零四条 因发包人的原因致使工程中途停建、缓建的,发包人应当采取措施弥补或者减少损失,赔偿承包人因此造成的停工、窝工、倒运、机械设备调迁、材料和构件积压等损失和实际费用。

第八百零五条 因发包人变更计划,提供的资料不准确,或者未按照期限提供必需的勘察、设计工作条件而造成勘察、设计的返工、停工或者修改设计,发包人应当按照勘察人、设计人实际消耗的工作量增付费用。

第八百零六条 承包人将建设工程转包、违法分包的,发包人可以解除合同。

发包人提供的主要建筑材料、建筑构配件和设备不符合强制性标准或者不履行协助义务，致使承包人无法施工，经催告后在合理期限内仍未履行相应义务的，承包人可以解除合同。

合同解除后，已经完成的建设工程质量合格的，发包人应当按照约定支付相应的工程价款；已经完成的建设工程质量不合格的，参照本法第七百九十三条的规定处理。

第八百零七条　发包人未按照约定支付价款的，承包人可以催告发包人在合理期限内支付价款。发包人逾期不支付的，除根据建设工程的性质不宜折价、拍卖外，承包人可以与发包人协议将该工程折价，也可以请求人民法院将该工程依法拍卖。建设工程的价款就该工程折价或者拍卖的价款优先受偿。

第八百零八条　本章没有规定的，适用承揽合同的有关规定。

第十九章　运输合同

第一节　一般规定

第八百零九条　运输合同是承运人将旅客或者货物从起运地点运输到约定地点，旅客、托运人或者收货人支付票款或者运输费用的合同。

第八百一十条　从事公共运输的承运人不得拒绝旅客、托运人通常、合理的运输要求。

第八百一十一条　承运人应当在约定期限或者合理期限内将旅客、货物安全运输到约定地点。

第八百一十二条　承运人应当按照约定的或者通常的运输路线将旅客、货物运输到约定地点。

第八百一十三条　旅客、托运人或者收货人应当支付票款或者运输费用。承运人未按照约定路线或者通常路线运输增加票款或者运输费用的，旅客、托运人或者收货人可以拒绝支付增加部分的票款或者运输费用。

第二节　客运合同

第八百一十四条　客运合同自承运人向旅客出具客票时成立，但是当事人另有约定或者另有交易习惯的除外。

第八百一十五条 旅客应当按照有效客票记载的时间、班次和座位号乘坐。旅客无票乘坐、超程乘坐、越级乘坐或者持不符合减价条件的优惠客票乘坐的,应当补交票款,承运人可以按照规定加收票款;旅客不支付票款的,承运人可以拒绝运输。

实名制客运合同的旅客丢失客票的,可以请求承运人挂失补办,承运人不得再次收取票款和其他不合理费用。

第八百一十六条 旅客因自己的原因不能按照客票记载的时间乘坐的,应当在约定的期限内办理退票或者变更手续;逾期办理的,承运人可以不退票款,并不再承担运输义务。

第八百一十七条 旅客随身携带行李应当符合约定的限量和品类要求;超过限量或者违反品类要求携带行李的,应当办理托运手续。

第八百一十八条 旅客不得随身携带或者在行李中夹带易燃、易爆、有毒、有腐蚀性、有放射性以及可能危及运输工具上人身和财产安全的危险物品或者违禁物品。

旅客违反前款规定的,承运人可以将危险物品或者违禁物品卸下、销毁或者送交有关部门。旅客坚持携带或者夹带危险物品或者违禁物品的,承运人应当拒绝运输。

第八百一十九条 承运人应当严格履行安全运输义务,及时告知旅客安全运输应当注意的事项。旅客对承运人为安全运输所作的合理安排应当积极协助和配合。

第八百二十条 承运人应当按照有效客票记载的时间、班次和座位号运输旅客。承运人迟延运输或者有其他不能正常运输情形的,应当及时告知和提醒旅客,采取必要的安置措施,并根据旅客的要求安排改乘其他班次或者退票;由此造成旅客损失的,承运人应当承担赔偿责任,但是不可归责于承运人的除外。

第八百二十一条 承运人擅自降低服务标准的,应当根据旅客的请求退票或者减收票款;提高服务标准的,不得加收票款。

第八百二十二条　承运人在运输过程中，应当尽力救助患有急病、分娩、遇险的旅客。

第八百二十三条　承运人应当对运输过程中旅客的伤亡承担赔偿责任；但是，伤亡是旅客自身健康原因造成的或者承运人证明伤亡是旅客故意、重大过失造成的除外。

前款规定适用于按照规定免票、持优待票或者经承运人许可搭乘的无票旅客。

第八百二十四条　在运输过程中旅客随身携带物品毁损、灭失，承运人有过错的，应当承担赔偿责任。

旅客托运的行李毁损、灭失的，适用货物运输的有关规定。

第三节　货运合同

第八百二十五条　托运人办理货物运输，应当向承运人准确表明收货人的姓名、名称或者凭指示的收货人，货物的名称、性质、重量、数量，收货地点等有关货物运输的必要情况。

因托运人申报不实或者遗漏重要情况，造成承运人损失的，托运人应当承担赔偿责任。

第八百二十六条　货物运输需要办理审批、检验等手续的，托运人应当将办理完有关手续的文件提交承运人。

第八百二十七条　托运人应当按照约定的方式包装货物。对包装方式没有约定或者约定不明确的，适用本法第六百一十九条的规定。

托运人违反前款规定的，承运人可以拒绝运输。

第八百二十八条　托运人托运易燃、易爆、有毒、有腐蚀性、有放射性等危险物品的，应当按照国家有关危险物品运输的规定对危险物品妥善包装，做出危险物品标志和标签，并将有关危险物品的名称、性质和防范措施的书面材料提交承运人。

托运人违反前款规定的，承运人可以拒绝运输，也可以采取相应措施以避免损失的发生，因此产生的费用由托运人负担。

第八百二十九条 在承运人将货物交付收货人之前,托运人可以要求承运人中止运输、返还货物、变更到达地或者将货物交给其他收货人,但是应当赔偿承运人因此受到的损失。

第八百三十条 货物运输到达后,承运人知道收货人的,应当及时通知收货人,收货人应当及时提货。收货人逾期提货的,应当向承运人支付保管费等费用。

第八百三十一条 收货人提货时应当按照约定的期限检验货物。对检验货物的期限没有约定或者约定不明确,依据本法第五百一十条的规定仍不能确定的,应当在合理期限内检验货物。收货人在约定的期限或者合理期限内对货物的数量、毁损等未提出异议的,视为承运人已经按照运输单证的记载交付的初步证据。

第八百三十二条 承运人对运输过程中货物的毁损、灭失承担赔偿责任。但是,承运人证明货物的毁损、灭失是因不可抗力、货物本身的自然性质或者合理损耗以及托运人、收货人的过错造成的,不承担赔偿责任。

第八百三十三条 货物的毁损、灭失的赔偿额,当事人有约定的,按照其约定;没有约定或者约定不明确,依据本法第五百一十条的规定仍不能确定的,按照交付或者应当交付时货物到达地的市场价格计算。法律、行政法规对赔偿额的计算方法和赔偿限额另有规定的,依照其规定。

第八百三十四条 两个以上承运人以同一运输方式联运的,与托运人订立合同的承运人应当对全程运输承担责任;损失发生在某一运输区段的,与托运人订立合同的承运人和该区段的承运人承担连带责任。

第八百三十五条 货物在运输过程中因不可抗力灭失,未收取运费的,承运人不得请求支付运费;已经收取运费的,托运人可以请求返还。法律另有规定的,依照其规定。

第八百三十六条 托运人或者收货人不支付运费、保管费或者其他费用的,承运人对相应的运输货物享有留置权,但是当事人另有约定的除外。

第八百三十七条 收货人不明或者收货人无正当理由拒绝受领货物的,承运人依法可以提存货物。

第四节　多式联运合同

第八百三十八条　多式联运经营人负责履行或者组织履行多式联运合同，对全程运输享有承运人的权利，承担承运人的义务。

第八百三十九条　多式联运经营人可以与参加多式联运的各区段承运人就多式联运合同的各区段运输约定相互之间的责任；但是，该约定不影响多式联运经营人对全程运输承担的义务。

第八百四十条　多式联运经营人收到托运人交付的货物时，应当签发多式联运单据。按照托运人的要求，多式联运单据可以是可转让单据，也可以是不可转让单据。

第八百四十一条　因托运人托运货物时的过错造成多式联运经营人损失的，即使托运人已经转让多式联运单据，托运人仍然应当承担赔偿责任。

第八百四十二条　货物的毁损、灭失发生于多式联运的某一运输区段的，多式联运经营人的赔偿责任和责任限额，适用调整该区段运输方式的有关法律规定；货物毁损、灭失发生的运输区段不能确定的，依照本章规定承担赔偿责任。

第二十章　技 术 合 同

第一节　一 般 规 定

第八百四十三条　技术合同是当事人就技术开发、转让、许可、咨询或者服务订立的确立相互之间权利和义务的合同。

第八百四十四条　订立技术合同，应当有利于知识产权的保护和科学技术的进步，促进科学技术成果的研发、转化、应用和推广。

第八百四十五条　技术合同的内容一般包括项目的名称，标的的内容、范围和要求，履行的计划、地点和方式，技术信息和资料的保密，技术成果的归属和收益的分配办法，验收标准和方法，名词和术语的解释等条款。

与履行合同有关的技术背景资料、可行性论证和技术评价报告、项目任务书和计划书、技术标准、技术规范、原始设计和工艺文件，以及其他技术文档,按照当事人的约定可以作为合同的组成部分。

技术合同涉及专利的,应当注明发明创造的名称、专利申请人和专利权人、申请日期、申请号、专利号以及专利权的有效期限。

第八百四十六条 技术合同价款、报酬或者使用费的支付方式由当事人约定,可以采取一次总算、一次总付或者一次总算、分期支付,也可以采取提成支付或者提成支付附加预付入门费的方式。

约定提成支付的,可以按照产品价格、实施专利和使用技术秘密后新增的产值、利润或者产品销售额的一定比例提成,也可以按照约定的其他方式计算。提成支付的比例可以采取固定比例、逐年递增比例或者逐年递减比例。

约定提成支付的,当事人可以约定查阅有关会计账目的办法。

第八百四十七条 职务技术成果的使用权、转让权属于法人或者非法人组织的,法人或者非法人组织可以就该项职务技术成果订立技术合同。法人或者非法人组织订立技术合同转让职务技术成果时,职务技术成果的完成人享有以同等条件优先受让的权利。

职务技术成果是执行法人或者非法人组织的工作任务,或者主要是利用法人或者非法人组织的物质技术条件所完成的技术成果。

第八百四十八条 非职务技术成果的使用权、转让权属于完成技术成果的个人,完成技术成果的个人可以就该项非职务技术成果订立技术合同。

第八百四十九条 完成技术成果的个人享有在有关技术成果文件上写明自己是技术成果完成者的权利和取得荣誉证书、奖励的权利。

第八百五十条 非法垄断技术或者侵害他人技术成果的技术合同无效。

第二节 技术开发合同

第八百五十一条 技术开发合同是当事人之间就新技术、新产品、新工艺、新品种或者新材料及其系统的研究开发所订立的合同。

技术开发合同包括委托开发合同和合作开发合同。

技术开发合同应当采用书面形式。

当事人之间就具有实用价值的科技成果实施转化订立的合同，参照适用技术开发合同的有关规定。

第八百五十二条　委托开发合同的委托人应当按照约定支付研究开发经费和报酬，提供技术资料，提出研究开发要求，完成协作事项，接受研究开发成果。

第八百五十三条　委托开发合同的研究开发人应当按照约定制定和实施研究开发计划，合理使用研究开发经费，按期完成研究开发工作，交付研究开发成果，提供有关的技术资料和必要的技术指导，帮助委托人掌握研究开发成果。

第八百五十四条　委托开发合同的当事人违反约定造成研究开发工作停滞、延误或者失败的，应当承担违约责任。

第八百五十五条　合作开发合同的当事人应当按照约定进行投资，包括以技术进行投资，分工参与研究开发工作，协作配合研究开发工作。

第八百五十六条　合作开发合同的当事人违反约定造成研究开发工作停滞、延误或者失败的，应当承担违约责任。

第八百五十七条　作为技术开发合同标的的技术已经由他人公开，致使技术开发合同的履行没有意义的，当事人可以解除合同。

第八百五十八条　技术开发合同履行过程中，因出现无法克服的技术困难，致使研究开发失败或者部分失败的，该风险由当事人约定；没有约定或者约定不明确，依据本法第五百一十条的规定仍不能确定的，风险由当事人合理分担。

当事人一方发现前款规定的可能致使研究开发失败或者部分失败的情形时，应当及时通知另一方并采取适当措施减少损失；没有及时通知并采取适当措施，致使损失扩大的，应当就扩大的损失承担责任。

第八百五十九条　委托开发完成的发明创造，除法律另有规定或者当事人另有约定外，申请专利的权利属于研究开发人。研究开发人取得专利权的，委托人可以依法实施该专利。

研究开发人转让专利申请权的,委托人享有以同等条件优先受让的权利。

第八百六十条　合作开发完成的发明创造,申请专利的权利属于合作开发的当事人共有;当事人一方转让其共有的专利申请权的,其他各方享有以同等条件优先受让的权利。但是,当事人另有约定的除外。

合作开发的当事人一方声明放弃其共有的专利申请权的,除当事人另有约定外,可以由另一方单独申请或者由其他各方共同申请。申请人取得专利权的,放弃专利申请权的一方可以免费实施该专利。

合作开发的当事人一方不同意申请专利的,另一方或者其他各方不得申请专利。

第八百六十一条　委托开发或者合作开发完成的技术秘密成果的使用权、转让权以及收益的分配办法,由当事人约定;没有约定或者约定不明确,依据本法第五百一十条的规定仍不能确定的,在没有相同技术方案被授予专利权前,当事人均有使用和转让的权利。但是,委托开发的研究开发人不得在向委托人交付研究开发成果之前,将研究开发成果转让给第三人。

第三节　技术转让合同和技术许可合同

第八百六十二条　技术转让合同是合法拥有技术的权利人,将现有特定的专利、专利申请、技术秘密的相关权利让与他人所订立的合同。

技术许可合同是合法拥有技术的权利人,将现有特定的专利、技术秘密的相关权利许可他人实施、使用所订立的合同。

技术转让合同和技术许可合同中关于提供实施技术的专用设备、原材料或者提供有关的技术咨询、技术服务的约定,属于合同的组成部分。

第八百六十三条　技术转让合同包括专利权转让、专利申请权转让、技术秘密转让等合同。

技术许可合同包括专利实施许可、技术秘密使用许可等合同。

技术转让合同和技术许可合同应当采用书面形式。

第八百六十四条　技术转让合同和技术许可合同可以约定实施专利或

者使用技术秘密的范围，但是不得限制技术竞争和技术发展。

第八百六十五条　专利实施许可合同仅在该专利权的存续期限内有效。专利权有效期限届满或者专利权被宣告无效的，专利权人不得就该专利与他人订立专利实施许可合同。

第八百六十六条　专利实施许可合同的许可人应当按照约定许可被许可人实施专利，交付实施专利有关的技术资料，提供必要的技术指导。

第八百六十七条　专利实施许可合同的被许可人应当按照约定实施专利，不得许可约定以外的第三人实施该专利，并按照约定支付使用费。

第八百六十八条　技术秘密转让合同的让与人和技术秘密使用许可合同的许可人应当按照约定提供技术资料，进行技术指导，保证技术的实用性、可靠性，承担保密义务。

前款规定的保密义务，不限制许可人申请专利，但是当事人另有约定的除外。

第八百六十九条　技术秘密转让合同的受让人和技术秘密使用许可合同的被许可人应当按照约定使用技术，支付转让费、使用费，承担保密义务。

第八百七十条　技术转让合同的让与人和技术许可合同的许可人应当保证自己是所提供的技术的合法拥有者，并保证所提供的技术完整、无误、有效，能够达到约定的目标。

第八百七十一条　技术转让合同的受让人和技术许可合同的被许可人应当按照约定的范围和期限，对让与人、许可人提供的技术中尚未公开的秘密部分，承担保密义务。

第八百七十二条　许可人未按照约定许可技术的，应当返还部分或者全部使用费，并应当承担违约责任；实施专利或者使用技术秘密超越约定的范围的，违反约定擅自许可第三人实施该项专利或者使用该项技术秘密的，应当停止违约行为，承担违约责任；违反约定的保密义务的，应当承担违约责任。

让与人承担违约责任，参照适用前款规定。

第八百七十三条　被许可人未按照约定支付使用费的，应当补交使用费并按照约定支付违约金;不补交使用费或者支付违约金的,应当停止实施专利或者使用技术秘密,交还技术资料,承担违约责任;实施专利或者使用技术秘密超越约定的范围的,未经许可人同意擅自许可第三人实施该专利或者使用该技术秘密的,应当停止违约行为,承担违约责任;违反约定的保密义务的,应当承担违约责任。

受让人承担违约责任,参照适用前款规定。

第八百七十四条 受让人或者被许可人按照约定实施专利、使用技术秘密侵害他人合法权益的,由让与人或者许可人承担责任,但是当事人另有约定的除外。

第八百七十五条 当事人可以按照互利的原则,在合同中约定实施专利、使用技术秘密后续改进的技术成果的分享办法;没有约定或者约定不明确,依据本法第五百一十条的规定仍不能确定的,一方后续改进的技术成果,其他各方无权分享。

第八百七十六条 集成电路布图设计专有权、植物新品种权、计算机软件著作权等其他知识产权的转让和许可,参照适用本节的有关规定。

第八百七十七条 法律、行政法规对技术进出口合同或者专利、专利申请合同另有规定的,依照其规定。

第四节 技术咨询合同和技术服务合同

第八百七十八条 技术咨询合同是当事人一方以技术知识为对方就特定技术项目提供可行性论证、技术预测、专题技术调查、分析评价报告等所订立的合同。

技术服务合同是当事人一方以技术知识为对方解决特定技术问题所订立的合同,不包括承揽合同和建设工程合同。

第八百七十九条 技术咨询合同的委托人应当按照约定阐明咨询的问题,提供技术背景材料及有关技术资料,接受受托人的工作成果,支付报酬。

第八百八十条 技术咨询合同的受托人应当按照约定的期限完成咨询报告或者解答问题,提出的咨询报告应当达到约定的要求。

第八百八十一条 技术咨询合同的委托人未按照约定提供必要的资料,影响工作进度和质量,不接受或者逾期接受工作成果的,支付的报酬不得追回,未支付的报酬应当支付。

技术咨询合同的受托人未按期提出咨询报告或者提出的咨询报告不符合约定的,应当承担减收或者免收报酬等违约责任。

技术咨询合同的委托人按照受托人符合约定要求的咨询报告和意见作出决策所造成的损失,由委托人承担,但是当事人另有约定的除外。

第八百八十二条 技术服务合同的委托人应当按照约定提供工作条件,完成配合事项,接受工作成果并支付报酬。

第八百八十三条 技术服务合同的受托人应当按照约定完成服务项目,解决技术问题,保证工作质量,并传授解决技术问题的知识。

第八百八十四条 技术服务合同的委托人不履行合同义务或者履行合同义务不符合约定,影响工作进度和质量,不接受或者逾期接受工作成果的,支付的报酬不得追回,未支付的报酬应当支付。

技术服务合同的受托人未按照约定完成服务工作的,应当承担免收报酬等违约责任。

第八百八十五条 技术咨询合同、技术服务合同履行过程中,受托人利用委托人提供的技术资料和工作条件完成的新的技术成果,属于受托人。委托人利用受托人的工作成果完成的新的技术成果,属于委托人。当事人另有约定的,按照其约定。

第八百八十六条 技术咨询合同和技术服务合同对受托人正常开展工作所需费用的负担没有约定或者约定不明确的,由受托人负担。

第八百八十七条 法律、行政法规对技术中介合同、技术培训合同另有规定的,依照其规定。

第二十一章 保管合同

第八百八十八条 保管合同是保管人保管寄存人交付的保管物,并返还该物的合同。

寄存人到保管人处从事购物、就餐、住宿等活动,将物品存放在指定场所的,视为保管,但是当事人另有约定或者另有交易习惯的除外。

第八百八十九条 寄存人应当按照约定向保管人支付保管费。

当事人对保管费没有约定或者约定不明确,依据本法第五百一十条的规定仍不能确定的,视为无偿保管。

第八百九十条 保管合同自保管物交付时成立,但是当事人另有约定的除外。

第八百九十一条 寄存人向保管人交付保管物的,保管人应当出具保管凭证,但是另有交易习惯的除外。

第八百九十二条 保管人应当妥善保管保管物。

当事人可以约定保管场所或者方法。除紧急情况或者为维护寄存人利益外,不得擅自改变保管场所或者方法。

第八百九十三条 寄存人交付的保管物有瑕疵或者根据保管物的性质需要采取特殊保管措施的,寄存人应当将有关情况告知保管人。寄存人未告知,致使保管物受损失的,保管人不承担赔偿责任;保管人因此受损失的,除保管人知道或者应当知道且未采取补救措施外,寄存人应当承担赔偿责任。

第八百九十四条 保管人不得将保管物转交第三人保管,但是当事人另有约定的除外。

保管人违反前款规定,将保管物转交第三人保管,造成保管物损失的,应当承担赔偿责任。

第八百九十五条 保管人不得使用或者许可第三人使用保管物,但是当事人另有约定的除外。

第八百九十六条 第三人对保管物主张权利的,除依法对保管物采取保全或者执行措施外,保管人应当履行向寄存人返还保管物的义务。

第三人对保管人提起诉讼或者对保管物申请扣押的,保管人应当及时通知寄存人。

第八百九十七条 保管期内,因保管人保管不善造成保管物毁损、灭失的，保管人应当承担赔偿责任。但是，无偿保管人证明自己没有故意或者重大过失的，不承担赔偿责任。

第八百九十八条　寄存人寄存货币、有价证券或者其他贵重物品的，应当向保管人声明，由保管人验收或者封存；寄存人未声明的，该物品毁损、灭失后，保管人可以按照一般物品予以赔偿。

第八百九十九条　寄存人可以随时领取保管物。

当事人对保管期限没有约定或者约定不明确的，保管人可以随时请求寄存人领取保管物；约定保管期限的，保管人无特别事由，不得请求寄存人提前领取保管物。

第九百条　保管期限届满或者寄存人提前领取保管物的，保管人应当将原物及其孳息归还寄存人。

第九百零一条　保管人保管货币的，可以返还相同种类、数量的货币；保管其他可替代物的，可以按照约定返还相同种类、品质、数量的物品。

第九百零二条　有偿的保管合同，寄存人应当按照约定的期限向保管人支付保管费。

当事人对支付期限没有约定或者约定不明确，依据本法第五百一十条的规定仍不能确定的，应当在领取保管物的同时支付。

第九百零三条　寄存人未按照约定支付保管费或者其他费用的，保管人对保管物享有留置权，但是当事人另有约定的除外。

第二十二章　仓储合同

第九百零四条　仓储合同是保管人储存存货人交付的仓储物，存货人支付仓储费的合同。

第九百零五条　仓储合同自保管人和存货人意思表示一致时成立。

第九百零六条　储存易燃、易爆、有毒、有腐蚀性、有放射性等危险物品或者易变质物品的，存货人应当说明该物品的性质，提供有关资料。

存货人违反前款规定的，保管人可以拒收仓储物，也可以采取相应措施以避免损失的发生，因此产生的费用由存货人负担。

保管人储存易燃、易爆、有毒、有腐蚀性、有放射性等危险物品的,应当具备相应的保管条件。

第九百零七条 保管人应当按照约定对入库仓储物进行验收。保管人验收时发现入库仓储物与约定不符合的,应当及时通知存货人。保管人验收后,发生仓储物的品种、数量、质量不符合约定的,保管人应当承担赔偿责任。

第九百零八条 存货人交付仓储物的,保管人应当出具仓单、入库单等凭证。

第九百零九条 保管人应当在仓单上签名或者盖章。仓单包括下列事项:

(一)存货人的姓名或者名称和住所;

(二)仓储物的品种、数量、质量、包装及其件数和标记;

(三)仓储物的损耗标准;

(四)储存场所;

(五)储存期限;

(六)仓储费;

(七)仓储物已经办理保险的,其保险金额、期间以及保险人的名称;

(八)填发人、填发地和填发日期。

第九百一十条 仓单是提取仓储物的凭证。存货人或者仓单持有人在仓单上背书并经保管人签名或者盖章的,可以转让提取仓储物的权利。

第九百一十一条 保管人根据存货人或者仓单持有人的要求,应当同意其检查仓储物或者提取样品。

第九百一十二条 保管人发现入库仓储物有变质或者其他损坏的,应当及时通知存货人或者仓单持有人。

第九百一十三条 保管人发现入库仓储物有变质或者其他损坏,危及其他仓储物的安全和正常保管的,应当催告存货人或者仓单持有人作出必要的处置。因情况紧急,保管人可以作出必要的处置;但是,事后应当将该情况及时通知存货人或者仓单持有人。

第九百一十四条　当事人对储存期限没有约定或者约定不明确的，存货人或者仓单持有人可以随时提取仓储物，保管人也可以随时请求存货人或者仓单持有人提取仓储物，但是应当给予必要的准备时间。

第九百一十五条　储存期限届满，存货人或者仓单持有人应当凭仓单、入库单等提取仓储物。存货人或者仓单持有人逾期提取的，应当加收仓储费；提前提取的，不减收仓储费。

第九百一十六条　储存期限届满，存货人或者仓单持有人不提取仓储物的，保管人可以催告其在合理期限内提取；逾期不提取的，保管人可以提存仓储物。

第九百一十七条　储存期内，因保管不善造成仓储物毁损、灭失的，保管人应当承担赔偿责任。因仓储物本身的自然性质、包装不符合约定或者超过有效储存期造成仓储物变质、损坏的，保管人不承担赔偿责任。

第九百一十八条　本章没有规定的，适用保管合同的有关规定。

第二十三章　委托合同

第九百一十九条　委托合同是委托人和受托人约定，由受托人处理委托人事务的合同。

第九百二十条　委托人可以特别委托受托人处理一项或者数项事务，也可以概括委托受托人处理一切事务。

第九百二十一条　委托人应当预付处理委托事务的费用。受托人为处理委托事务垫付的必要费用，委托人应当偿还该费用并支付利息。

第九百二十二条　受托人应当按照委托人的指示处理委托事务。需要变更委托人指示的，应当经委托人同意；因情况紧急，难以和委托人取得联系的，受托人应当妥善处理委托事务，但是事后应当将该情况及时报告委托人。

第九百二十三条　受托人应当亲自处理委托事务。经委托人同意，受托人可以转委托。转委托经同意或者追认的，委托人可以就委托事务直接指示转委托的第三人，受托人仅就第三人的选任及其对第三人的指示承担责任。转委托未经同意或者追认的,受托人应当对转委托的第三人的行为承担责任;但是,在紧急情况下受托人为了维护委托人的利益需要转委托第三人的除外。

第九百二十四条 受托人应当按照委托人的要求,报告委托事务的处理情况。委托合同终止时,受托人应当报告委托事务的结果。

第九百二十五条 受托人以自己的名义,在委托人的授权范围内与第三人订立的合同,第三人在订立合同时知道受托人与委托人之间的代理关系的,该合同直接约束委托人和第三人;但是,有确切证据证明该合同只约束受托人和第三人的除外。

第九百二十六条 受托人以自己的名义与第三人订立合同时,第三人不知道受托人与委托人之间的代理关系的,受托人因第三人的原因对委托人不履行义务,受托人应当向委托人披露第三人,委托人因此可以行使受托人对第三人的权利。但是,第三人与受托人订立合同时如果知道该委托人就不会订立合同的除外。

受托人因委托人的原因对第三人不履行义务,受托人应当向第三人披露委托人,第三人因此可以选择受托人或者委托人作为相对人主张其权利,但是第三人不得变更选定的相对人。

委托人行使受托人对第三人的权利的,第三人可以向委托人主张其对受托人的抗辩。第三人选定委托人作为其相对人的,委托人可以向第三人主张其对受托人的抗辩以及受托人对第三人的抗辩。

第九百二十七条 受托人处理委托事务取得的财产,应当转交给委托人。

第九百二十八条 受托人完成委托事务的,委托人应当按照约定向其支付报酬。

因不可归责于受托人的事由,委托合同解除或者委托事务不能完成的,委托人应当向受托人支付相应的报酬。当事人另有约定的,按照其约定。

第九百二十九条 有偿的委托合同,因受托人的过错造成委托人损失的，委托人可以请求赔偿损失。无偿的委托合同，因受托人的故意或者重大过失造成委托人损失的，委托人可以请求赔偿损失。

受托人超越权限造成委托人损失的，应当赔偿损失。

第九百三十条　受托人处理委托事务时，因不可归责于自己的事由受到损失的，可以向委托人请求赔偿损失。

第九百三十一条　委托人经受托人同意，可以在受托人之外委托第三人处理委托事务。因此造成受托人损失的，受托人可以向委托人请求赔偿损失。

第九百三十二条　两个以上的受托人共同处理委托事务的，对委托人承担连带责任。

第九百三十三条　委托人或者受托人可以随时解除委托合同。因解除合同造成对方损失的，除不可归责于该当事人的事由外，无偿委托合同的解除方应当赔偿因解除时间不当造成的直接损失，有偿委托合同的解除方应当赔偿对方的直接损失和合同履行后可以获得的利益。

第九百三十四条　委托人死亡、终止或者受托人死亡、丧失民事行为能力、终止的，委托合同终止；但是，当事人另有约定或者根据委托事务的性质不宜终止的除外。

第九百三十五条　因委托人死亡或者被宣告破产、解散，致使委托合同终止将损害委托人利益的，在委托人的继承人、遗产管理人或者清算人承受委托事务之前，受托人应当继续处理委托事务。

第九百三十六条　因受托人死亡、丧失民事行为能力或者被宣告破产、解散，致使委托合同终止的，受托人的继承人、遗产管理人、法定代理人或者清算人应当及时通知委托人。因委托合同终止将损害委托人利益的，在委托人作出善后处理之前，受托人的继承人、遗产管理人、法定代理人或者清算人应当采取必要措施。

第二十四章　物业服务合同

第九百三十七条　物业服务合同是物业服务人在物业服务区域内，为业主提供建筑物及其附属设施的维修养护、环境卫生和相关秩序的管理维护等物业服务,业主支付物业费的合同。

物业服务人包括物业服务企业和其他管理人。

第九百三十八条 物业服务合同的内容一般包括服务事项、服务质量、服务费用的标准和收取办法、维修资金的使用、服务用房的管理和使用、服务期限、服务交接等条款。

物业服务人公开作出的有利于业主的服务承诺,为物业服务合同的组成部分。

物业服务合同应当采用书面形式。

第九百三十九条 建设单位依法与物业服务人订立的前期物业服务合同,以及业主委员会与业主大会依法选聘的物业服务人订立的物业服务合同,对业主具有法律约束力。

第九百四十条 建设单位依法与物业服务人订立的前期物业服务合同约定的服务期限届满前,业主委员会或者业主与新物业服务人订立的物业服务合同生效的,前期物业服务合同终止。

第九百四十一条 物业服务人将物业服务区域内的部分专项服务事项委托给专业性服务组织或者其他第三人的,应当就该部分专项服务事项向业主负责。

物业服务人不得将其应当提供的全部物业服务转委托给第三人,或者将全部物业服务支解后分别转委托给第三人。

第九百四十二条 物业服务人应当按照约定和物业的使用性质,妥善维修、养护、清洁、绿化和经营管理物业服务区域内的业主共有部分,维护物业服务区域内的基本秩序,采取合理措施保护业主的人身、财产安全。

对物业服务区域内违反有关治安、环保、消防等法律法规的行为,物业服务人应当及时采取合理措施制止、向有关行政主管部门报告并协助处理。

第九百四十三条 物业服务人应当定期将服务的事项、负责人员、质量要求、收费项目、收费标准、履行情况,以及维修资金使用情况、业主共有部分的经营与收益情况等以合理方式向业主公开并向业主大会、业主委员会报告。

第九百四十四条 业主应当按照约定向物业服务人支付物业费。物业服务人已经按照约定和有关规定提供服务的,业主不得以未接受或者无需接受相关物业服务为由拒绝支付物业费。

业主违反约定逾期不支付物业费的,物业服务人可以催告其在合理期限内支付;合理期限届满仍不支付的,物业服务人可以提起诉讼或者申请仲裁。

物业服务人不得采取停止供电、供水、供热、供燃气等方式催交物业费。

第九百四十五条 业主装饰装修房屋的,应当事先告知物业服务人,遵守物业服务人提示的合理注意事项,并配合其进行必要的现场检查。

业主转让、出租物业专有部分、设立居住权或者依法改变共有部分用途的,应当及时将相关情况告知物业服务人。

第九百四十六条 业主依照法定程序共同决定解聘物业服务人的,可以解除物业服务合同。决定解聘的,应当提前六十日书面通知物业服务人,但是合同对通知期限另有约定的除外。

依据前款规定解除合同造成物业服务人损失的,除不可归责于业主的事由外,业主应当赔偿损失。

第九百四十七条 物业服务期限届满前,业主依法共同决定续聘的,应当与原物业服务人在合同期限届满前续订物业服务合同。

物业服务期限届满前,物业服务人不同意续聘的,应当在合同期限届满前九十日书面通知业主或者业主委员会,但是合同对通知期限另有约定的除外。

第九百四十八条 物业服务期限届满后,业主没有依法作出续聘或者另聘物业服务人的决定,物业服务人继续提供物业服务的,原物业服务合同继续有效,但是服务期限为不定期。

当事人可以随时解除不定期物业服务合同,但是应当提前六十日书面通知对方。

第九百四十九条 物业服务合同终止的,原物业服务人应当在约定期限或者合理期限内退出物业服务区域,将物业服务用房、相关设施、物业服务所必需的相关资料等交还给业主委员会、决定自行管理的业主或者其指定的人,配合新物业服务人做好交接工作,并如实告知物业的使用和管理状况。

原物业服务人违反前款规定的,不得请求业主支付物业服务合同终止后的物业费;造成业主损失的,应当赔偿损失。

第九百五十条 物业服务合同终止后,在业主或者业主大会选聘的新物业服务人或者决定自行管理的业主接管之前,原物业服务人应当继续处理物业服务事项,并可以请求业主支付该期间的物业费。

第二十五章 行纪合同

第九百五十一条 行纪合同是行纪人以自己的名义为委托人从事贸易活动,委托人支付报酬的合同。

第九百五十二条 行纪人处理委托事务支出的费用,由行纪人负担,但是当事人另有约定的除外。

第九百五十三条 行纪人占有委托物的,应当妥善保管委托物。

第九百五十四条 委托物交付给行纪人时有瑕疵或者容易腐烂、变质的,经委托人同意,行纪人可以处分该物;不能与委托人及时取得联系的,行纪人可以合理处分。

第九百五十五条 行纪人低于委托人指定的价格卖出或者高于委托人指定的价格买入的,应当经委托人同意;未经委托人同意,行纪人补偿其差额的,该买卖对委托人发生效力。

行纪人高于委托人指定的价格卖出或者低于委托人指定的价格买入的,可以按照约定增加报酬;没有约定或者约定不明确,依据本法第五百一十条的规定仍不能确定的,该利益属于委托人。

委托人对价格有特别指示的,行纪人不得违背该指示卖出或者买入。

第九百五十六条 行纪人卖出或者买入具有市场定价的商品,除委托人有相反的意思表示外,行纪人自己可以作为买受人或者出卖人。

行纪人有前款规定情形的,仍然可以请求委托人支付报酬。

第九百五十七条 行纪人按照约定买入委托物,委托人应当及时受领。经行纪人催告,委托人无正当理由拒绝受领的,行纪人依法可以提存委托物。

委托物不能卖出或者委托人撤回出卖,经行纪人催告,委托人不取回或者不处分该物的,行纪人依法可以提存委托物。

第九百五十八条 行纪人与第三人订立合同的,行纪人对该合同直接享有权利、承担义务。

第三人不履行义务致使委托人受到损害的,行纪人应当承担赔偿责任,但是行纪人与委托人另有约定的除外。

第九百五十九条 行纪人完成或者部分完成委托事务的,委托人应当向其支付相应的报酬。委托人逾期不支付报酬的,行纪人对委托物享有留置权,但是当事人另有约定的除外。

第九百六十条 本章没有规定的,参照适用委托合同的有关规定。

第二十六章 中介合同

第九百六十一条 中介合同是中介人向委托人报告订立合同的机会或者提供订立合同的媒介服务,委托人支付报酬的合同。

第九百六十二条 中介人应当就有关订立合同的事项向委托人如实报告。

中介人故意隐瞒与订立合同有关的重要事实或者提供虚假情况,损害委托人利益的,不得请求支付报酬并应当承担赔偿责任。

第九百六十三条 中介人促成合同成立的,委托人应当按照约定支付报酬。对中介人的报酬没有约定或者约定不明确,依据本法第五百一十条的规定仍不能确定的,根据中介人的劳务合理确定。因中介人提供订立合同的媒介服务而促成合同成立的,由该合同的当事人平均负担中介人的报酬。

中介人促成合同成立的,中介活动的费用,由中介人负担。

第九百六十四条 中介人未促成合同成立的,不得请求支付报酬;但是,可以按照约定请求委托人支付从事中介活动支出的必要费用。

第九百六十五条 委托人在接受中介人的服务后,利用中介人提供的交易机会或者媒介服务,绕开中介人直接订立合同的,应当向中介人支付报酬。

第九百六十六条 本章没有规定的,参照适用委托合同的有关规定。

第二十七章 合伙合同

第九百六十七条 合伙合同是两个以上合伙人为了共同的事业目的,订立的共享利益、共担风险的协议。

第九百六十八条 合伙人应当按照约定的出资方式、数额和缴付期限,履行出资义务。

第九百六十九条 合伙人的出资、因合伙事务依法取得的收益和其他财产,属于合伙财产。

合伙合同终止前,合伙人不得请求分割合伙财产。

第九百七十条 合伙人就合伙事务作出决定的,除合伙合同另有约定外,应当经全体合伙人一致同意。

合伙事务由全体合伙人共同执行。按照合伙合同的约定或者全体合伙人的决定,可以委托一个或者数个合伙人执行合伙事务;其他合伙人不再执行合伙事务,但是有权监督执行情况。

合伙人分别执行合伙事务的,执行事务合伙人可以对其他合伙人执行的事务提出异议;提出异议后,其他合伙人应当暂停该项事务的执行。

第九百七十一条 合伙人不得因执行合伙事务而请求支付报酬,但是合伙合同另有约定的除外。

第九百七十二条 合伙的利润分配和亏损分担,按照合伙合同的约定办理;合伙合同没有约定或者约定不明确的,由合伙人协商决定;协商不成的,由合伙人按照实缴出资比例分配、分担;无法确定出资比例的,由合伙人平均分配、分担。

第九百七十三条 合伙人对合伙债务承担连带责任。清偿合伙债务超过自己应当承担份额的合伙人,有权向其他合伙人追偿。

第九百七十四条 除合伙合同另有约定外,合伙人向合伙人以外的人转让其全部或者部分财产份额的,须经其他合伙人一致同意。

第九百七十五条 合伙人的债权人不得代位行使合伙人依照本章规定和合伙合同享有的权利,但是合伙人享有的利益分配请求权除外。

第九百七十六条 合伙人对合伙期限没有约定或者约定不明确,依据本法第五百一十条的规定仍不能确定的,视为不定期合伙。

合伙期限届满,合伙人继续执行合伙事务,其他合伙人没有提出异议的,原合伙合同继续有效,但是合伙期限为不定期。

合伙人可以随时解除不定期合伙合同,但是应当在合理期限之前通知其他合伙人。

第九百七十七条 合伙人死亡、丧失民事行为能力或者终止的,合伙合同终止;但是,合伙合同另有约定或者根据合伙事务的性质不宜终止的除外。

第九百七十八条 合伙合同终止后,合伙财产在支付因终止而产生的费用以及清偿合伙债务后有剩余的,依据本法第九百七十二条的规定进行分配。

第三分编 准 合 同

第二十八章 无 因 管 理

第九百七十九条 管理人没有法定的或者约定的义务,为避免他人利益受损失而管理他人事务的,可以请求受益人偿还因管理事务而支出的必要费用;管理人因管理事务受到损失的,可以请求受益人给予适当补偿。

管理事务不符合受益人真实意思的,管理人不享有前款规定的权利;但是,受益人的真实意思违反法律或者违背公序良俗的除外。

第九百八十条 管理人管理事务不属于前条规定的情形,但是受益人享有管理利益的,受益人应当在其获得的利益范围内向管理人承担前条第一款规定的义务。

第九百八十一条 管理人管理他人事务,应当采取有利于受益人的方法。中断管理对受益人不利的,无正当理由不得中断。

第九百八十二条 管理人管理他人事务,能够通知受益人的,应当及时通知受益人。管理的事务不需要紧急处理的,应当等待受益人的指示。

第九百八十三条 管理结束后,管理人应当向受益人报告管理事务的情况。管理人管理事务取得的财产,应当及时转交给受益人。

第九百八十四条 管理人管理事务经受益人事后追认的,从管理事务开始时起,适用委托合同的有关规定,但是管理人另有意思表示的除外。

第二十九章 不当得利

第九百八十五条 得利人没有法律根据取得不当利益的,受损失的人可以请求得利人返还取得的利益,但是有下列情形之一的除外:

(一)为履行道德义务进行的给付;

(二)债务到期之前的清偿;

(三)明知无给付义务而进行的债务清偿。

第九百八十六条 得利人不知道且不应当知道取得的利益没有法律根据,取得的利益已经不存在的,不承担返还该利益的义务。

第九百八十七条 得利人知道或者应当知道取得的利益没有法律根据的,受损失的人可以请求得利人返还其取得的利益并依法赔偿损失。

第九百八十八条 得利人已经将取得的利益无偿转让给第三人的,受损失的人可以请求第三人在相应范围内承担返还义务。

第四编 人 格 权

第一章 一 般 规 定

第九百八十九条 本编调整因人格权的享有和保护产生的民事关系。

第九百九十条 人格权是民事主体享有的生命权、身体权、健康权、姓名权、名称权、肖像权、名誉权、荣誉权、隐私权等权利。

除前款规定的人格权外，自然人享有基于人身自由、人格尊严产生的其他人格权益。

第九百九十一条 民事主体的人格权受法律保护，任何组织或者个人不得侵害。

第九百九十二条 人格权不得放弃、转让或者继承。

第九百九十三条 民事主体可以将自己的姓名、名称、肖像等许可他人使用，但是依照法律规定或者根据其性质不得许可的除外。

第九百九十四条 死者的姓名、肖像、名誉、荣誉、隐私、遗体等受到侵害的，其配偶、子女、父母有权依法请求行为人承担民事责任；死者没有配偶、子女且父母已经死亡的，其他近亲属有权依法请求行为人承担民事责任。

第九百九十五条 人格权受到侵害的，受害人有权依照本法和其他法律的规定请求行为人承担民事责任。受害人的停止侵害、排除妨碍、消除危险、消除影响、恢复名誉、赔礼道歉请求权，不适用诉讼时效的规定。

第九百九十六条 因当事人一方的违约行为，损害对方人格权并造成严重精神损害，受损害方选择请求其承担违约责任的，不影响受损害方请求精神损害赔偿。

第九百九十七条 民事主体有证据证明行为人正在实施或者即将实施

侵害其人格权的违法行为,不及时制止将使其合法权益受到难以弥补的损害的,有权依法向人民法院申请采取责令行为人停止有关行为的措施。

第九百九十八条 认定行为人承担侵害除生命权、身体权和健康权外的人格权的民事责任,应当考虑行为人和受害人的职业、影响范围、过错程度,以及行为的目的、方式、后果等因素。

第九百九十九条 为公共利益实施新闻报道、舆论监督等行为的,可以合理使用民事主体的姓名、名称、肖像、个人信息等;使用不合理侵害民事主体人格权的,应当依法承担民事责任。

第一千条 行为人因侵害人格权承担消除影响、恢复名誉、赔礼道歉等民事责任的,应当与行为的具体方式和造成的影响范围相当。

行为人拒不承担前款规定的民事责任的,人民法院可以采取在报刊、网络等媒体上发布公告或者公布生效裁判文书等方式执行,产生的费用由行为人负担。

第一千零一条 对自然人因婚姻家庭关系等产生的身份权利的保护,适用本法第一编、第五编和其他法律的相关规定;没有规定的,可以根据其性质参照适用本编人格权保护的有关规定。

第二章　生命权、身体权和健康权

第一千零二条 自然人享有生命权。自然人的生命安全和生命尊严受法律保护。任何组织或者个人不得侵害他人的生命权。

第一千零三条 自然人享有身体权。自然人的身体完整和行动自由受法律保护。任何组织或者个人不得侵害他人的身体权。

第一千零四条 自然人享有健康权。自然人的身心健康受法律保护。任何组织或者个人不得侵害他人的健康权。

第一千零五条 自然人的生命权、身体权、健康权受到侵害或者处于其他危难情形的,负有法定救助义务的组织或者个人应当及时施救。

第一千零六条 完全民事行为能力人有权依法自主决定无偿捐献其人体细胞、人体组织、人体器官、遗体。任何组织或者个人不得强迫、欺骗、利诱其捐献。

完全民事行为能力人依据前款规定同意捐献的，应当采用书面形式，也可以订立遗嘱。

自然人生前未表示不同意捐献的，该自然人死亡后，其配偶、成年子女、父母可以共同决定捐献，决定捐献应当采用书面形式。

第一千零七条　禁止以任何形式买卖人体细胞、人体组织、人体器官、遗体。

违反前款规定的买卖行为无效。

第一千零八条　为研制新药、医疗器械或者发展新的预防和治疗方法，需要进行临床试验的，应当依法经相关主管部门批准并经伦理委员会审查同意，向受试者或者受试者的监护人告知试验目的、用途和可能产生的风险等详细情况，并经其书面同意。

进行临床试验的，不得向受试者收取试验费用。

第一千零九条　从事与人体基因、人体胚胎等有关的医学和科研活动，应当遵守法律、行政法规和国家有关规定，不得危害人体健康，不得违背伦理道德，不得损害公共利益。

第一千零一十条　违背他人意愿，以言语、文字、图像、肢体行为等方式对他人实施性骚扰的，受害人有权依法请求行为人承担民事责任。

机关、企业、学校等单位应当采取合理的预防、受理投诉、调查处置等措施，防止和制止利用职权、从属关系等实施性骚扰。

第一千零一十一条　以非法拘禁等方式剥夺、限制他人的行动自由，或者非法搜查他人身体的，受害人有权依法请求行为人承担民事责任。

第三章　姓名权和名称权

第一千零一十二条　自然人享有姓名权，有权依法决定、使用、变更或者许可他人使用自己的姓名，但是不得违背公序良俗。

第一千零一十三条　法人、非法人组织享有名称权，有权依法决定、使用、变更、转让或者许可他人使用自己的名称。

第一千零一十四条 任何组织或者个人不得以干涉、盗用、假冒等方式侵害他人的姓名权或者名称权。

第一千零一十五条 自然人应当随父姓或者母姓,但是有下列情形之一的,可以在父姓和母姓之外选取姓氏:

(一)选取其他直系长辈血亲的姓氏;

(二)因由法定扶养人以外的人扶养而选取扶养人姓氏;

(三)有不违背公序良俗的其他正当理由。

少数民族自然人的姓氏可以遵从本民族的文化传统和风俗习惯。

第一千零一十六条 自然人决定、变更姓名,或者法人、非法人组织决定、变更、转让名称的,应当依法向有关机关办理登记手续,但是法律另有规定的除外。

民事主体变更姓名、名称的,变更前实施的民事法律行为对其具有法律约束力。

第一千零一十七条 具有一定社会知名度,被他人使用足以造成公众混淆的笔名、艺名、网名、译名、字号、姓名和名称的简称等,参照适用姓名权和名称权保护的有关规定。

第四章 肖 像 权

第一千零一十八条 自然人享有肖像权,有权依法制作、使用、公开或者许可他人使用自己的肖像。

肖像是通过影像、雕塑、绘画等方式在一定载体上所反映的特定自然人可以被识别的外部形象。

第一千零一十九条 任何组织或者个人不得以丑化、污损,或者利用信息技术手段伪造等方式侵害他人的肖像权。未经肖像权人同意,不得制作、使用、公开肖像权人的肖像,但是法律另有规定的除外。

未经肖像权人同意,肖像作品权利人不得以发表、复制、发行、出租、展览等方式使用或者公开肖像权人的肖像。

第一千零二十条 合理实施下列行为的,可以不经肖像权人同意:

（一）为个人学习、艺术欣赏、课堂教学或者科学研究，在必要范围内使用肖像权人已经公开的肖像；

（二）为实施新闻报道，不可避免地制作、使用、公开肖像权人的肖像；

（三）为依法履行职责，国家机关在必要范围内制作、使用、公开肖像权人的肖像；

（四）为展示特定公共环境，不可避免地制作、使用、公开肖像权人的肖像；

（五）为维护公共利益或者肖像权人合法权益，制作、使用、公开肖像权人的肖像的其他行为。

第一千零二十一条　当事人对肖像许可使用合同中关于肖像使用条款的理解有争议的，应当作出有利于肖像权人的解释。

第一千零二十二条　当事人对肖像许可使用期限没有约定或者约定不明确的，任何一方当事人可以随时解除肖像许可使用合同，但是应当在合理期限之前通知对方。

当事人对肖像许可使用期限有明确约定，肖像权人有正当理由的，可以解除肖像许可使用合同，但是应当在合理期限之前通知对方。因解除合同造成对方损失的，除不可归责于肖像权人的事由外，应当赔偿损失。

第一千零二十三条　对姓名等的许可使用，参照适用肖像许可使用的有关规定。

对自然人声音的保护，参照适用肖像权保护的有关规定。

第五章　名誉权和荣誉权

第一千零二十四条　民事主体享有名誉权。任何组织或者个人不得以侮辱、诽谤等方式侵害他人的名誉权。

名誉是对民事主体的品德、声望、才能、信用等的社会评价。

第一千零二十五条　行为人为公共利益实施新闻报道、舆论监督等行为，影响他人名誉的，不承担民事责任，但是有下列情形之一的除外：

（一）捏造、歪曲事实；

(二)对他人提供的严重失实内容未尽到合理核实义务;

(三)使用侮辱性言辞等贬损他人名誉。

第一千零二十六条 认定行为人是否尽到前条第二项规定的合理核实义务,应当考虑下列因素:

(一)内容来源的可信度;

(二)对明显可能引发争议的内容是否进行了必要的调查;

(三)内容的时限性;

(四)内容与公序良俗的关联性;

(五)受害人名誉受贬损的可能性;

(六)核实能力和核实成本。

第一千零二十七条 行为人发表的文学、艺术作品以真人真事或者特定人为描述对象,含有侮辱、诽谤内容,侵害他人名誉权的,受害人有权依法请求该行为人承担民事责任。

行为人发表的文学、艺术作品不以特定人为描述对象,仅其中的情节与该特定人的情况相似的,不承担民事责任。

第一千零二十八条 民事主体有证据证明报刊、网络等媒体报道的内容失实,侵害其名誉权的,有权请求该媒体及时采取更正或者删除等必要措施。

第一千零二十九条 民事主体可以依法查询自己的信用评价;发现信用评价不当的,有权提出异议并请求采取更正、删除等必要措施。信用评价人应当及时核查,经核查属实的,应当及时采取必要措施。

第一千零三十条 民事主体与征信机构等信用信息处理者之间的关系,适用本编有关个人信息保护的规定和其他法律、行政法规的有关规定。

第一千零三十一条 民事主体享有荣誉权。任何组织或者个人不得非法剥夺他人的荣誉称号,不得诋毁、贬损他人的荣誉。

获得的荣誉称号应当记载而没有记载的,民事主体可以请求记载;获得的荣誉称号记载错误的,民事主体可以请求更正。

第六章 隐私权和个人信息保护

第一千零三十二条 自然人享有隐私权。任何组织或者个人不得以刺探、侵扰、泄露、公开等方式侵害他人的隐私权。

隐私是自然人的私人生活安宁和不愿为他人知晓的私密空间、私密活动、私密信息。

第一千零三十三条 除法律另有规定或者权利人明确同意外,任何组织或者个人不得实施下列行为:

(一)以电话、短信、即时通讯工具、电子邮件、传单等方式侵扰他人的私人生活安宁;

(二)进入、拍摄、窥视他人的住宅、宾馆房间等私密空间;

(三)拍摄、窥视、窃听、公开他人的私密活动;

(四)拍摄、窥视他人身体的私密部位;

(五)处理他人的私密信息;

(六)以其他方式侵害他人的隐私权。

第一千零三十四条 自然人的个人信息受法律保护。

个人信息是以电子或者其他方式记录的能够单独或者与其他信息结合识别特定自然人的各种信息,包括自然人的姓名、出生日期、身份证件号码、生物识别信息、住址、电话号码、电子邮箱、健康信息、行踪信息等。

个人信息中的私密信息,适用有关隐私权的规定;没有规定的,适用有关个人信息保护的规定。

第一千零三十五条 处理个人信息的,应当遵循合法、正当、必要原则,不得过度处理,并符合下列条件:

(一)征得该自然人或者其监护人同意,但是法律、行政法规另有规定的除外;

(二)公开处理信息的规则;

(三)明示处理信息的目的、方式和范围;

(四)不违反法律、行政法规的规定和双方的约定。

个人信息的处理包括个人信息的收集、存储、使用、加工、传输、提供、公开等。

第一千零三十六条 处理个人信息,有下列情形之一的,行为人不承担民事责任:

(一)在该自然人或者其监护人同意的范围内合理实施的行为;

(二)合理处理该自然人自行公开的或者其他已经合法公开的信息,但是该自然人明确拒绝或者处理该信息侵害其重大利益的除外;

(三)为维护公共利益或者该自然人合法权益,合理实施的其他行为。

第一千零三十七条 自然人可以依法向信息处理者查阅或者复制其个人信息;发现信息有错误的,有权提出异议并请求及时采取更正等必要措施。

自然人发现信息处理者违反法律、行政法规的规定或者双方的约定处理其个人信息的,有权请求信息处理者及时删除。

第一千零三十八条 信息处理者不得泄露或者篡改其收集、存储的个人信息;未经自然人同意,不得向他人非法提供其个人信息,但是经过加工无法识别特定个人且不能复原的除外。

信息处理者应当采取技术措施和其他必要措施,确保其收集、存储的个人信息安全,防止信息泄露、篡改、丢失;发生或者可能发生个人信息泄露、篡改、丢失的,应当及时采取补救措施,按照规定告知自然人并向有关主管部门报告。

第一千零三十九条 国家机关、承担行政职能的法定机构及其工作人员对于履行职责过程中知悉的自然人的隐私和个人信息,应当予以保密,不得泄露或者向他人非法提供。

第五编 婚姻家庭

第一章 一般规定

第一千零四十条 本编调整因婚姻家庭产生的民事关系。

第一千零四十一条 婚姻家庭受国家保护。

实行婚姻自由、一夫一妻、男女平等的婚姻制度。

保护妇女、未成年人、老年人、残疾人的合法权益。

第一千零四十二条 禁止包办、买卖婚姻和其他干涉婚姻自由的行为。禁止借婚姻索取财物。

禁止重婚。禁止有配偶者与他人同居。

禁止家庭暴力。禁止家庭成员间的虐待和遗弃。

第一千零四十三条 家庭应当树立优良家风,弘扬家庭美德,重视家庭文明建设。

夫妻应当互相忠实,互相尊重,互相关爱;家庭成员应当敬老爱幼,互相帮助,维护平等、和睦、文明的婚姻家庭关系。

第一千零四十四条 收养应当遵循最有利于被收养人的原则,保障被收养人和收养人的合法权益。

禁止借收养名义买卖未成年人。

第一千零四十五条 亲属包括配偶、血亲和姻亲。

配偶、父母、子女、兄弟姐妹、祖父母、外祖父母、孙子女、外孙子女为近亲属。

配偶、父母、子女和其他共同生活的近亲属为家庭成员。

第二章 结 婚

第一千零四十六条 结婚应当男女双方完全自愿,禁止任何一方对另一方加以强迫,禁止任何组织或者个人加以干涉。

第一千零四十七条 结婚年龄,男不得早于二十二周岁,女不得早于二十周岁。

第一千零四十八条 直系血亲或者三代以内的旁系血亲禁止结婚。

第一千零四十九条 要求结婚的男女双方应当亲自到婚姻登记机关申请结婚登记。符合本法规定的,予以登记,发给结婚证。完成结婚登记,即确立婚姻关系。未办理结婚登记的,应当补办登记。

第一千零五十条 登记结婚后,按照男女双方约定,女方可以成为男方家庭的成员,男方可以成为女方家庭的成员。

第一千零五十一条 有下列情形之一的,婚姻无效:

(一)重婚;

(二)有禁止结婚的亲属关系;

(三)未到法定婚龄。

第一千零五十二条 因胁迫结婚的,受胁迫的一方可以向人民法院请求撤销婚姻。

请求撤销婚姻的,应当自胁迫行为终止之日起一年内提出。

被非法限制人身自由的当事人请求撤销婚姻的,应当自恢复人身自由之日起一年内提出。

第一千零五十三条 一方患有重大疾病的,应当在结婚登记前如实告知另一方;不如实告知的,另一方可以向人民法院请求撤销婚姻。

请求撤销婚姻的,应当自知道或者应当知道撤销事由之日起一年内提出。

第一千零五十四条 无效的或者被撤销的婚姻自始没有法律约束力,当事人不具有夫妻的权利和义务。同居期间所得的财产,由当事人协议处理;协议不成的,由人民法院根据照顾无过错方的原则判决。对重婚导致的无效婚姻的财产处理,不得侵害合法婚姻当事人的财产权益。当事人所生的子女,适用本法关于父母子女的规定。

婚姻无效或者被撤销的,无过错方有权请求损害赔偿。

第三章　家庭关系

第一节　夫妻关系

第一千零五十五条　夫妻在婚姻家庭中地位平等。

第一千零五十六条　夫妻双方都有各自使用自己姓名的权利。

第一千零五十七条　夫妻双方都有参加生产、工作、学习和社会活动的自由，一方不得对另一方加以限制或者干涉。

第一千零五十八条　夫妻双方平等享有对未成年子女抚养、教育和保护的权利，共同承担对未成年子女抚养、教育和保护的义务。

第一千零五十九条　夫妻有相互扶养的义务。

需要扶养的一方，在另一方不履行扶养义务时，有要求其给付扶养费的权利。

第一千零六十条　夫妻一方因家庭日常生活需要而实施的民事法律行为，对夫妻双方发生效力，但是夫妻一方与相对人另有约定的除外。

夫妻之间对一方可以实施的民事法律行为范围的限制，不得对抗善意相对人。

第一千零六十一条　夫妻有相互继承遗产的权利。

第一千零六十二条　夫妻在婚姻关系存续期间所得的下列财产，为夫妻的共同财产，归夫妻共同所有：

（一）工资、奖金、劳务报酬；

（二）生产、经营、投资的收益；

（三）知识产权的收益；

（四）继承或者受赠的财产，但是本法第一千零六十三条第三项规定的除外；

（五）其他应当归共同所有的财产。

夫妻对共同财产，有平等的处理权。

第一千零六十三条　下列财产为夫妻一方的个人财产：

（一）一方的婚前财产；

(二)一方因受到人身损害获得的赔偿或者补偿;

(三)遗嘱或者赠与合同中确定只归一方的财产;

(四)一方专用的生活用品;

(五)其他应当归一方的财产。

第一千零六十四条 夫妻双方共同签名或者夫妻一方事后追认等共同意思表示所负的债务,以及夫妻一方在婚姻关系存续期间以个人名义为家庭日常生活需要所负的债务,属于夫妻共同债务。

夫妻一方在婚姻关系存续期间以个人名义超出家庭日常生活需要所负的债务,不属于夫妻共同债务;但是,债权人能够证明该债务用于夫妻共同生活、共同生产经营或者基于夫妻双方共同意思表示的除外。

第一千零六十五条 男女双方可以约定婚姻关系存续期间所得的财产以及婚前财产归各自所有、共同所有或者部分各自所有、部分共同所有。约定应当采用书面形式。没有约定或者约定不明确的,适用本法第一千零六十二条、第一千零六十三条的规定。

夫妻对婚姻关系存续期间所得的财产以及婚前财产的约定,对双方具有法律约束力。

夫妻对婚姻关系存续期间所得的财产约定归各自所有,夫或者妻一方对外所负的债务,相对人知道该约定的,以夫或者妻一方的个人财产清偿。

第一千零六十六条 婚姻关系存续期间,有下列情形之一的,夫妻一方可以向人民法院请求分割共同财产:

(一)一方有隐藏、转移、变卖、毁损、挥霍夫妻共同财产或者伪造夫妻共同债务等严重损害夫妻共同财产利益的行为;

(二)一方负有法定扶养义务的人患重大疾病需要医治,另一方不同意支付相关医疗费用。

第二节 父母子女关系和其他近亲属关系

第一千零六十七条 父母不履行抚养义务的,未成年子女或者不能独立生活的成年子女,有要求父母给付抚养费的权利。

成年子女不履行赡养义务的，缺乏劳动能力或者生活困难的父母，有要求成年子女给付赡养费的权利。

第一千零六十八条　父母有教育、保护未成年子女的权利和义务。未成年子女造成他人损害的，父母应当依法承担民事责任。

第一千零六十九条　子女应当尊重父母的婚姻权利，不得干涉父母离婚、再婚以及婚后的生活。子女对父母的赡养义务，不因父母的婚姻关系变化而终止。

第一千零七十条　父母和子女有相互继承遗产的权利。

第一千零七十一条　非婚生子女享有与婚生子女同等的权利，任何组织或者个人不得加以危害和歧视。

不直接抚养非婚生子女的生父或者生母，应当负担未成年子女或者不能独立生活的成年子女的抚养费。

第一千零七十二条　继父母与继子女间，不得虐待或者歧视。

继父或者继母和受其抚养教育的继子女间的权利义务关系，适用本法关于父母子女关系的规定。

第一千零七十三条　对亲子关系有异议且有正当理由的，父或者母可以向人民法院提起诉讼，请求确认或者否认亲子关系。

对亲子关系有异议且有正当理由的，成年子女可以向人民法院提起诉讼，请求确认亲子关系。

第一千零七十四条　有负担能力的祖父母、外祖父母，对于父母已经死亡或者父母无力抚养的未成年孙子女、外孙子女，有抚养的义务。

有负担能力的孙子女、外孙子女，对于子女已经死亡或者子女无力赡养的祖父母、外祖父母，有赡养的义务。

第一千零七十五条　有负担能力的兄、姐，对于父母已经死亡或者父母无力抚养的未成年弟、妹，有扶养的义务。

由兄、姐扶养长大的有负担能力的弟、妹，对于缺乏劳动能力又缺乏生活来源的兄、姐，有扶养的义务。

第四章　离　　婚

第一千零七十六条　夫妻双方自愿离婚的,应当签订书面离婚协议,并亲自到婚姻登记机关申请离婚登记。

离婚协议应当载明双方自愿离婚的意思表示和对子女抚养、财产以及债务处理等事项协商一致的意见。

第一千零七十七条　自婚姻登记机关收到离婚登记申请之日起三十日内,任何一方不愿意离婚的,可以向婚姻登记机关撤回离婚登记申请。

前款规定期限届满后三十日内,双方应当亲自到婚姻登记机关申请发给离婚证;未申请的,视为撤回离婚登记申请。

第一千零七十八条　婚姻登记机关查明双方确实是自愿离婚,并已经对子女抚养、财产以及债务处理等事项协商一致的,予以登记,发给离婚证。

第一千零七十九条　夫妻一方要求离婚的,可以由有关组织进行调解或者直接向人民法院提起离婚诉讼。

人民法院审理离婚案件,应当进行调解;如果感情确已破裂,调解无效的,应当准予离婚。

有下列情形之一,调解无效的,应当准予离婚:

(一)重婚或者与他人同居;

(二)实施家庭暴力或者虐待、遗弃家庭成员;

(三)有赌博、吸毒等恶习屡教不改;

(四)因感情不和分居满二年;

(五)其他导致夫妻感情破裂的情形。

一方被宣告失踪,另一方提起离婚诉讼的,应当准予离婚。

经人民法院判决不准离婚后,双方又分居满一年,一方再次提起离婚诉讼的,应当准予离婚。

第一千零八十条　完成离婚登记,或者离婚判决书、调解书生效,即解除婚姻关系。

第一千零八十一条　现役军人的配偶要求离婚,应当征得军人同意,但是军人一方有重大过错的除外。

第一千零八十二条　女方在怀孕期间、分娩后一年内或者终止妊娠后六个月内,男方不得提出离婚;但是,女方提出离婚或者人民法院认为确有必要受理男方离婚请求的除外。

第一千零八十三条　离婚后,男女双方自愿恢复婚姻关系的,应当到婚姻登记机关重新进行结婚登记。

第一千零八十四条　父母与子女间的关系,不因父母离婚而消除。离婚后,子女无论由父或者母直接抚养,仍是父母双方的子女。

离婚后,父母对于子女仍有抚养、教育、保护的权利和义务。

离婚后,不满两周岁的子女,以由母亲直接抚养为原则。已满两周岁的子女,父母双方对抚养问题协议不成的,由人民法院根据双方的具体情况,按照最有利于未成年子女的原则判决。子女已满八周岁的,应当尊重其真实意愿。

第一千零八十五条　离婚后,子女由一方直接抚养的,另一方应当负担部分或者全部抚养费。负担费用的多少和期限的长短,由双方协议;协议不成的,由人民法院判决。

前款规定的协议或者判决,不妨碍子女在必要时向父母任何一方提出超过协议或者判决原定数额的合理要求。

第一千零八十六条　离婚后,不直接抚养子女的父或者母,有探望子女的权利,另一方有协助的义务。

行使探望权利的方式、时间由当事人协议;协议不成的,由人民法院判决。

父或者母探望子女,不利于子女身心健康的,由人民法院依法中止探望;中止的事由消失后,应当恢复探望。

第一千零八十七条　离婚时,夫妻的共同财产由双方协议处理;协议不成的,由人民法院根据财产的具体情况,按照照顾子女、女方和无过错方权益的原则判决。

对夫或者妻在家庭土地承包经营中享有的权益等,应当依法予以保护。

第一千零八十八条 夫妻一方因抚育子女、照料老年人、协助另一方工作等负担较多义务的,离婚时有权向另一方请求补偿,另一方应当给予补偿。具体办法由双方协议;协议不成的,由人民法院判决。

第一千零八十九条 离婚时,夫妻共同债务应当共同偿还。共同财产不足清偿或者财产归各自所有的,由双方协议清偿;协议不成的,由人民法院判决。

第一千零九十条 离婚时,如果一方生活困难,有负担能力的另一方应当给予适当帮助。具体办法由双方协议;协议不成的,由人民法院判决。

第一千零九十一条 有下列情形之一,导致离婚的,无过错方有权请求损害赔偿:

(一)重婚;

(二)与他人同居;

(三)实施家庭暴力;

(四)虐待、遗弃家庭成员;

(五)有其他重大过错。

第一千零九十二条 夫妻一方隐藏、转移、变卖、毁损、挥霍夫妻共同财产,或者伪造夫妻共同债务企图侵占另一方财产的,在离婚分割夫妻共同财产时,对该方可以少分或者不分。离婚后,另一方发现有上述行为的,可以向人民法院提起诉讼,请求再次分割夫妻共同财产。

第五章 收 养

第一节 收养关系的成立

第一千零九十三条 下列未成年人,可以被收养:

(一)丧失父母的孤儿;

(二)查找不到生父母的未成年人;

(三)生父母有特殊困难无力抚养的子女。

第一千零九十四条 下列个人、组织可以作送养人:

（一）孤儿的监护人；

（二）儿童福利机构；

（三）有特殊困难无力抚养子女的生父母。

第一千零九十五条　未成年人的父母均不具备完全民事行为能力且可能严重危害该未成年人的，该未成年人的监护人可以将其送养。

第一千零九十六条　监护人送养孤儿的，应当征得有抚养义务的人同意。有抚养义务的人不同意送养、监护人不愿意继续履行监护职责的，应当依照本法第一编的规定另行确定监护人。

第一千零九十七条　生父母送养子女，应当双方共同送养。生父母一方不明或者查找不到的，可以单方送养。

第一千零九十八条　收养人应当同时具备下列条件：

（一）无子女或者只有一名子女；

（二）有抚养、教育和保护被收养人的能力；

（三）未患有在医学上认为不应当收养子女的疾病；

（四）无不利于被收养人健康成长的违法犯罪记录；

（五）年满三十周岁。

第一千零九十九条　收养三代以内旁系同辈血亲的子女，可以不受本法第一千零九十三条第三项、第一千零九十四条第三项和第一千一百零二条规定的限制。

华侨收养三代以内旁系同辈血亲的子女，还可以不受本法第一千零九十八条第一项规定的限制。

第一千一百条　无子女的收养人可以收养两名子女；有子女的收养人只能收养一名子女。

收养孤儿、残疾未成年人或者儿童福利机构抚养的查找不到生父母的未成年人，可以不受前款和本法第一千零九十八条第一项规定的限制。

第一千一百零一条　有配偶者收养子女，应当夫妻共同收养。

第一千一百零二条　无配偶者收养异性子女的，收养人与被收养人的年龄应当相差四十周岁以上。

第一千一百零三条 继父或者继母经继子女的生父母同意,可以收养继子女,并可以不受本法第一千零九十三条第三项、第一千零九十四条第三项、第一千零九十八条和第一千一百条第一款规定的限制。

第一千一百零四条 收养人收养与送养人送养,应当双方自愿。收养八周岁以上未成年人的,应当征得被收养人的同意。

第一千一百零五条 收养应当向县级以上人民政府民政部门登记。收养关系自登记之日起成立。

收养查找不到生父母的未成年人的,办理登记的民政部门应当在登记前予以公告。

收养关系当事人愿意签订收养协议的,可以签订收养协议。

收养关系当事人各方或者一方要求办理收养公证的,应当办理收养公证。

县级以上人民政府民政部门应当依法进行收养评估。

第一千一百零六条 收养关系成立后,公安机关应当按照国家有关规定为被收养人办理户口登记。

第一千一百零七条 孤儿或者生父母无力抚养的子女,可以由生父母的亲属、朋友抚养;抚养人与被抚养人的关系不适用本章规定。

第一千一百零八条 配偶一方死亡,另一方送养未成年子女的,死亡一方的父母有优先抚养的权利。

第一千一百零九条 外国人依法可以在中华人民共和国收养子女。

外国人在中华人民共和国收养子女,应当经其所在国主管机关依照该国法律审查同意。收养人应当提供由其所在国有权机构出具的有关其年龄、婚姻、职业、财产、健康、有无受过刑事处罚等状况的证明材料,并与送养人签订书面协议,亲自向省、自治区、直辖市人民政府民政部门登记。

前款规定的证明材料应当经收养人所在国外交机关或者外交机关授权的机构认证,并经中华人民共和国驻该国使领馆认证,但是国家另有规定的除外。

第一千一百一十条 收养人、送养人要求保守收养秘密的,其他人应当尊重其意愿,不得泄露。

第二节 收养的效力

第一千一百一十一条 自收养关系成立之日起,养父母与养子女间的权利义务关系,适用本法关于父母子女关系的规定;养子女与养父母的近亲属间的权利义务关系,适用本法关于子女与父母的近亲属关系的规定。

养子女与生父母以及其他近亲属间的权利义务关系,因收养关系的成立而消除。

第一千一百一十二条 养子女可以随养父或者养母的姓氏,经当事人协商一致,也可以保留原姓氏。

第一千一百一十三条 有本法第一编关于民事法律行为无效规定情形或者违反本编规定的收养行为无效。

无效的收养行为自始没有法律约束力。

第三节 收养关系的解除

第一千一百一十四条 收养人在被收养人成年以前,不得解除收养关系,但是收养人、送养人双方协议解除的除外。养子女八周岁以上的,应当征得本人同意。

收养人不履行抚养义务,有虐待、遗弃等侵害未成年养子女合法权益行为的,送养人有权要求解除养父母与养子女间的收养关系。送养人、收养人不能达成解除收养关系协议的,可以向人民法院提起诉讼。

第一千一百一十五条 养父母与成年养子女关系恶化、无法共同生活的,可以协议解除收养关系。不能达成协议的,可以向人民法院提起诉讼。

第一千一百一十六条 当事人协议解除收养关系的,应当到民政部门办理解除收养关系登记。

第一千一百一十七条 收养关系解除后,养子女与养父母以及其他近亲属间的权利义务关系即行消除,与生父母以及其他近亲属间的权利义务关系自行恢复。但是,成年养子女与生父母以及其他近亲属间的权利义务关系是否恢复,可以协商确定。

第一千一百一十八条 收养关系解除后,经养父母抚养的成年养子女,对缺乏劳动能力又缺乏生活来源的养父母,应当给付生活费。因养子女成年后虐待、遗弃养父母而解除收养关系的,养父母可以要求养子女补偿收养期间支出的抚养费。

生父母要求解除收养关系的,养父母可以要求生父母适当补偿收养期间支出的抚养费;但是,因养父母虐待、遗弃养子女而解除收养关系的除外。

第六编　继　　承

第一章　一般规定

第一千一百一十九条　本编调整因继承产生的民事关系。

第一千一百二十条　国家保护自然人的继承权。

第一千一百二十一条　继承从被继承人死亡时开始。

相互有继承关系的数人在同一事件中死亡，难以确定死亡时间的，推定没有其他继承人的人先死亡。都有其他继承人，辈份不同的，推定长辈先死亡；辈份相同的，推定同时死亡，相互不发生继承。

第一千一百二十二条　遗产是自然人死亡时遗留的个人合法财产。

依照法律规定或者根据其性质不得继承的遗产，不得继承。

第一千一百二十三条　继承开始后，按照法定继承办理；有遗嘱的，按照遗嘱继承或者遗赠办理；有遗赠扶养协议的，按照协议办理。

第一千一百二十四条　继承开始后，继承人放弃继承的，应当在遗产处理前，以书面形式作出放弃继承的表示；没有表示的，视为接受继承。

受遗赠人应当在知道受遗赠后六十日内，作出接受或者放弃受遗赠的表示；到期没有表示的，视为放弃受遗赠。

第一千一百二十五条　继承人有下列行为之一的，丧失继承权：

（一）故意杀害被继承人；

（二）为争夺遗产而杀害其他继承人；

（三）遗弃被继承人，或者虐待被继承人情节严重；

（四）伪造、篡改、隐匿或者销毁遗嘱，情节严重；

（五）以欺诈、胁迫手段迫使或者妨碍被继承人设立、变更或者撤回遗嘱，情节严重。

继承人有前款第三项至第五项行为,确有悔改表现,被继承人表示宽恕或者事后在遗嘱中将其列为继承人的,该继承人不丧失继承权。

受遗赠人有本条第一款规定行为的,丧失受遗赠权。

第二章　法定继承

第一千一百二十六条　继承权男女平等。

第一千一百二十七条　遗产按照下列顺序继承:

(一)第一顺序:配偶、子女、父母;

(二)第二顺序:兄弟姐妹、祖父母、外祖父母。

继承开始后,由第一顺序继承人继承,第二顺序继承人不继承;没有第一顺序继承人继承的,由第二顺序继承人继承。

本编所称子女,包括婚生子女、非婚生子女、养子女和有扶养关系的继子女。

本编所称父母,包括生父母、养父母和有扶养关系的继父母。

本编所称兄弟姐妹,包括同父母的兄弟姐妹、同父异母或者同母异父的兄弟姐妹、养兄弟姐妹、有扶养关系的继兄弟姐妹。

第一千一百二十八条　被继承人的子女先于被继承人死亡的,由被继承人的子女的直系晚辈血亲代位继承。

被继承人的兄弟姐妹先于被继承人死亡的,由被继承人的兄弟姐妹的子女代位继承。

代位继承人一般只能继承被代位继承人有权继承的遗产份额。

第一千一百二十九条　丧偶儿媳对公婆,丧偶女婿对岳父母,尽了主要赡养义务的,作为第一顺序继承人。

第一千一百三十条　同一顺序继承人继承遗产的份额,一般应当均等。

对生活有特殊困难又缺乏劳动能力的继承人,分配遗产时,应当予以照顾。

对被继承人尽了主要扶养义务或者与被继承人共同生活的继承人,分配遗产时,可以多分。

有扶养能力和有扶养条件的继承人,不尽扶养义务的,分配遗产时,应当不分或者少分。

继承人协商同意的,也可以不均等。

第一千一百三十一条　对继承人以外的依靠被继承人扶养的人,或者继承人以外的对被继承人扶养较多的人,可以分给适当的遗产。

第一千一百三十二条　继承人应当本着互谅互让、和睦团结的精神,协商处理继承问题。遗产分割的时间、办法和份额,由继承人协商确定;协商不成的,可以由人民调解委员会调解或者向人民法院提起诉讼。

第三章　遗嘱继承和遗赠

第一千一百三十三条　自然人可以依照本法规定立遗嘱处分个人财产,并可以指定遗嘱执行人。

自然人可以立遗嘱将个人财产指定由法定继承人中的一人或者数人继承。

自然人可以立遗嘱将个人财产赠与国家、集体或者法定继承人以外的组织、个人。

自然人可以依法设立遗嘱信托。

第一千一百三十四条　自书遗嘱由遗嘱人亲笔书写,签名,注明年、月、日。

第一千一百三十五条　代书遗嘱应当有两个以上见证人在场见证,由其中一人代书,并由遗嘱人、代书人和其他见证人签名,注明年、月、日。

第一千一百三十六条　打印遗嘱应当有两个以上见证人在场见证。遗嘱人和见证人应当在遗嘱每一页签名,注明年、月、日。

第一千一百三十七条　以录音录像形式立的遗嘱,应当有两个以上见证人在场见证。遗嘱人和见证人应当在录音录像中记录其姓名或者肖像,以及年、月、日。

第一千一百三十八条　遗嘱人在危急情况下,可以立口头遗嘱。口头遗嘱应当有两个以上见证人在场见证。危急情况消除后,遗嘱人能够以书面或者录音录像形式立遗嘱的,所立的口头遗嘱无效。

第一千一百三十九条 公证遗嘱由遗嘱人经公证机构办理。

第一千一百四十条 下列人员不能作为遗嘱见证人:

(一)无民事行为能力人、限制民事行为能力人以及其他不具有见证能力的人;

(二)继承人、受遗赠人;

(三)与继承人、受遗赠人有利害关系的人。

第一千一百四十一条 遗嘱应当为缺乏劳动能力又没有生活来源的继承人保留必要的遗产份额。

第一千一百四十二条 遗嘱人可以撤回、变更自己所立的遗嘱。

立遗嘱后,遗嘱人实施与遗嘱内容相反的民事法律行为的,视为对遗嘱相关内容的撤回。

立有数份遗嘱,内容相抵触的,以最后的遗嘱为准。

第一千一百四十三条 无民事行为能力人或者限制民事行为能力人所立的遗嘱无效。

遗嘱必须表示遗嘱人的真实意思,受欺诈、胁迫所立的遗嘱无效。

伪造的遗嘱无效。

遗嘱被篡改的,篡改的内容无效。

第一千一百四十四条 遗嘱继承或者遗赠附有义务的,继承人或者受遗赠人应当履行义务。没有正当理由不履行义务的,经利害关系人或者有关组织请求,人民法院可以取消其接受附义务部分遗产的权利。

第四章 遗产的处理

第一千一百四十五条 继承开始后,遗嘱执行人为遗产管理人;没有遗嘱执行人的,继承人应当及时推选遗产管理人;继承人未推选的,由继承人共同担任遗产管理人;没有继承人或者继承人均放弃继承的,由被继承人生前住所地的民政部门或者村民委员会担任遗产管理人。

第一千一百四十六条 对遗产管理人的确定有争议的,利害关系人可以向人民法院申请指定遗产管理人。

第一千一百四十七条　遗产管理人应当履行下列职责：

(一)清理遗产并制作遗产清单；

(二)向继承人报告遗产情况；

(三)采取必要措施防止遗产毁损、灭失；

(四)处理被继承人的债权债务；

(五)按照遗嘱或者依照法律规定分割遗产；

(六)实施与管理遗产有关的其他必要行为。

第一千一百四十八条　遗产管理人应当依法履行职责，因故意或者重大过失造成继承人、受遗赠人、债权人损害的，应当承担民事责任。

第一千一百四十九条　遗产管理人可以依照法律规定或者按照约定获得报酬。

第一千一百五十条　继承开始后，知道被继承人死亡的继承人应当及时通知其他继承人和遗嘱执行人。继承人中无人知道被继承人死亡或者知道被继承人死亡而不能通知的，由被继承人生前所在单位或者住所地的居民委员会、村民委员会负责通知。

第一千一百五十一条　存有遗产的人，应当妥善保管遗产，任何组织或者个人不得侵吞或者争抢。

第一千一百五十二条　继承开始后，继承人于遗产分割前死亡，并没有放弃继承的，该继承人应当继承的遗产转给其继承人，但是遗嘱另有安排的除外。

第一千一百五十三条　夫妻共同所有的财产，除有约定的外，遗产分割时，应当先将共同所有的财产的一半分出为配偶所有，其余的为被继承人的遗产。

遗产在家庭共有财产之中的，遗产分割时，应当先分出他人的财产。

第一千一百五十四条　有下列情形之一的，遗产中的有关部分按照法定继承办理：

(一)遗嘱继承人放弃继承或者受遗赠人放弃受遗赠;

(二)遗嘱继承人丧失继承权或者受遗赠人丧失受遗赠权;

(三)遗嘱继承人、受遗赠人先于遗嘱人死亡或者终止;

(四)遗嘱无效部分所涉及的遗产;

(五)遗嘱未处分的遗产。

第一千一百五十五条　遗产分割时,应当保留胎儿的继承份额。胎儿娩出时是死体的,保留的份额按照法定继承办理。

第一千一百五十六条　遗产分割应当有利于生产和生活需要,不损害遗产的效用。

不宜分割的遗产,可以采取折价、适当补偿或者共有等方法处理。

第一千一百五十七条　夫妻一方死亡后另一方再婚的,有权处分所继承的财产,任何组织或者个人不得干涉。

第一千一百五十八条　自然人可以与继承人以外的组织或者个人签订遗赠扶养协议。按照协议,该组织或者个人承担该自然人生养死葬的义务,享有受遗赠的权利。

第一千一百五十九条　分割遗产,应当清偿被继承人依法应当缴纳的税款和债务;但是,应当为缺乏劳动能力又没有生活来源的继承人保留必要的遗产。

第一千一百六十条　无人继承又无人受遗赠的遗产,归国家所有,用于公益事业;死者生前是集体所有制组织成员的,归所在集体所有制组织所有。

第一千一百六十一条　继承人以所得遗产实际价值为限清偿被继承人依法应当缴纳的税款和债务。超过遗产实际价值部分,继承人自愿偿还的不在此限。

继承人放弃继承的,对被继承人依法应当缴纳的税款和债务可以不负清偿责任。

第一千一百六十二条　执行遗赠不得妨碍清偿遗赠人依法应当缴纳的

税款和债务。

第一千一百六十三条 既有法定继承又有遗嘱继承、遗赠的,由法定继承人清偿被继承人依法应当缴纳的税款和债务;超过法定继承遗产实际价值部分,由遗嘱继承人和受遗赠人按比例以所得遗产清偿。

第七编　侵权责任

第一章　一般规定

第一千一百六十四条　本编调整因侵害民事权益产生的民事关系。

第一千一百六十五条　行为人因过错侵害他人民事权益造成损害的，应当承担侵权责任。

依照法律规定推定行为人有过错，其不能证明自己没有过错的，应当承担侵权责任。

第一千一百六十六条　行为人造成他人民事权益损害，不论行为人有无过错，法律规定应当承担侵权责任的，依照其规定。

第一千一百六十七条　侵权行为危及他人人身、财产安全的，被侵权人有权请求侵权人承担停止侵害、排除妨碍、消除危险等侵权责任。

第一千一百六十八条　二人以上共同实施侵权行为，造成他人损害的，应当承担连带责任。

第一千一百六十九条　教唆、帮助他人实施侵权行为的，应当与行为人承担连带责任。

教唆、帮助无民事行为能力人、限制民事行为能力人实施侵权行为的，应当承担侵权责任；该无民事行为能力人、限制民事行为能力人的监护人未尽到监护职责的，应当承担相应的责任。

第一千一百七十条　二人以上实施危及他人人身、财产安全的行为，其中一人或者数人的行为造成他人损害，能够确定具体侵权人的，由侵权人承担责任；不能确定具体侵权人的，行为人承担连带责任。

第一千一百七十一条　二人以上分别实施侵权行为造成同一损害，每个人的侵权行为都足以造成全部损害的，行为人承担连带责任。

第一千一百七十二条 二人以上分别实施侵权行为造成同一损害,能够确定责任大小的,各自承担相应的责任;难以确定责任大小的,平均承担责任。

第一千一百七十三条 被侵权人对同一损害的发生或者扩大有过错的,可以减轻侵权人的责任。

第一千一百七十四条 损害是因受害人故意造成的,行为人不承担责任。

第一千一百七十五条 损害是因第三人造成的,第三人应当承担侵权责任。

第一千一百七十六条 自愿参加具有一定风险的文体活动,因其他参加者的行为受到损害的,受害人不得请求其他参加者承担侵权责任;但是,其他参加者对损害的发生有故意或者重大过失的除外。

活动组织者的责任适用本法第一千一百九十八条至第一千二百零一条的规定。

第一千一百七十七条 合法权益受到侵害,情况紧迫且不能及时获得国家机关保护,不立即采取措施将使其合法权益受到难以弥补的损害的,受害人可以在保护自己合法权益的必要范围内采取扣留侵权人的财物等合理措施;但是,应当立即请求有关国家机关处理。

受害人采取的措施不当造成他人损害的,应当承担侵权责任。

第一千一百七十八条 本法和其他法律对不承担责任或者减轻责任的情形另有规定的,依照其规定。

第二章 损害赔偿

第一千一百七十九条 侵害他人造成人身损害的,应当赔偿医疗费、护理费、交通费、营养费、住院伙食补助费等为治疗和康复支出的合理费用,以及因误工减少的收入。造成残疾的,还应当赔偿辅助器具费和残疾赔偿金;造成死亡的,还应当赔偿丧葬费和死亡赔偿金。

第一千一百八十条 因同一侵权行为造成多人死亡的,可以以相同数额确定死亡赔偿金。

第一千一百八十一条 被侵权人死亡的,其近亲属有权请求侵权人承担侵权责任。被侵权人为组织,该组织分立、合并的,承继权利的组织有权请求侵权人承担侵权责任。

被侵权人死亡的,支付被侵权人医疗费、丧葬费等合理费用的人有权请求侵权人赔偿费用,但是侵权人已经支付该费用的除外。

第一千一百八十二条 侵害他人人身权益造成财产损失的,按照被侵权人因此受到的损失或者侵权人因此获得的利益赔偿;被侵权人因此受到的损失以及侵权人因此获得的利益难以确定,被侵权人和侵权人就赔偿数额协商不一致,向人民法院提起诉讼的,由人民法院根据实际情况确定赔偿数额。

第一千一百八十三条 侵害自然人人身权益造成严重精神损害的,被侵权人有权请求精神损害赔偿。

因故意或者重大过失侵害自然人具有人身意义的特定物造成严重精神损害的,被侵权人有权请求精神损害赔偿。

第一千一百八十四条 侵害他人财产的,财产损失按照损失发生时的市场价格或者其他合理方式计算。

第一千一百八十五条 故意侵害他人知识产权,情节严重的,被侵权人有权请求相应的惩罚性赔偿。

第一千一百八十六条 受害人和行为人对损害的发生都没有过错的,依照法律的规定由双方分担损失。

第一千一百八十七条 损害发生后,当事人可以协商赔偿费用的支付方式。协商不一致的,赔偿费用应当一次性支付;一次性支付确有困难的,可以分期支付,但是被侵权人有权请求提供相应的担保。

第三章 责任主体的特殊规定

第一千一百八十八条 无民事行为能力人、限制民事行为能力人造成他人损害的,由监护人承担侵权责任。监护人尽到监护职责的,可以减轻其侵权责任。

有财产的无民事行为能力人、限制民事行为能力人造成他人损害的，从本人财产中支付赔偿费用；不足部分，由监护人赔偿。

第一千一百八十九条 无民事行为能力人、限制民事行为能力人造成他人损害，监护人将监护职责委托给他人的，监护人应当承担侵权责任；受托人有过错的，承担相应的责任。

第一千一百九十条 完全民事行为能力人对自己的行为暂时没有意识或者失去控制造成他人损害有过错的，应当承担侵权责任；没有过错的，根据行为人的经济状况对受害人适当补偿。

完全民事行为能力人因醉酒、滥用麻醉药品或者精神药品对自己的行为暂时没有意识或者失去控制造成他人损害的，应当承担侵权责任。

第一千一百九十一条 用人单位的工作人员因执行工作任务造成他人损害的，由用人单位承担侵权责任。用人单位承担侵权责任后，可以向有故意或者重大过失的工作人员追偿。

劳务派遣期间，被派遣的工作人员因执行工作任务造成他人损害的，由接受劳务派遣的用工单位承担侵权责任；劳务派遣单位有过错的，承担相应的责任。

第一千一百九十二条 个人之间形成劳务关系，提供劳务一方因劳务造成他人损害的，由接受劳务一方承担侵权责任。接受劳务一方承担侵权责任后，可以向有故意或者重大过失的提供劳务一方追偿。提供劳务一方因劳务受到损害的，根据双方各自的过错承担相应的责任。

提供劳务期间，因第三人的行为造成提供劳务一方损害的，提供劳务一方有权请求第三人承担侵权责任，也有权请求接受劳务一方给予补偿。接受劳务一方补偿后，可以向第三人追偿。

第一千一百九十三条 承揽人在完成工作过程中造成第三人损害或者自己损害的，定作人不承担侵权责任。但是，定作人对定作、指示或者选任有过错的，应当承担相应的责任。

第一千一百九十四条 网络用户、网络服务提供者利用网络侵害他人民事权益的,应当承担侵权责任。法律另有规定的,依照其规定。

第一千一百九十五条 网络用户利用网络服务实施侵权行为的,权利人有权通知网络服务提供者采取删除、屏蔽、断开链接等必要措施。通知应当包括构成侵权的初步证据及权利人的真实身份信息。

网络服务提供者接到通知后,应当及时将该通知转送相关网络用户,并根据构成侵权的初步证据和服务类型采取必要措施;未及时采取必要措施的,对损害的扩大部分与该网络用户承担连带责任。

权利人因错误通知造成网络用户或者网络服务提供者损害的,应当承担侵权责任。法律另有规定的,依照其规定。

第一千一百九十六条 网络用户接到转送的通知后,可以向网络服务提供者提交不存在侵权行为的声明。声明应当包括不存在侵权行为的初步证据及网络用户的真实身份信息。

网络服务提供者接到声明后,应当将该声明转送发出通知的权利人,并告知其可以向有关部门投诉或者向人民法院提起诉讼。网络服务提供者在转送声明到达权利人后的合理期限内,未收到权利人已经投诉或者提起诉讼通知的,应当及时终止所采取的措施。

第一千一百九十七条 网络服务提供者知道或者应当知道网络用户利用其网络服务侵害他人民事权益,未采取必要措施的,与该网络用户承担连带责任。

第一千一百九十八条 宾馆、商场、银行、车站、机场、体育场馆、娱乐场所等经营场所、公共场所的经营者、管理者或者群众性活动的组织者,未尽到安全保障义务,造成他人损害的,应当承担侵权责任。

因第三人的行为造成他人损害的,由第三人承担侵权责任;经营者、管理者或者组织者未尽到安全保障义务的,承担相应的补充责任。经营者、管理者或者组织者承担补充责任后,可以向第三人追偿。

第一千一百九十九条 无民事行为能力人在幼儿园、学校或者其他教育机构学习、生活期间受到人身损害的,幼儿园、学校或者其他教育机构应当承担侵权责任;但是,能够证明尽到教育、管理职责的,不承担侵权责任。

第一千二百条　限制民事行为能力人在学校或者其他教育机构学习、生活期间受到人身损害，学校或者其他教育机构未尽到教育、管理职责的，应当承担侵权责任。

第一千二百零一条　无民事行为能力人或者限制民事行为能力人在幼儿园、学校或者其他教育机构学习、生活期间，受到幼儿园、学校或者其他教育机构以外的第三人人身损害的，由第三人承担侵权责任；幼儿园、学校或者其他教育机构未尽到管理职责的，承担相应的补充责任。幼儿园、学校或者其他教育机构承担补充责任后，可以向第三人追偿。

第四章　产品责任

第一千二百零二条　因产品存在缺陷造成他人损害的，生产者应当承担侵权责任。

第一千二百零三条　因产品存在缺陷造成他人损害的，被侵权人可以向产品的生产者请求赔偿，也可以向产品的销售者请求赔偿。

产品缺陷由生产者造成的，销售者赔偿后，有权向生产者追偿。因销售者的过错使产品存在缺陷的，生产者赔偿后，有权向销售者追偿。

第一千二百零四条　因运输者、仓储者等第三人的过错使产品存在缺陷，造成他人损害的，产品的生产者、销售者赔偿后，有权向第三人追偿。

第一千二百零五条　因产品缺陷危及他人人身、财产安全的，被侵权人有权请求生产者、销售者承担停止侵害、排除妨碍、消除危险等侵权责任。

第一千二百零六条　产品投入流通后发现存在缺陷的，生产者、销售者应当及时采取停止销售、警示、召回等补救措施；未及时采取补救措施或者补救措施不力造成损害扩大的，对扩大的损害也应当承担侵权责任。

依据前款规定采取召回措施的，生产者、销售者应当负担被侵权人因此支出的必要费用。

第一千二百零七条　明知产品存在缺陷仍然生产、销售，或者没有依据前条规定采取有效补救措施，造成他人死亡或者健康严重损害的，被侵权人有权请求相应的惩罚性赔偿。

第五章　机动车交通事故责任

第一千二百零八条　机动车发生交通事故造成损害的,依照道路交通安全法律和本法的有关规定承担赔偿责任。

第一千二百零九条　因租赁、借用等情形机动车所有人、管理人与使用人不是同一人时,发生交通事故造成损害,属于该机动车一方责任的,由机动车使用人承担赔偿责任;机动车所有人、管理人对损害的发生有过错的,承担相应的赔偿责任。

第一千二百一十条　当事人之间已经以买卖或者其他方式转让并交付机动车但是未办理登记,发生交通事故造成损害,属于该机动车一方责任的,由受让人承担赔偿责任。

第一千二百一十一条　以挂靠形式从事道路运输经营活动的机动车,发生交通事故造成损害,属于该机动车一方责任的,由挂靠人和被挂靠人承担连带责任。

第一千二百一十二条　未经允许驾驶他人机动车,发生交通事故造成损害,属于该机动车一方责任的,由机动车使用人承担赔偿责任;机动车所有人、管理人对损害的发生有过错的,承担相应的赔偿责任,但是本章另有规定的除外。

第一千二百一十三条　机动车发生交通事故造成损害,属于该机动车一方责任的,先由承保机动车强制保险的保险人在强制保险责任限额范围内予以赔偿;不足部分,由承保机动车商业保险的保险人按照保险合同的约定予以赔偿;仍然不足或者没有投保机动车商业保险的,由侵权人赔偿。

第一千二百一十四条　以买卖或者其他方式转让拼装或者已经达到报废标准的机动车,发生交通事故造成损害的,由转让人和受让人承担连带责任。

第一千二百一十五条　盗窃、抢劫或者抢夺的机动车发生交通事故造成损害的,由盗窃人、抢劫人或者抢夺人承担赔偿责任。盗窃人、抢劫人或者抢夺人与机动车使用人不是同一人,发生交通事故造成损害,属于该机动车一方责任的，由盗窃人、抢劫人或者抢夺人与机动车使用人承担连带责任。

保险人在机动车强制保险责任限额范围内垫付抢救费用的，有权向交通事故责任人追偿。

第一千二百一十六条　机动车驾驶人发生交通事故后逃逸，该机动车参加强制保险的，由保险人在机动车强制保险责任限额范围内予以赔偿；机动车不明、该机动车未参加强制保险或者抢救费用超过机动车强制保险责任限额，需要支付被侵权人人身伤亡的抢救、丧葬等费用的，由道路交通事故社会救助基金垫付。道路交通事故社会救助基金垫付后，其管理机构有权向交通事故责任人追偿。

第一千二百一十七条　非营运机动车发生交通事故造成无偿搭乘人损害，属于该机动车一方责任的，应当减轻其赔偿责任，但是机动车使用人有故意或者重大过失的除外。

第六章　医疗损害责任

第一千二百一十八条　患者在诊疗活动中受到损害，医疗机构或者其医务人员有过错的，由医疗机构承担赔偿责任。

第一千二百一十九条　医务人员在诊疗活动中应当向患者说明病情和医疗措施。需要实施手术、特殊检查、特殊治疗的，医务人员应当及时向患者具体说明医疗风险、替代医疗方案等情况，并取得其明确同意；不能或者不宜向患者说明的，应当向患者的近亲属说明，并取得其明确同意。

医务人员未尽到前款义务，造成患者损害的，医疗机构应当承担赔偿责任。

第一千二百二十条　因抢救生命垂危的患者等紧急情况，不能取得患者或者其近亲属意见的，经医疗机构负责人或者授权的负责人批准，可以立即实施相应的医疗措施。

第一千二百二十一条　医务人员在诊疗活动中未尽到与当时的医疗水平相应的诊疗义务，造成患者损害的，医疗机构应当承担赔偿责任。

第一千二百二十二条 患者在诊疗活动中受到损害,有下列情形之一的,推定医疗机构有过错:

(一)违反法律、行政法规、规章以及其他有关诊疗规范的规定;

(二)隐匿或者拒绝提供与纠纷有关的病历资料;

(三)遗失、伪造、篡改或者违法销毁病历资料。

第一千二百二十三条 因药品、消毒产品、医疗器械的缺陷,或者输入不合格的血液造成患者损害的,患者可以向药品上市许可持有人、生产者、血液提供机构请求赔偿,也可以向医疗机构请求赔偿。患者向医疗机构请求赔偿的,医疗机构赔偿后,有权向负有责任的药品上市许可持有人、生产者、血液提供机构追偿。

第一千二百二十四条 患者在诊疗活动中受到损害,有下列情形之一的,医疗机构不承担赔偿责任:

(一)患者或者其近亲属不配合医疗机构进行符合诊疗规范的诊疗;

(二)医务人员在抢救生命垂危的患者等紧急情况下已经尽到合理诊疗义务;

(三)限于当时的医疗水平难以诊疗。

前款第一项情形中,医疗机构或者其医务人员也有过错的,应当承担相应的赔偿责任。

第一千二百二十五条 医疗机构及其医务人员应当按照规定填写并妥善保管住院志、医嘱单、检验报告、手术及麻醉记录、病理资料、护理记录等病历资料。

患者要求查阅、复制前款规定的病历资料的,医疗机构应当及时提供。

第一千二百二十六条 医疗机构及其医务人员应当对患者的隐私和个人信息保密。泄露患者的隐私和个人信息,或者未经患者同意公开其病历资料的,应当承担侵权责任。

第一千二百二十七条 医疗机构及其医务人员不得违反诊疗规范实施不必要的检查。

第一千二百二十八条 医疗机构及其医务人员的合法权益受法律

保护。

干扰医疗秩序，妨碍医务人员工作、生活，侵害医务人员合法权益的，应当依法承担法律责任。

第七章 环境污染和生态破坏责任

第一千二百二十九条 因污染环境、破坏生态造成他人损害的，侵权人应当承担侵权责任。

第一千二百三十条 因污染环境、破坏生态发生纠纷，行为人应当就法律规定的不承担责任或者减轻责任的情形及其行为与损害之间不存在因果关系承担举证责任。

第一千二百三十一条 两个以上侵权人污染环境、破坏生态的，承担责任的大小，根据污染物的种类、浓度、排放量，破坏生态的方式、范围、程度，以及行为对损害后果所起的作用等因素确定。

第一千二百三十二条 侵权人违反法律规定故意污染环境、破坏生态造成严重后果的，被侵权人有权请求相应的惩罚性赔偿。

第一千二百三十三条 因第三人的过错污染环境、破坏生态的，被侵权人可以向侵权人请求赔偿，也可以向第三人请求赔偿。侵权人赔偿后，有权向第三人追偿。

第一千二百三十四条 违反国家规定造成生态环境损害，生态环境能够修复的，国家规定的机关或者法律规定的组织有权请求侵权人在合理期限内承担修复责任。侵权人在期限内未修复的，国家规定的机关或者法律规定的组织可以自行或者委托他人进行修复，所需费用由侵权人负担。

第一千二百三十五条 违反国家规定造成生态环境损害的，国家规定的机关或者法律规定的组织有权请求侵权人赔偿下列损失和费用：

（一）生态环境受到损害至修复完成期间服务功能丧失导致的损失；

（二）生态环境功能永久性损害造成的损失；

（三）生态环境损害调查、鉴定评估等费用；

（四）清除污染、修复生态环境费用；

(五)防止损害的发生和扩大所支出的合理费用。

第八章　高度危险责任

第一千二百三十六条　从事高度危险作业造成他人损害的,应当承担侵权责任。

第一千二百三十七条　民用核设施或者运入运出核设施的核材料发生核事故造成他人损害的,民用核设施的营运单位应当承担侵权责任;但是,能够证明损害是因战争、武装冲突、暴乱等情形或者受害人故意造成的,不承担责任。

第一千二百三十八条　民用航空器造成他人损害的,民用航空器的经营者应当承担侵权责任;但是,能够证明损害是因受害人故意造成的,不承担责任。

第一千二百三十九条　占有或者使用易燃、易爆、剧毒、高放射性、强腐蚀性、高致病性等高度危险物造成他人损害的,占有人或者使用人应当承担侵权责任;但是,能够证明损害是因受害人故意或者不可抗力造成的,不承担责任。被侵权人对损害的发生有重大过失的,可以减轻占有人或者使用人的责任。

第一千二百四十条　从事高空、高压、地下挖掘活动或者使用高速轨道运输工具造成他人损害的,经营者应当承担侵权责任;但是,能够证明损害是因受害人故意或者不可抗力造成的,不承担责任。被侵权人对损害的发生有重大过失的,可以减轻经营者的责任。

第一千二百四十一条　遗失、抛弃高度危险物造成他人损害的,由所有人承担侵权责任。所有人将高度危险物交由他人管理的,由管理人承担侵权责任;所有人有过错的,与管理人承担连带责任。

第一千二百四十二条　非法占有高度危险物造成他人损害的,由非法占有人承担侵权责任。所有人、管理人不能证明对防止非法占有尽到高度注意义务的,与非法占有人承担连带责任。

第一千二百四十三条　未经许可进入高度危险活动区域或者高度危险

物存放区域受到损害，管理人能够证明已经采取足够安全措施并尽到充分警示义务的，可以减轻或者不承担责任。

第一千二百四十四条　承担高度危险责任，法律规定赔偿限额的，依照其规定，但是行为人有故意或者重大过失的除外。

第九章　饲养动物损害责任

第一千二百四十五条　饲养的动物造成他人损害的，动物饲养人或者管理人应当承担侵权责任；但是，能够证明损害是因被侵权人故意或者重大过失造成的，可以不承担或者减轻责任。

第一千二百四十六条　违反管理规定，未对动物采取安全措施造成他人损害的，动物饲养人或者管理人应当承担侵权责任；但是，能够证明损害是因被侵权人故意造成的，可以减轻责任。

第一千二百四十七条　禁止饲养的烈性犬等危险动物造成他人损害的，动物饲养人或者管理人应当承担侵权责任。

第一千二百四十八条　动物园的动物造成他人损害的，动物园应当承担侵权责任；但是，能够证明尽到管理职责的，不承担侵权责任。

第一千二百四十九条　遗弃、逃逸的动物在遗弃、逃逸期间造成他人损害的，由动物原饲养人或者管理人承担侵权责任。

第一千二百五十条　因第三人的过错致使动物造成他人损害的，被侵权人可以向动物饲养人或者管理人请求赔偿，也可以向第三人请求赔偿。动物饲养人或者管理人赔偿后，有权向第三人追偿。

第一千二百五十一条　饲养动物应当遵守法律法规，尊重社会公德，不得妨碍他人生活。

第十章　建筑物和物件损害责任

第一千二百五十二条　建筑物、构筑物或者其他设施倒塌、塌陷造成他人损害的，由建设单位与施工单位承担连带责任，但是建设单位与施工单位能够证明不存在质量缺陷的除外。建设单位、施工单位赔偿后,有其他责任人的,有权向其他责任人追偿。

因所有人、管理人、使用人或者第三人的原因,建筑物、构筑物或者其他设施倒塌、塌陷造成他人损害的,由所有人、管理人、使用人或者第三人承担侵权责任。

第一千二百五十三条 建筑物、构筑物或者其他设施及其搁置物、悬挂物发生脱落、坠落造成他人损害,所有人、管理人或者使用人不能证明自己没有过错的,应当承担侵权责任。所有人、管理人或者使用人赔偿后,有其他责任人的,有权向其他责任人追偿。

第一千二百五十四条 禁止从建筑物中抛掷物品。从建筑物中抛掷物品或者从建筑物上坠落的物品造成他人损害的,由侵权人依法承担侵权责任;经调查难以确定具体侵权人的,除能够证明自己不是侵权人的外,由可能加害的建筑物使用人给予补偿。可能加害的建筑物使用人补偿后,有权向侵权人追偿。

物业服务企业等建筑物管理人应当采取必要的安全保障措施防止前款规定情形的发生;未采取必要的安全保障措施的,应当依法承担未履行安全保障义务的侵权责任。

发生本条第一款规定的情形的,公安等机关应当依法及时调查,查清责任人。

第一千二百五十五条 堆放物倒塌、滚落或者滑落造成他人损害,堆放人不能证明自己没有过错的,应当承担侵权责任。

第一千二百五十六条 在公共道路上堆放、倾倒、遗撒妨碍通行的物品造成他人损害的,由行为人承担侵权责任。公共道路管理人不能证明已经尽到清理、防护、警示等义务的,应当承担相应的责任。

第一千二百五十七条 因林木折断、倾倒或者果实坠落等造成他人损害,林木的所有人或者管理人不能证明自己没有过错的,应当承担侵权责任。

第一千二百五十八条 在公共场所或者道路上挖掘、修缮安装地下设施等造成他人损害，施工人不能证明已经设置明显标志和采取安全措施的，应当承担侵权责任。

窨井等地下设施造成他人损害，管理人不能证明尽到管理职责的，应当承担侵权责任。

附　　则

第一千二百五十九条　民法所称的“以上”、“以下”、“以内”、“届满”,包括本数;所称的“不满”、“超过”、“以外”,不包括本数。

第一千二百六十条　本法自2021年1月1日起施行。《中华人民共和国婚姻法》、《中华人民共和国继承法》、《中华人民共和国民法通则》、《中华人民共和国收养法》、《中华人民共和国担保法》、《中华人民共和国合同法》、《中华人民共和国物权法》、《中华人民共和国侵权责任法》、《中华人民共和国民法总则》同时废止。